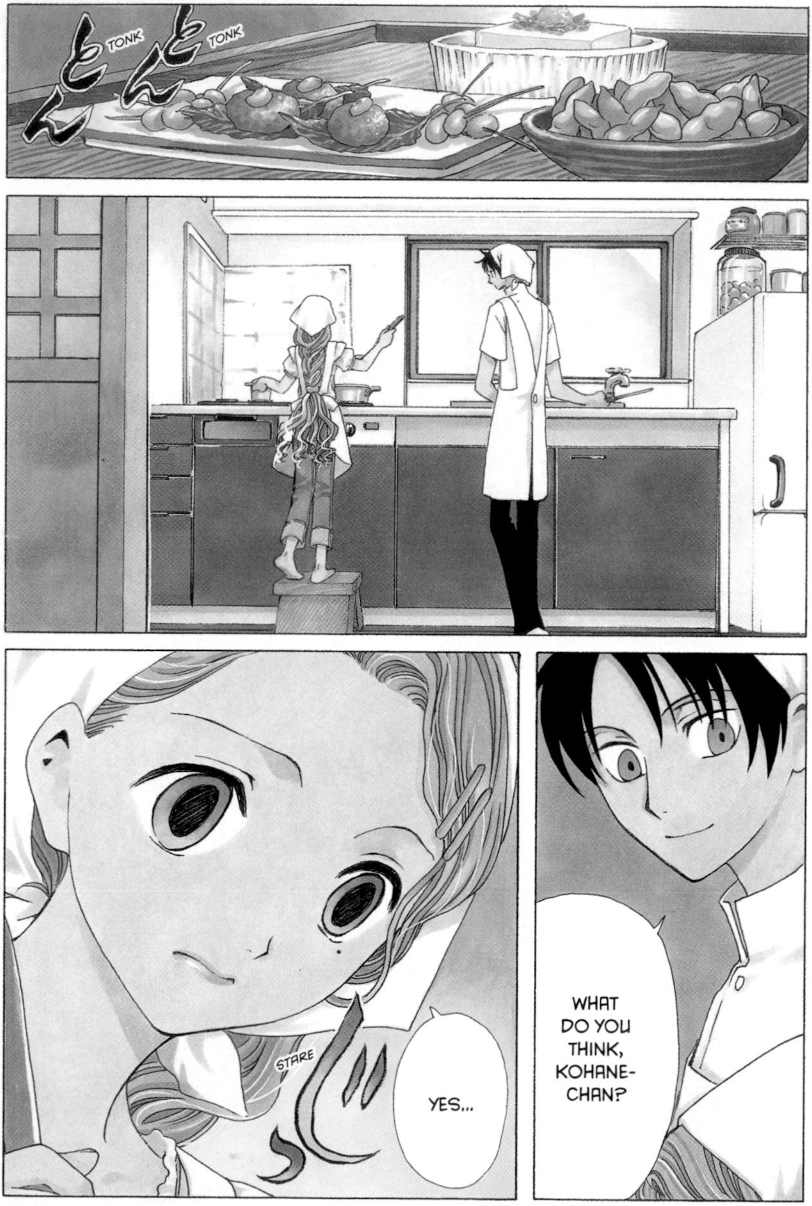
TONK
TONK
WHAT DO YOU THINK, KOHANE-CHAN?
STARE
YES...

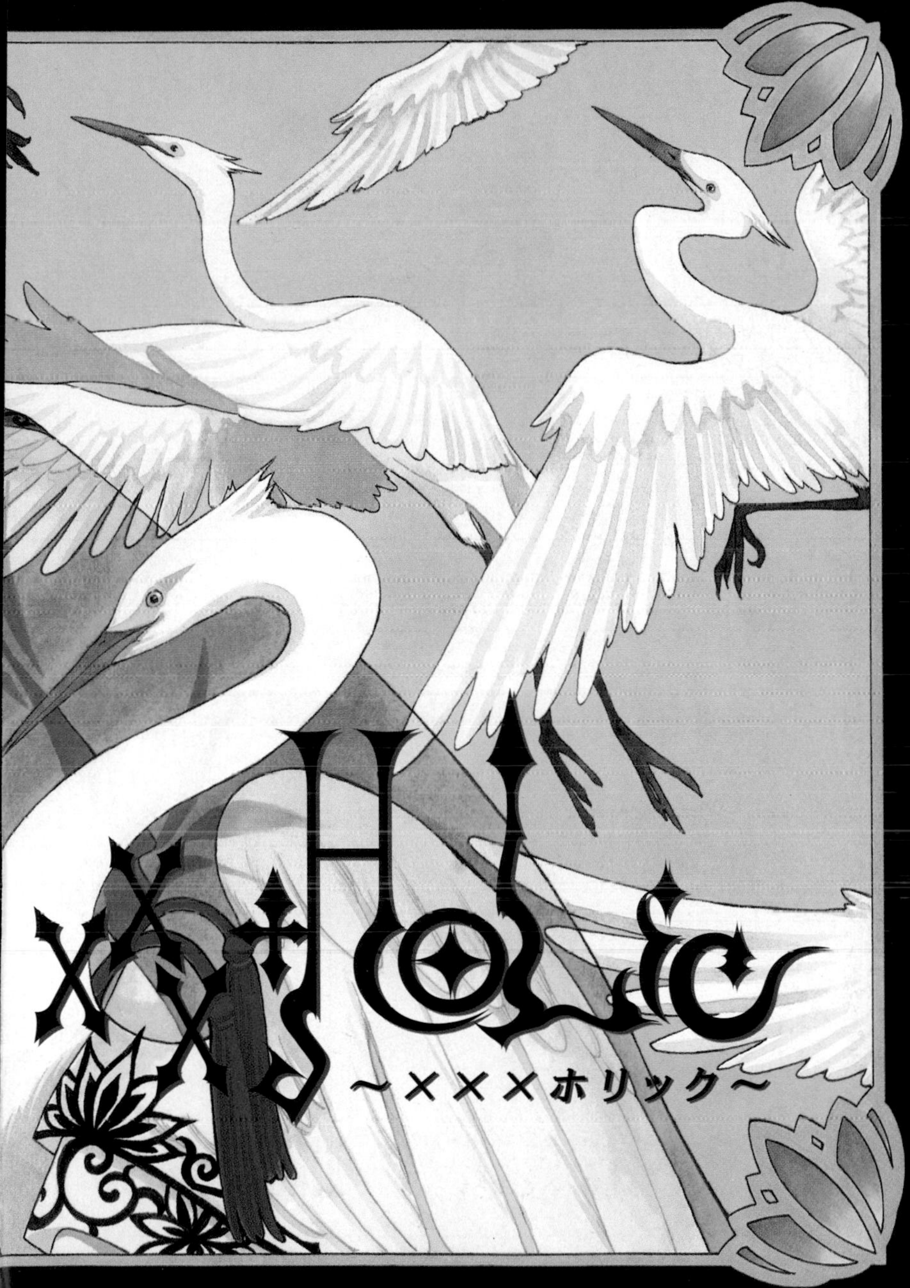
xxxHOLiC
〜×××ホリック〜

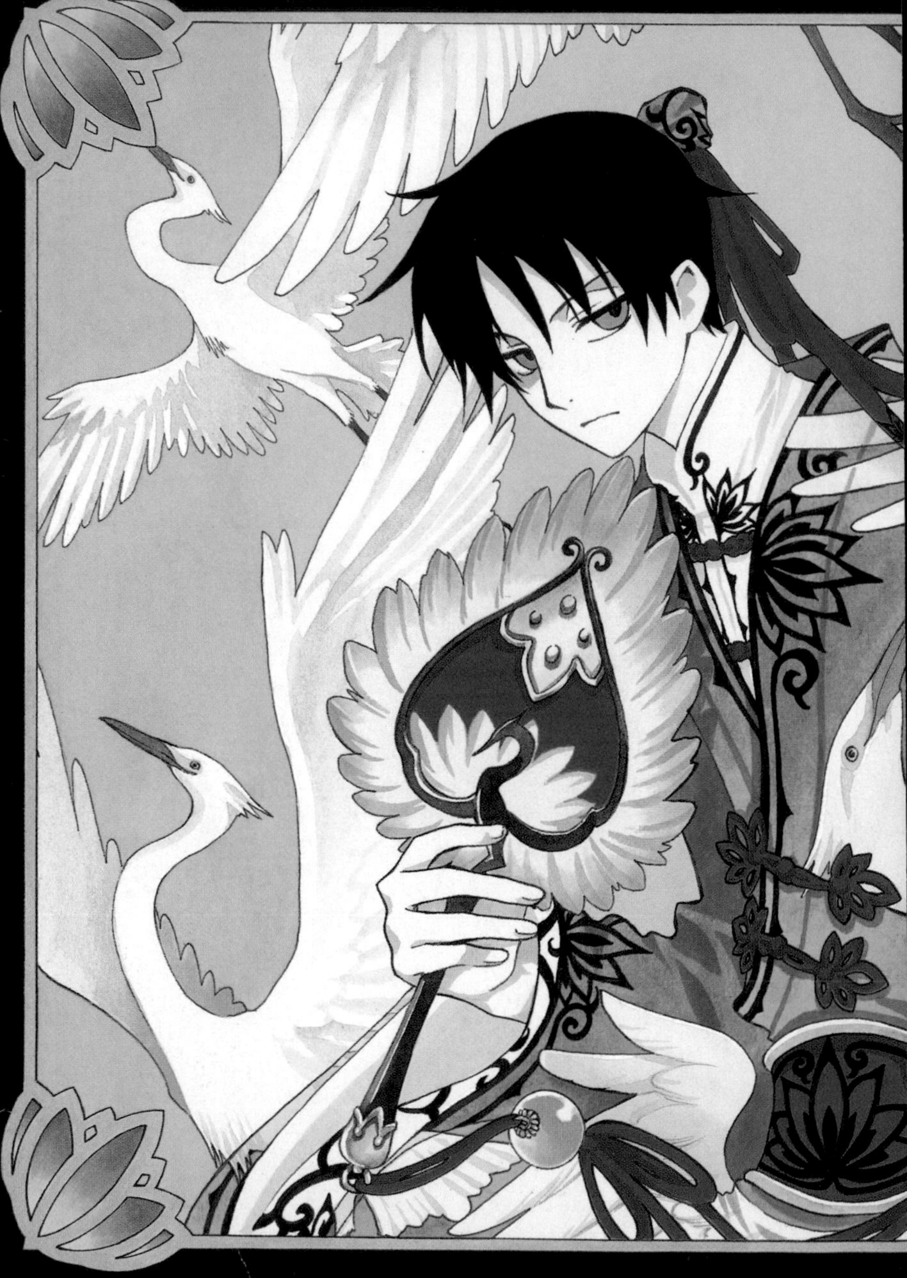

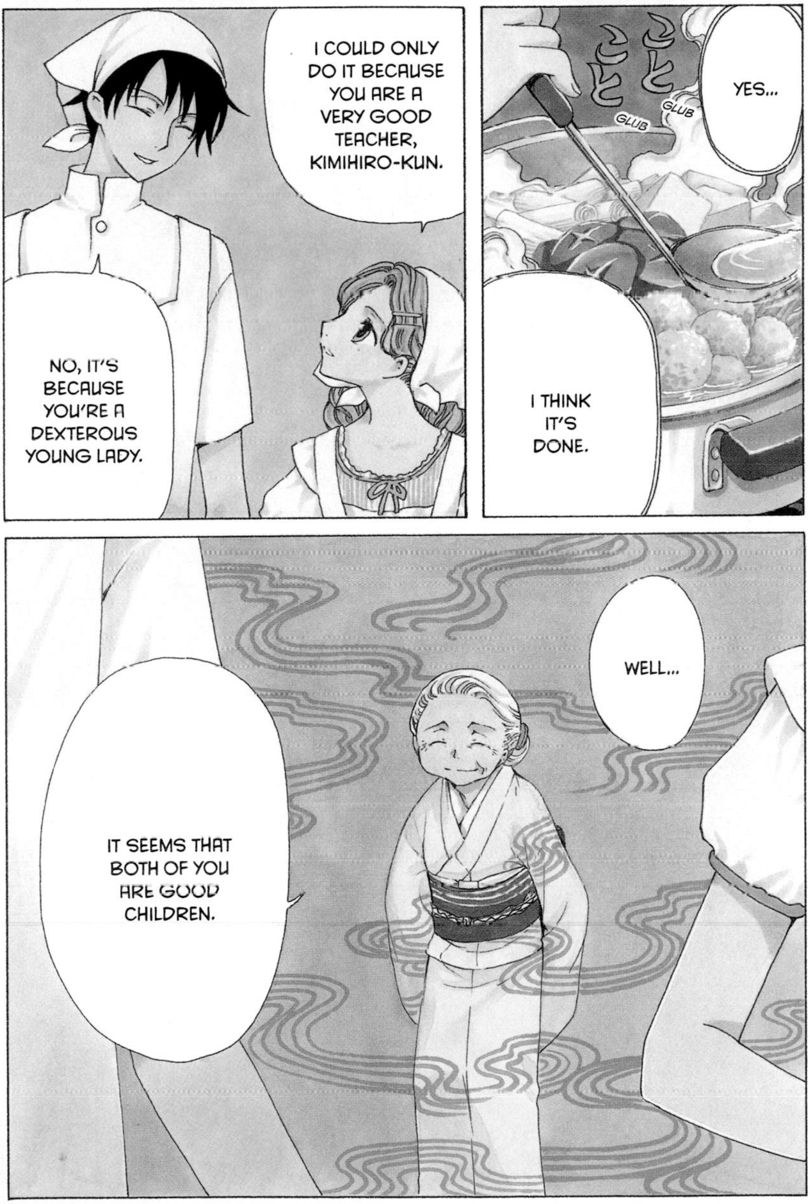
ことこと
GLUB
GLUB
YES...
I THINK IT'S DONE.
I COULD ONLY DO IT BECAUSE YOU ARE A VERY GOOD TEACHER, KIMIHIRO-KUN.
NO, IT'S BECAUSE YOU'RE A DEXTEROUS YOUNG LADY.
WELL...
IT SEEMS THAT BOTH OF YOU ARE GOOD CHILDREN.

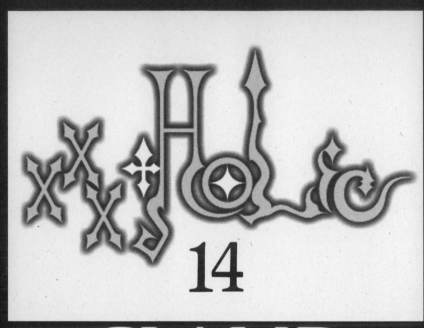

14

CLAMP

TRANSLATED AND ADAPTED BY
William Flanagan

LETTERED BY
North Market Street Graphics

BALLANTINE BOOKS • NEW YORK

1/10 11.00

xxxHOLiC, volume 14 is a work of fiction. Names, characters, places, and incidents are the products of the author's imagination or are used fictitiously. Any resemblance to actual events, locales, or persons, living or dead, is entirely coincidental.

A Del Rey Manga/Kodansha Trade Paperback Original

Published in the United States by Del Rey Books, an imprint of The Random House Publishing Group, a division of Random House, Inc., New York.

Del Rey is a registered trademark and the Del Rey colophon is a trademark of Random House, Inc.

Publication rights arranged through Kodansha Ltd.

First published in Japan in 2009 by Kodansha Ltd., Tokyo

ISBN 978-0-345-51843-9

Printed in the United States of America

www.delreymanga.com

9 8 7 6 5 4 3 2 1

Translator and Adapter—William Flanagan
Lettering—North Market Street Graphics

xxxHOLiC crosses over with *Tsubasa*. Although it isn't necessary to read *Tsubasa* to understand the events in *xxxHOLiC*, you'll get to see the same events from different perspectives if you read both series!

Contents

Honorifics Explained

Throughout the Del Rey Manga books, you will find Japanese honorifics left intact in the translations. For those not familiar with how the Japanese use honorifics and, more important, how they differ from American honorifics, we present this brief overview.

Politeness has always been a critical facet of Japanese culture. Ever since the feudal era, when Japan was a highly stratified society, use of honorifics—which can be defined as polite speech that indicates relationship or status—has played an essential role in the Japanese language. When you address someone in Japanese, an honorific usually takes the form of a suffix attached to one's name (example: "Asuna-san"), is used as a title at the end of one's name, or appears in place of the name itself (example: "Negi-sensei," or simply "Sensei!").

Honorifics can be expressions of respect or endearment. In the context of manga and anime, honorifics give insight into the nature of the relationship between characters. Many English translations leave out these important honorifics and therefore distort the feel of the original Japanese. Because Japanese honorifics contain nuances that English honorifics lack, it is our policy at Del Rey not to translate them. Here, instead, is a guide to some of the honorifics you may encounter in Del Rey Manga.

-san: This is the most common honorific and is equivalent to Mr., Miss, Ms., or Mrs. It is the all-purpose honorific and can be used in any situation where politeness is required.

-sama: This is one level higher than "-san" and is used to confer great respect.

-dono: This comes from the word "tono," which means "lord." It is an even higher level than "-sama" and confers utmost respect.

-kun: This suffix is used at the end of boys' names to express familiarity or endearment. It is also sometimes used by men among friends, or when addressing someone younger or of a lower station.

-chan: This is used to express endearment, mostly toward girls. It is also used for little boys, pets, and even among lovers. It gives a sense of childish cuteness.

Bozu: This is an informal way to refer to a boy, similar to the English terms "kid" and "squirt."

Sempai/Senpai: This title suggests that the addressee is one's senior in a group or organization. It is most often used in a school setting, where underclassmen refer to their upperclassmen as "sempai." It can also be used in the workplace, such as when a newer employee addresses an employee who has seniority in the company.

Kohai: This is the opposite of "sempai" and is used toward under-classmen in school or newcomers in the workplace. It connotes that the addressee is of a lower station.

Sensei: Literally meaning "one who has come before," this title is used for teachers, doctors, or masters of any profession or art.

-[blank]: This is usually forgotten in these lists, but it is perhaps the most significant difference between Japanese and English. The lack of honorific means that the speaker has permission to address the person in a very intimate way. Usually, only family, spouses, or very close friends have this kind of permission. Known as *yobisute*, it can be gratifying when someone who has earned the intimacy starts to call one by one's name without an honorific. But when that intimacy hasn't been earned, it can be very insulting.

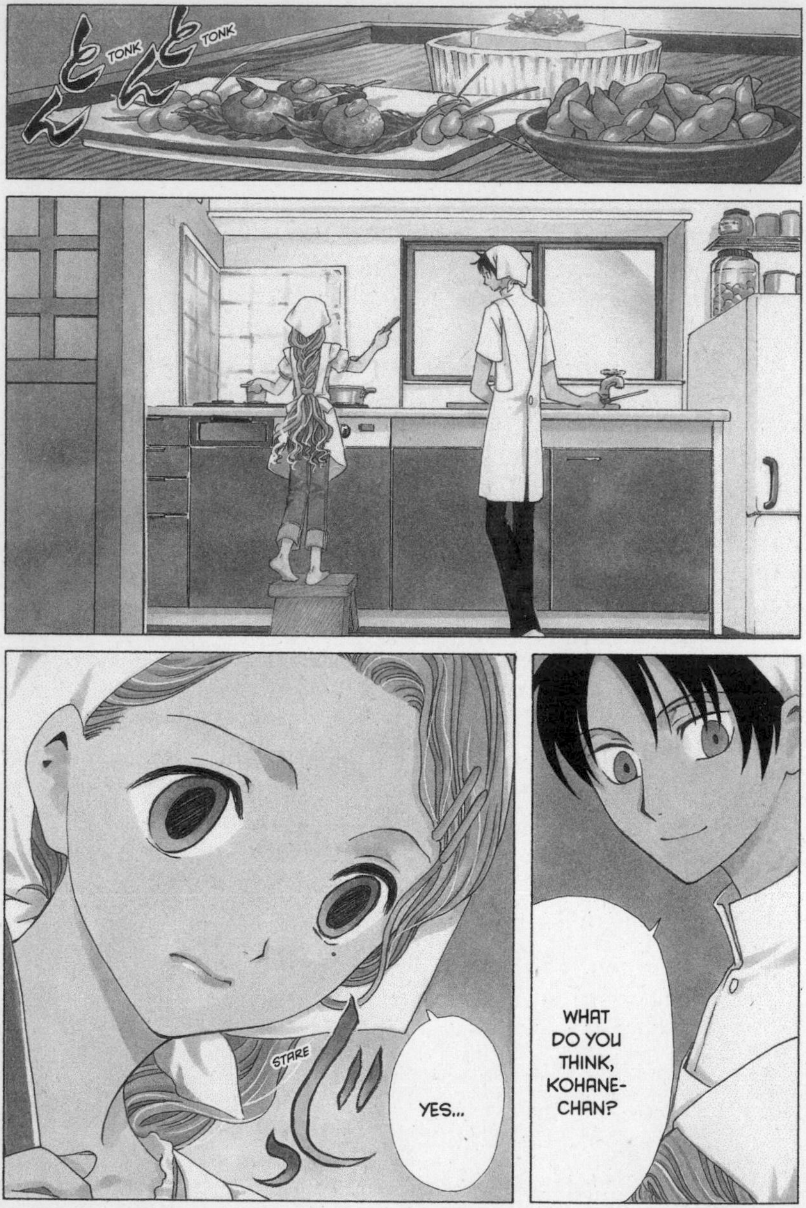
TONK
TONK
WHAT DO YOU THINK, KOHANE-CHAN?
YES...
STARE

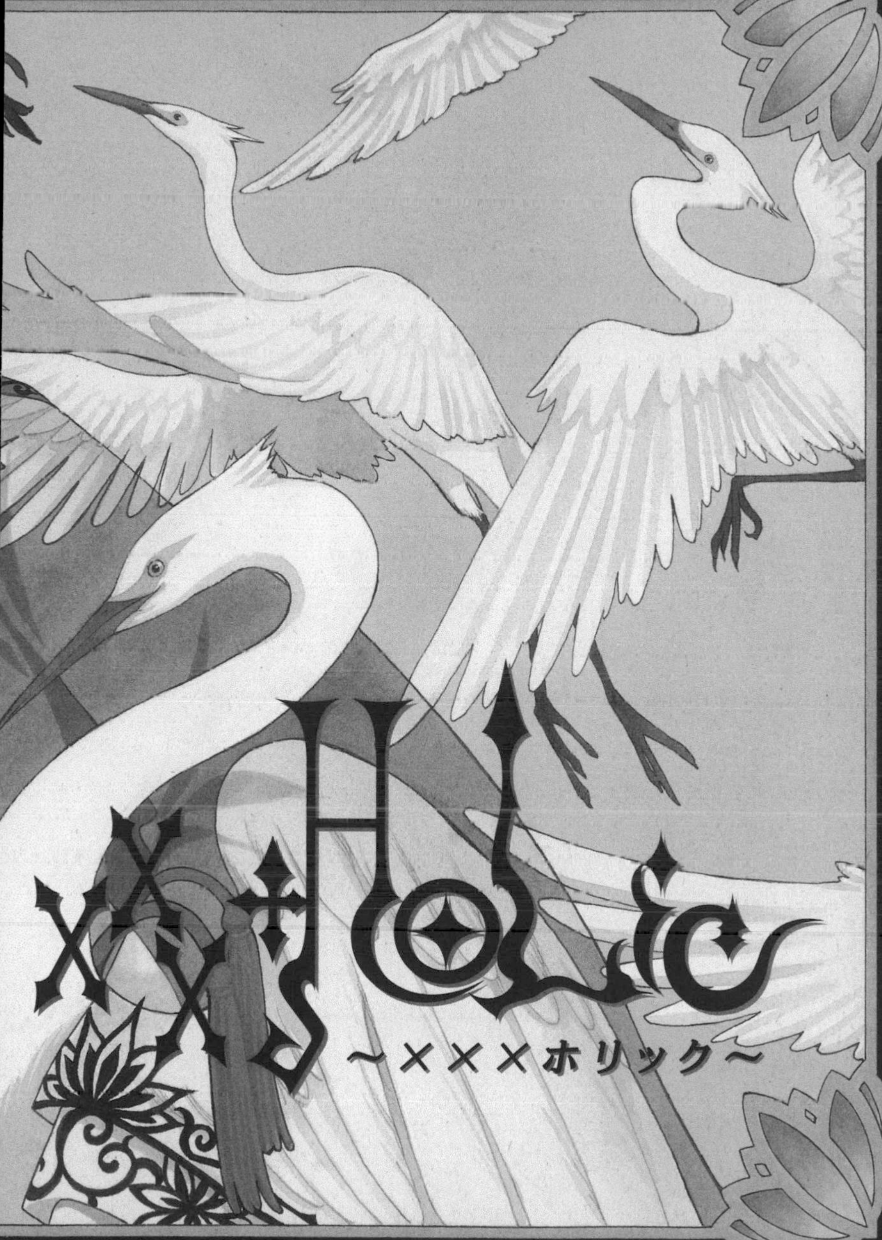
xxxHOLiC
〜×××ホリック〜

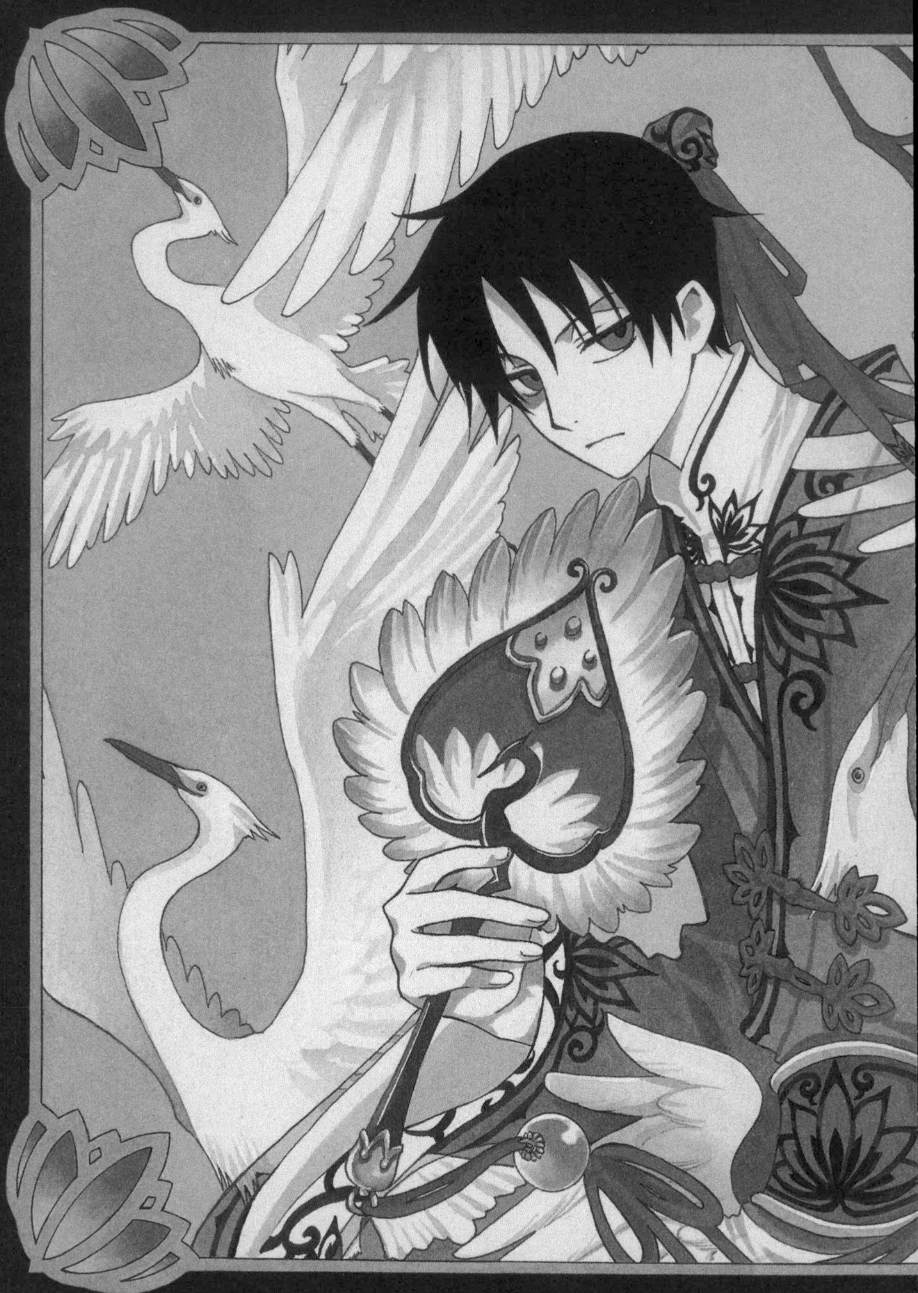

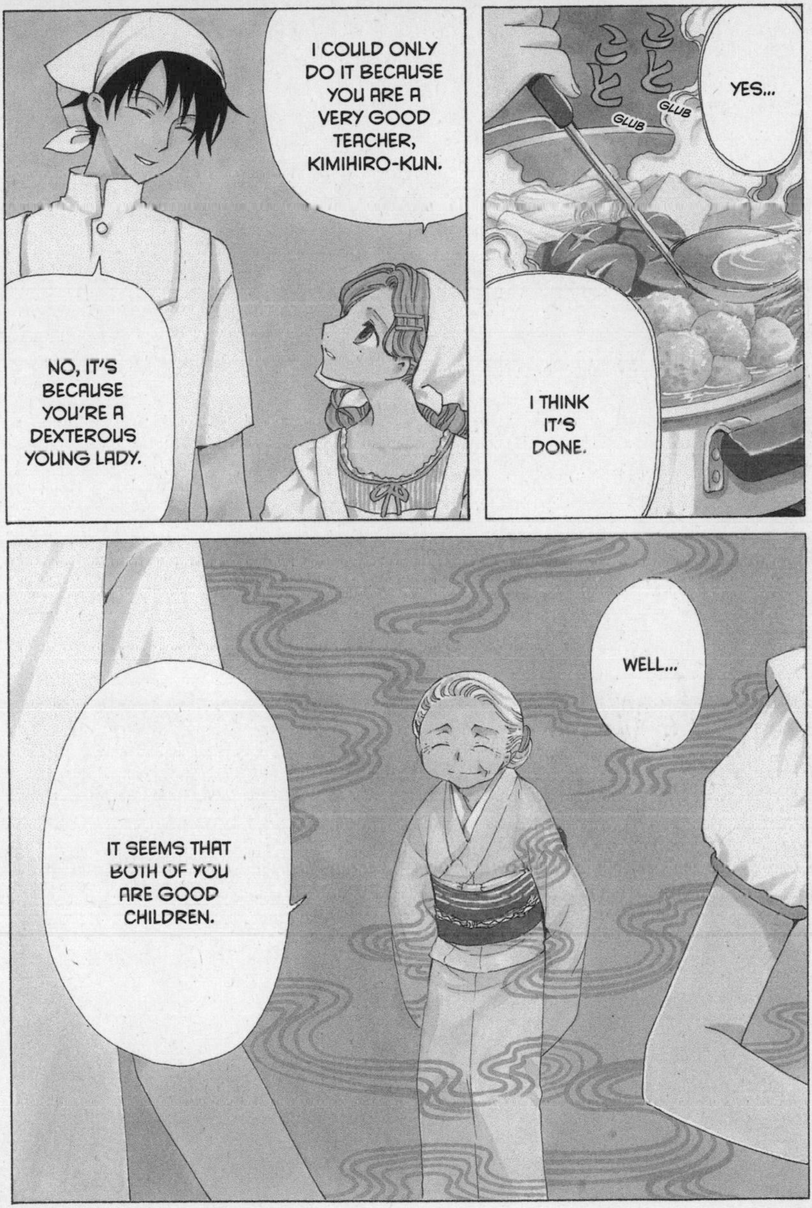
YES...
ことこと
GLUB
GLUB
I THINK IT'S DONE.
I COULD ONLY DO IT BECAUSE YOU ARE A VERY GOOD TEACHER, KIMIHIRO-KUN.
NO, IT'S BECAUSE YOU'RE A DEXTEROUS YOUNG LADY.
WELL...
IT SEEMS THAT BOTH OF YOU ARE GOOD CHILDREN.

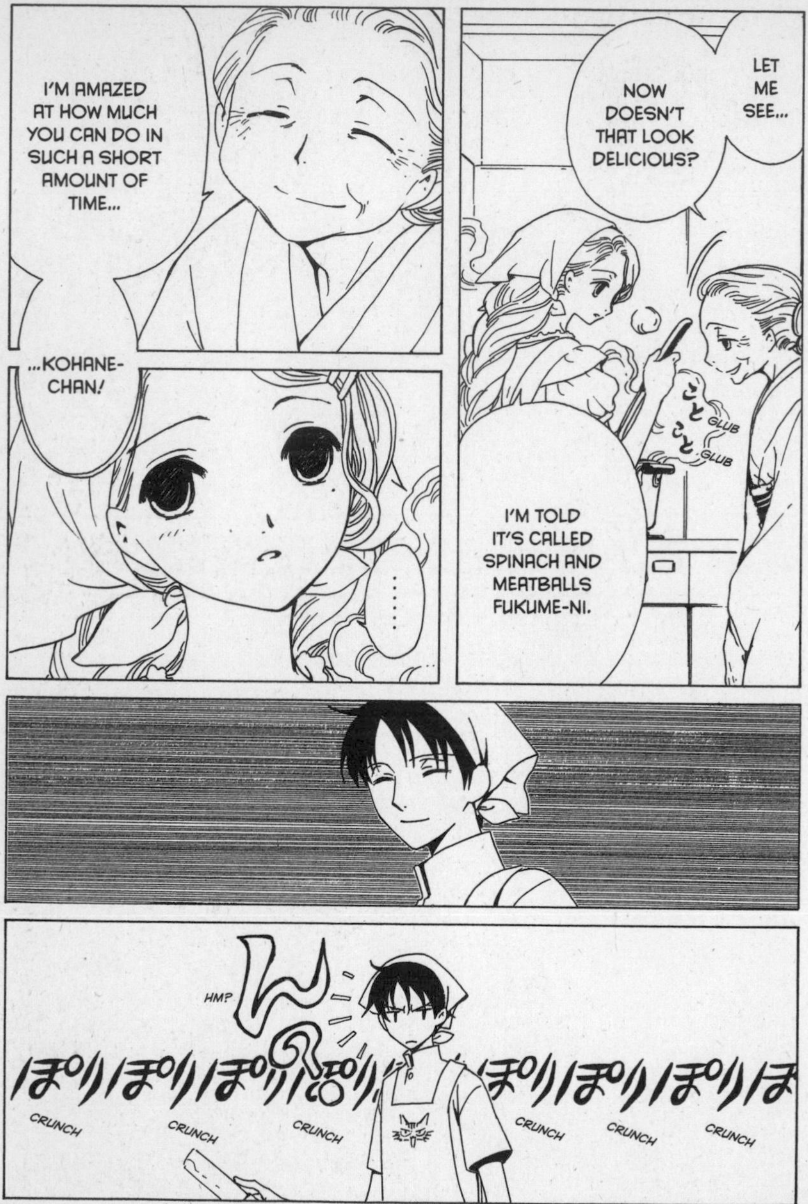
LET ME SEE...
NOW DOESN'T THAT LOOK DELICIOUS?
ことこと
GLUB
GLUB
I'M TOLD IT'S CALLED SPINACH AND MEATBALLS FUKUME-NI.
I'M AMAZED AT HOW MUCH YOU CAN DO IN SUCH A SHORT AMOUNT OF TIME...
...KOHANE-CHAN!
......
ん?
HM?
ぽりぽりぽりぽりぽりぽりぽりぽ
CRUNCH
CRUNCH
CRUNCH
CRUNCH
CRUNCH
CRUNCH

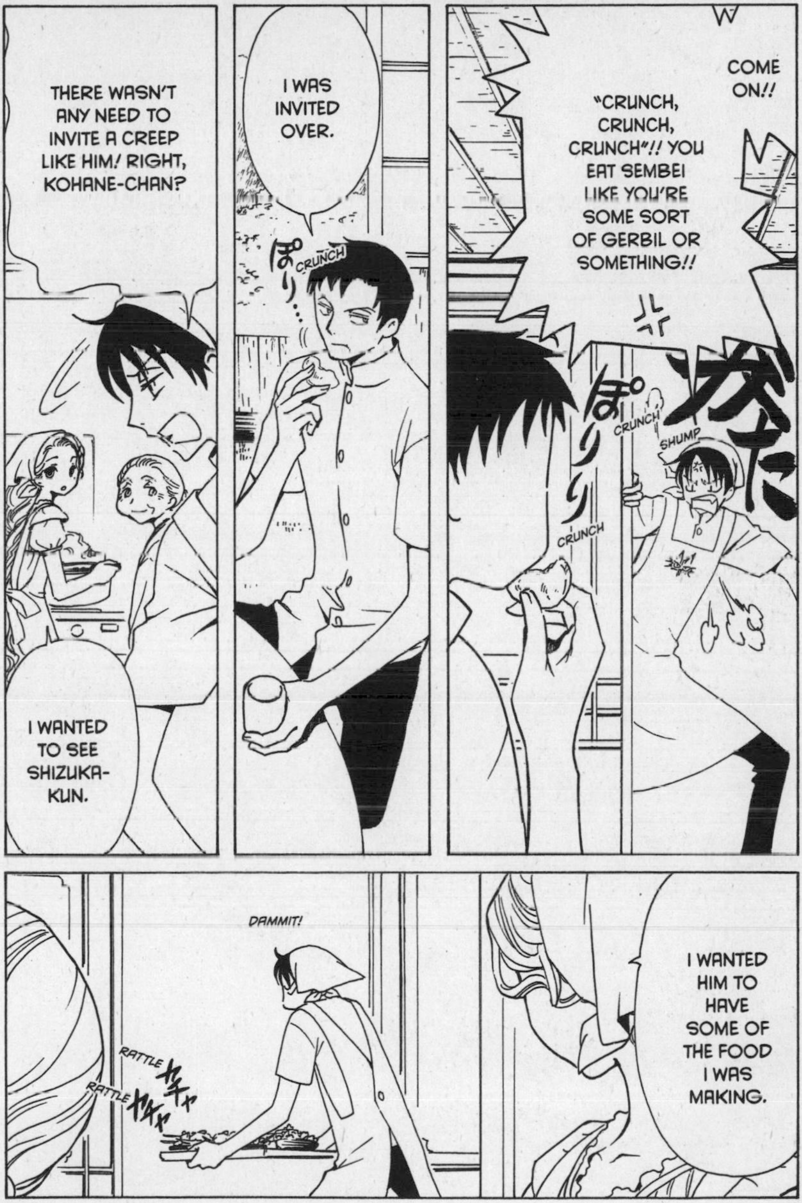
COME ON!!
"CRUNCH, CRUNCH, CRUNCH"!! YOU EAT SEMBEI LIKE YOU'RE SOME SORT OF GERBIL OR SOMETHING!!
SHUMP
CRUNCH
CRUNCH
I WAS INVITED OVER.
CRUNCH
THERE WASN'T ANY NEED TO INVITE A CREEP LIKE HIM! RIGHT, KOHANE-CHAN?
I WANTED TO SEE SHIZUKA-KUN.
I WANTED HIM TO HAVE SOME OF THE FOOD I WAS MAKING.
DAMMIT!
RATTLE
RATTLE

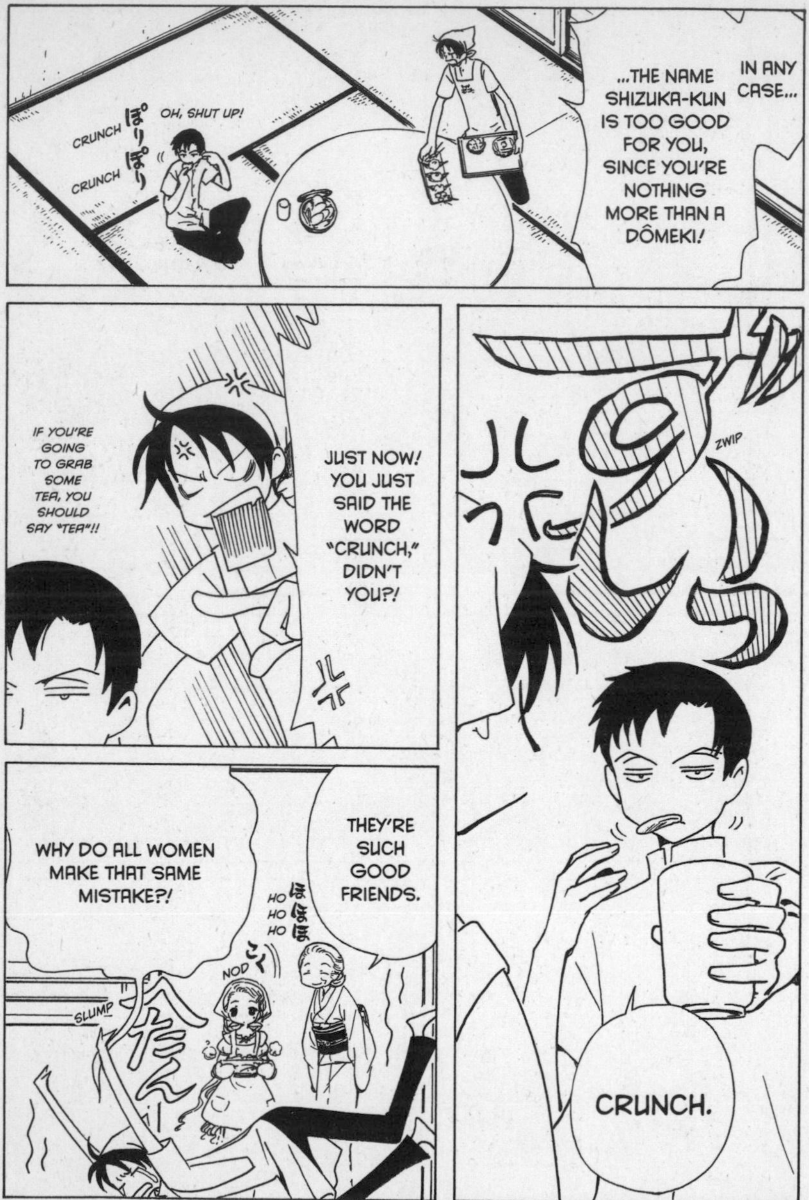
IN ANY CASE...
...THE NAME SHIZUKA-KUN IS TOO GOOD FOR YOU, SINCE YOU'RE NOTHING MORE THAN A DÔMEKI!
OH, SHUT UP!
ぽりぽり
CRUNCH CRUNCH
ZWIP
CRUNCH.
JUST NOW! YOU JUST SAID THE WORD "CRUNCH," DIDN'T YOU?!
IF YOU'RE GOING TO GRAB SOME TEA, YOU SHOULD SAY "TEA"!!
THEY'RE SUCH GOOD FRIENDS.
ほほほ
HO HO HO
こく
NOD
WHY DO ALL WOMEN MAKE THAT SAME MISTAKE?!
SLUMP

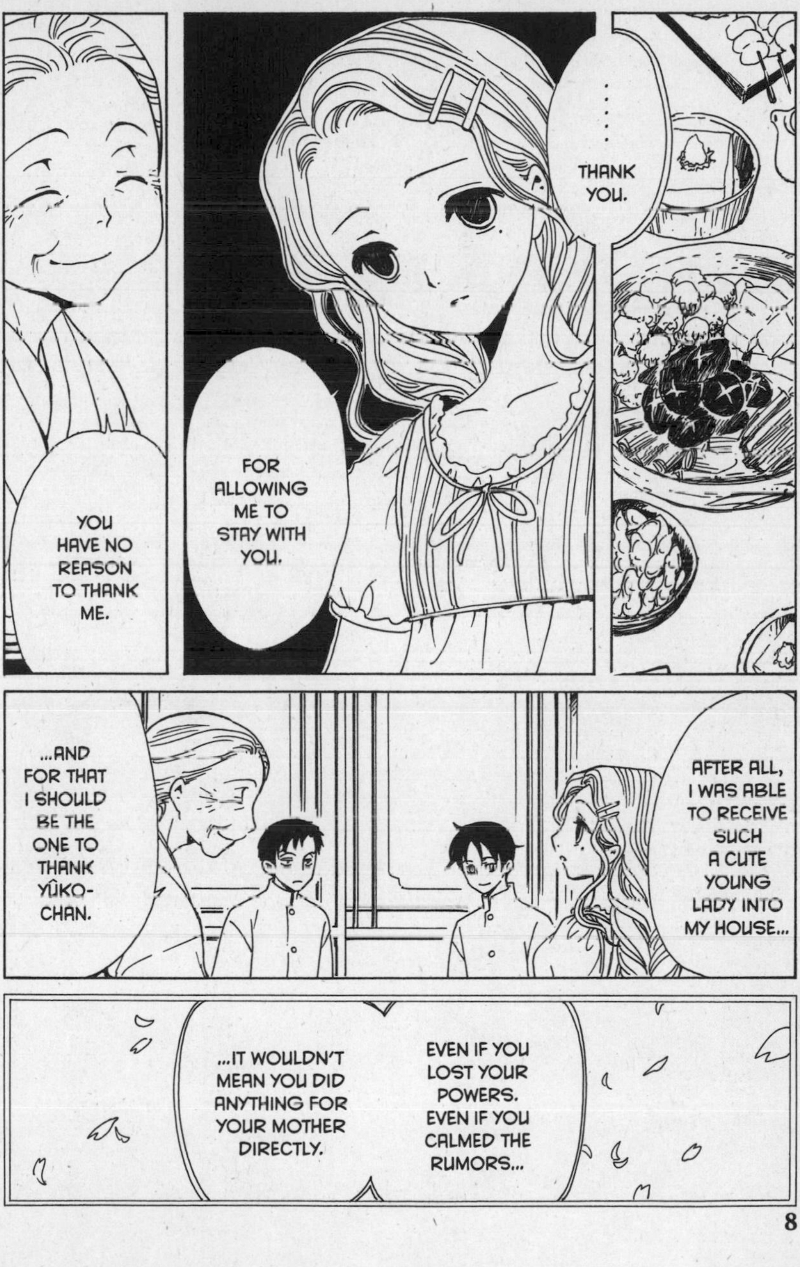
......
THANK YOU.
FOR ALLOWING ME TO STAY WITH YOU.
YOU HAVE NO REASON TO THANK ME.
AFTER ALL, I WAS ABLE TO RECEIVE SUCH A CUTE YOUNG LADY INTO MY HOUSE...
...AND FOR THAT I SHOULD BE THE ONE TO THANK YÛKO-CHAN.
EVEN IF YOU LOST YOUR POWERS. EVEN IF YOU CALMED THE RUMORS...
...IT WOULDN'T MEAN YOU DID ANYTHING FOR YOUR MOTHER DIRECTLY.

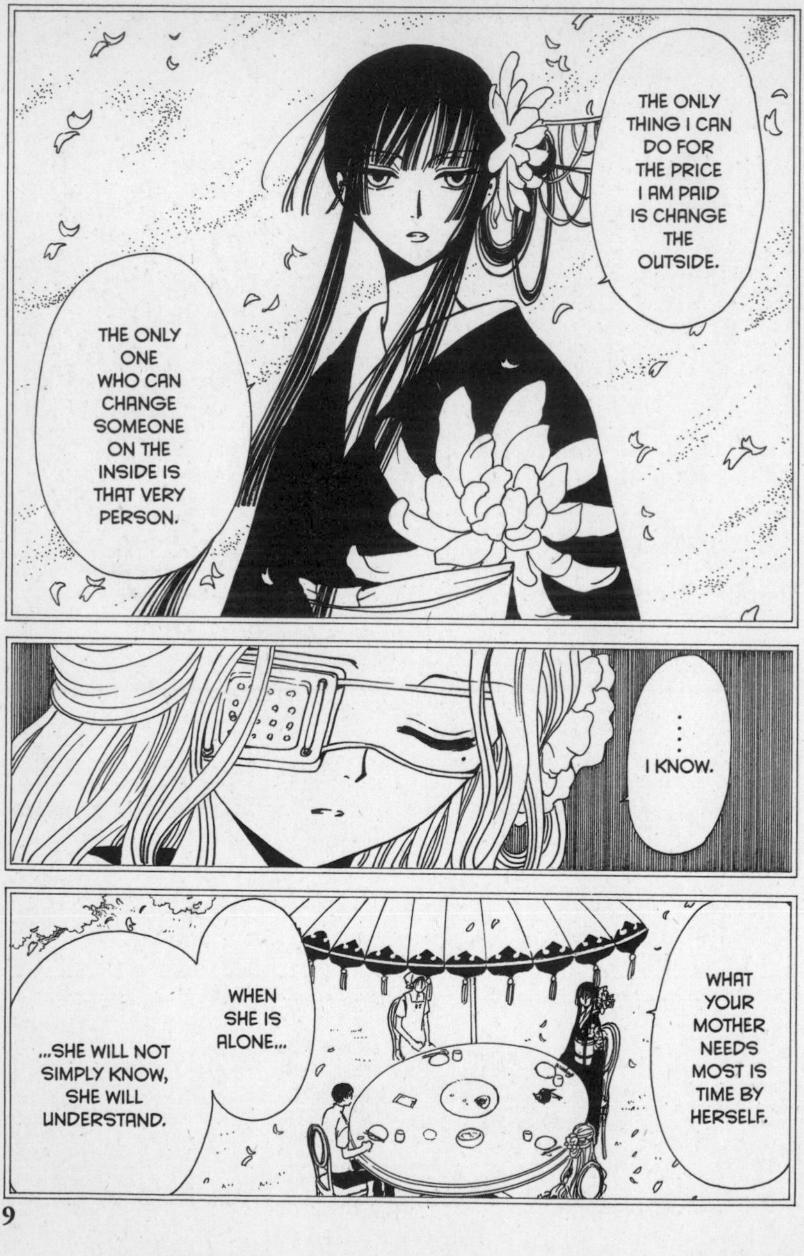
THE ONLY THING I CAN DO FOR THE PRICE I AM PAID IS CHANGE THE OUTSIDE.
THE ONLY ONE WHO CAN CHANGE SOMEONE ON THE INSIDE IS THAT VERY PERSON.
...... I KNOW.
WHAT YOUR MOTHER NEEDS MOST IS TIME BY HERSELF.
WHEN SHE IS ALONE...
...SHE WILL NOT SIMPLY KNOW, SHE WILL UNDERSTAND.

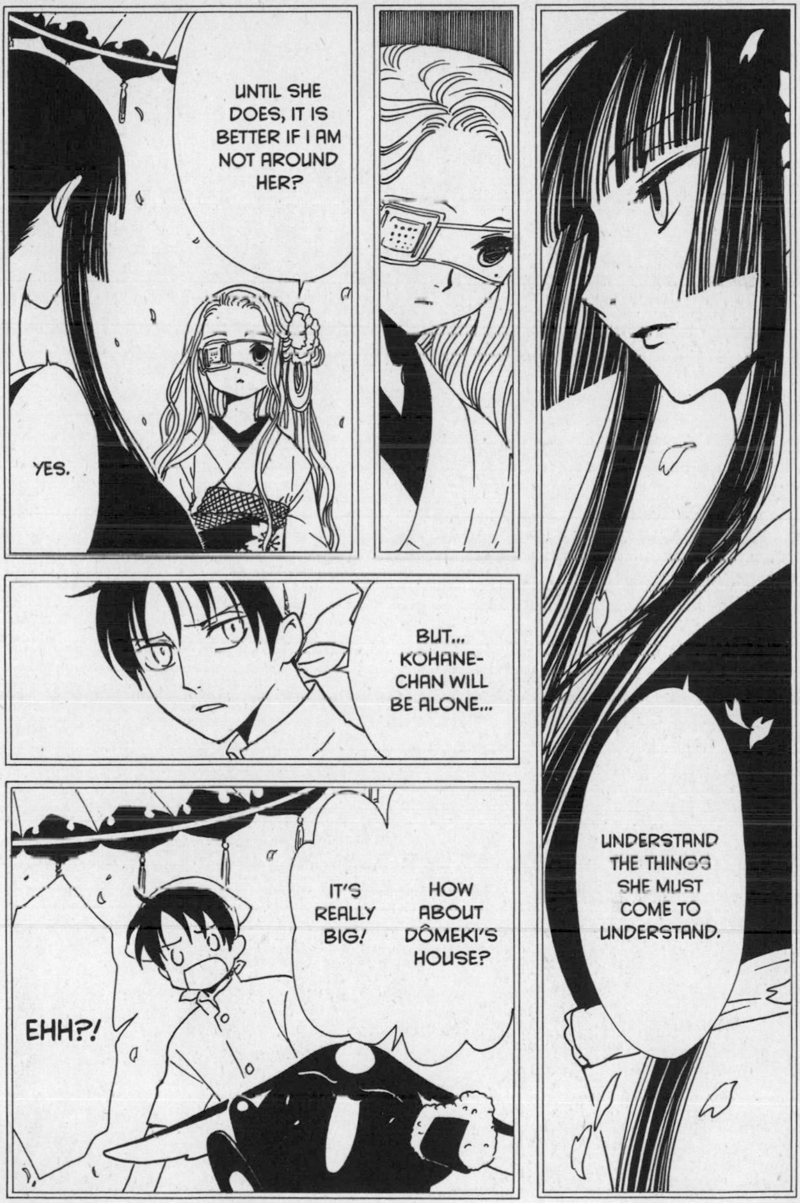
UNDERSTAND THE THINGS SHE MUST COME TO UNDERSTAND.
UNTIL SHE DOES, IT IS BETTER IF I AM NOT AROUND HER?
YES.
BUT... KOHANE-CHAN WILL BE ALONE...
HOW ABOUT DÔMEKI'S HOUSE?
IT'S REALLY BIG!
EHH?!

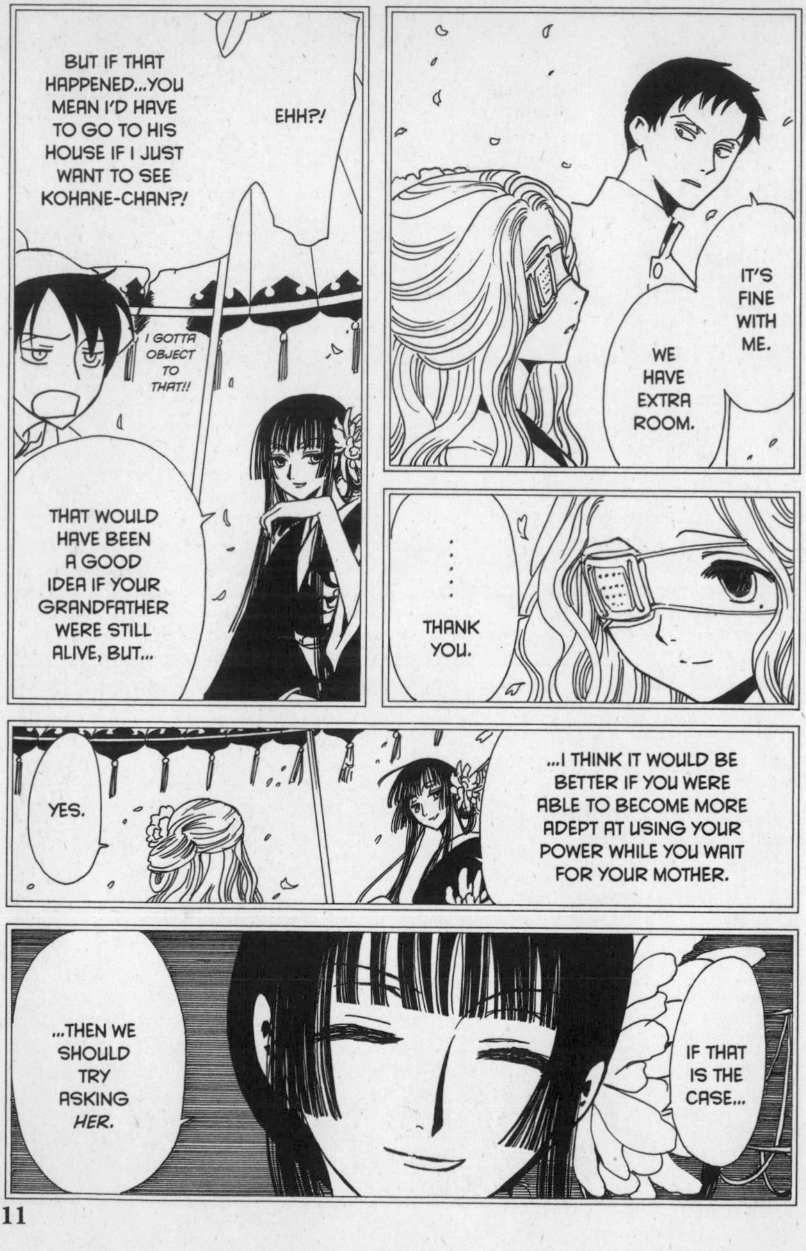
IT'S FINE WITH ME.
WE HAVE EXTRA ROOM.
......
THANK YOU.
EHH?!
BUT IF THAT HAPPENED...YOU MEAN I'D HAVE TO GO TO HIS HOUSE IF I JUST WANT TO SEE KOHANE-CHAN?!
I GOTTA OBJECT TO THAT!!
THAT WOULD HAVE BEEN A GOOD IDEA IF YOUR GRANDFATHER WERE STILL ALIVE, BUT...
...I THINK IT WOULD BE BETTER IF YOU WERE ABLE TO BECOME MORE ADEPT AT USING YOUR POWER WHILE YOU WAIT FOR YOUR MOTHER.
YES.
IF THAT IS THE CASE...
...THEN WE SHOULD TRY ASKING *HER*.

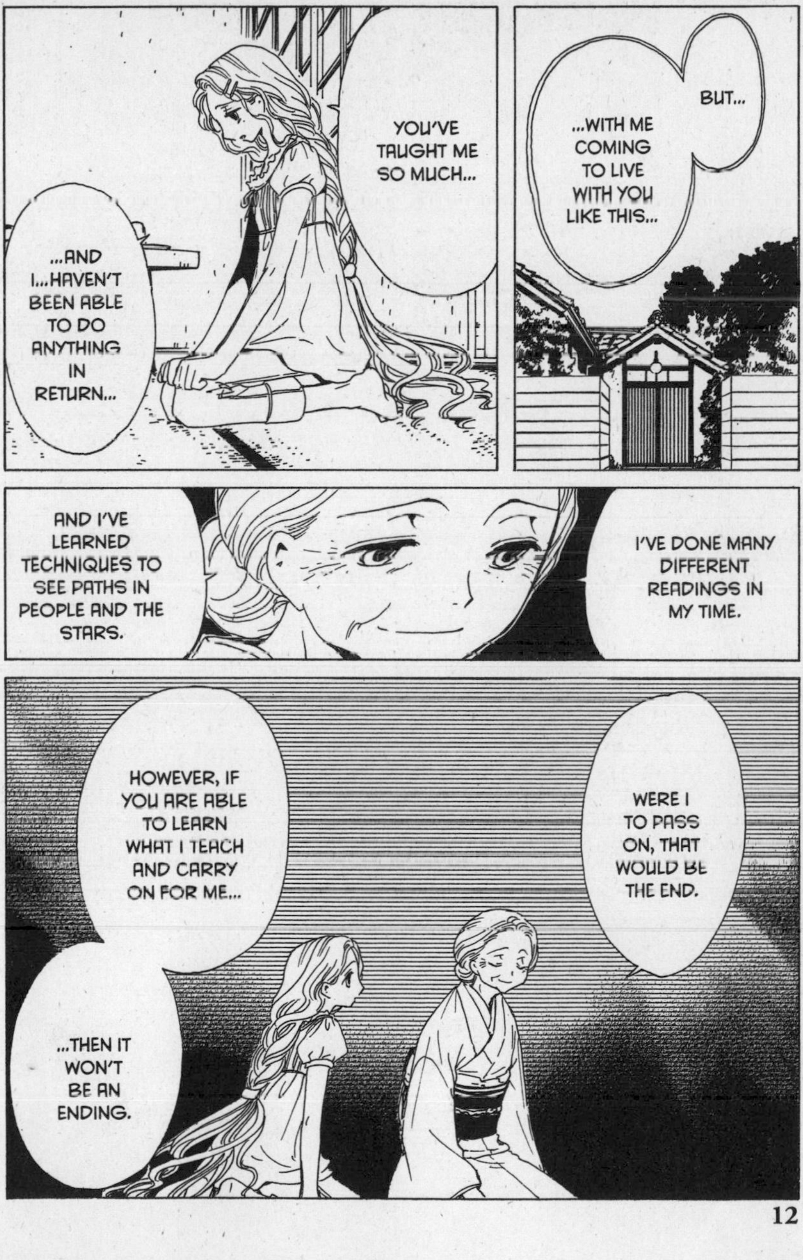
BUT...
...WITH ME COMING TO LIVE WITH YOU LIKE THIS...
YOU'VE TAUGHT ME SO MUCH...
...AND I...HAVEN'T BEEN ABLE TO DO ANYTHING IN RETURN...
I'VE DONE MANY DIFFERENT READINGS IN MY TIME.
AND I'VE LEARNED TECHNIQUES TO SEE PATHS IN PEOPLE AND THE STARS.
WERE I TO PASS ON, THAT WOULD BE THE END.
HOWEVER, IF YOU ARE ABLE TO LEARN WHAT I TEACH AND CARRY ON FOR ME...
...THEN IT WON'T BE AN ENDING.

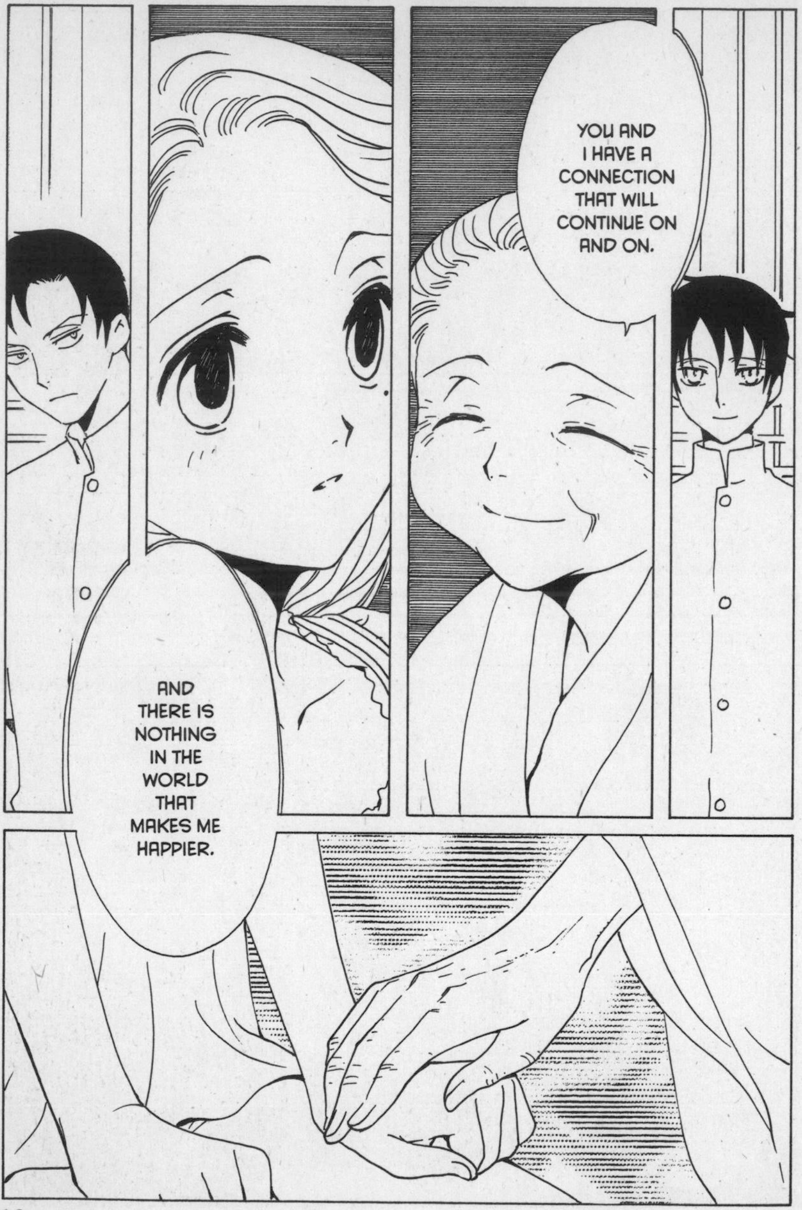
YOU AND I HAVE A CONNECTION THAT WILL CONTINUE ON AND ON.
AND THERE IS NOTHING IN THE WORLD THAT MAKES ME HAPPIER.

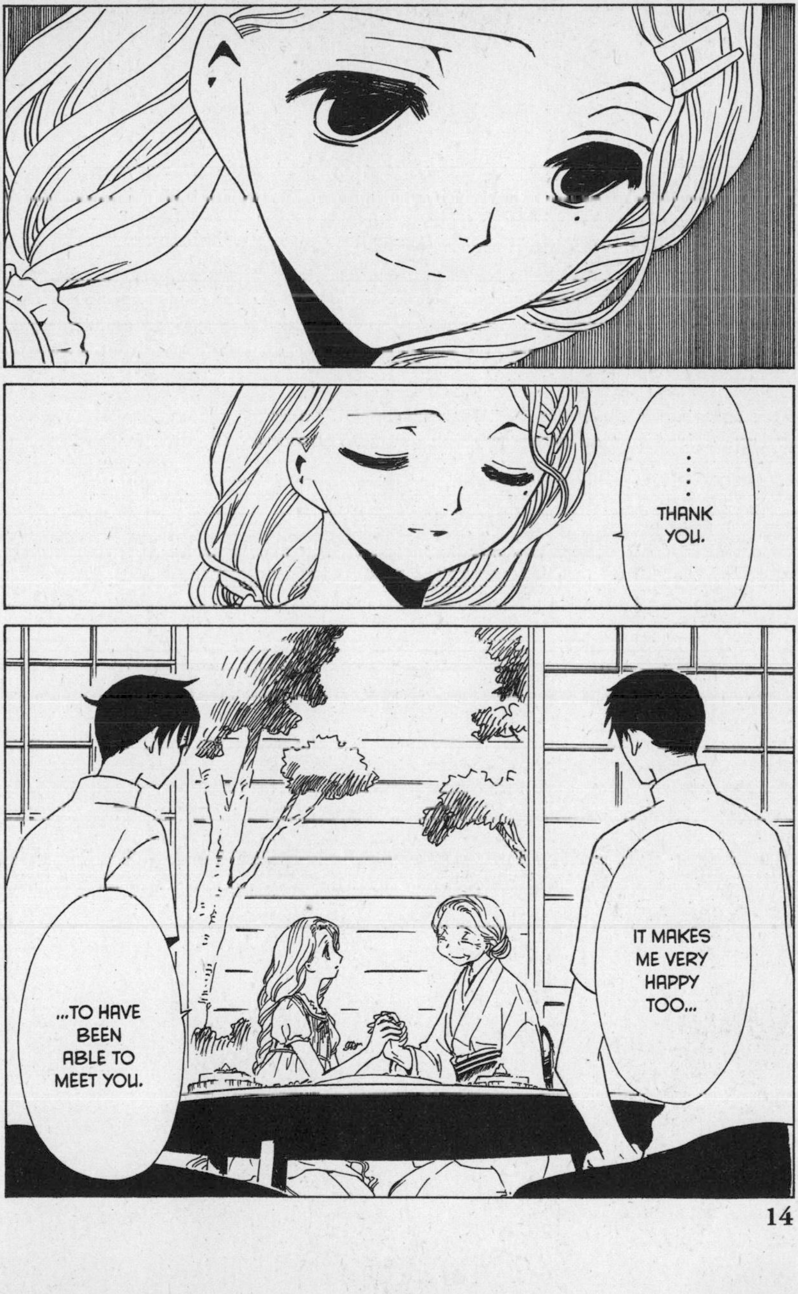
.... THANK YOU.
IT MAKES ME VERY HAPPY TOO...
...TO HAVE BEEN ABLE TO MEET YOU.

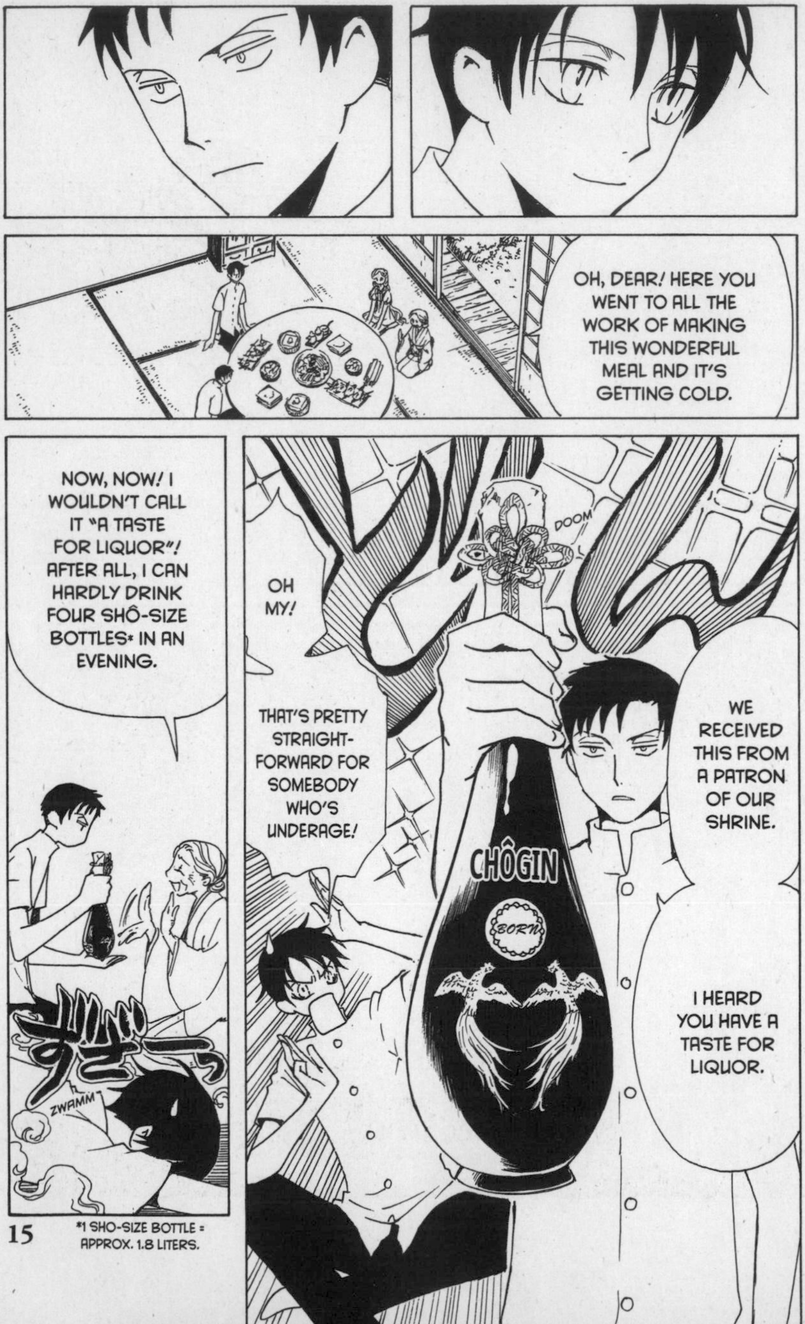
OH, DEAR! HERE YOU WENT TO ALL THE WORK OF MAKING THIS WONDERFUL MEAL AND IT'S GETTING COLD.
WE RECEIVED THIS FROM A PATRON OF OUR SHRINE.
I HEARD YOU HAVE A TASTE FOR LIQUOR.
DOOM
CHÔGIN
BORN
OH MY!
THAT'S PRETTY STRAIGHT-FORWARD FOR SOMEBODY WHO'S UNDERAGE!
NOW, NOW! I WOULDN'T CALL IT "A TASTE FOR LIQUOR"! AFTER ALL, I CAN HARDLY DRINK FOUR SHÔ-SIZE BOTTLES* IN AN EVENING.
ZWAMM

*1 SHO-SIZE BOTTLE = APPROX. 1.8 LITERS.

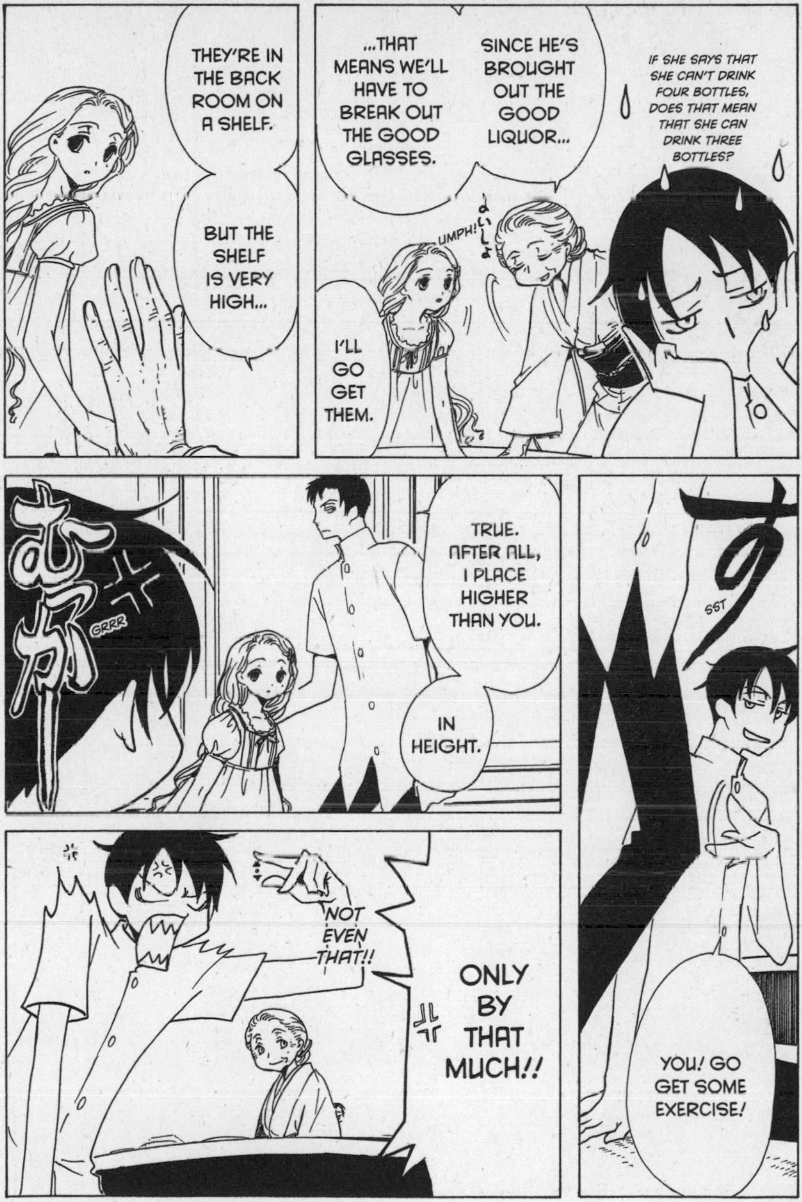
IF SHE SAYS THAT SHE CAN'T DRINK FOUR BOTTLES, DOES THAT MEAN THAT SHE CAN DRINK THREE BOTTLES?
SINCE HE'S BROUGHT OUT THE GOOD LIQUOR...
...THAT MEANS WE'LL HAVE TO BREAK OUT THE GOOD GLASSES.
よいしょ
UMPH!
I'LL GO GET THEM.
THEY'RE IN THE BACK ROOM ON A SHELF.
BUT THE SHELF IS VERY HIGH...
す
SST
YOU! GO GET SOME EXERCISE!
TRUE. AFTER ALL, I PLACE HIGHER THAN YOU.
IN HEIGHT.
むか
GRRR
NOT EVEN THAT!!
ONLY BY THAT MUCH!!

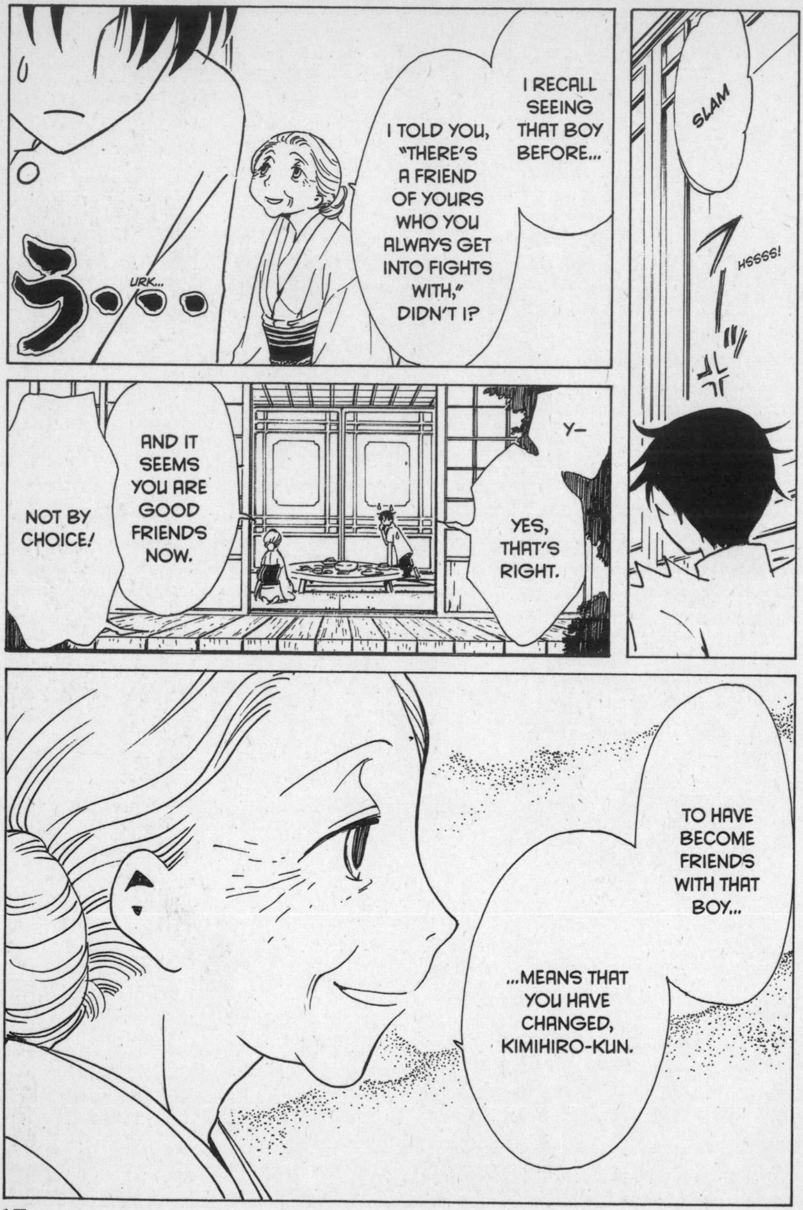
SLAM
HSSSS!
I RECALL SEEING THAT BOY BEFORE...
I TOLD YOU, "THERE'S A FRIEND OF YOURS WHO YOU ALWAYS GET INTO FIGHTS WITH," DIDN'T I?
URK...
Y—
YES, THAT'S RIGHT.
AND IT SEEMS YOU ARE GOOD FRIENDS NOW.
NOT BY CHOICE!
TO HAVE BECOME FRIENDS WITH THAT BOY...
...MEANS THAT YOU HAVE CHANGED, KIMIHIRO-KUN.

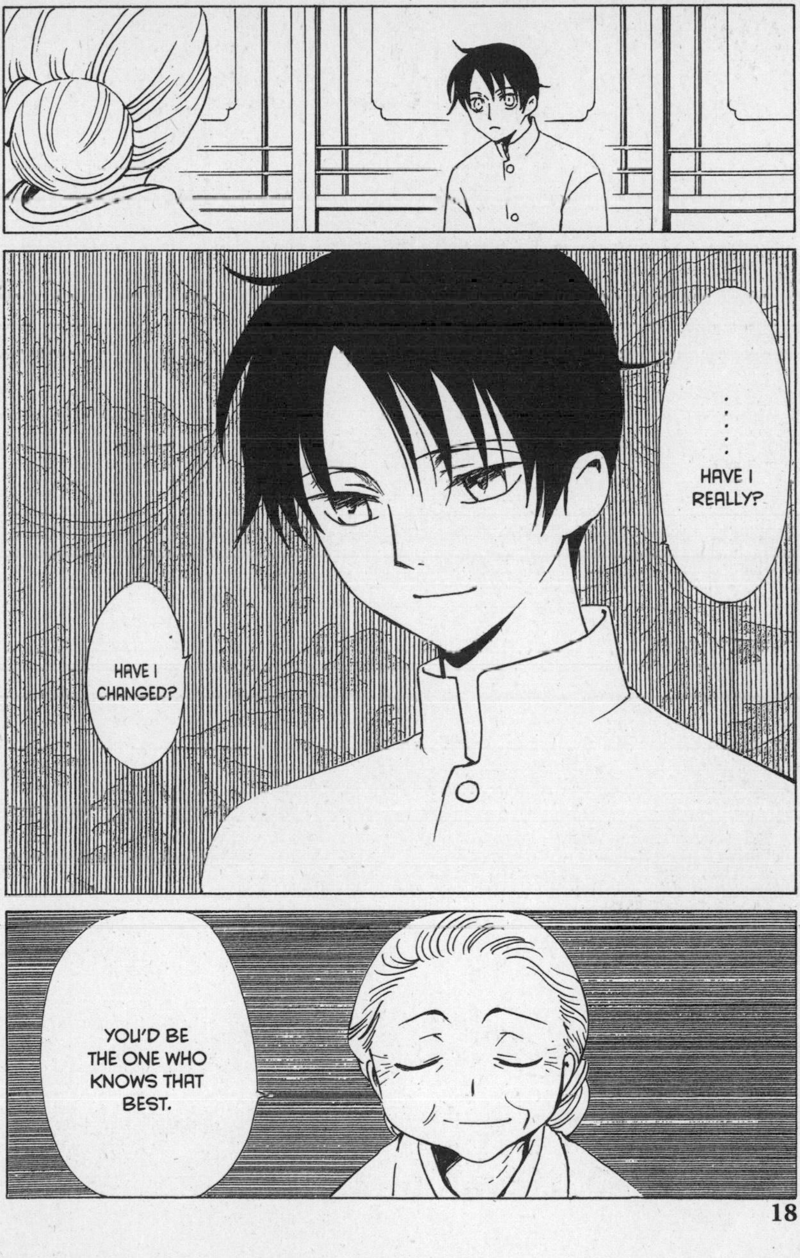
......
HAVE I REALLY?
HAVE I CHANGED?
YOU'D BE THE ONE WHO KNOWS THAT BEST.

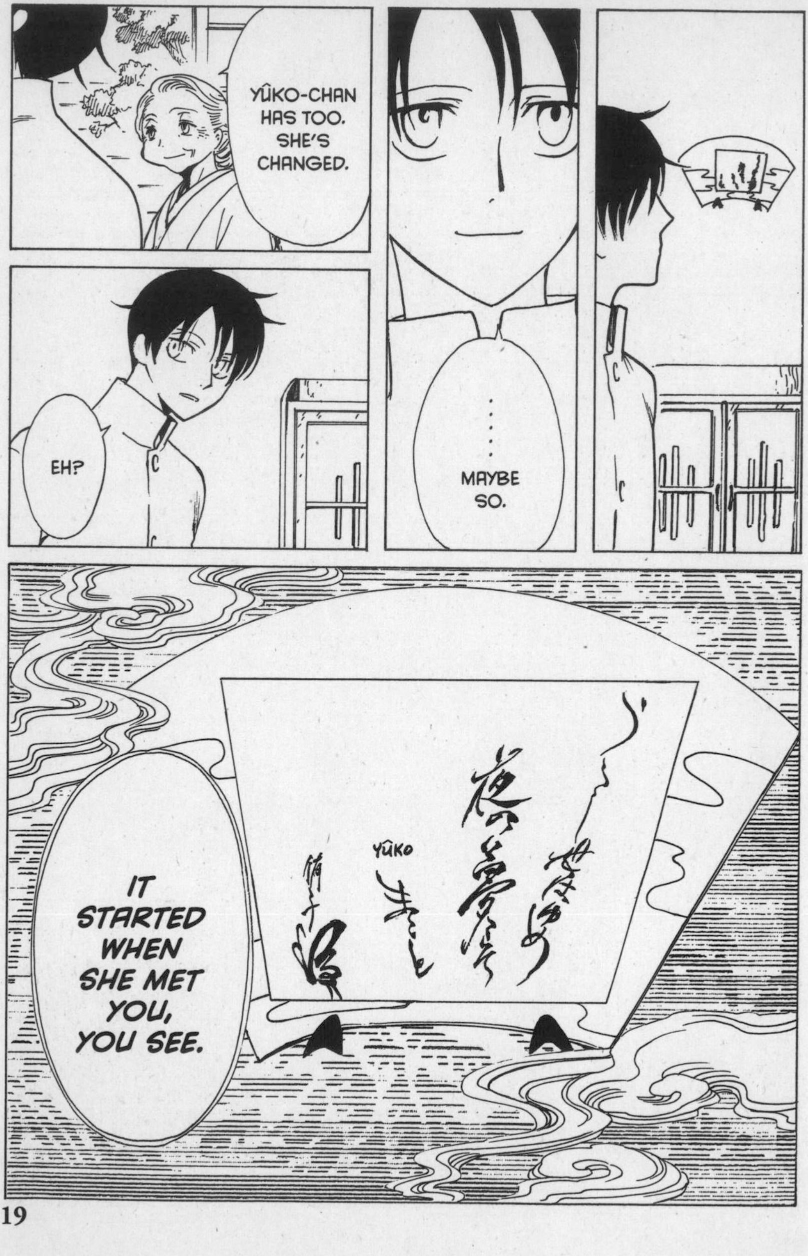
......
MAYBE SO.
YÛKO-CHAN HAS TOO. SHE'S CHANGED.
EH?
IT STARTED WHEN SHE MET YOU, YOU SEE.
YÛKO

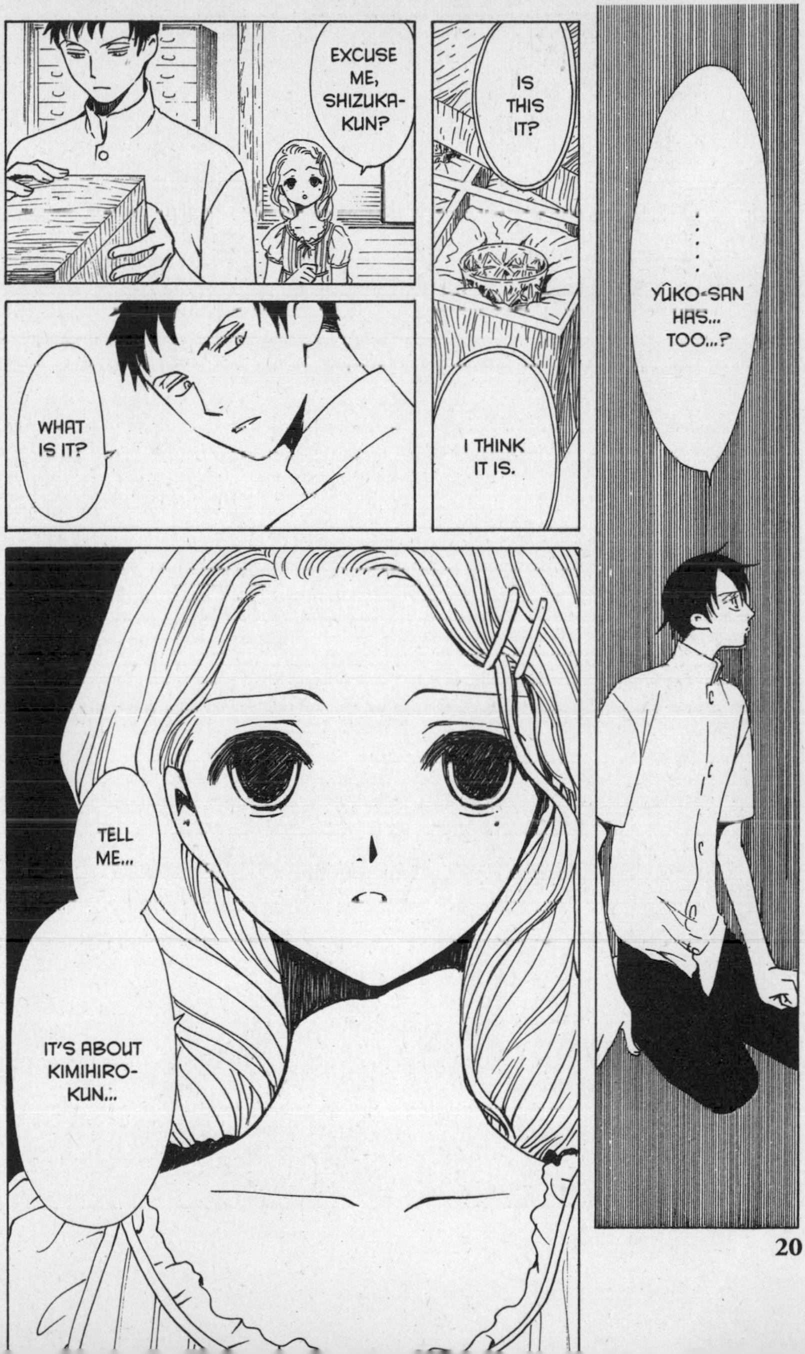
......
YÛKO-SAN HAS... TOO...?
IS THIS IT?
EXCUSE ME, SHIZUKA-KUN?
I THINK IT IS.
WHAT IS IT?
TELL ME...
IT'S ABOUT KIMIHIRO-KUN...

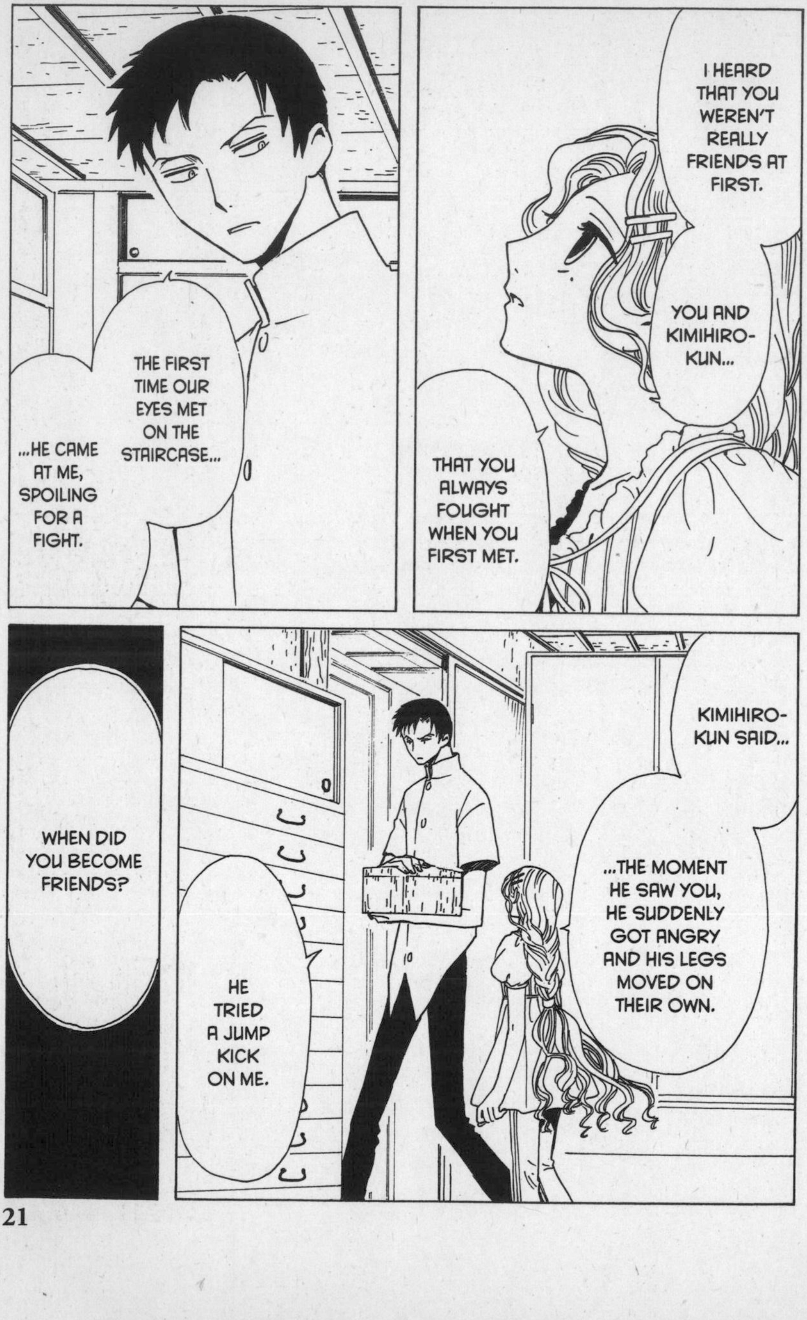
I HEARD THAT YOU WEREN'T REALLY FRIENDS AT FIRST.
YOU AND KIMIHIRO-KUN...
THAT YOU ALWAYS FOUGHT WHEN YOU FIRST MET.
THE FIRST TIME OUR EYES MET ON THE STAIRCASE...
...HE CAME AT ME, SPOILING FOR A FIGHT.
KIMIHIRO-KUN SAID...
...THE MOMENT HE SAW YOU, HE SUDDENLY GOT ANGRY AND HIS LEGS MOVED ON THEIR OWN.
HE TRIED A JUMP KICK ON ME.
WHEN DID YOU BECOME FRIENDS?

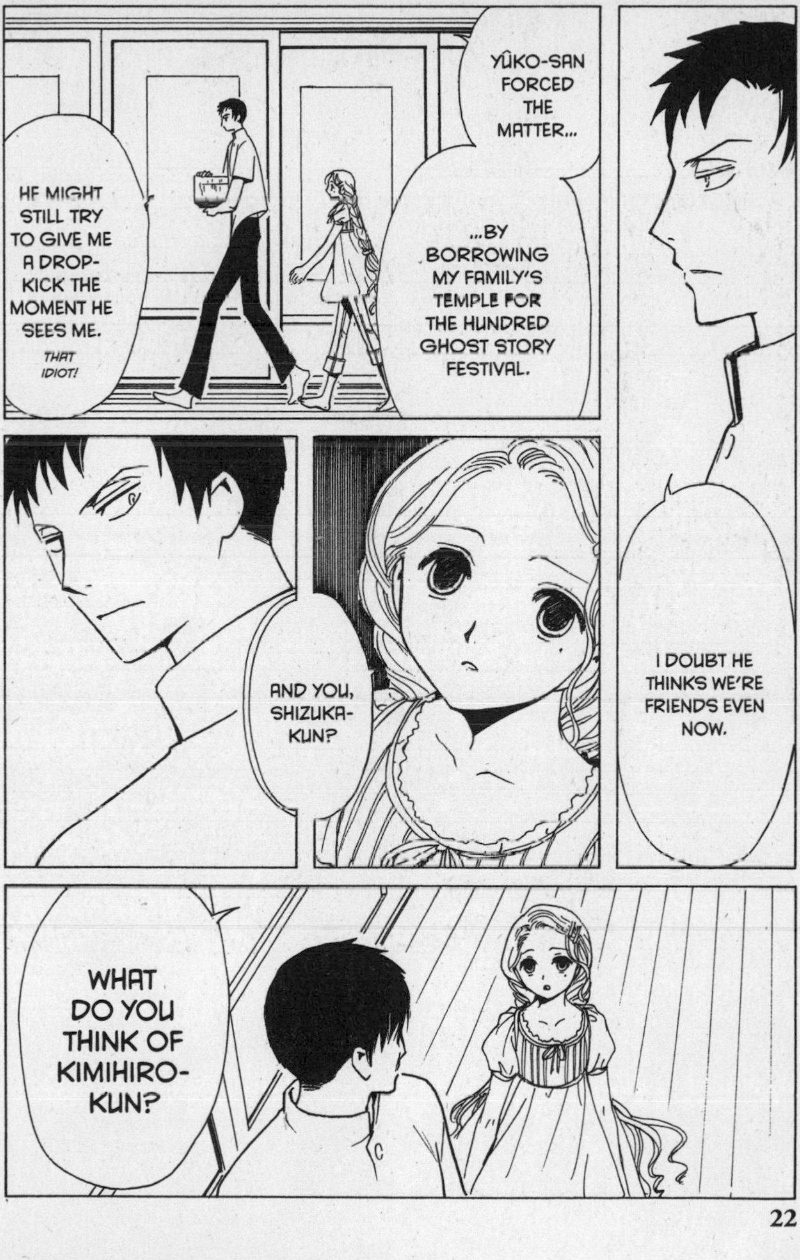
I DOUBT HE THINKS WE'RE FRIENDS EVEN NOW.
YÛKO-SAN FORCED THE MATTER...
...BY BORROWING MY FAMILY'S TEMPLE FOR THE HUNDRED GHOST STORY FESTIVAL.
HE MIGHT STILL TRY TO GIVE ME A DROP-KICK THE MOMENT HE SEES ME.
THAT IDIOT!
AND YOU, SHIZUKA-KUN?
WHAT DO YOU THINK OF KIMIHIRO-KUN?

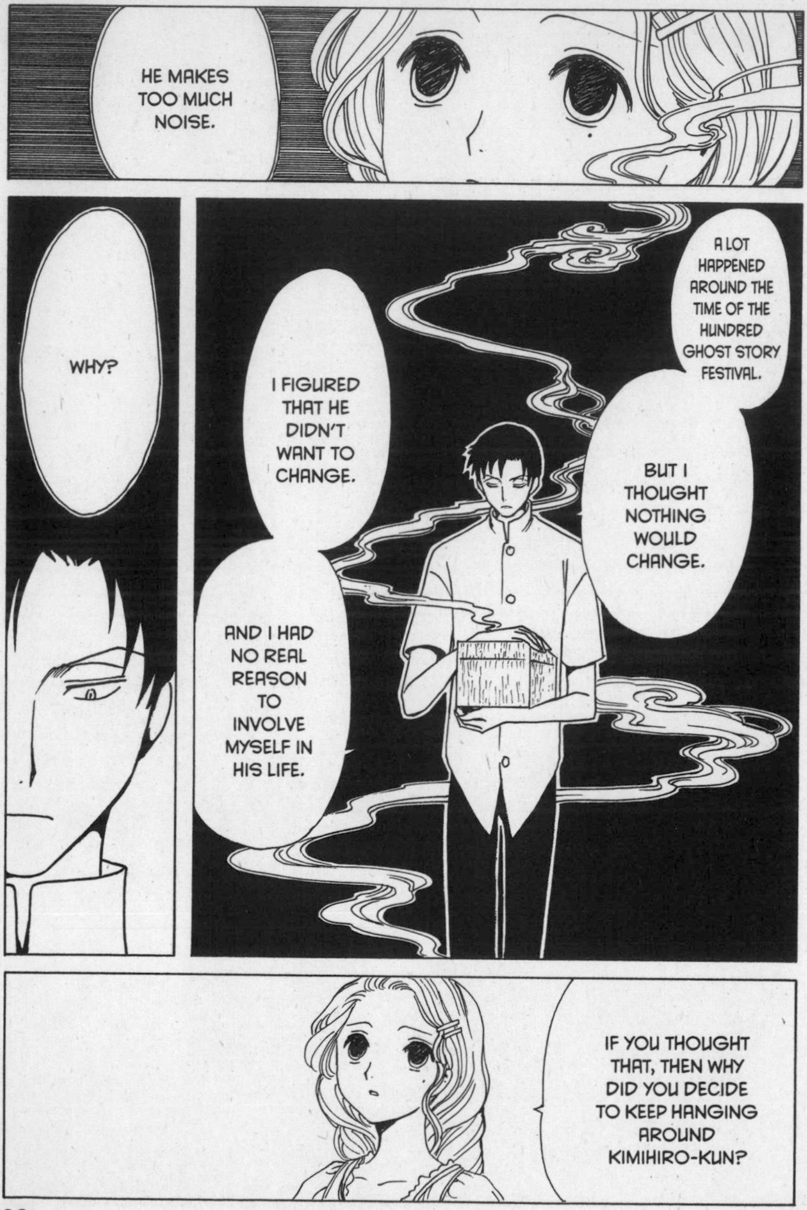
HE MAKES TOO MUCH NOISE.
A LOT HAPPENED AROUND THE TIME OF THE HUNDRED GHOST STORY FESTIVAL.
BUT I THOUGHT NOTHING WOULD CHANGE.
I FIGURED THAT HE DIDN'T WANT TO CHANGE.
AND I HAD NO REAL REASON TO INVOLVE MYSELF IN HIS LIFE.
WHY?
IF YOU THOUGHT THAT, THEN WHY DID YOU DECIDE TO KEEP HANGING AROUND KIMIHIRO-KUN?

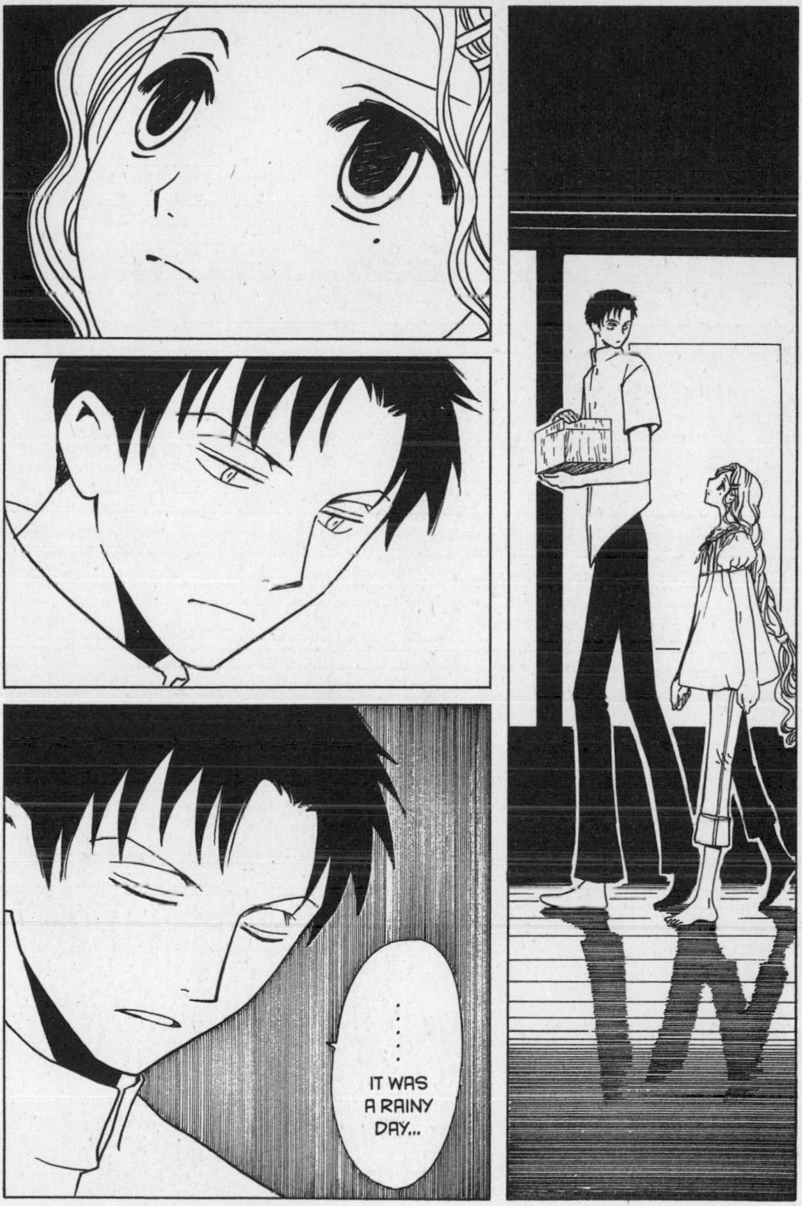
......
IT WAS A RAINY DAY...

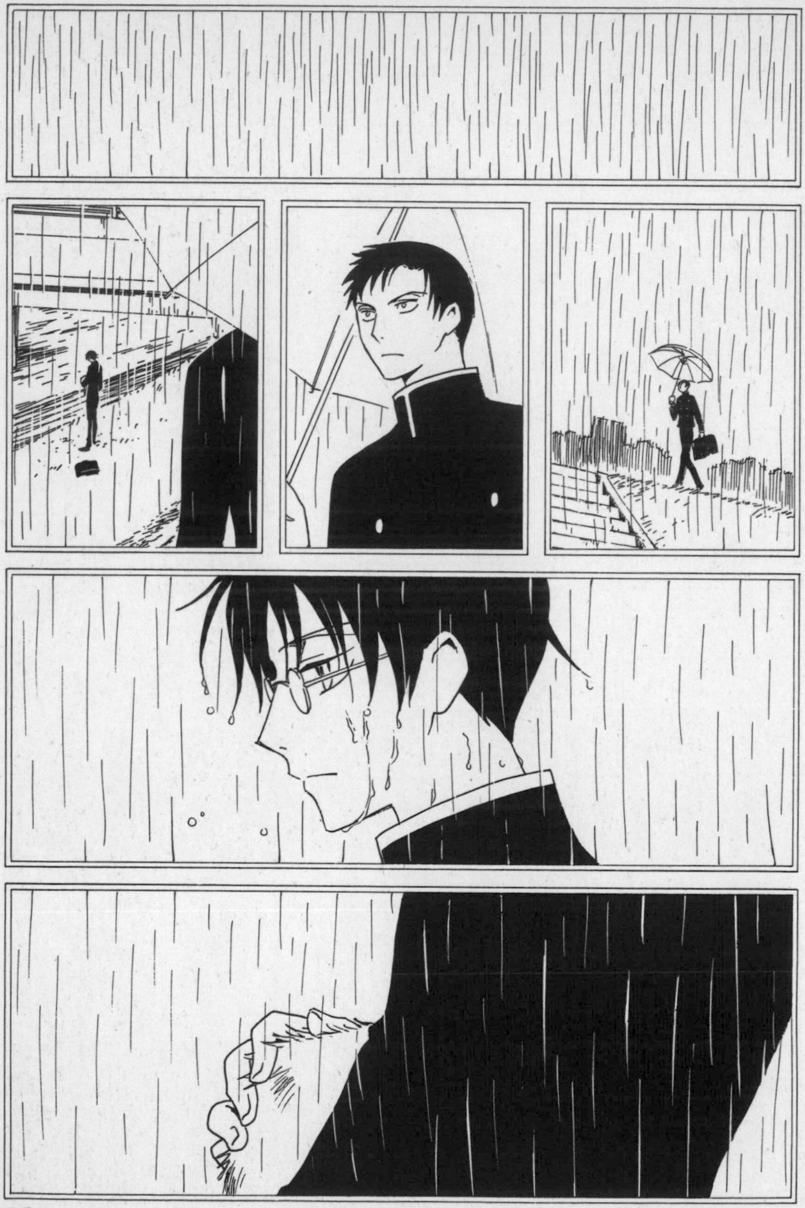

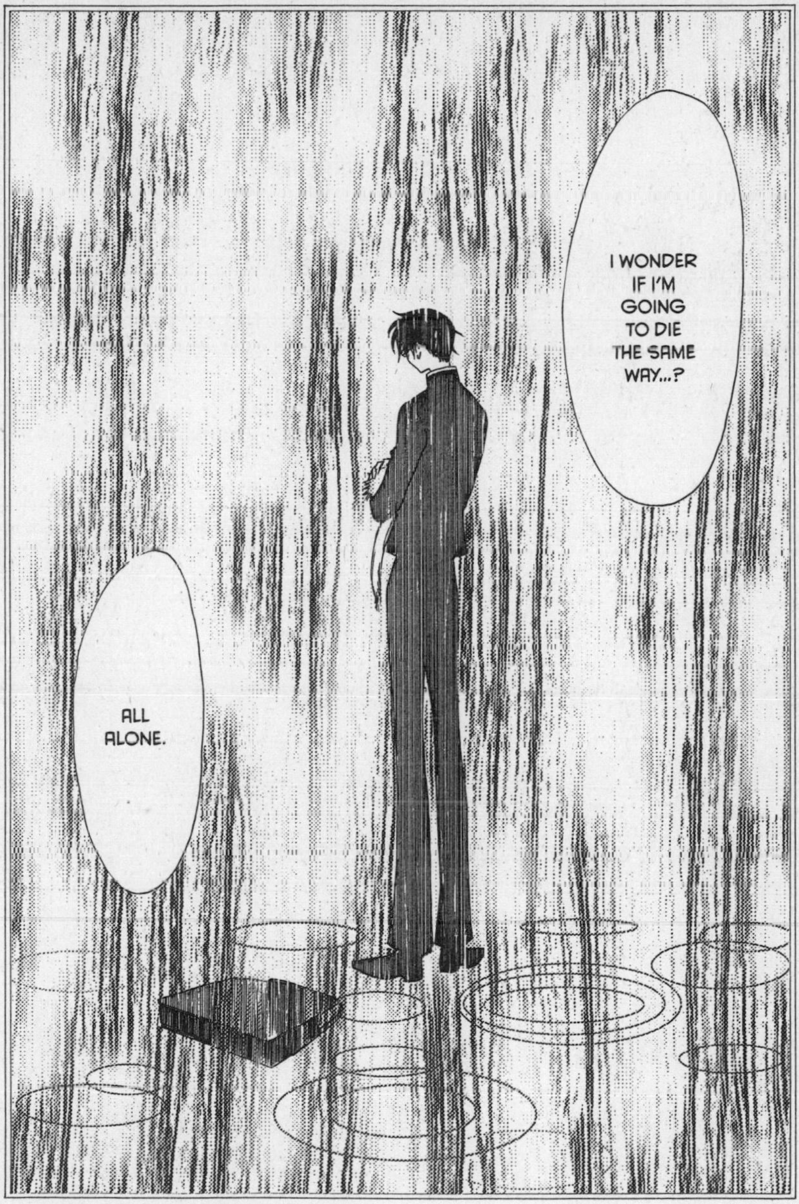
I WONDER IF I'M GOING TO DIE THE SAME WAY...?
ALL ALONE.

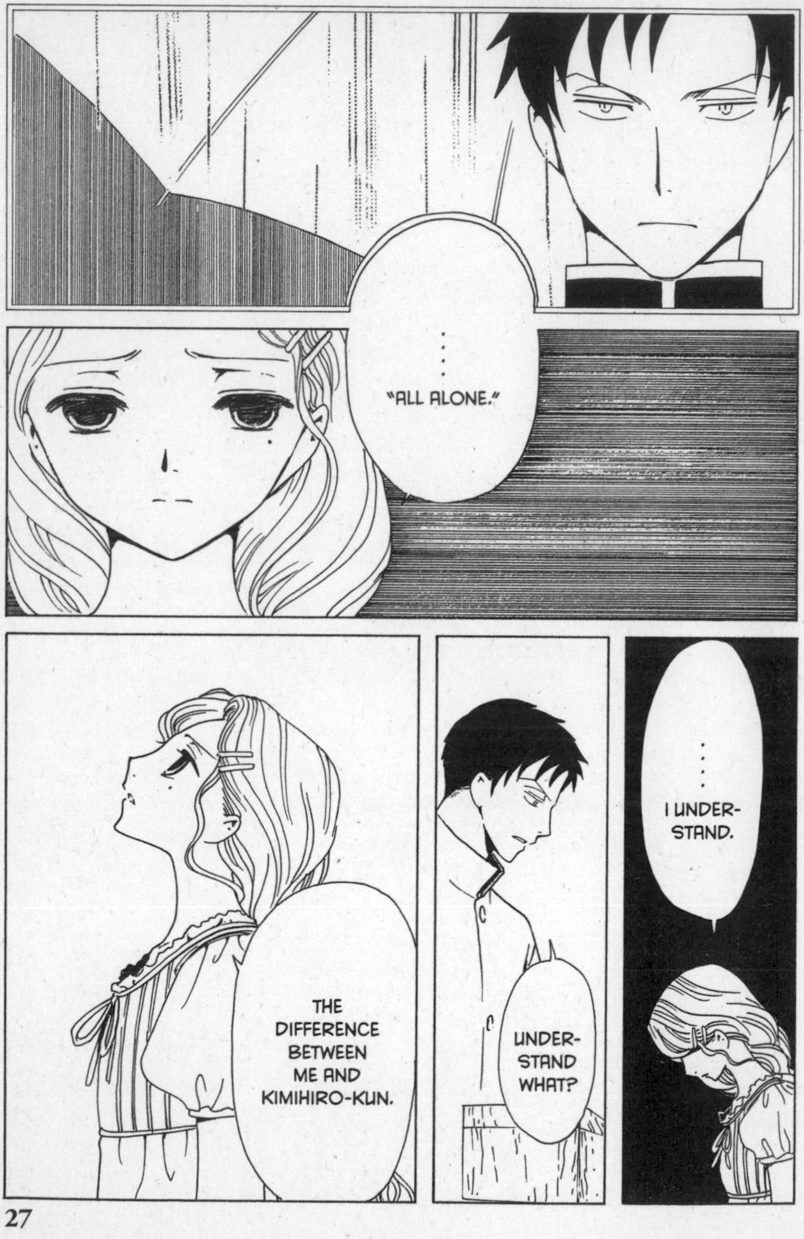

... "ALL ALONE."
... I UNDER-STAND.
UNDER-STAND WHAT?
THE DIFFERENCE BETWEEN ME AND KIMIHIRO-KUN.

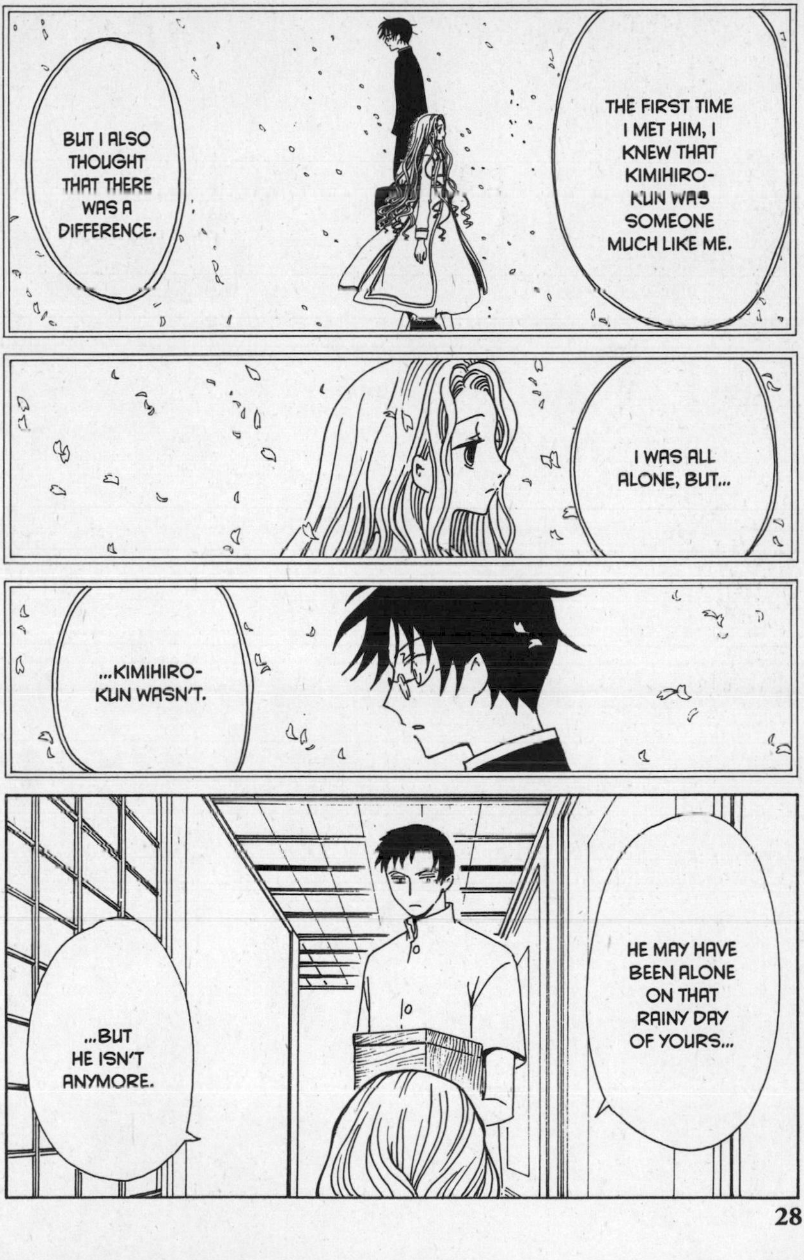
THE FIRST TIME I MET HIM, I KNEW THAT KIMIHIRO-KUN WAS SOMEONE MUCH LIKE ME.
BUT I ALSO THOUGHT THAT THERE WAS A DIFFERENCE.
I WAS ALL ALONE, BUT...
...KIMIHIRO-KUN WASN'T.
HE MAY HAVE BEEN ALONE ON THAT RAINY DAY OF YOURS...
...BUT HE ISN'T ANYMORE.

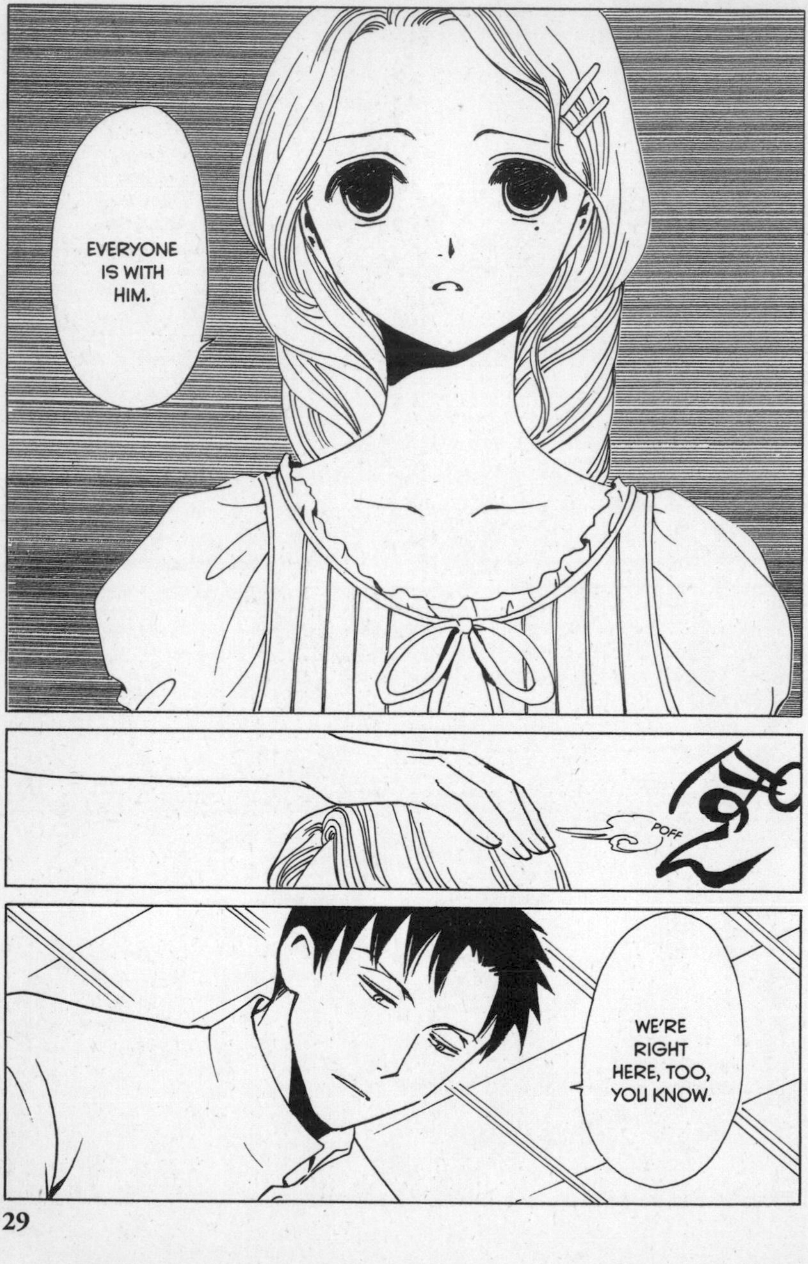
EVERYONE IS WITH HIM.
POFF
WE'RE RIGHT HERE, TOO, YOU KNOW.

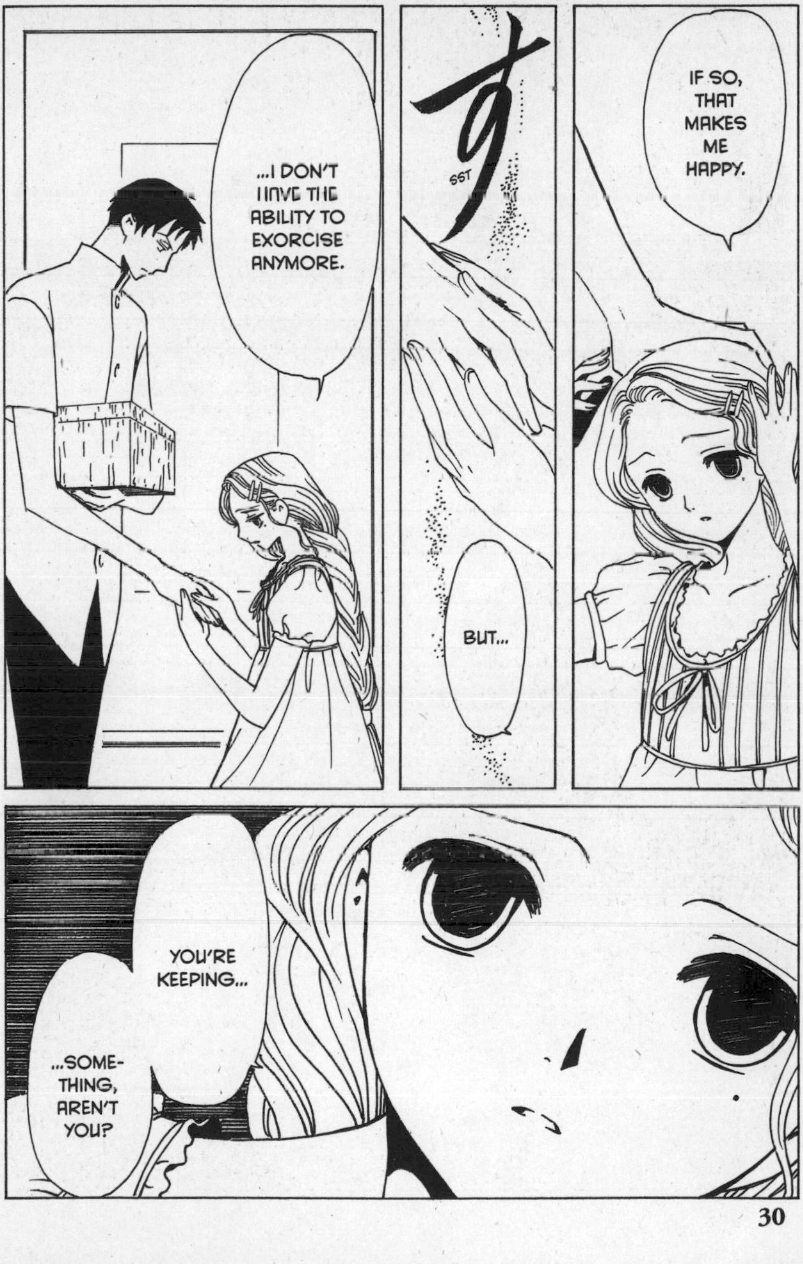
IF SO, THAT MAKES ME HAPPY.
す
SST
BUT...
...I DON'T HAVE THE ABILITY TO EXORCISE ANYMORE.
YOU'RE KEEPING...
...SOME-THING, AREN'T YOU?

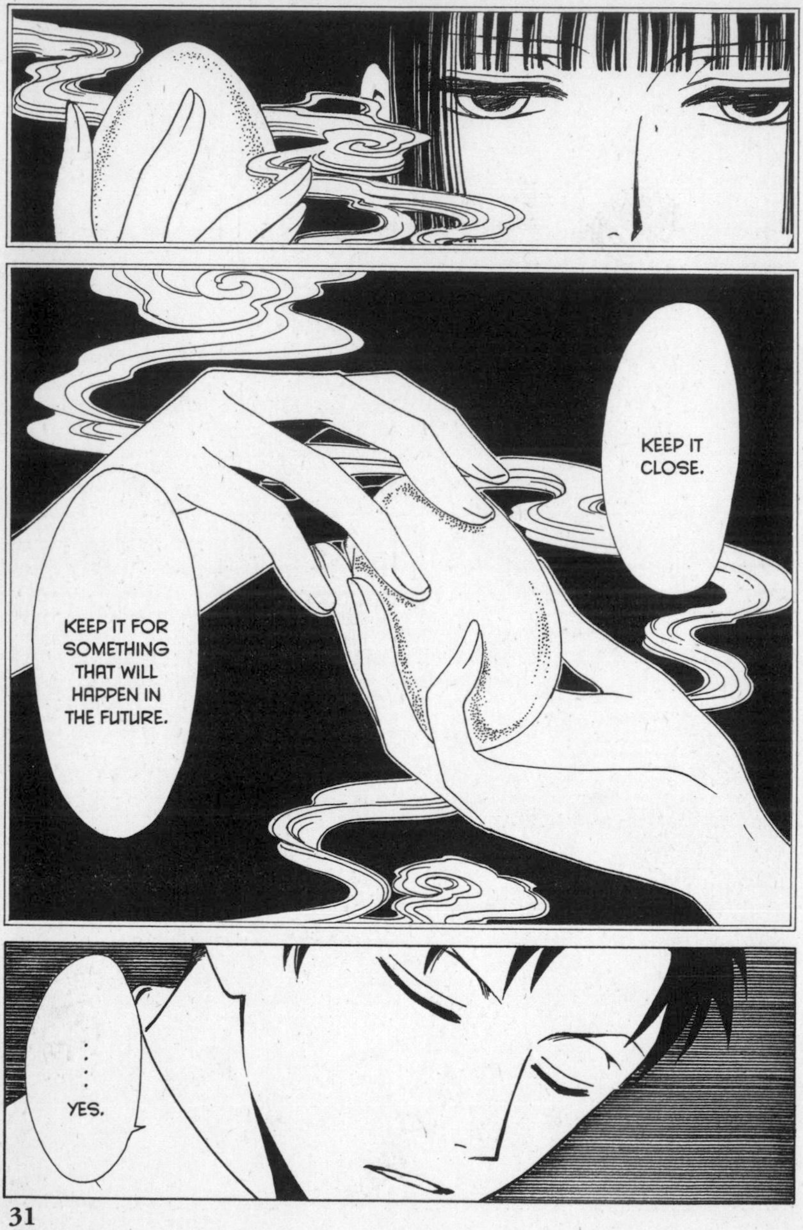
KEEP IT CLOSE.
KEEP IT FOR SOMETHING THAT WILL HAPPEN IN THE FUTURE.
.... YES.

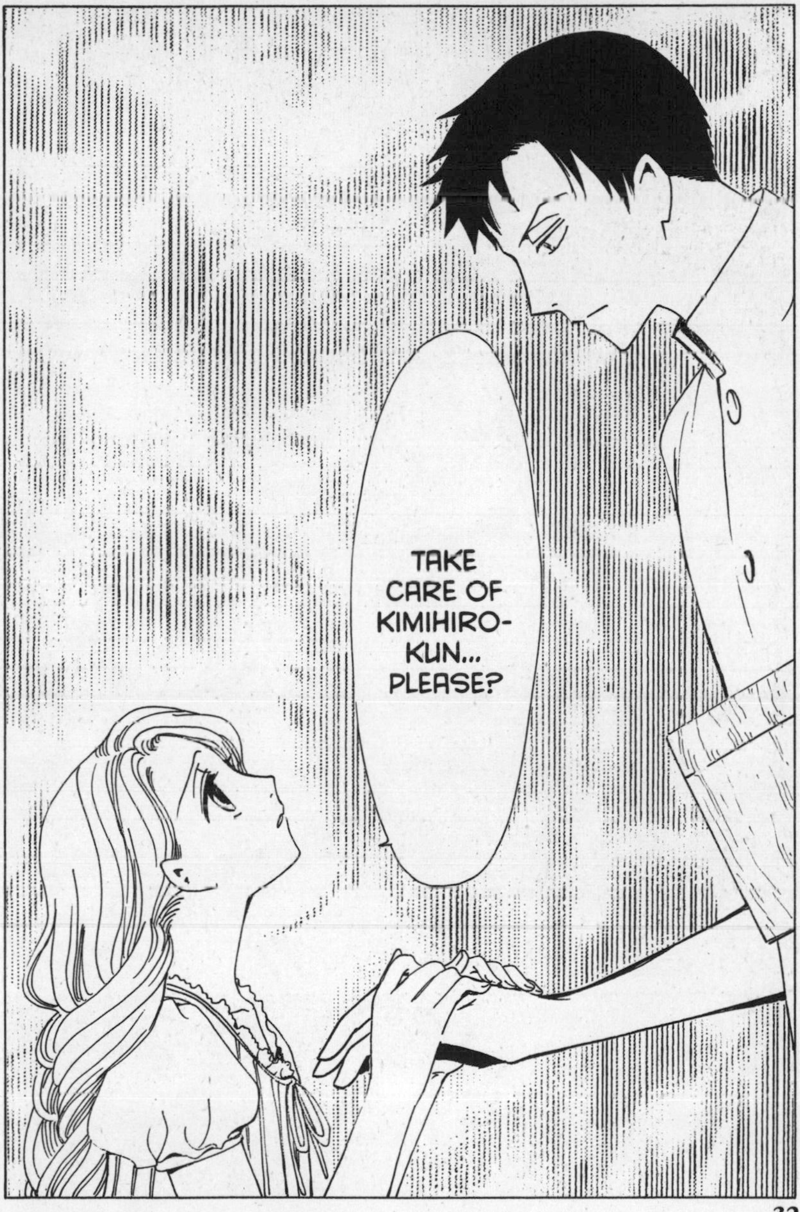
TAKE CARE OF KIMIHIRO-KUN... PLEASE?

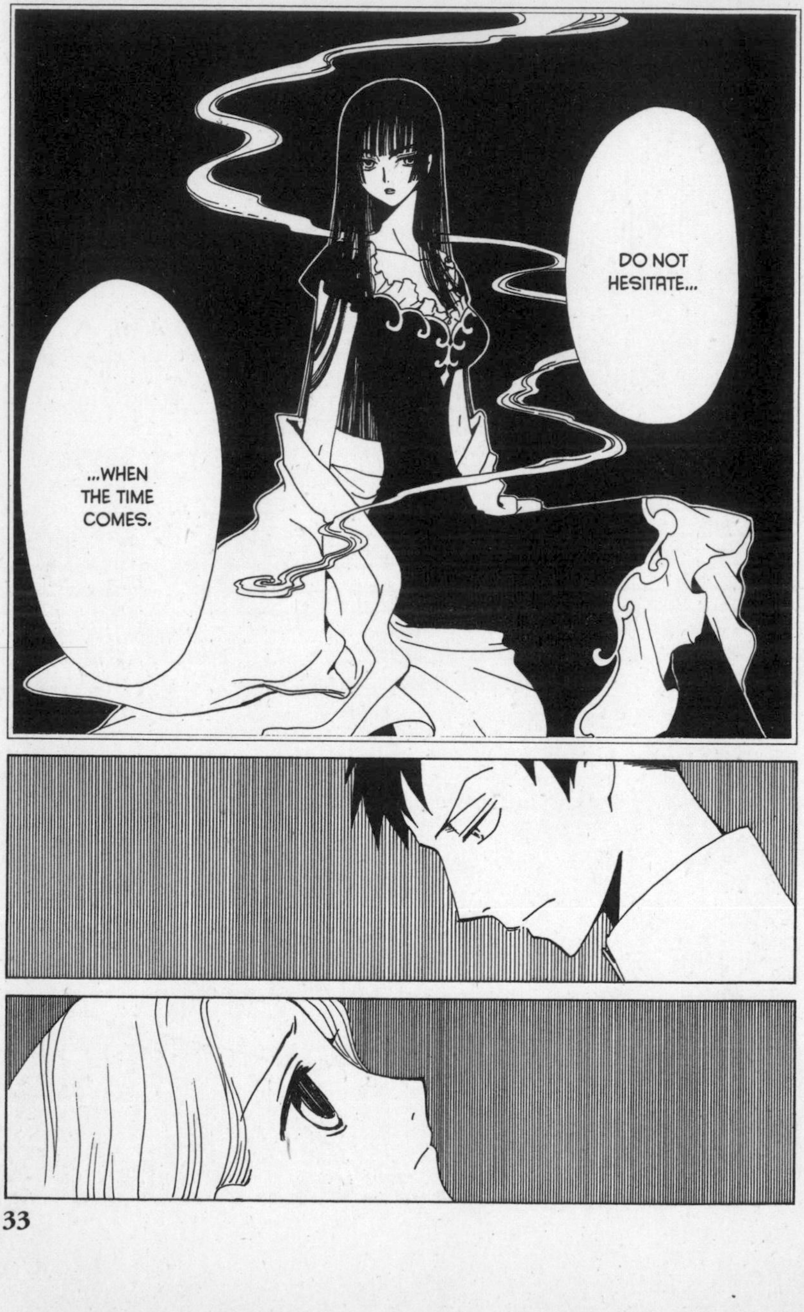
DO NOT HESITATE...
...WHEN THE TIME COMES.

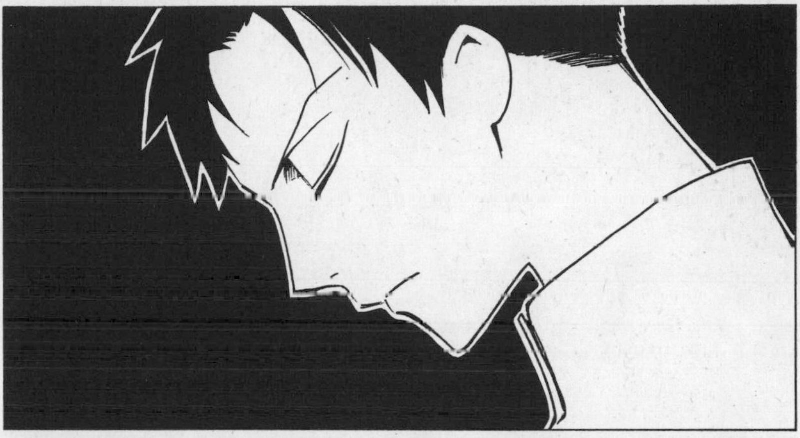

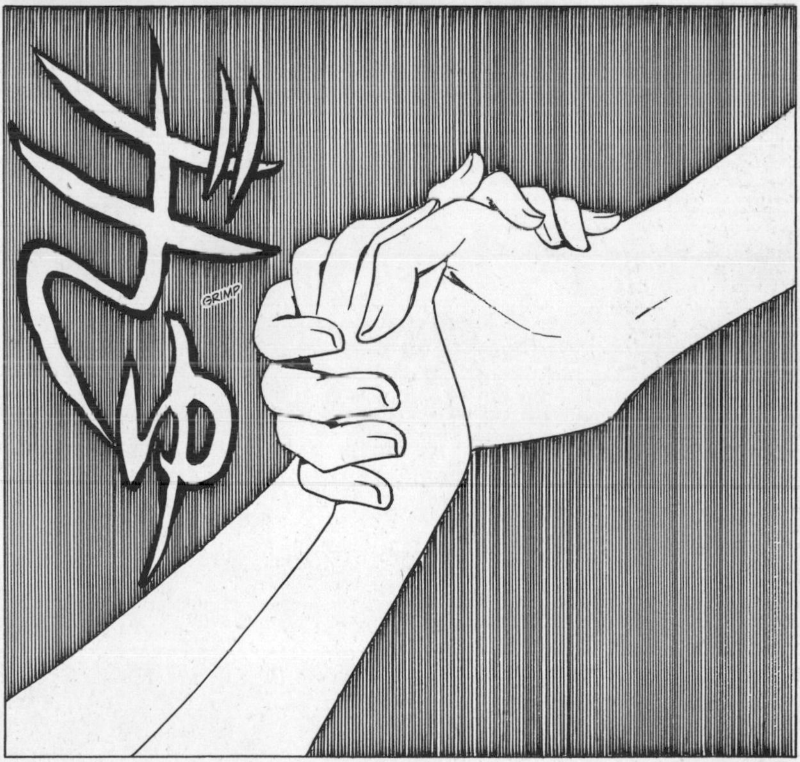
GRIMP

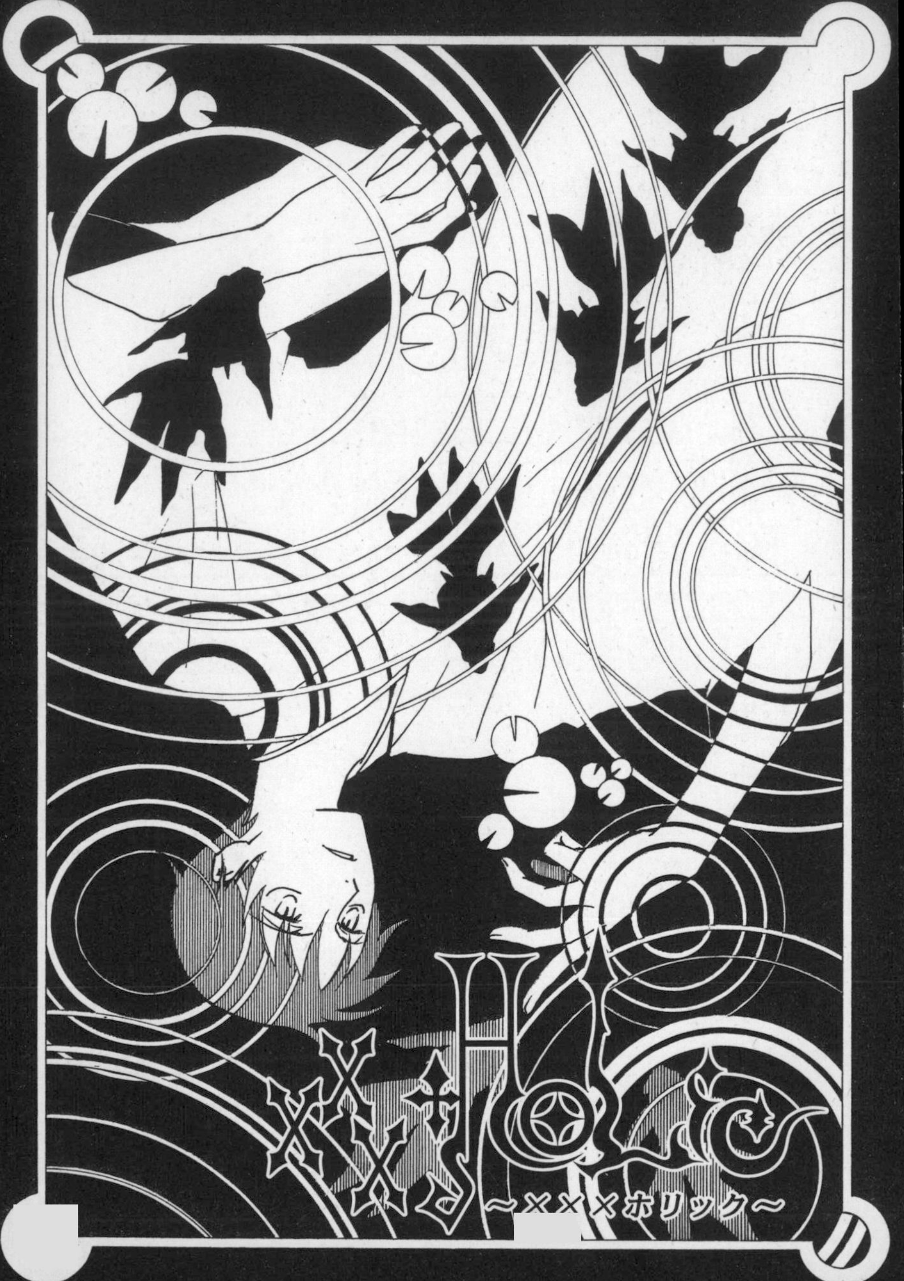
xxxHOLiC
～×××ホリック～

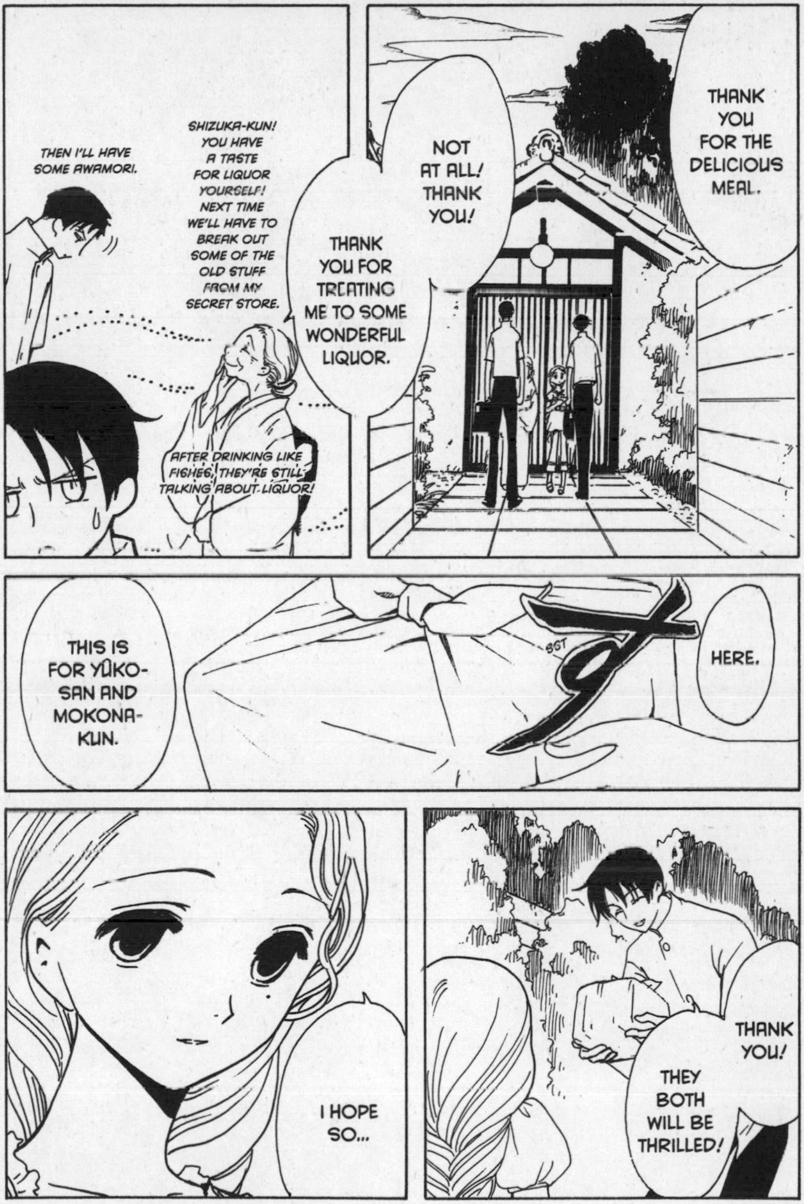
THANK YOU FOR THE DELICIOUS MEAL.
NOT AT ALL! THANK YOU!
THANK YOU FOR TREATING ME TO SOME WONDERFUL LIQUOR.
SHIZUKA-KUN! YOU HAVE A TASTE FOR LIQUOR YOURSELF! NEXT TIME WE'LL HAVE TO BREAK OUT SOME OF THE OLD STUFF FROM MY SECRET STORE.
THEN I'LL HAVE SOME AWAMORI.
AFTER DRINKING LIKE FISHES, THEY'RE STILL TALKING ABOUT LIQUOR!
HERE.
SST
THIS IS FOR YŪKO-SAN AND MOKONA-KUN.
THANK YOU!
THEY BOTH WILL BE THRILLED!
I HOPE SO...

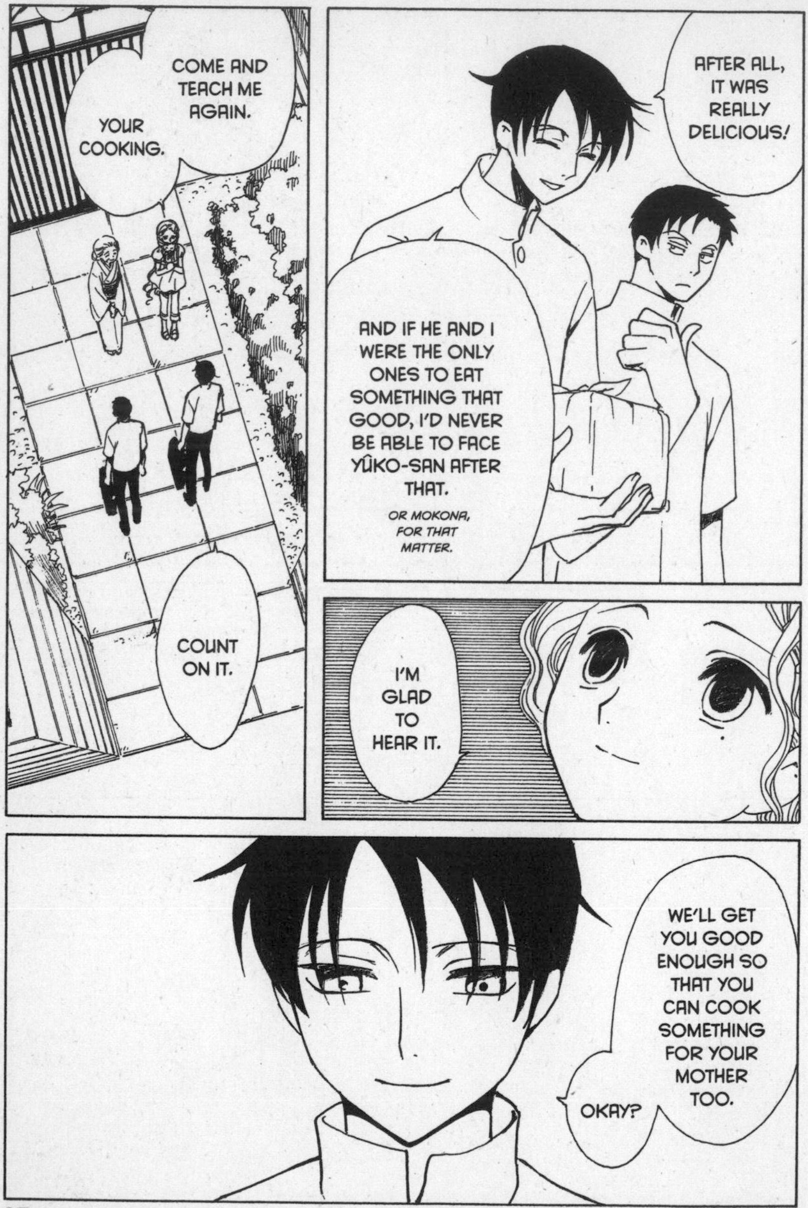
AFTER ALL, IT WAS REALLY DELICIOUS!
AND IF HE AND I WERE THE ONLY ONES TO EAT SOMETHING THAT GOOD, I'D NEVER BE ABLE TO FACE YÛKO-SAN AFTER THAT.
OR MOKONA, FOR THAT MATTER.
I'M GLAD TO HEAR IT.
COME AND TEACH ME AGAIN.
YOUR COOKING.
COUNT ON IT.
WE'LL GET YOU GOOD ENOUGH SO THAT YOU CAN COOK SOMETHING FOR YOUR MOTHER TOO.
OKAY?

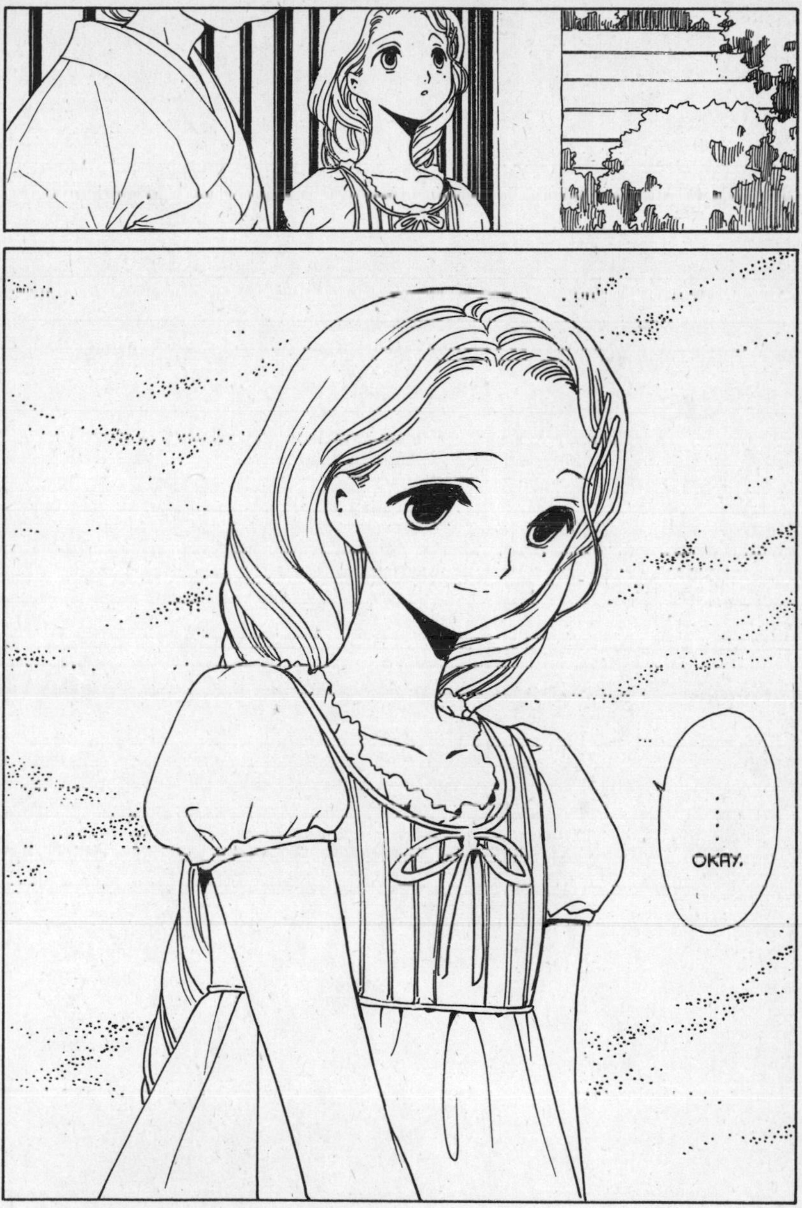
... OKAY.

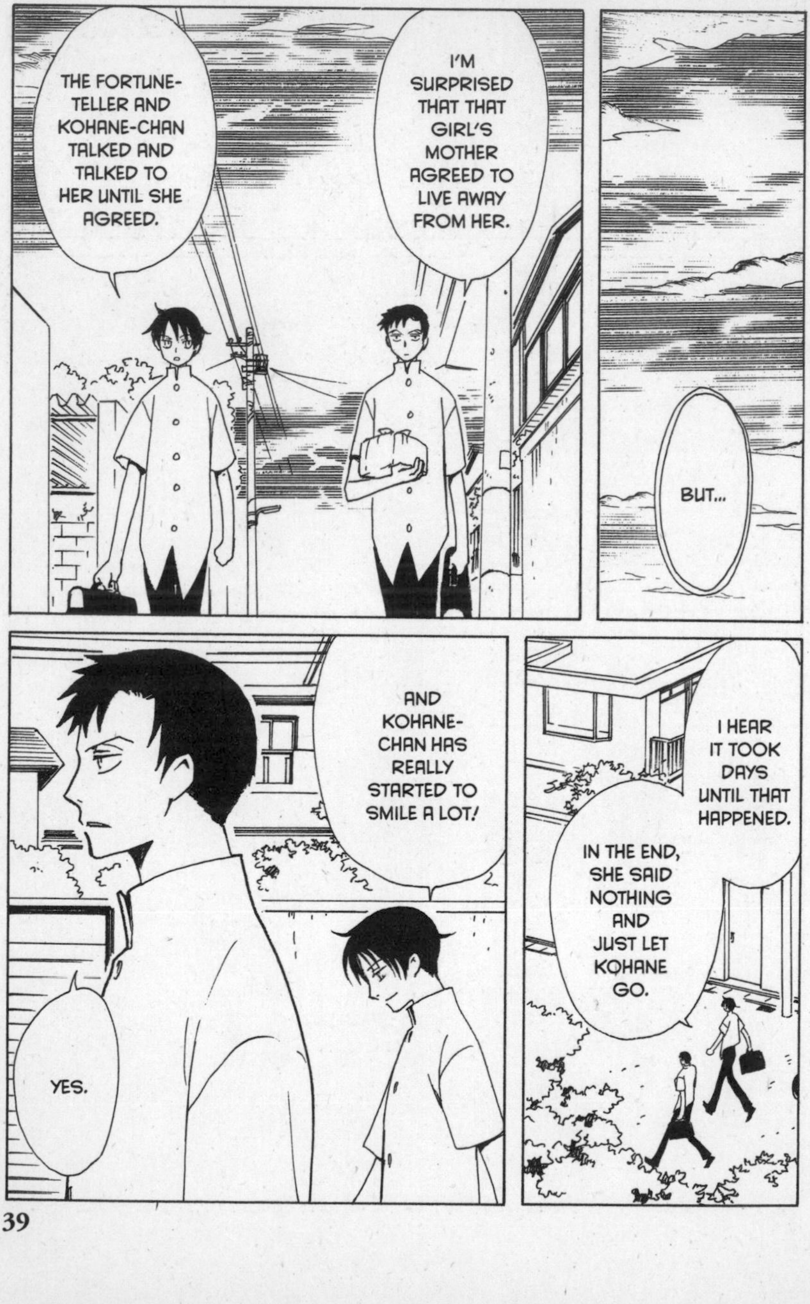
BUT...
I'M SURPRISED THAT THAT GIRL'S MOTHER AGREED TO LIVE AWAY FROM HER.
THE FORTUNE-TELLER AND KOHANE-CHAN TALKED AND TALKED TO HER UNTIL SHE AGREED.
I HEAR IT TOOK DAYS UNTIL THAT HAPPENED.
IN THE END, SHE SAID NOTHING AND JUST LET KOHANE GO.
AND KOHANE-CHAN HAS REALLY STARTED TO SMILE A LOT!
YES.

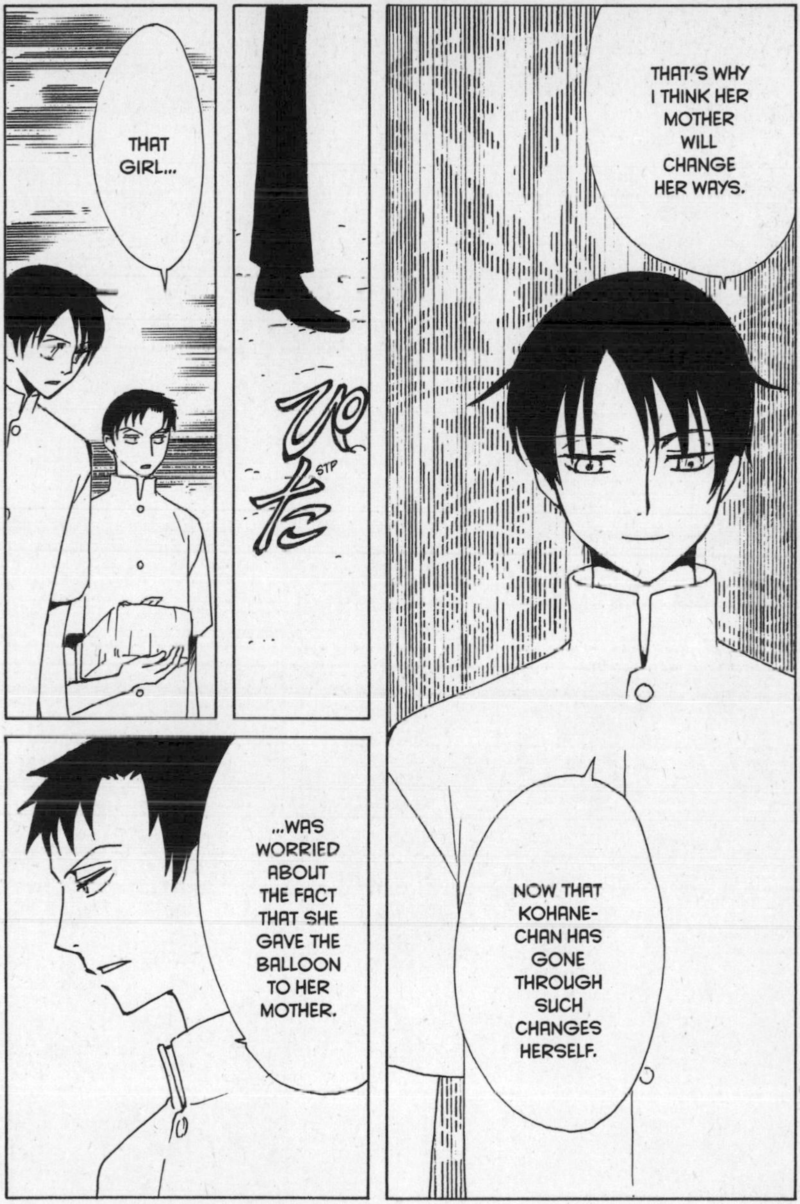
THAT'S WHY I THINK HER MOTHER WILL CHANGE HER WAYS.
NOW THAT KOHANE-CHAN HAS GONE THROUGH SUCH CHANGES HERSELF.
ぴた
STP
THAT GIRL...
...WAS WORRIED ABOUT THE FACT THAT SHE GAVE THE BALLOON TO HER MOTHER.

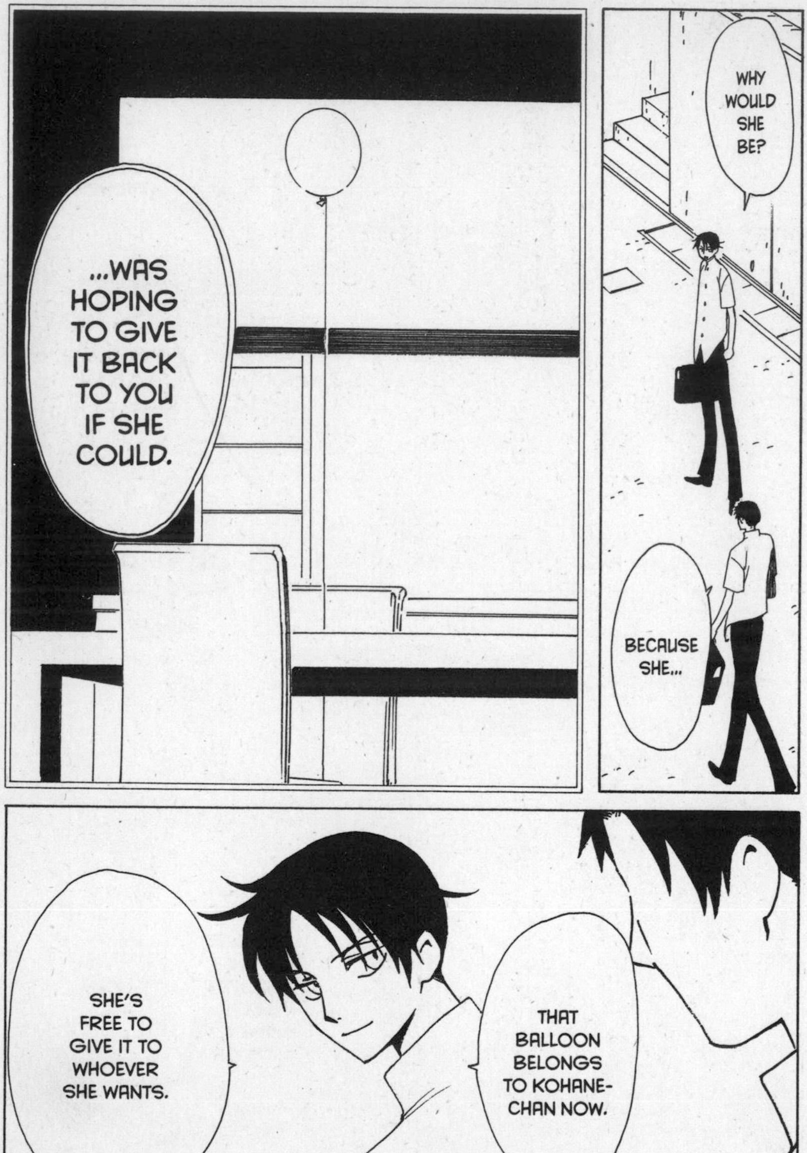
WHY WOULD SHE BE?
BECAUSE SHE...
...WAS HOPING TO GIVE IT BACK TO YOU IF SHE COULD.
THAT BALLOON BELONGS TO KOHANE-CHAN NOW.
SHE'S FREE TO GIVE IT TO WHOEVER SHE WANTS.

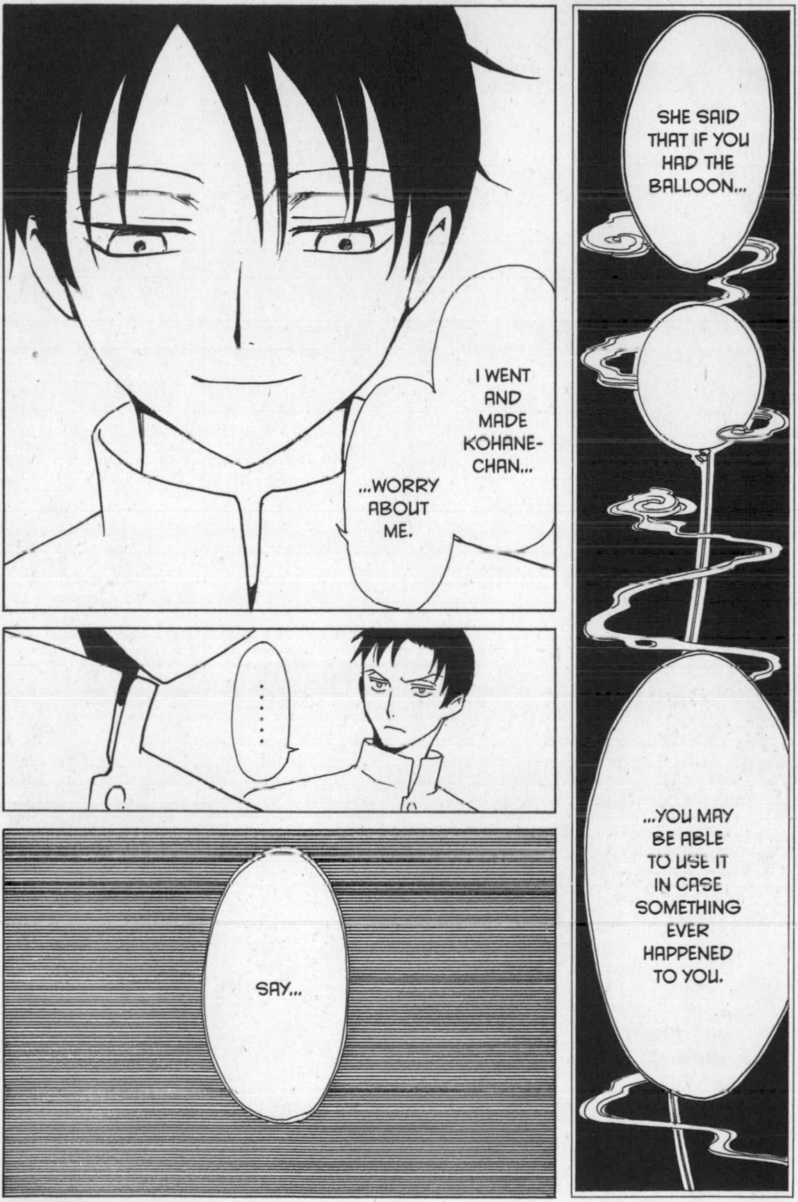
SHE SAID THAT IF YOU HAD THE BALLOON...
...YOU MAY BE ABLE TO USE IT IN CASE SOMETHING EVER HAPPENED TO YOU.
I WENT AND MADE KOHANE-CHAN...
...WORRY ABOUT ME.
......
SAY...

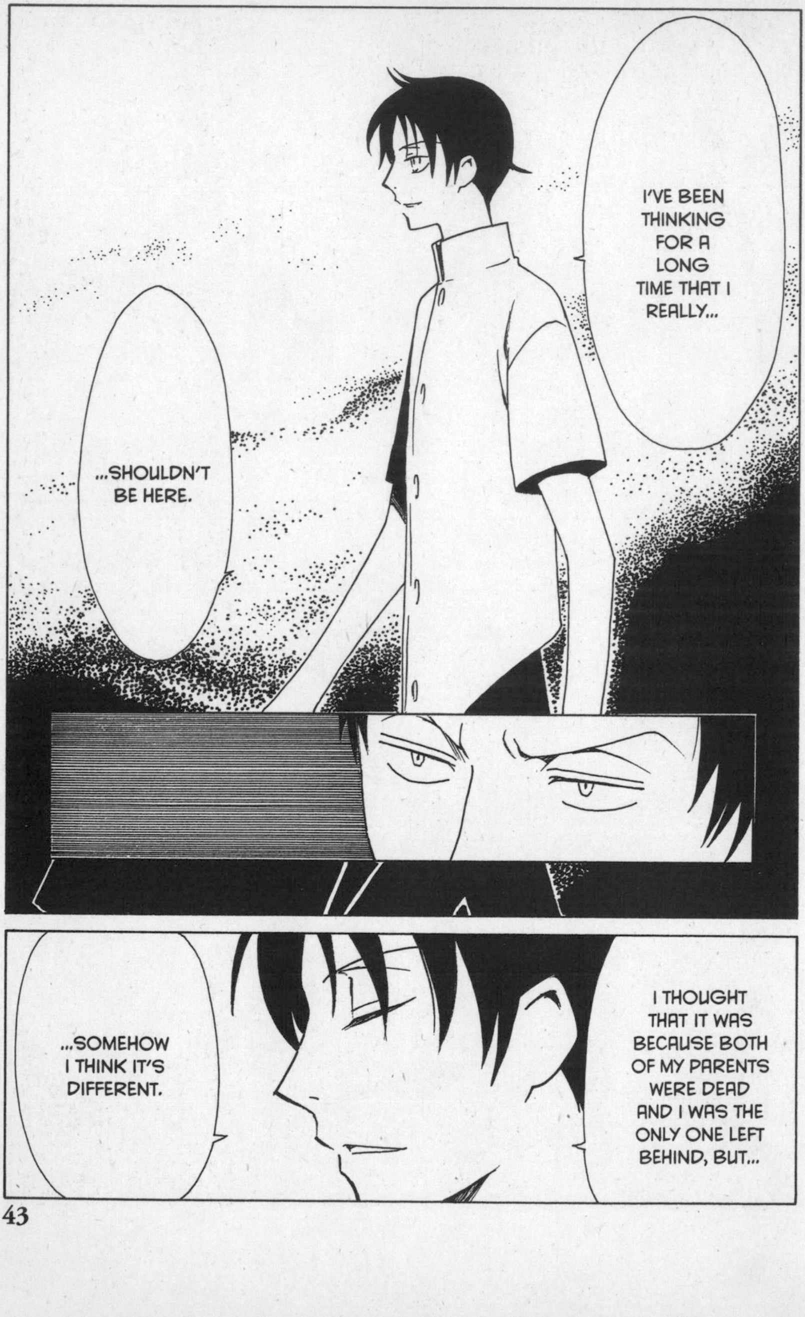
I'VE BEEN THINKING FOR A LONG TIME THAT I REALLY...
...SHOULDN'T BE HERE.
I THOUGHT THAT IT WAS BECAUSE BOTH OF MY PARENTS WERE DEAD AND I WAS THE ONLY ONE LEFT BEHIND, BUT...
...SOMEHOW I THINK IT'S DIFFERENT.

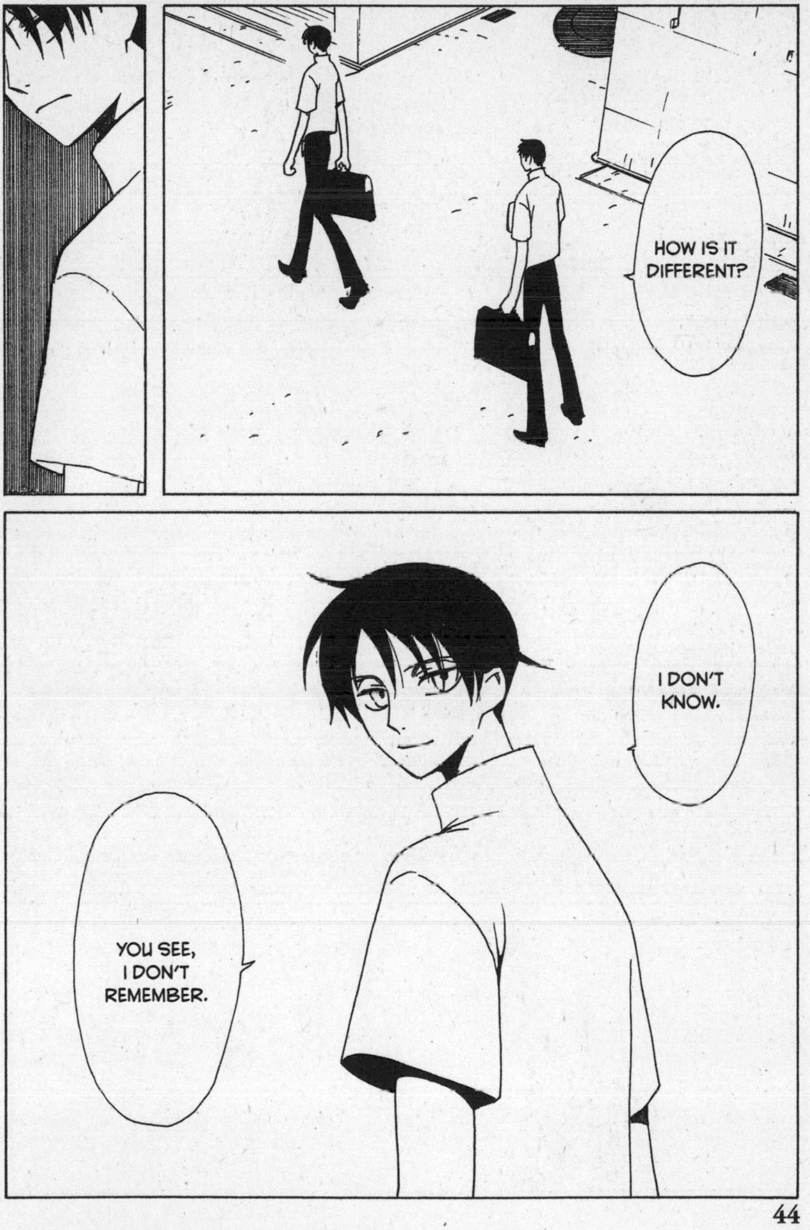
HOW IS IT DIFFERENT?
I DON'T KNOW.
YOU SEE, I DON'T REMEMBER.

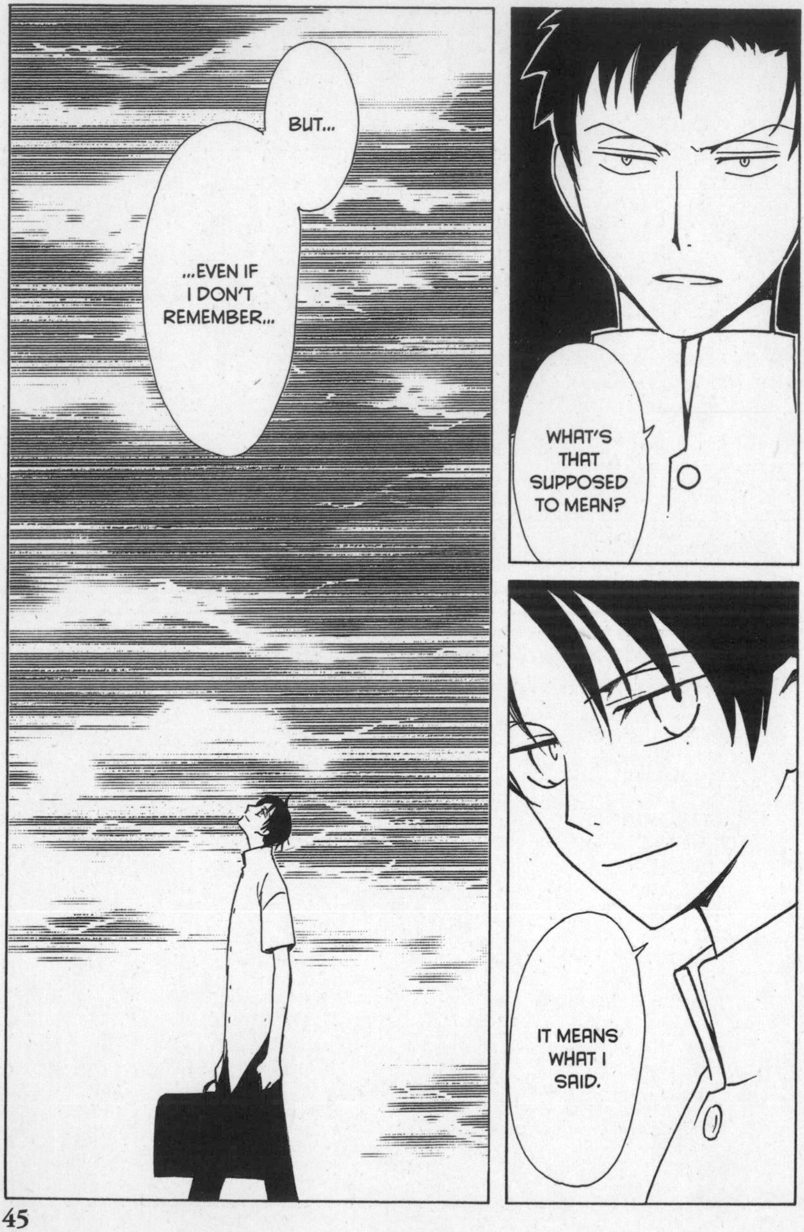
WHAT'S THAT SUPPOSED TO MEAN?
IT MEANS WHAT I SAID.
BUT...
...EVEN IF I DON'T REMEMBER...

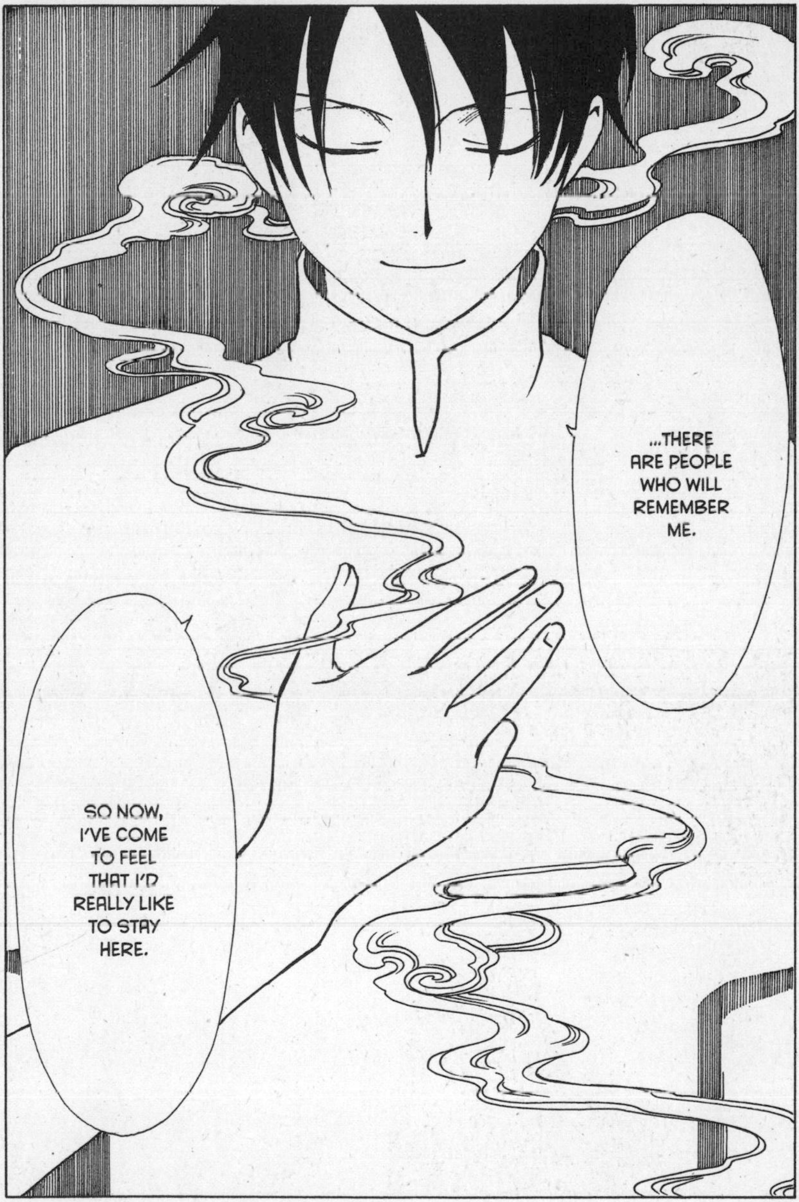
...THERE ARE PEOPLE WHO WILL REMEMBER ME.
SO NOW, I'VE COME TO FEEL THAT I'D REALLY LIKE TO STAY HERE.

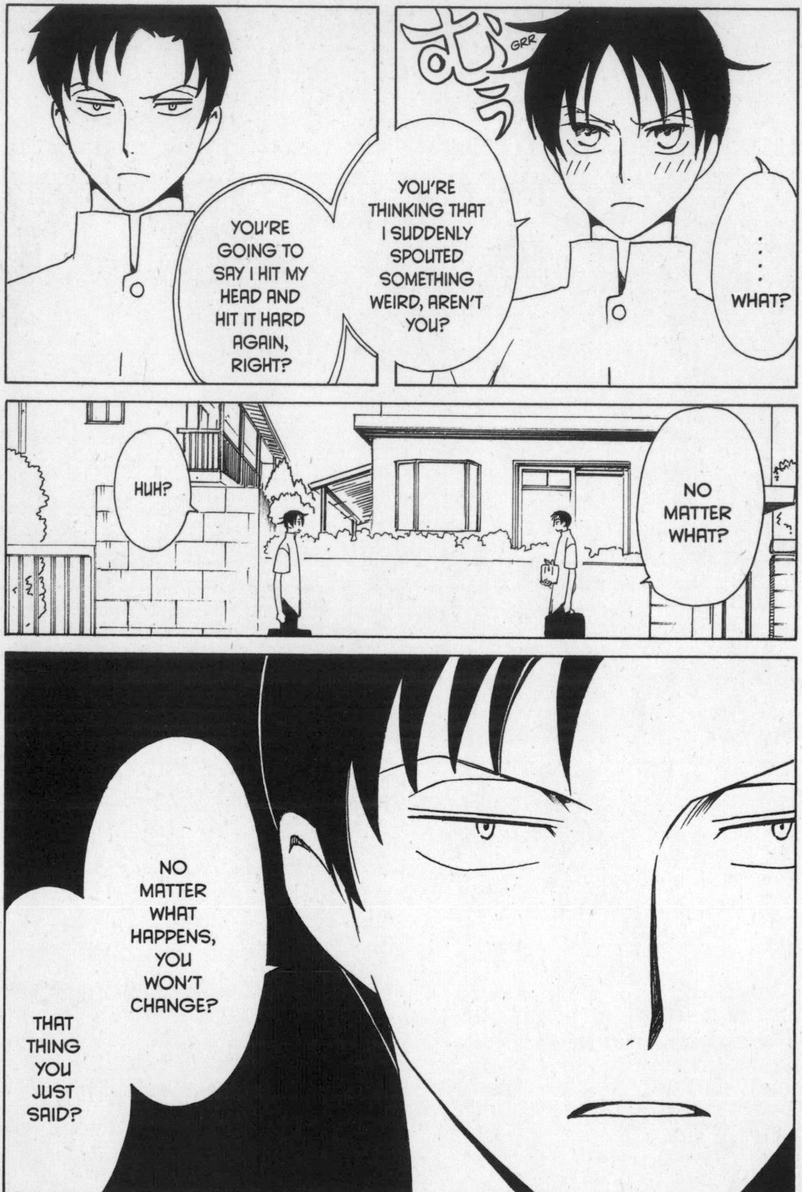
むぅ GRR
...... WHAT?
YOU'RE THINKING THAT I SUDDENLY SPOUTED SOMETHING WEIRD, AREN'T YOU?
YOU'RE GOING TO SAY I HIT MY HEAD AND HIT IT HARD AGAIN, RIGHT?
NO MATTER WHAT?
HUH?
NO MATTER WHAT HAPPENS, YOU WON'T CHANGE?
THAT THING YOU JUST SAID?

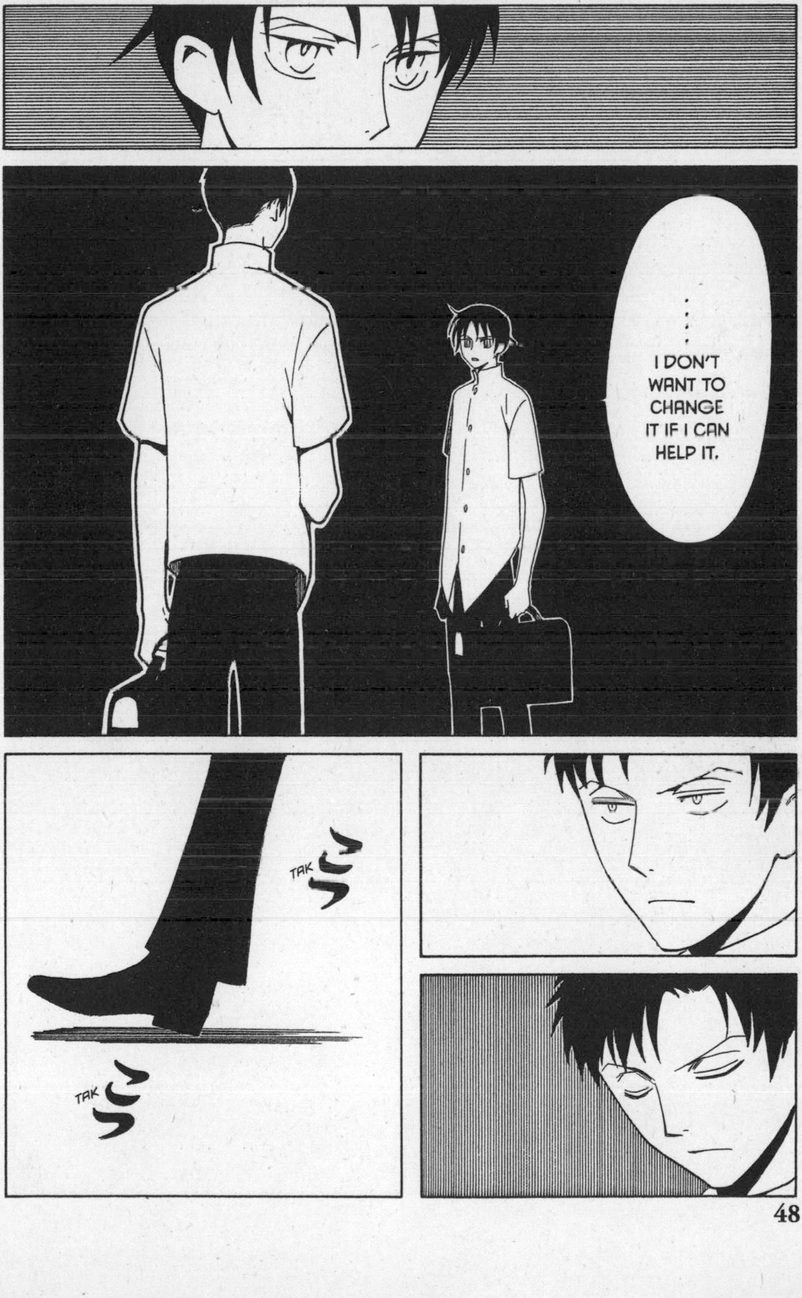
.... I DON'T WANT TO CHANGE IT IF I CAN HELP IT.
TAK
TAK

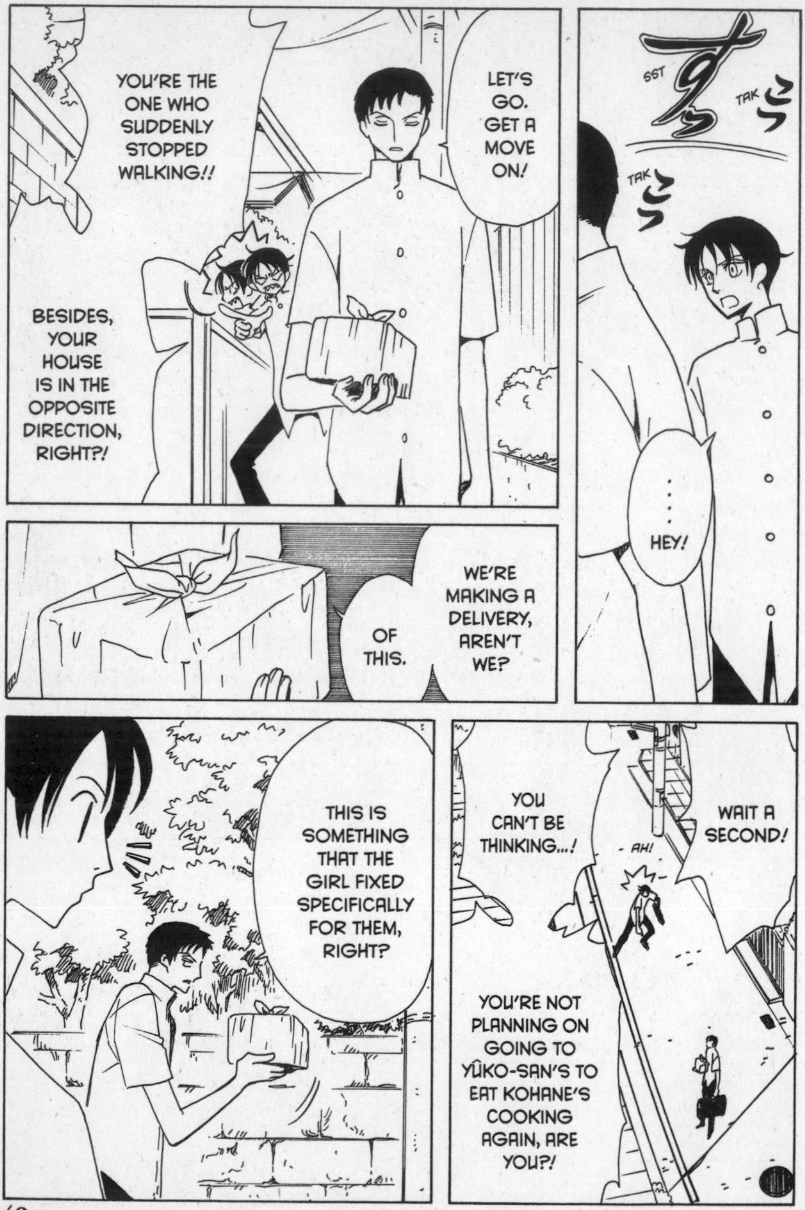
SST
TAK
TAK
...HEY!
LET'S GO. GET A MOVE ON!
YOU'RE THE ONE WHO SUDDENLY STOPPED WALKING!!
BESIDES, YOUR HOUSE IS IN THE OPPOSITE DIRECTION, RIGHT?!
WE'RE MAKING A DELIVERY, AREN'T WE?
OF THIS.
WAIT A SECOND!
AH!
YOU CAN'T BE THINKING...!
YOU'RE NOT PLANNING ON GOING TO YÛKO-SAN'S TO EAT KOHANE'S COOKING AGAIN, ARE YOU?!
THIS IS SOMETHING THAT THE GIRL FIXED SPECIFICALLY FOR THEM, RIGHT?

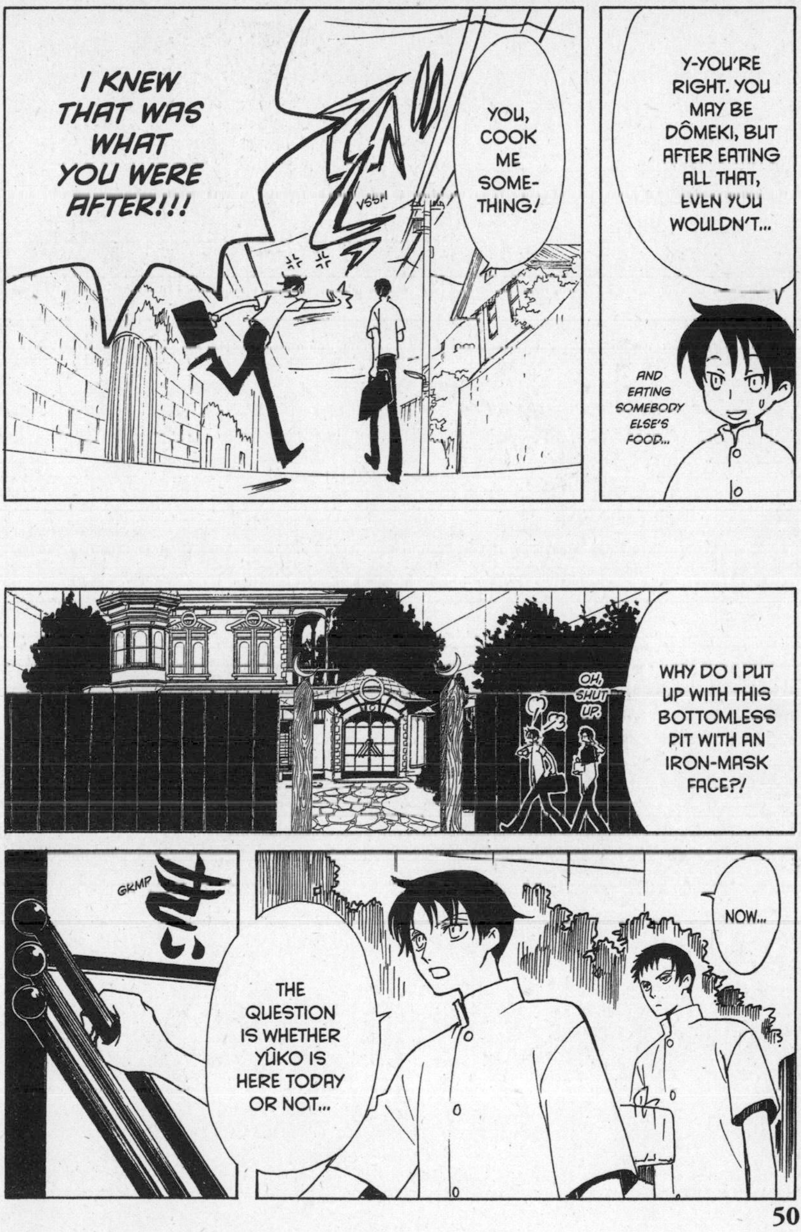
Y-YOU'RE RIGHT. YOU MAY BE DÔMEKI, BUT AFTER EATING ALL THAT, EVEN YOU WOULDN'T...
AND EATING SOMEBODY ELSE'S FOOD...
YOU, COOK ME SOME-THING!
VSSH
I KNEW THAT WAS WHAT YOU WERE AFTER!!!
WHY DO I PUT UP WITH THIS BOTTOMLESS PIT WITH AN IRON-MASK FACE?!
OH, SHUT UP.
NOW...
THE QUESTION IS WHETHER YÛKO IS HERE TODAY OR NOT...
GKMP

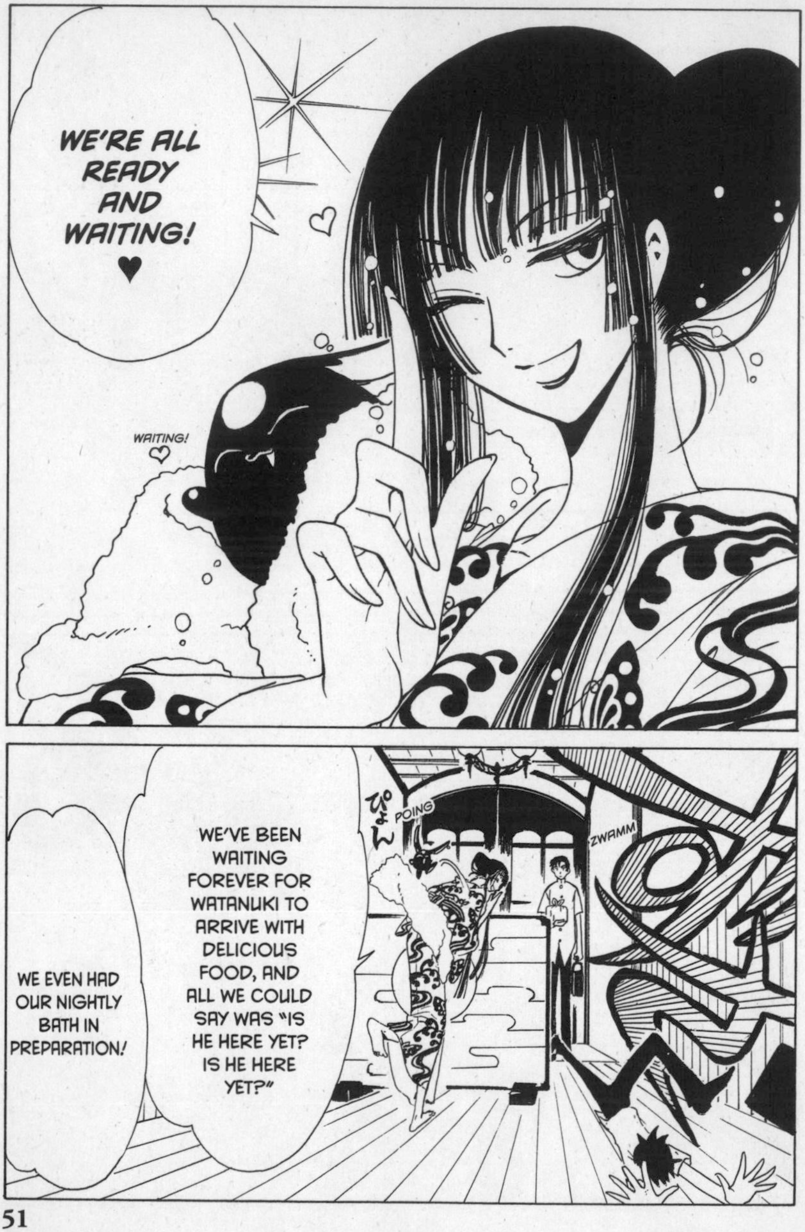
WE'RE ALL READY AND WAITING! ♥
WAITING! ♡
ZWAMM
ぴょん
POING
WE'VE BEEN WAITING FOREVER FOR WATANUKI TO ARRIVE WITH DELICIOUS FOOD, AND ALL WE COULD SAY WAS "IS HE HERE YET? IS HE HERE YET?"
WE EVEN HAD OUR NIGHTLY BATH IN PREPARATION!

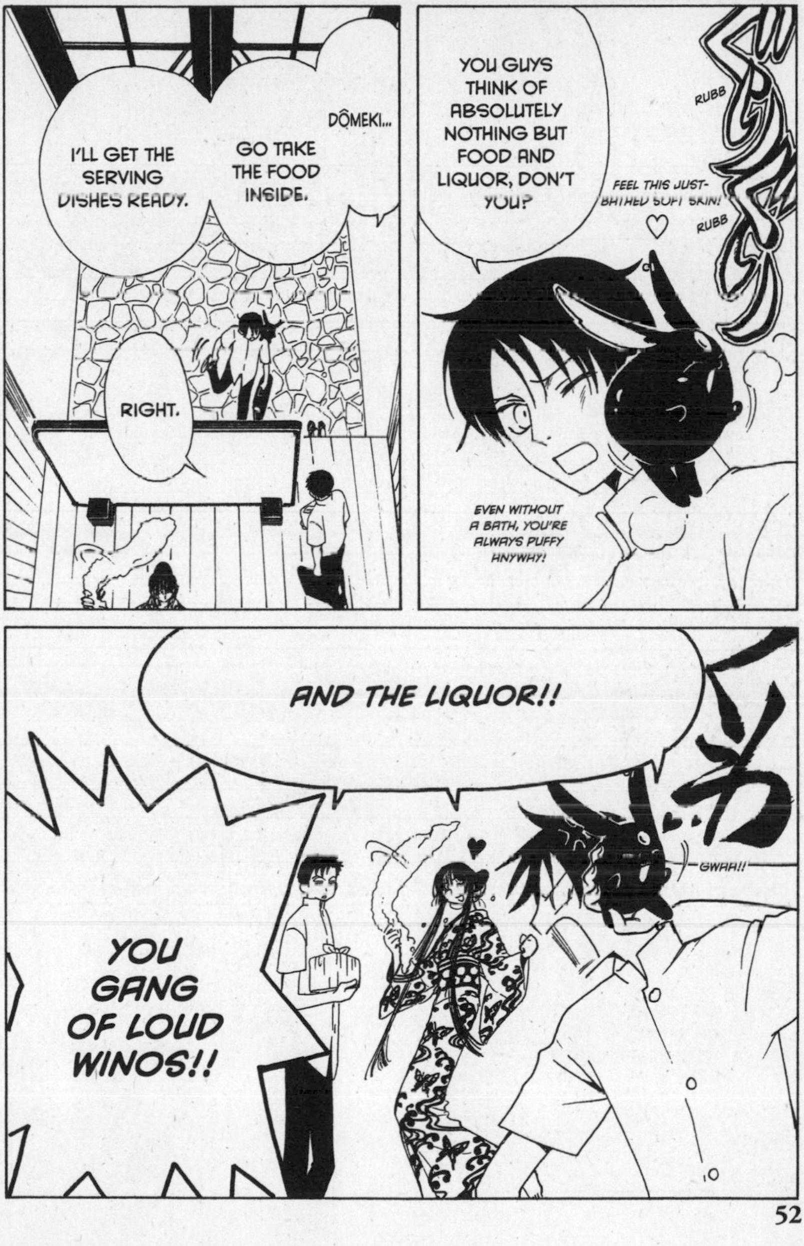
YOU GUYS THINK OF ABSOLUTELY NOTHING BUT FOOD AND LIQUOR, DON'T YOU?
RUBB
FEEL THIS JUST-BATHED SOFT SKIN! ♡
RUBB
EVEN WITHOUT A BATH, YOU'RE ALWAYS PUFFY ANYWAY!
DÔMEKI...
GO TAKE THE FOOD INSIDE.
I'LL GET THE SERVING DISHES READY.
RIGHT.
AND THE LIQUOR!!
GWAH!!
YOU GANG OF LOUD WINOS!!

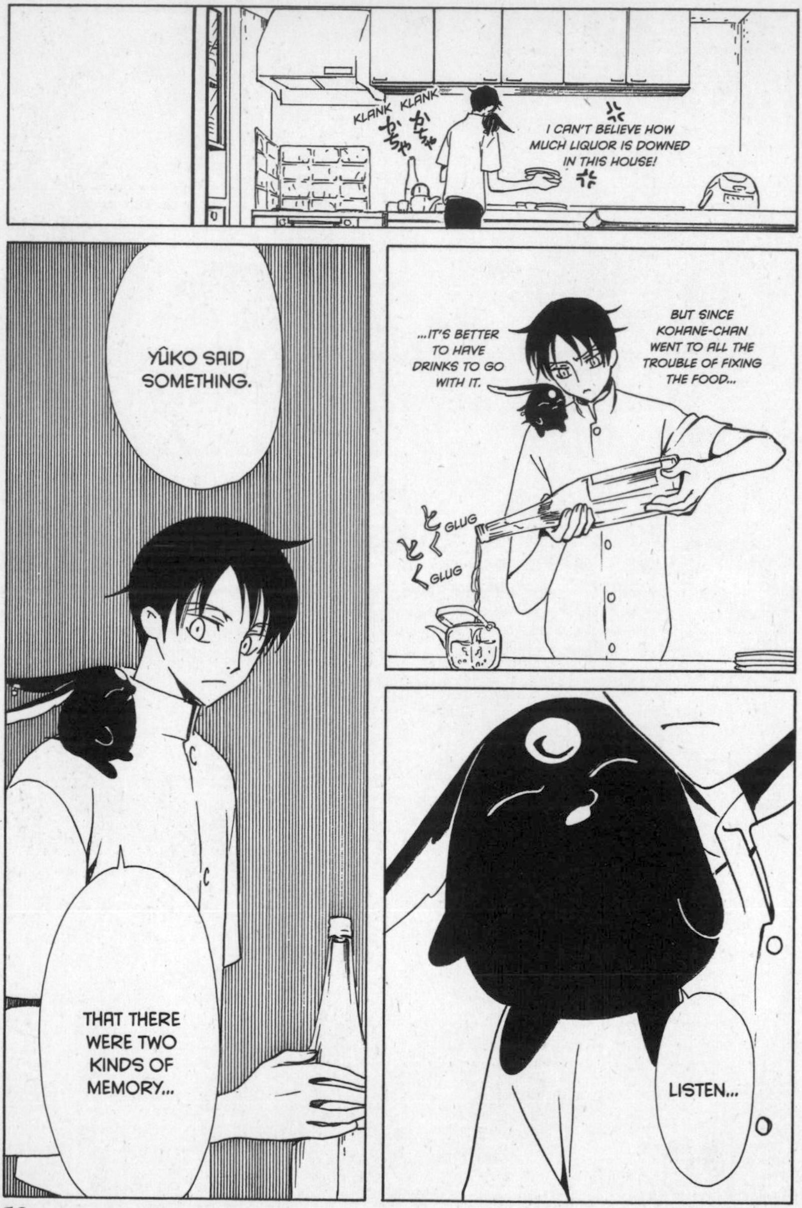
KLANK KLANK
かちゃかちゃ
I CAN'T BELIEVE HOW MUCH LIQUOR IS DOWNED IN THIS HOUSE!
BUT SINCE KOHANE-CHAN WENT TO ALL THE TROUBLE OF FIXING THE FOOD...
...IT'S BETTER TO HAVE DRINKS TO GO WITH IT.
とくとく
GLUG GLUG
LISTEN...
YÛKO SAID SOMETHING.
THAT THERE WERE TWO KINDS OF MEMORY...

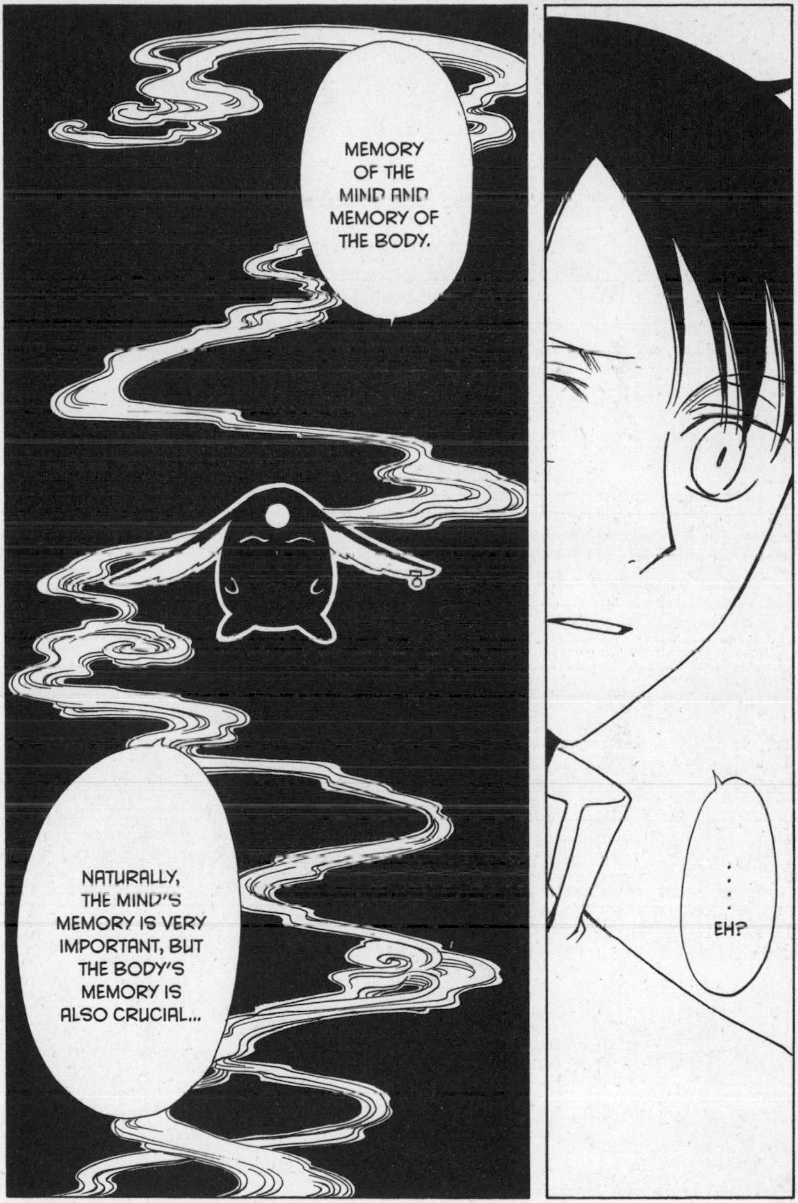
....EH?
MEMORY OF THE MIND AND MEMORY OF THE BODY.
NATURALLY, THE MIND'S MEMORY IS VERY IMPORTANT, BUT THE BODY'S MEMORY IS ALSO CRUCIAL...

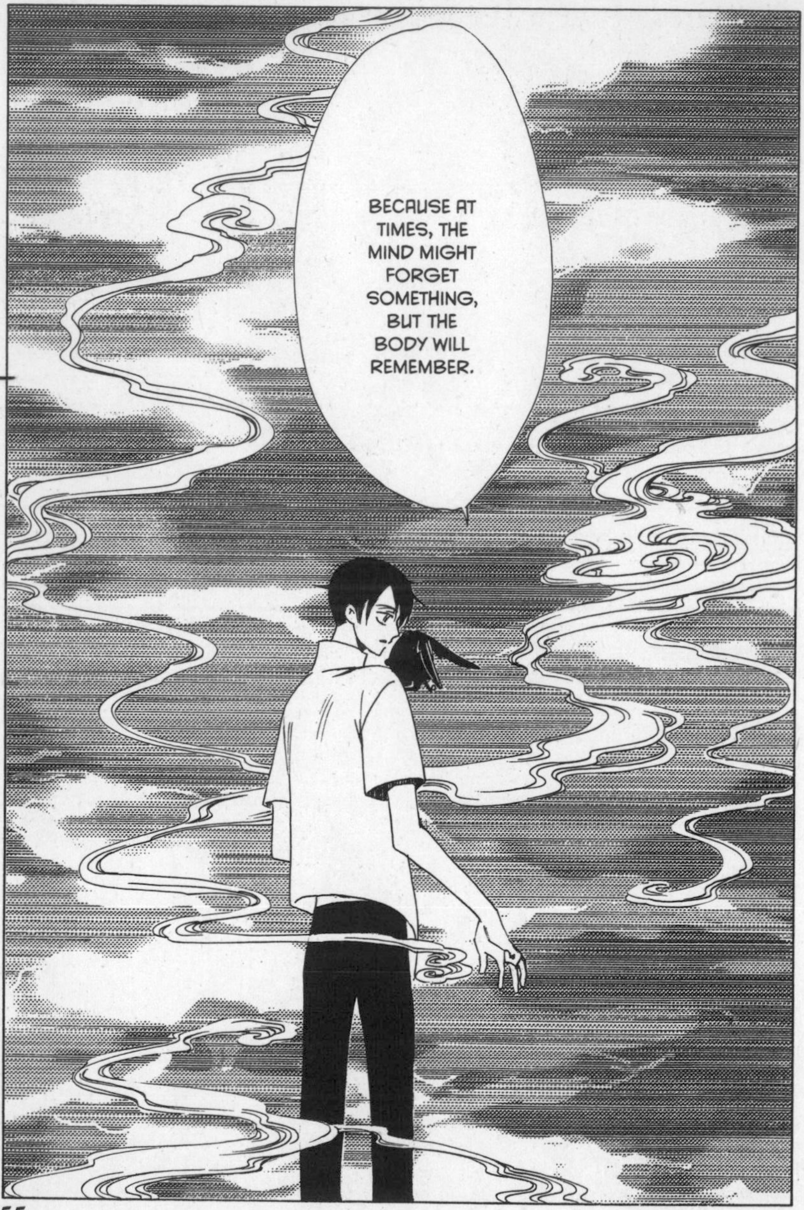
BECAUSE AT TIMES, THE MIND MIGHT FORGET SOMETHING, BUT THE BODY WILL REMEMBER.

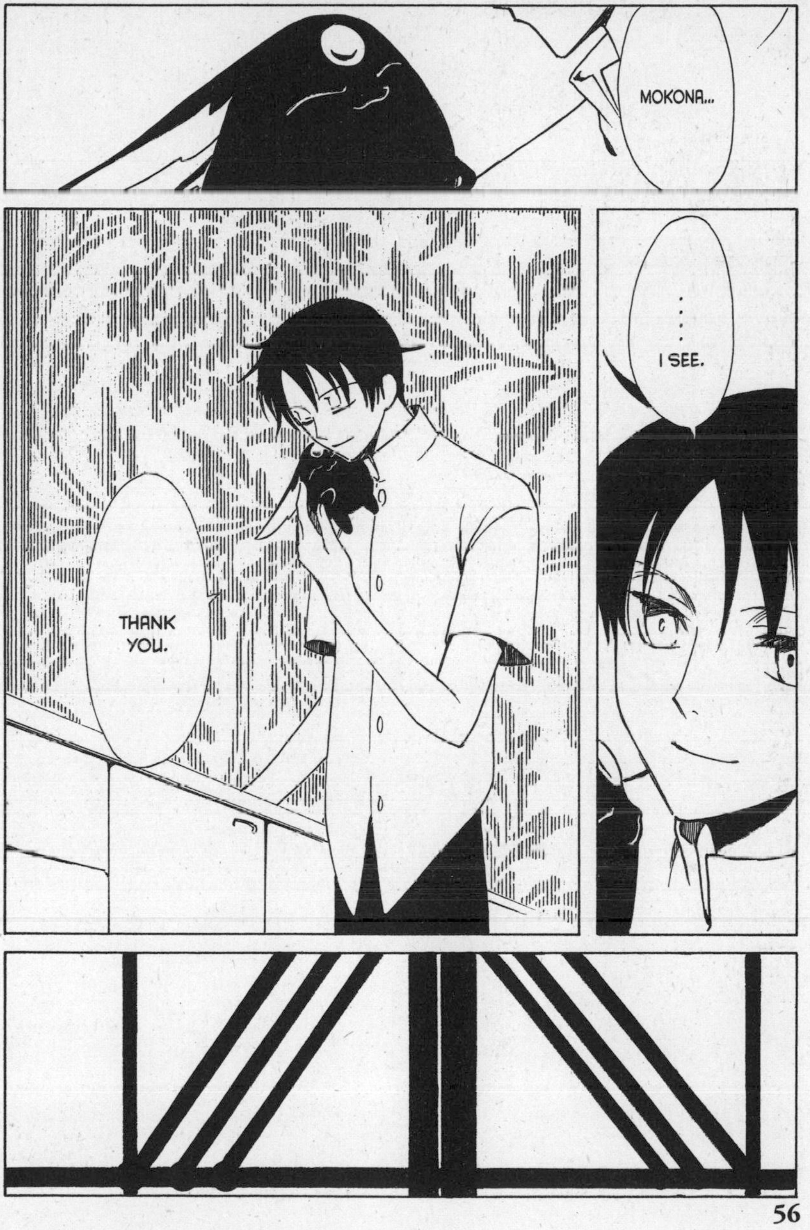
MOKONA...
...... I SEE.
THANK YOU.

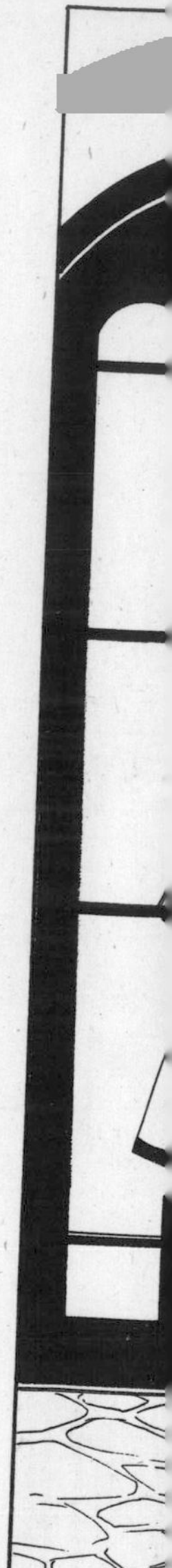

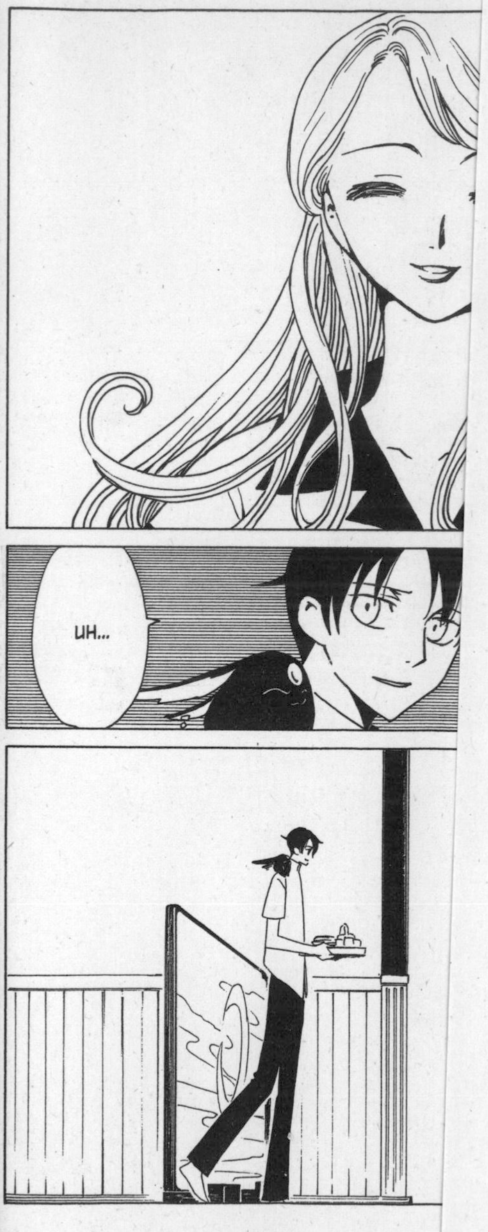
UH...

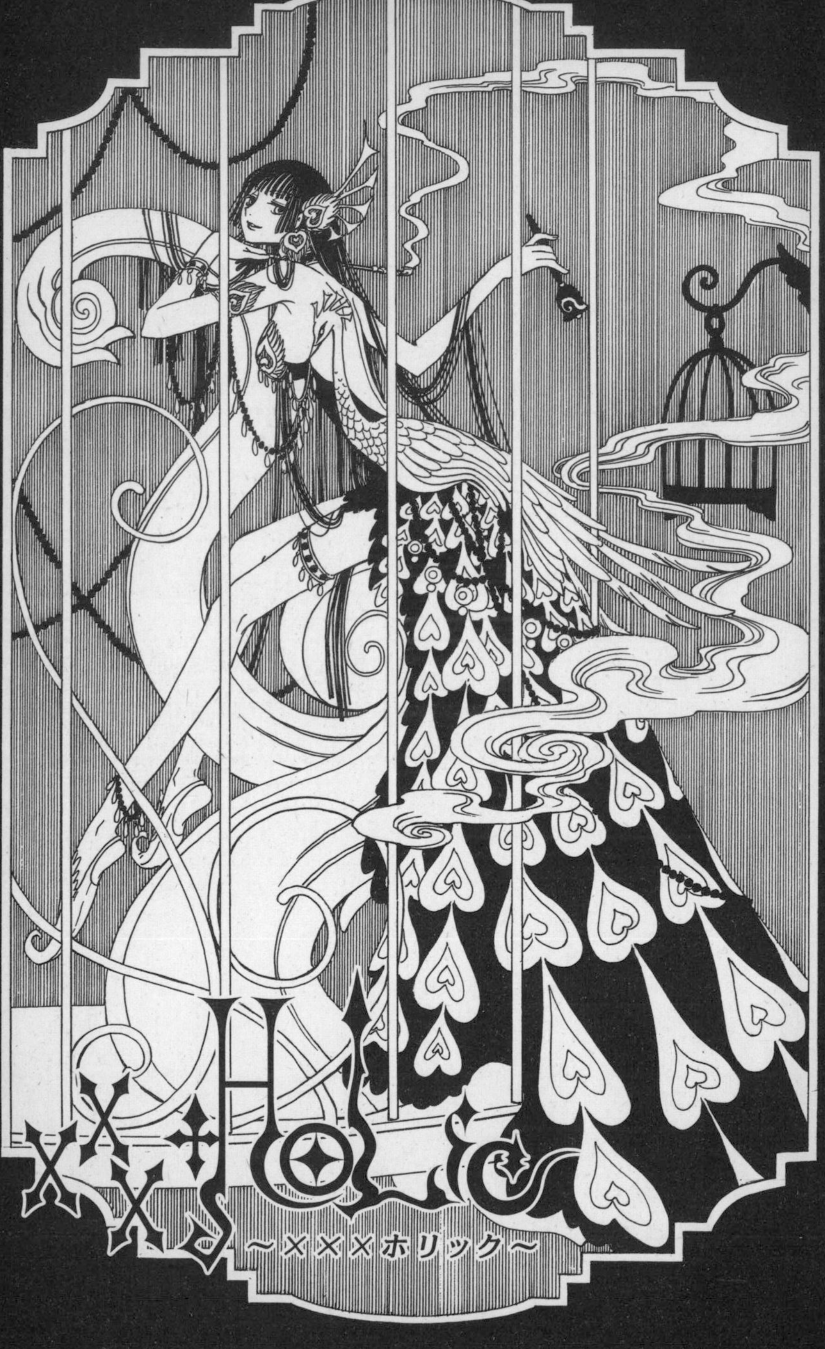
xxxHOLiC
~×××ホリック~

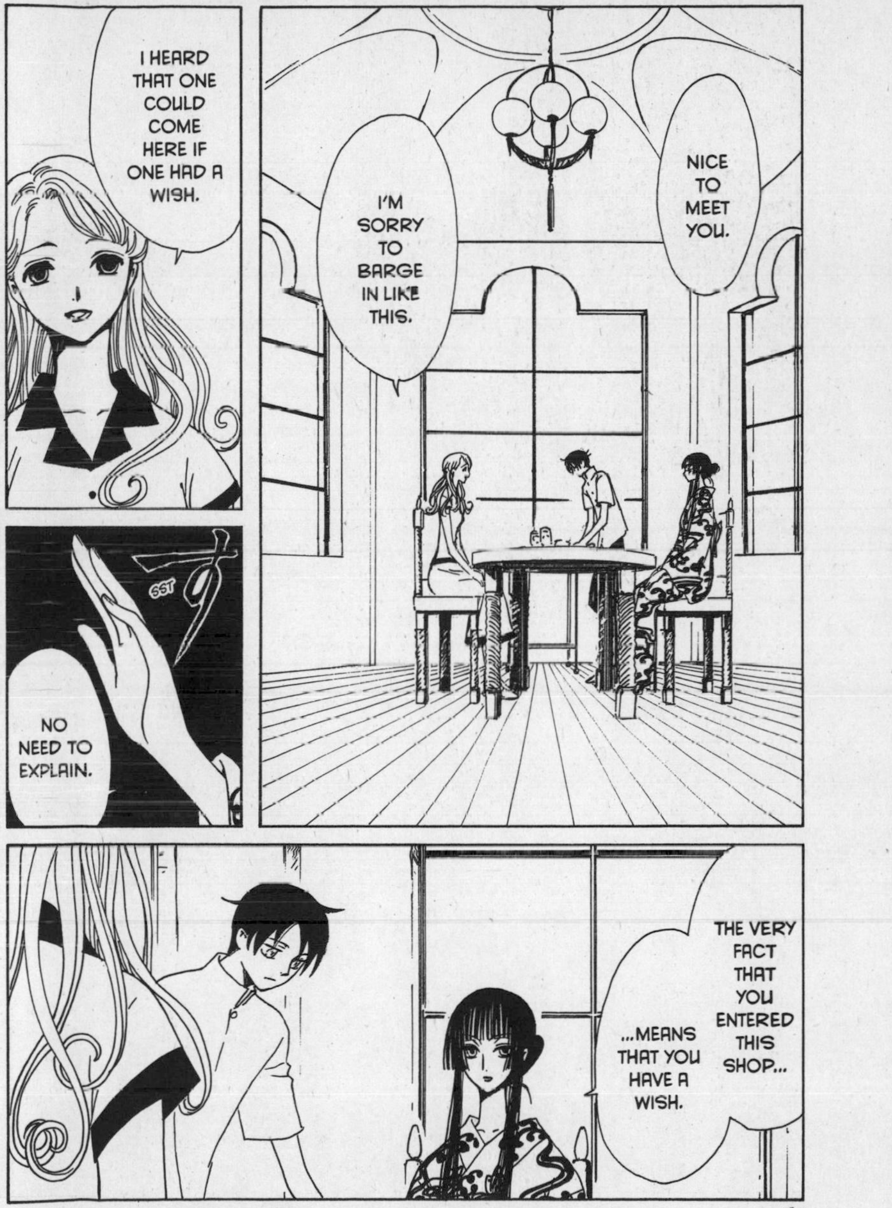
NICE TO MEET YOU.
I'M SORRY TO BARGE IN LIKE THIS.
I HEARD THAT ONE COULD COME HERE IF ONE HAD A WISH.
SST
NO NEED TO EXPLAIN.
THE VERY FACT THAT YOU ENTERED THIS SHOP...
...MEANS THAT YOU HAVE A WISH.

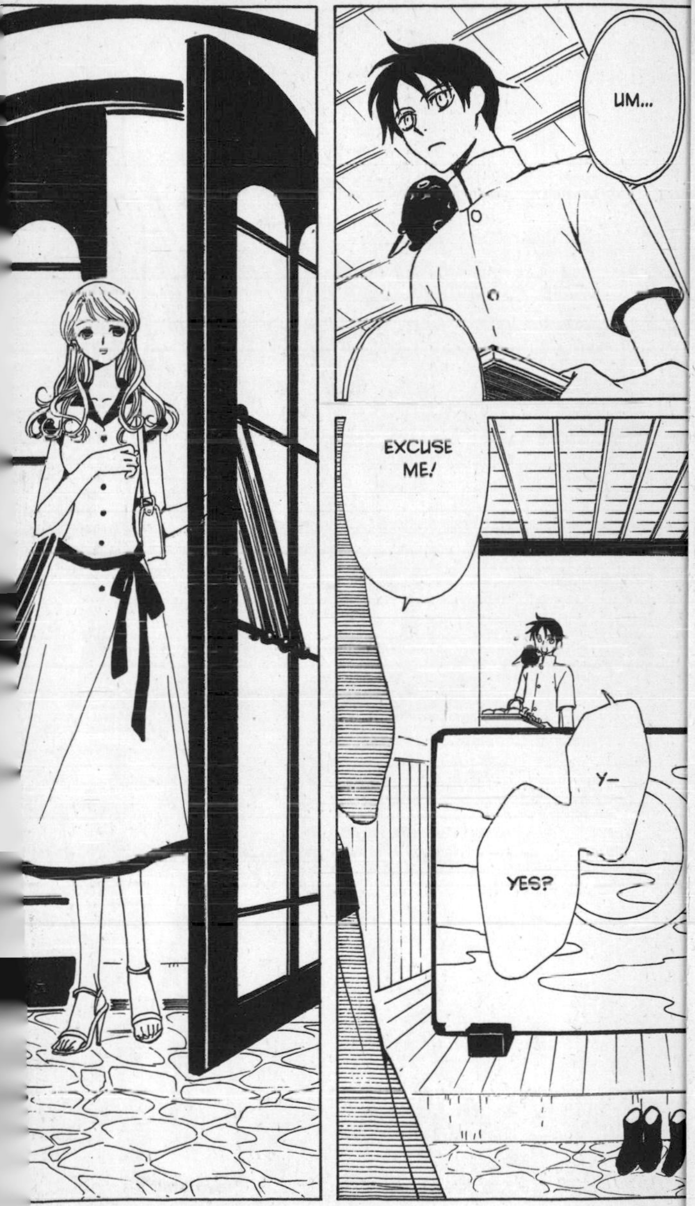
UM...
EXCUSE ME!
Y—
YES?

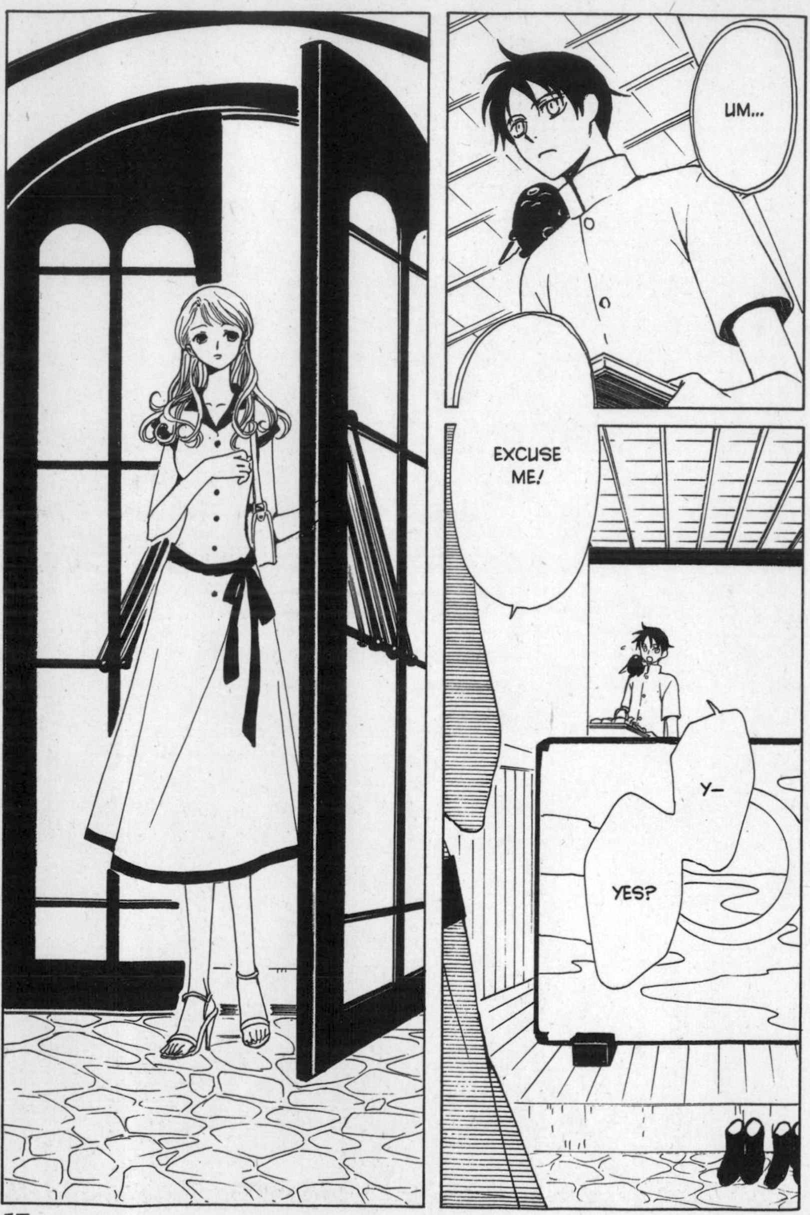
UM...
EXCUSE ME!
Y—
YES?

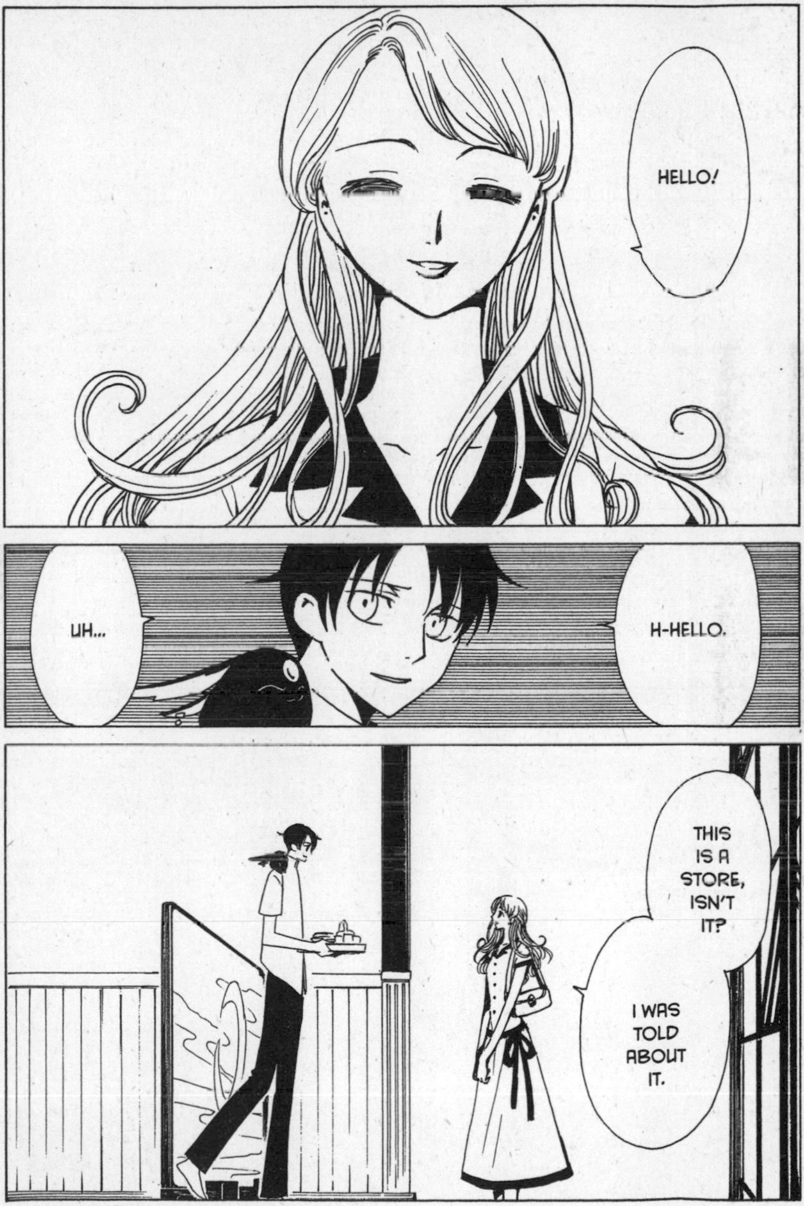
HELLO!
H-HELLO.
UH...
THIS IS A STORE, ISN'T IT?
I WAS TOLD ABOUT IT.

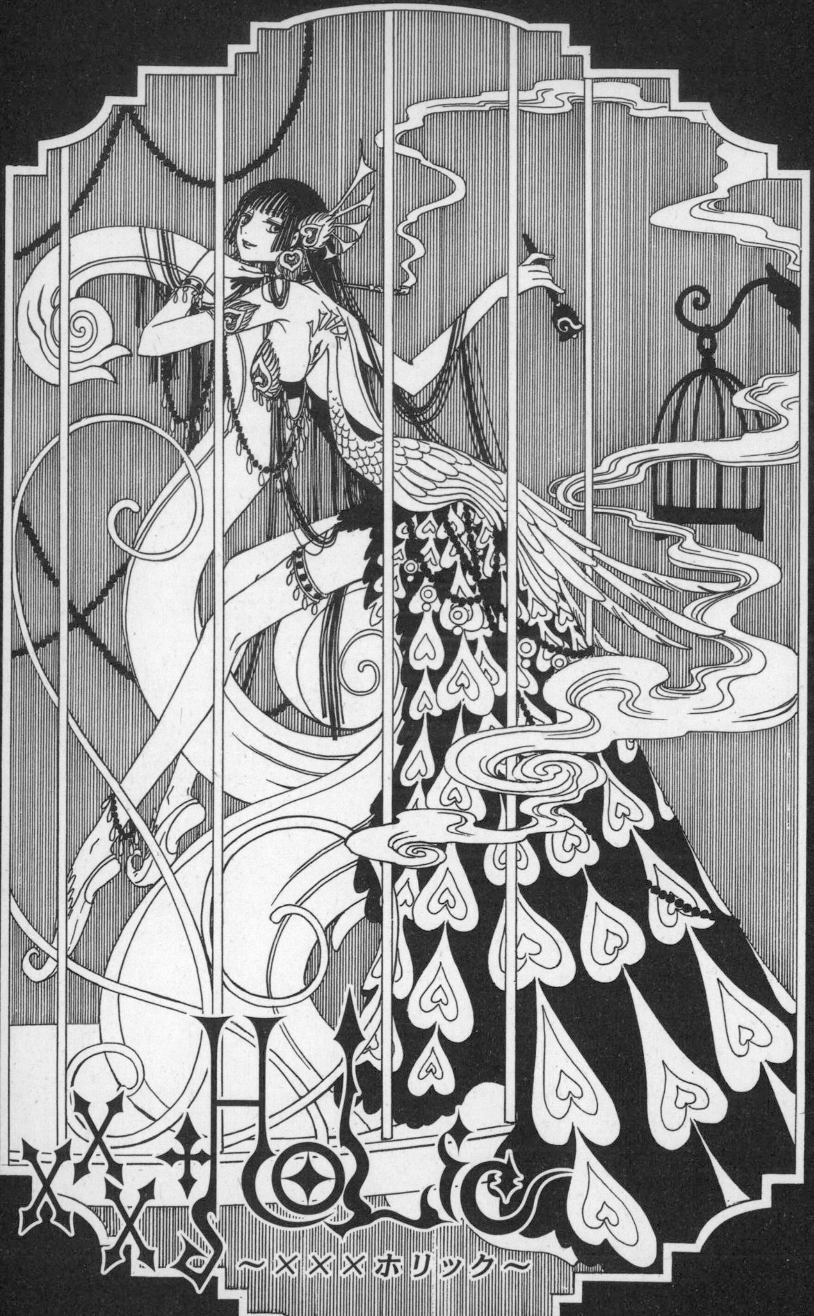
xxxHOLiC
〜×××ホリック〜

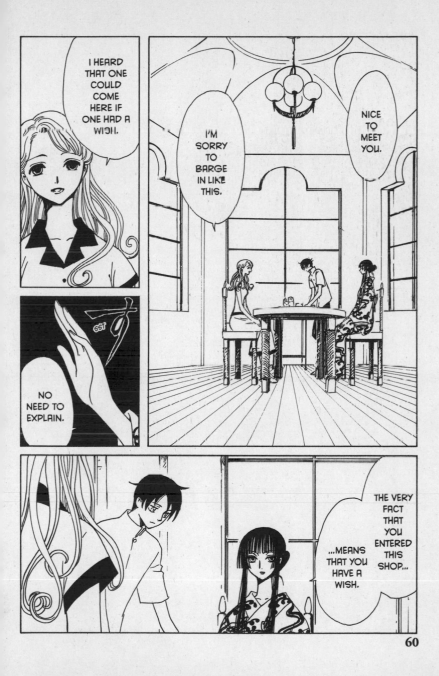

60

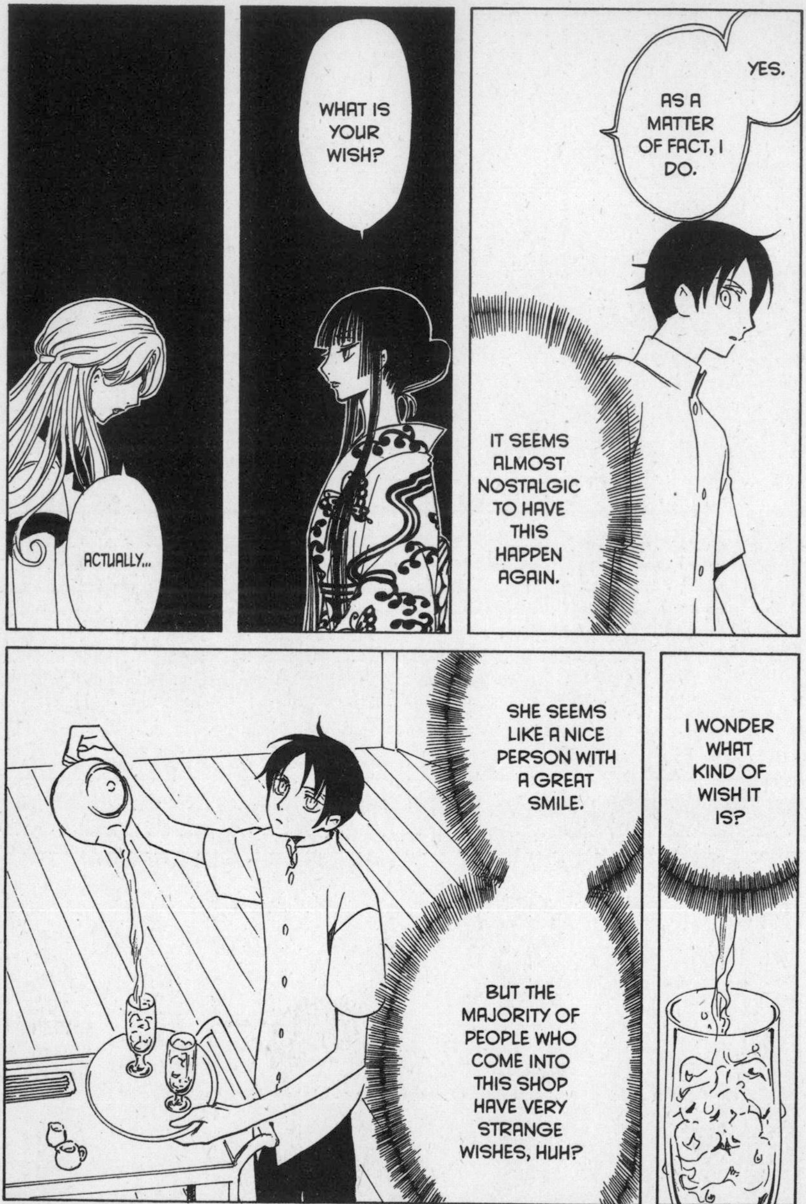
YES.
AS A MATTER OF FACT, I DO.
IT SEEMS ALMOST NOSTALGIC TO HAVE THIS HAPPEN AGAIN.
WHAT IS YOUR WISH?
ACTUALLY...
I WONDER WHAT KIND OF WISH IT IS?
SHE SEEMS LIKE A NICE PERSON WITH A GREAT SMILE.
BUT THE MAJORITY OF PEOPLE WHO COME INTO THIS SHOP HAVE VERY STRANGE WISHES, HUH?

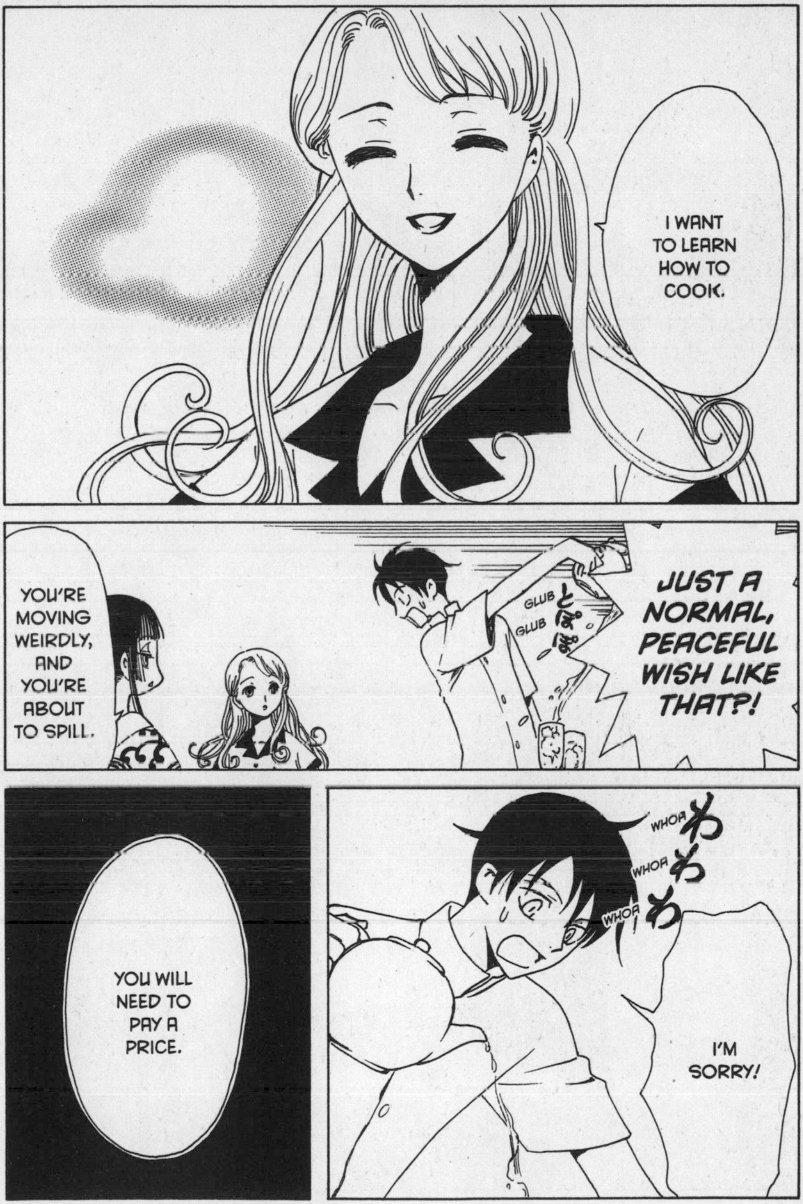
I WANT TO LEARN HOW TO COOK.
JUST A NORMAL, PEACEFUL WISH LIKE THAT?!
GLUB GLUB
とぽぽ
YOU'RE MOVING WEIRDLY, AND YOU'RE ABOUT TO SPILL.
WHOA WHOA WHOA
わわわ
I'M SORRY!
YOU WILL NEED TO PAY A PRICE.

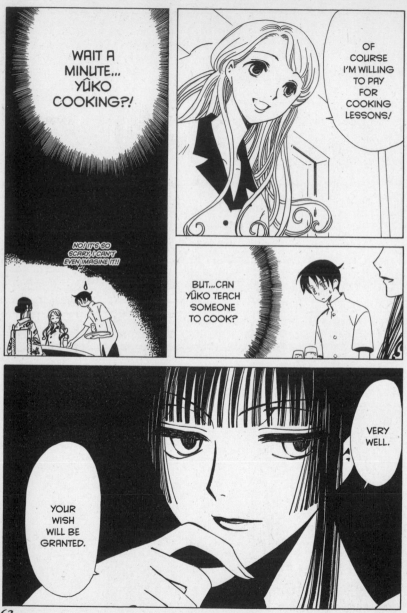

OF COURSE I'M WILLING TO PAY FOR COOKING LESSONS!
BUT...CAN YÛKO TEACH SOMEONE TO COOK?
WAIT A MINUTE... YÛKO COOKING?!
NO! IT'S SO SCARY, I CAN'T EVEN IMAGINE IT!!
VERY WELL.
YOUR WISH WILL BE GRANTED.

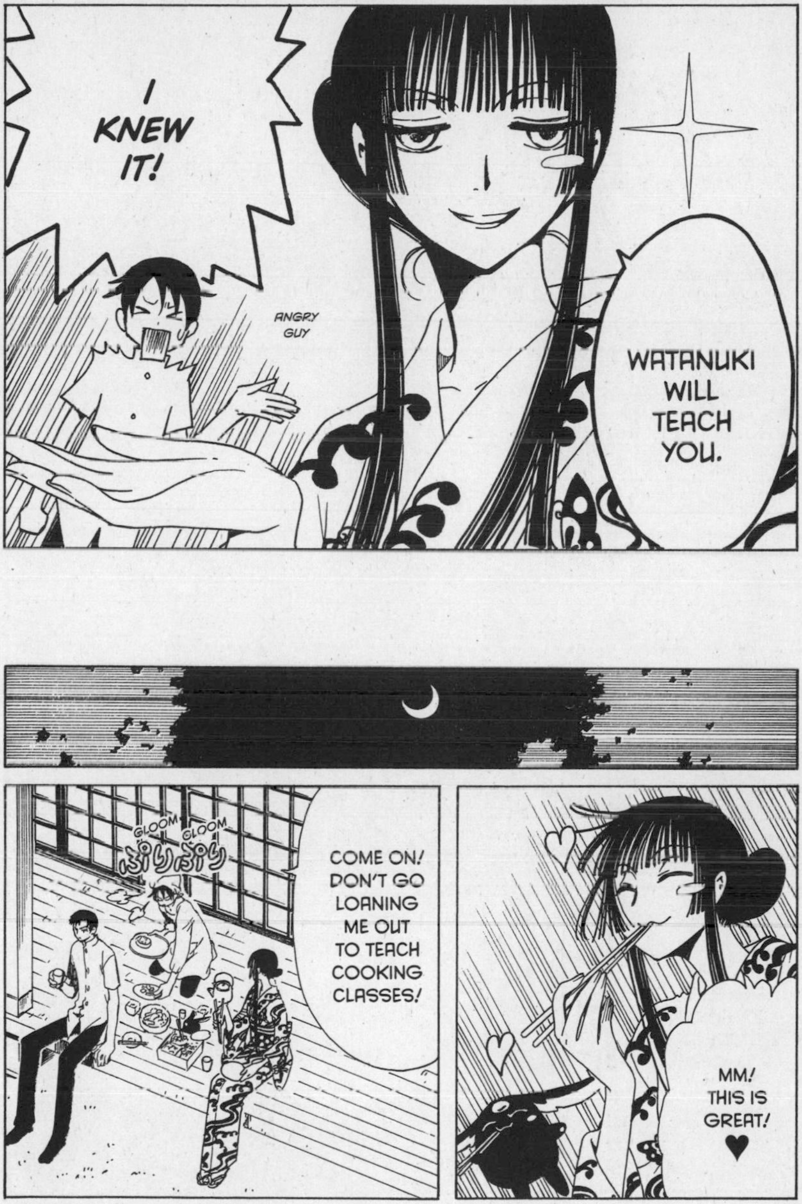
WATANUKI WILL TEACH YOU.
I KNEW IT!
ANGRY GUY
MM! THIS IS GREAT! ♥
COME ON! DON'T GO LOANING ME OUT TO TEACH COOKING CLASSES!
GLOOM GLOOM
ぷりぷり

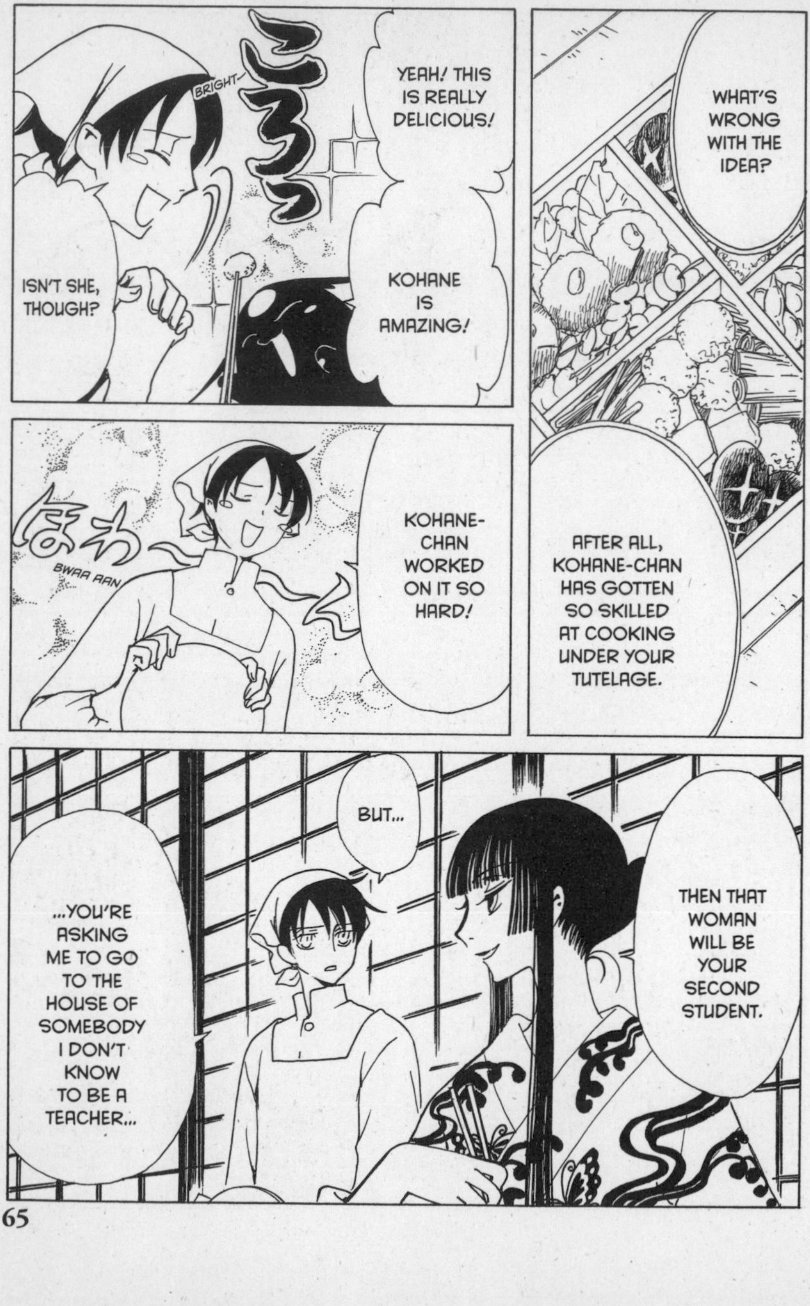
WHAT'S WRONG WITH THE IDEA?
AFTER ALL, KOHANE-CHAN HAS GOTTEN SO SKILLED AT COOKING UNDER YOUR TUTELAGE.
BRIGHT—
YEAH! THIS IS REALLY DELICIOUS!
KOHANE IS AMAZING!
ISN'T SHE, THOUGH?
KOHANE-CHAN WORKED ON IT SO HARD!
ほわ
BWAA AAN
THEN THAT WOMAN WILL BE YOUR SECOND STUDENT.
BUT...
...YOU'RE ASKING ME TO GO TO THE HOUSE OF SOMEBODY I DON'T KNOW TO BE A TEACHER...

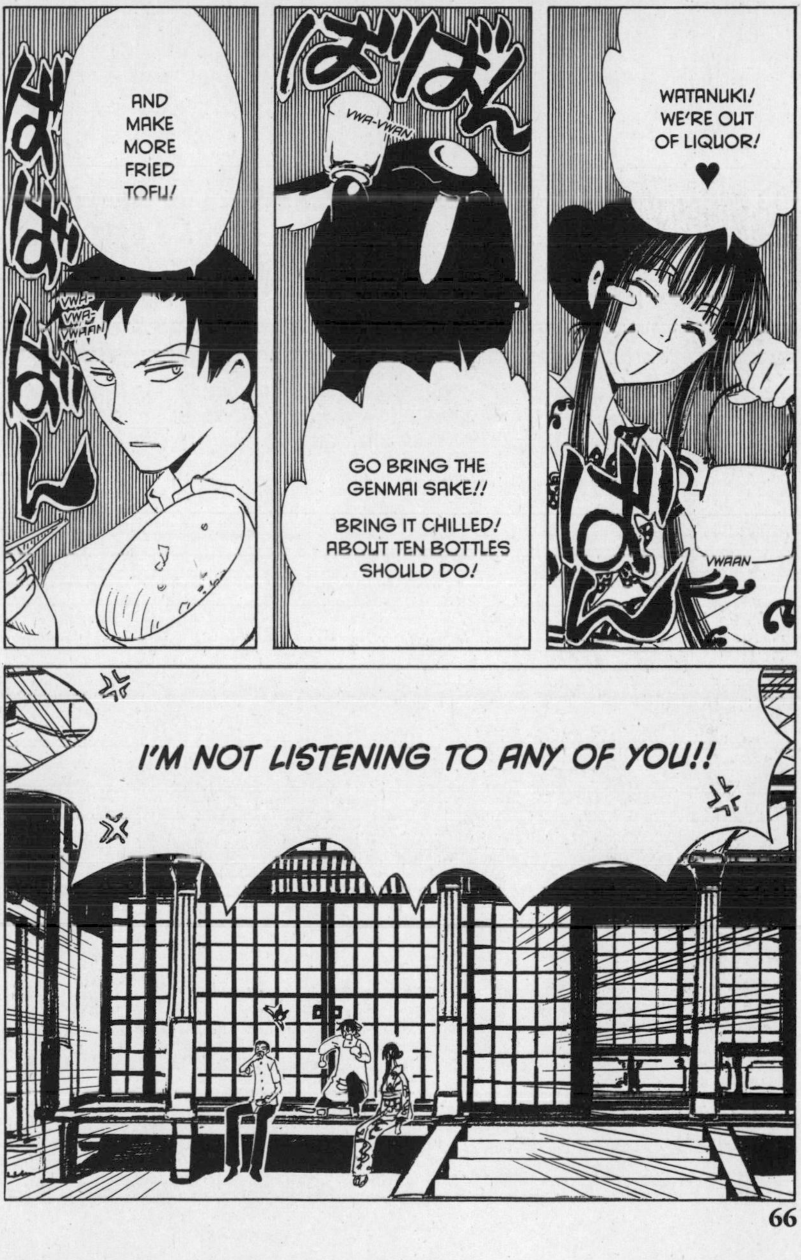
WATANUKI! WE'RE OUT OF LIQUOR! ♥
VWAAN
VWA-VWAN
GO BRING THE GENMAI SAKE!!
BRING IT CHILLED! ABOUT TEN BOTTLES SHOULD DO!
AND MAKE MORE FRIED TOFU!
VWA-VWA-VWAAN
I'M NOT LISTENING TO ANY OF YOU!!

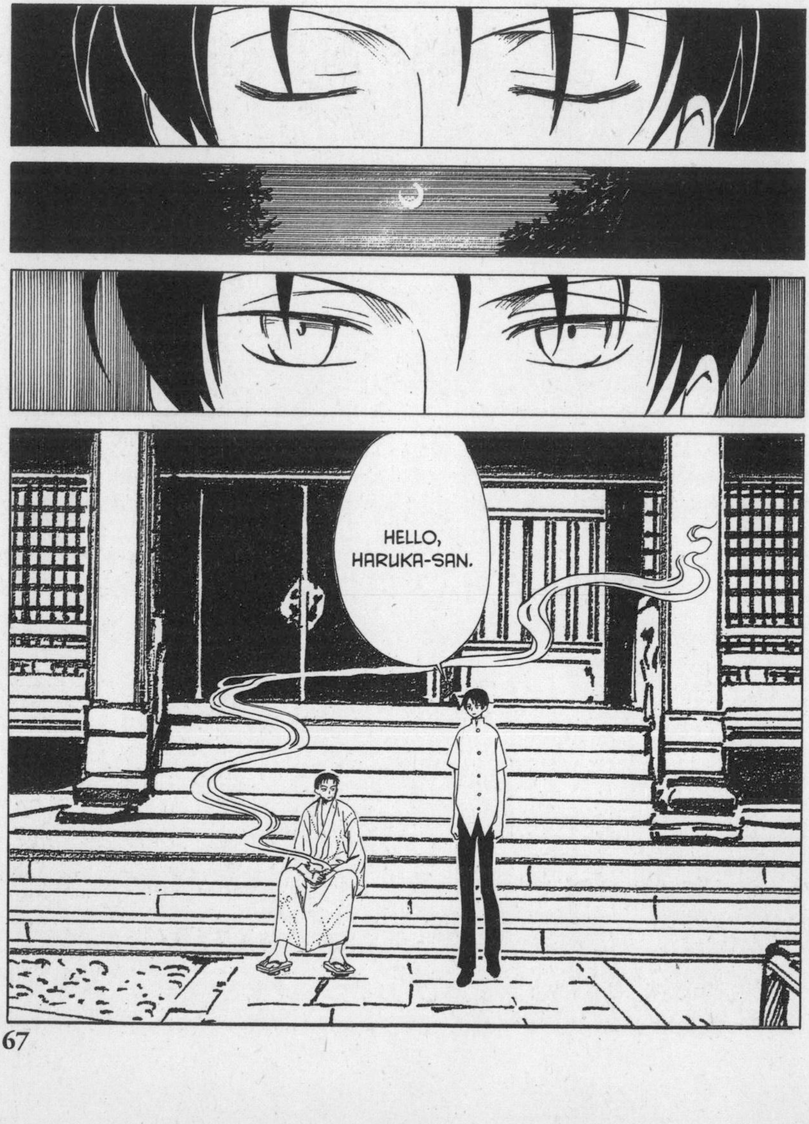
HELLO, HARUKA-SAN.

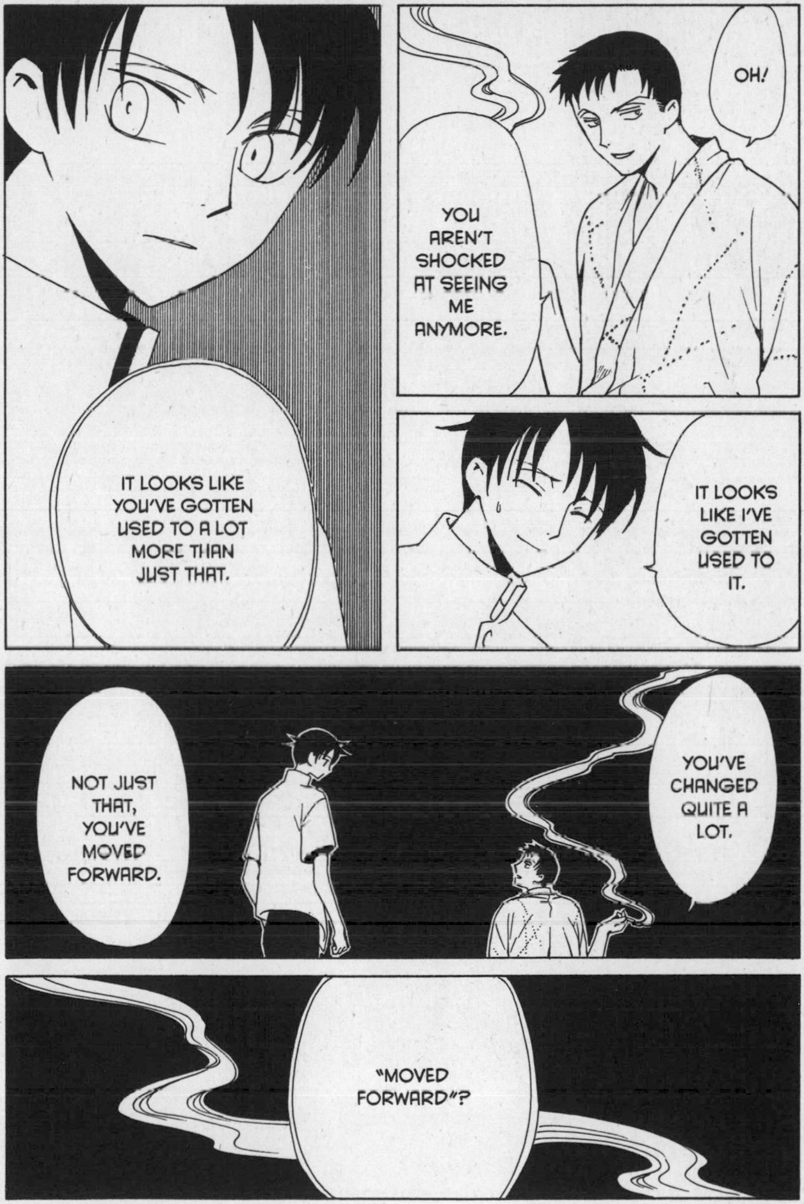
OH!
YOU AREN'T SHOCKED AT SEEING ME ANYMORE.
IT LOOKS LIKE I'VE GOTTEN USED TO IT.
IT LOOKS LIKE YOU'VE GOTTEN USED TO A LOT MORE THAN JUST THAT.
YOU'VE CHANGED QUITE A LOT.
NOT JUST THAT, YOU'VE MOVED FORWARD.
"MOVED FORWARD"?

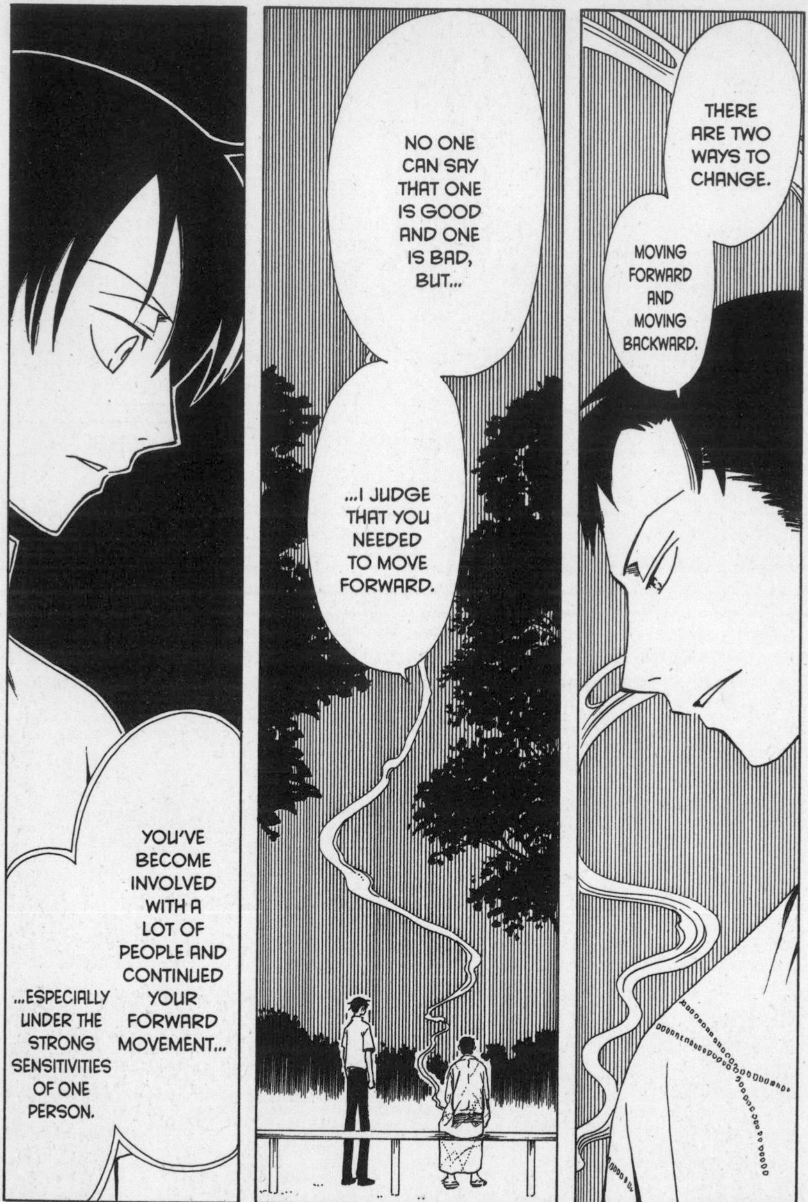
THERE ARE TWO WAYS TO CHANGE.
MOVING FORWARD AND MOVING BACKWARD.
NO ONE CAN SAY THAT ONE IS GOOD AND ONE IS BAD, BUT...
...I JUDGE THAT YOU NEEDED TO MOVE FORWARD.
YOU'VE BECOME INVOLVED WITH A LOT OF PEOPLE AND CONTINUED YOUR FORWARD MOVEMENT...
...ESPECIALLY UNDER THE STRONG SENSITIVITIES OF ONE PERSON.

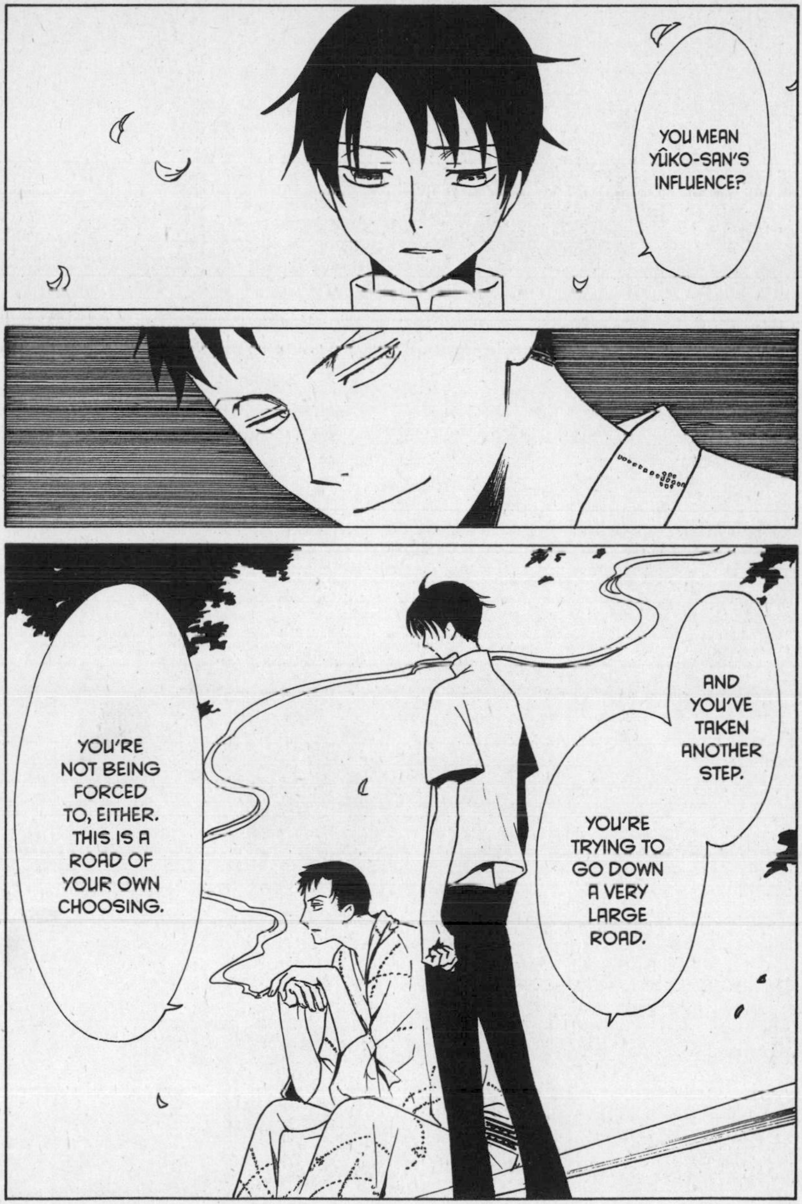
YOU MEAN YÛKO-SAN'S INFLUENCE?
AND YOU'VE TAKEN ANOTHER STEP.
YOU'RE TRYING TO GO DOWN A VERY LARGE ROAD.
YOU'RE NOT BEING FORCED TO, EITHER. THIS IS A ROAD OF YOUR OWN CHOOSING.

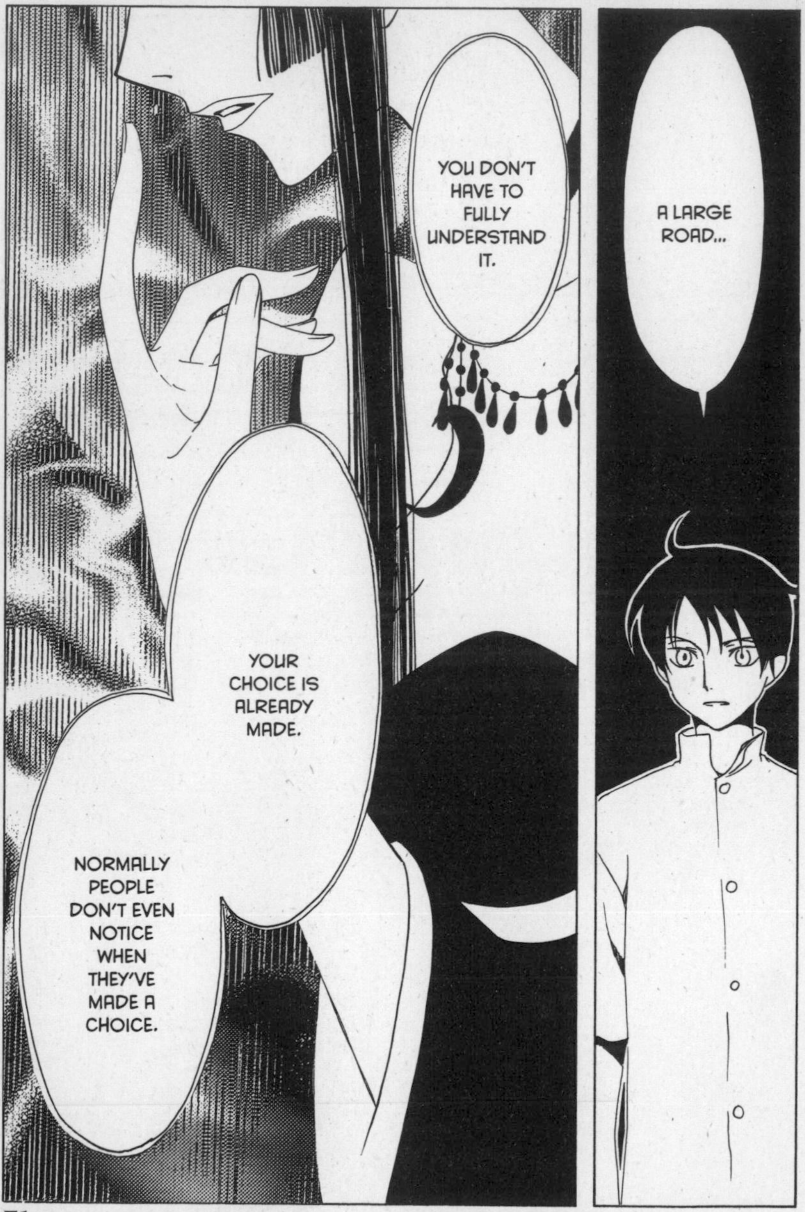
A LARGE ROAD...
YOU DON'T HAVE TO FULLY UNDERSTAND IT.
YOUR CHOICE IS ALREADY MADE.
NORMALLY PEOPLE DON'T EVEN NOTICE WHEN THEY'VE MADE A CHOICE.

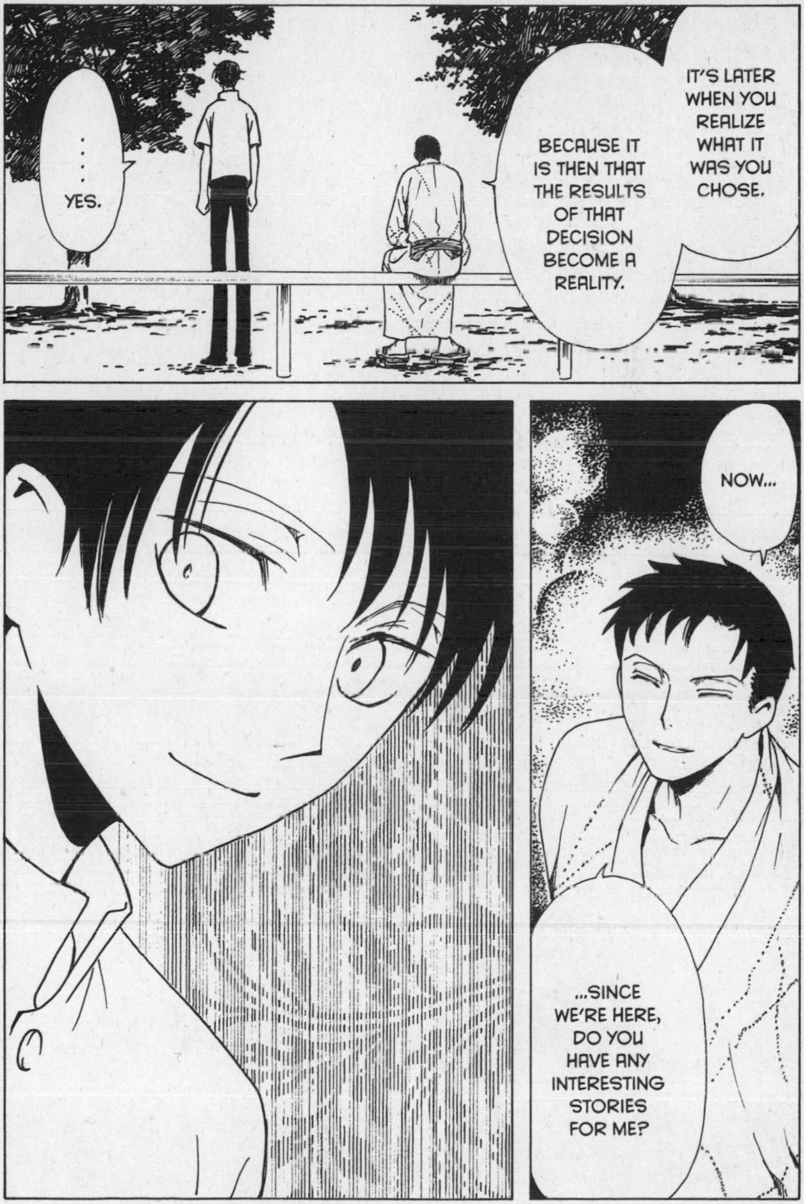
IT'S LATER WHEN YOU REALIZE WHAT IT WAS YOU CHOSE.
BECAUSE IT IS THEN THAT THE RESULTS OF THAT DECISION BECOME A REALITY.
.....YES.
NOW...
...SINCE WE'RE HERE, DO YOU HAVE ANY INTERESTING STORIES FOR ME?

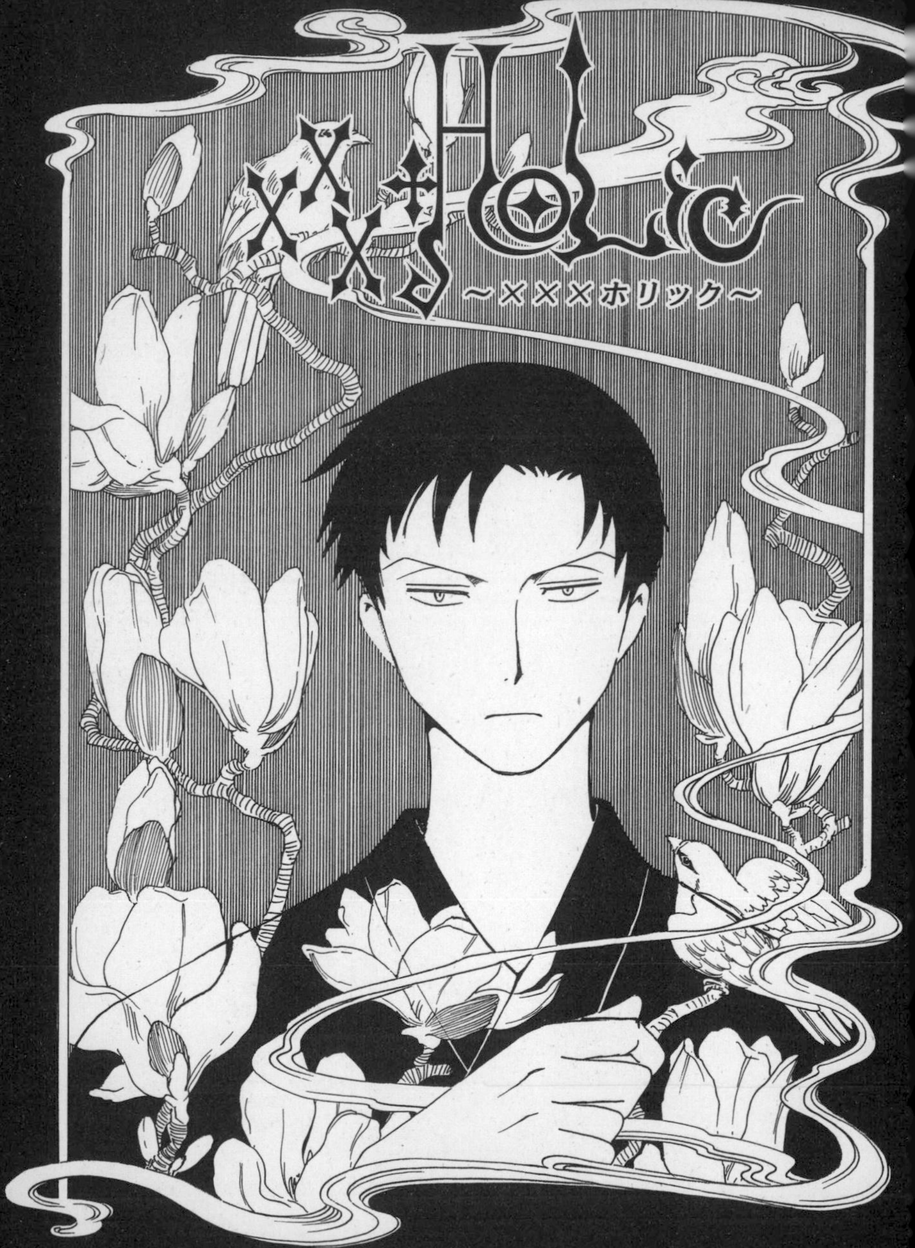
xxxHOLiC
～×××ホリック～

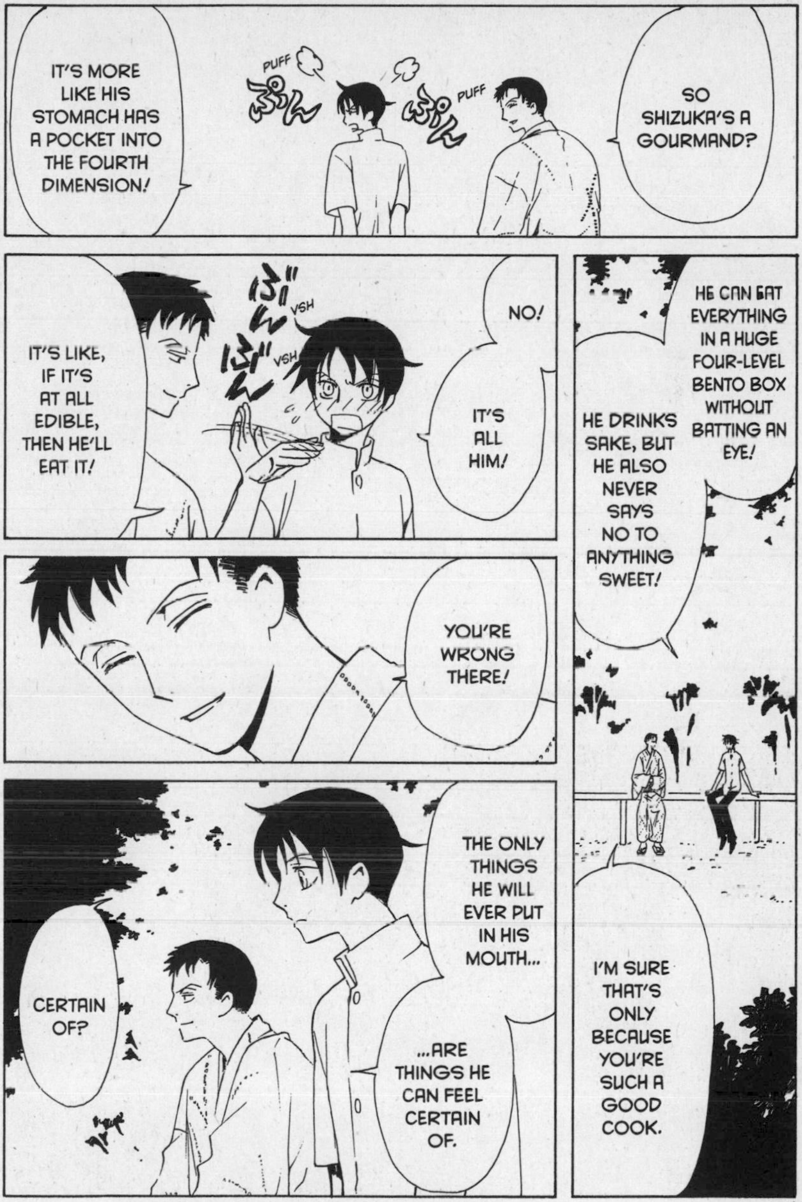
SO SHIZUKA'S A GOURMAND?
ぷん PUFF
ぷん PUFF
IT'S MORE LIKE HIS STOMACH HAS A POCKET INTO THE FOURTH DIMENSION!
HE CAN EAT EVERYTHING IN A HUGE FOUR-LEVEL BENTO BOX WITHOUT BATTING AN EYE!
HE DRINKS SAKE, BUT HE ALSO NEVER SAYS NO TO ANYTHING SWEET!
I'M SURE THAT'S ONLY BECAUSE YOU'RE SUCH A GOOD COOK.
NO!
IT'S ALL HIM!
ぶん VSH
ぶん VSH
IT'S LIKE, IF IT'S AT ALL EDIBLE, THEN HE'LL EAT IT!
YOU'RE WRONG THERE!
THE ONLY THINGS HE WILL EVER PUT IN HIS MOUTH...
...ARE THINGS HE CAN FEEL CERTAIN OF.
CERTAIN OF?

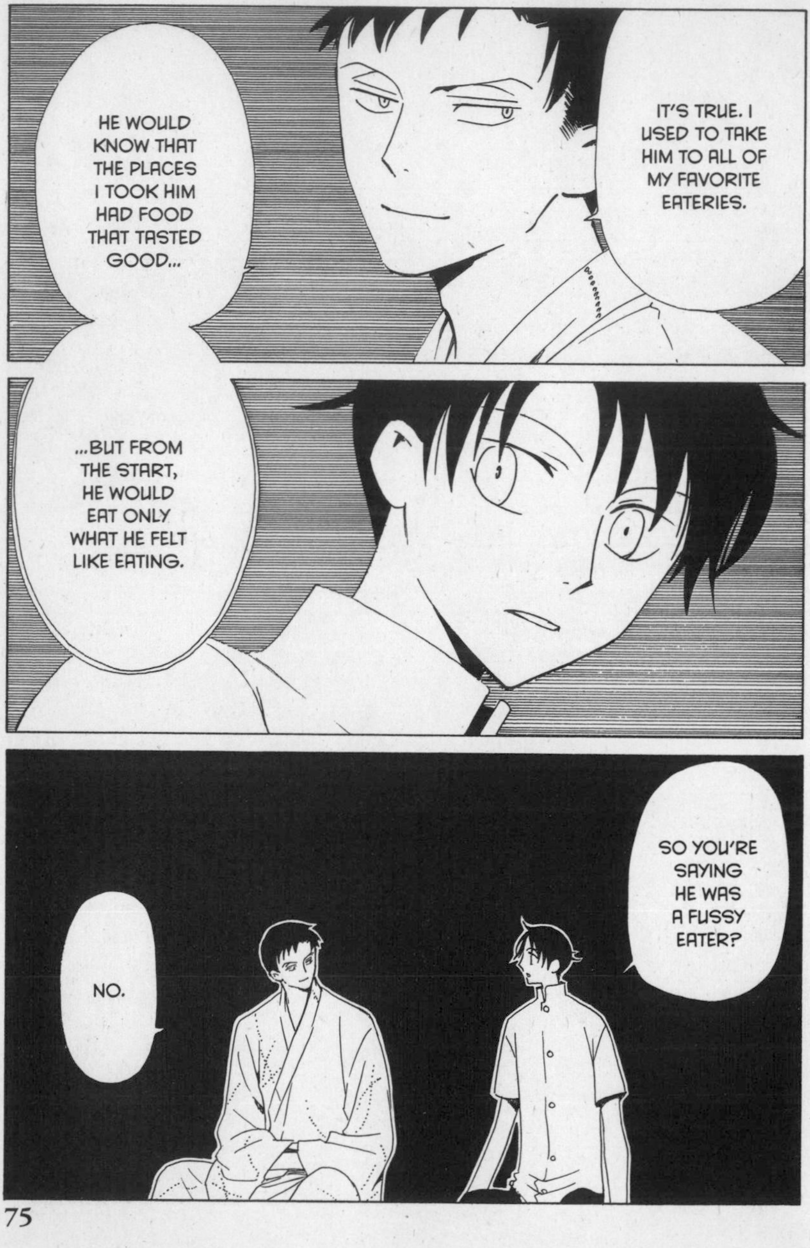
IT'S TRUE. I USED TO TAKE HIM TO ALL OF MY FAVORITE EATERIES.
HE WOULD KNOW THAT THE PLACES I TOOK HIM HAD FOOD THAT TASTED GOOD...
...BUT FROM THE START, HE WOULD EAT ONLY WHAT HE FELT LIKE EATING.
SO YOU'RE SAYING HE WAS A FUSSY EATER?
NO.

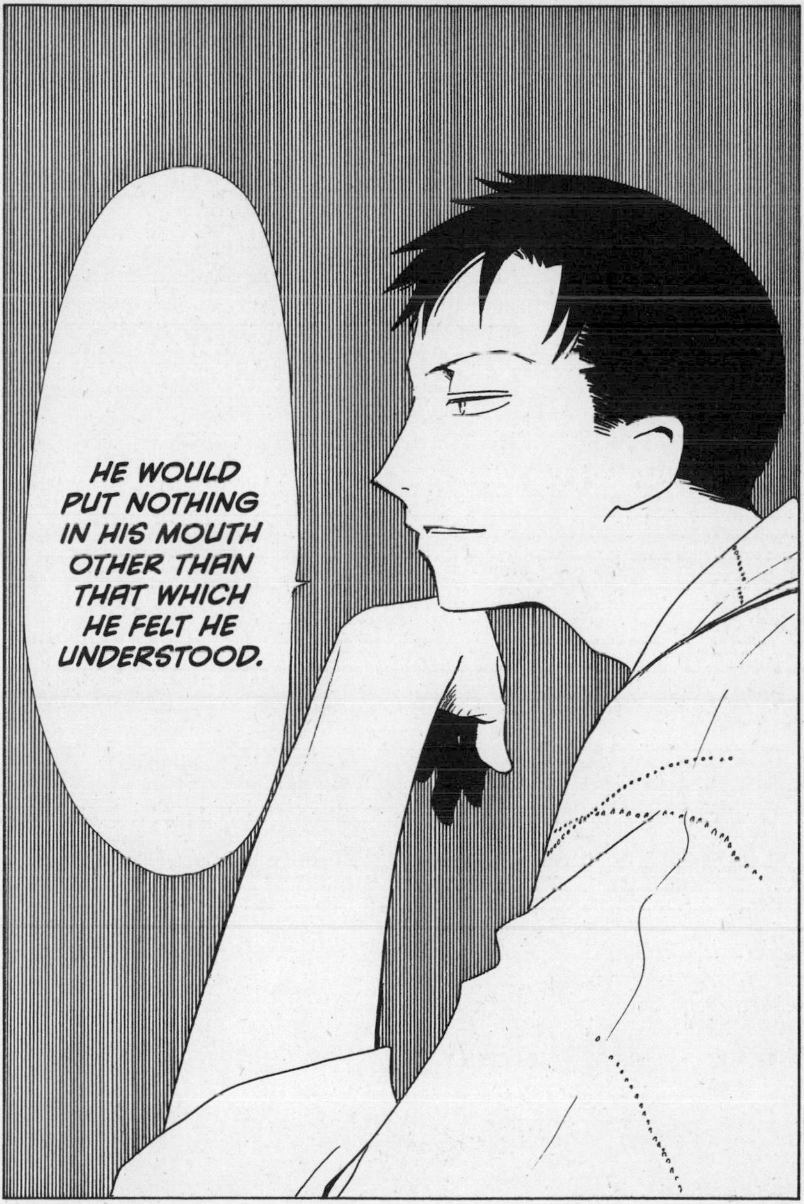
HE WOULD PUT NOTHING IN HIS MOUTH OTHER THAN THAT WHICH HE FELT HE UNDERSTOOD.

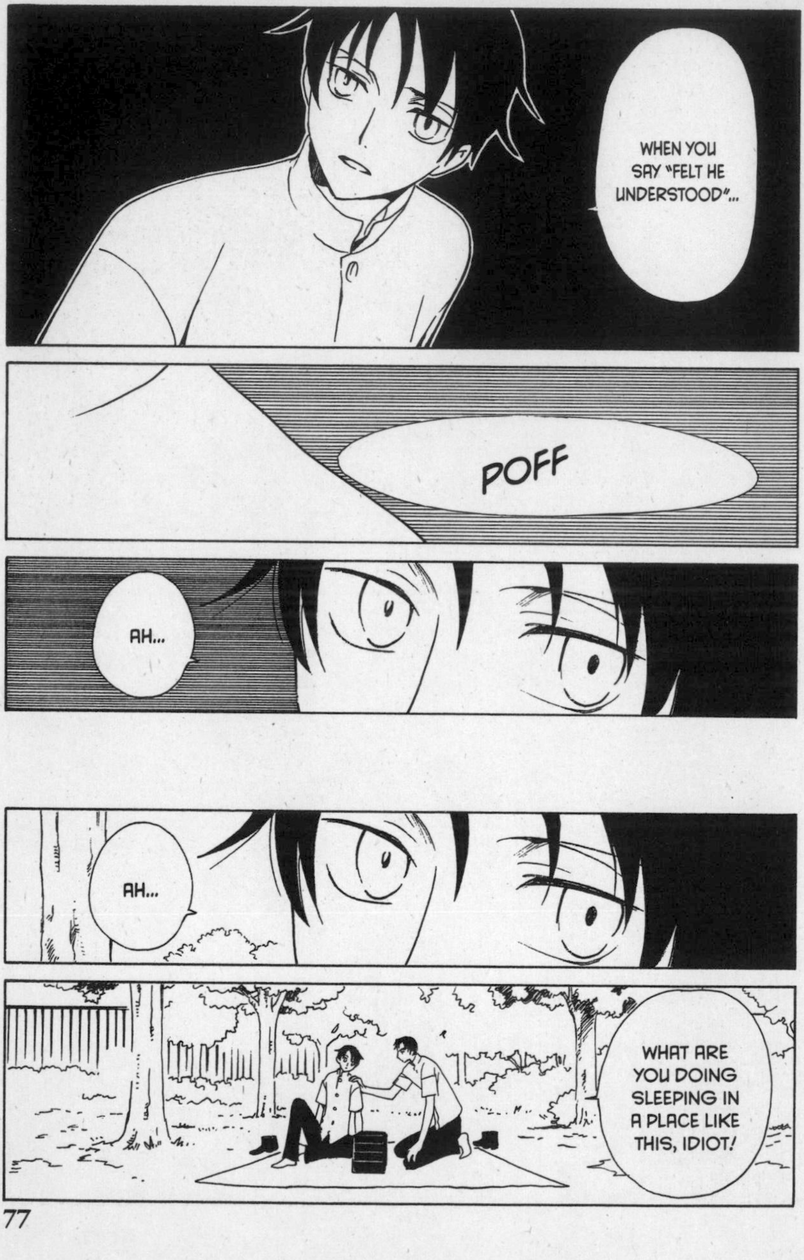
WHEN YOU SAY "FELT HE UNDERSTOOD"...
POFF
AH...
AH...
WHAT ARE YOU DOING SLEEPING IN A PLACE LIKE THIS, IDIOT!

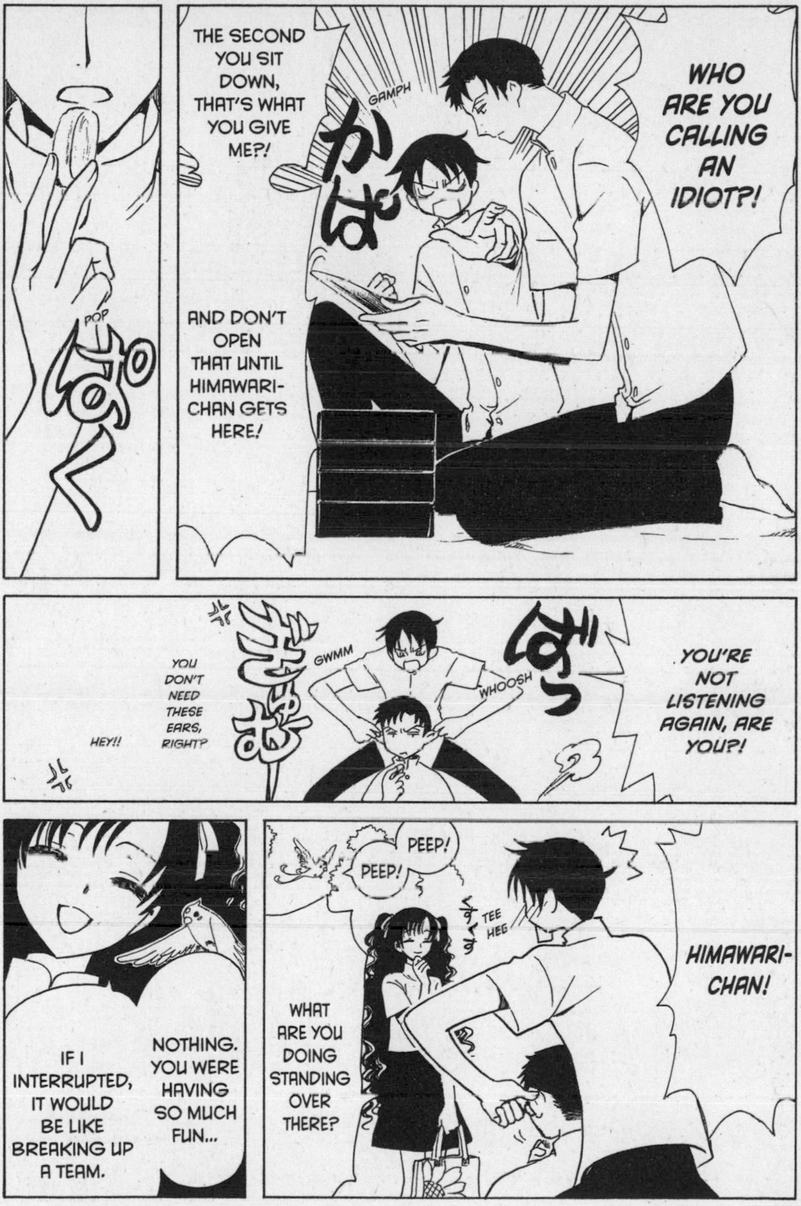
WHO ARE YOU CALLING AN IDIOT?!
GAMPH
THE SECOND YOU SIT DOWN, THAT'S WHAT YOU GIVE ME?!
AND DON'T OPEN THAT UNTIL HIMAWARI-CHAN GETS HERE!
POP
YOU'RE NOT LISTENING AGAIN, ARE YOU?!
WHOOSH
GWMM
YOU DON'T NEED THESE EARS, RIGHT?
HEY!!
HIMAWARI-CHAN!
TEE HEE
PEEP!
PEEP!
WHAT ARE YOU DOING STANDING OVER THERE?
NOTHING. YOU WERE HAVING SO MUCH FUN...
IF I INTERRUPTED, IT WOULD BE LIKE BREAKING UP A TEAM.

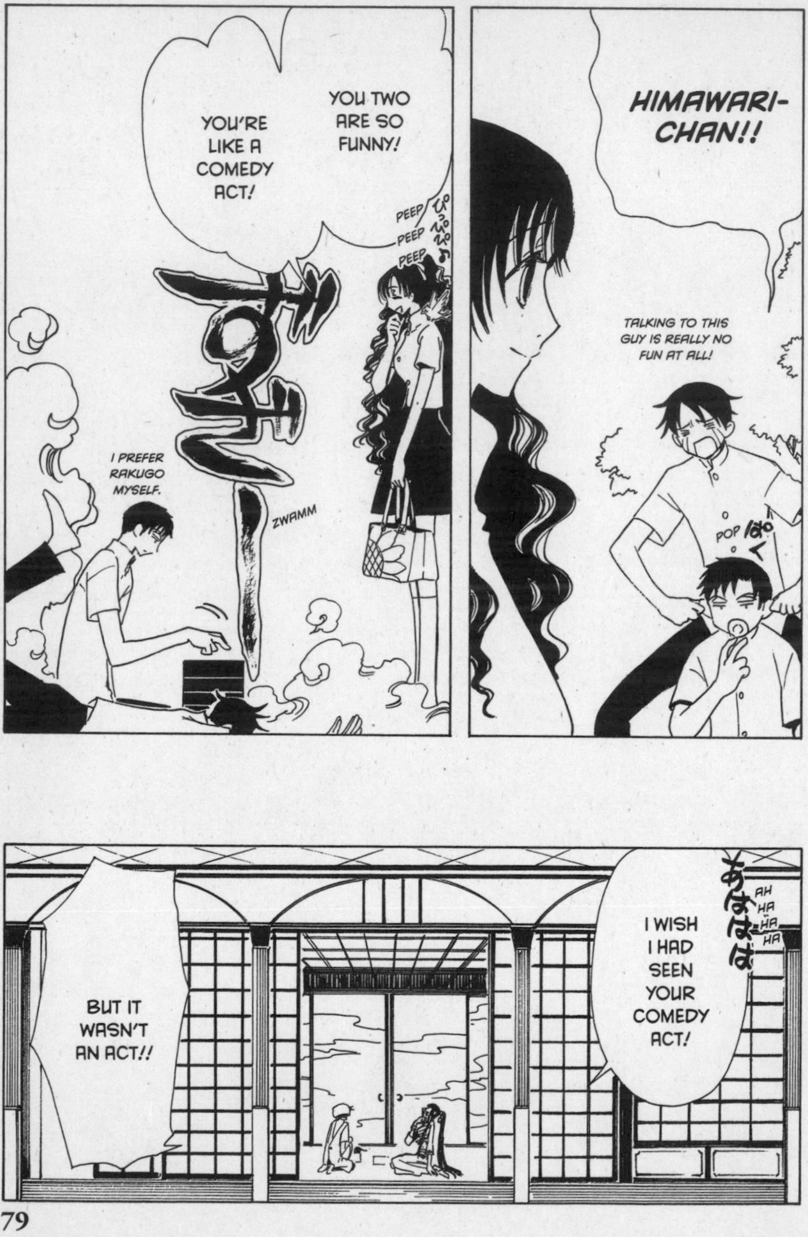
HIMAWARI-CHAN!!
TALKING TO THIS GUY IS REALLY NO FUN AT ALL!
POP ぱく
YOU TWO ARE SO FUNNY!
YOU'RE LIKE A COMEDY ACT!
PEEP PEEP PEEP
ぴっぴっぴ♪
ZWAMM
I PREFER RAKUGO MYSELF.
あははは
AH HA HA HA
I WISH I HAD SEEN YOUR COMEDY ACT!
BUT IT WASN'T AN ACT!!

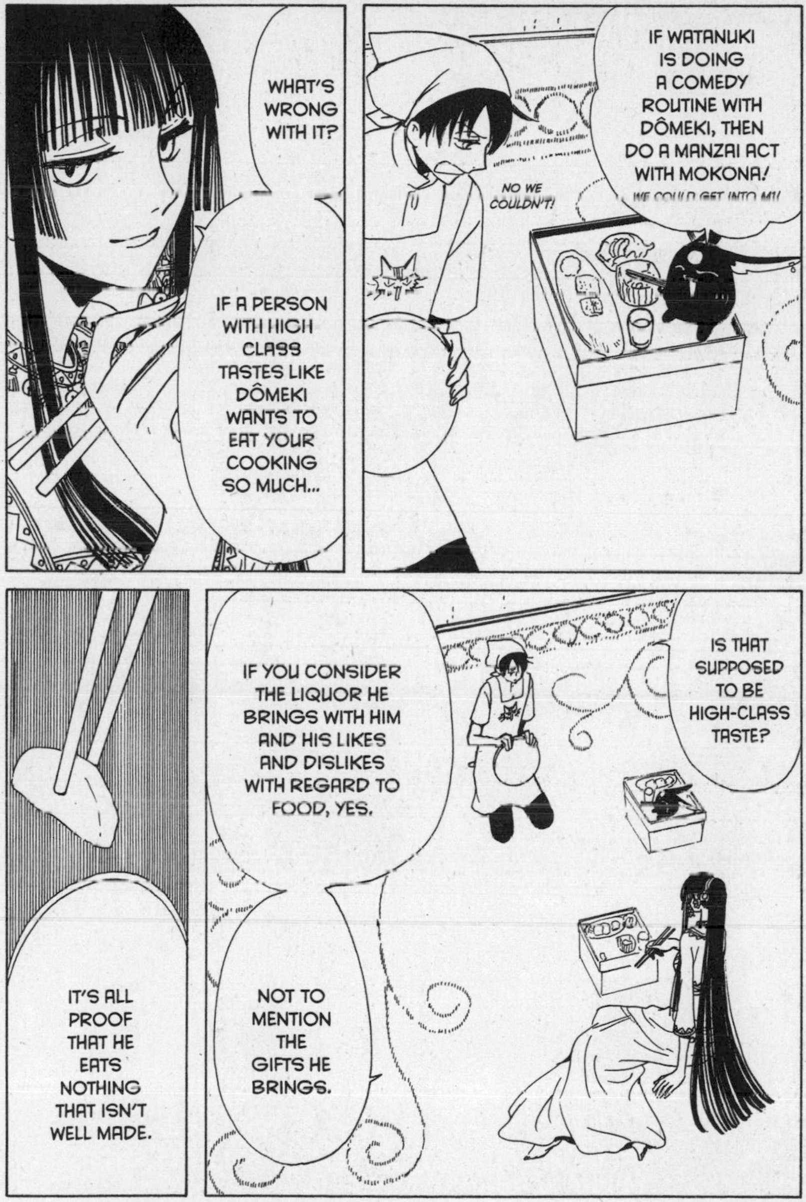
IF WATANUKI IS DOING A COMEDY ROUTINE WITH DÔMEKI, THEN DO A MANZAI ACT WITH MOKONA!
WE COULD GET INTO M1!
NO WE COULDN'T!
WHAT'S WRONG WITH IT?
IF A PERSON WITH HIGH CLASS TASTES LIKE DÔMEKI WANTS TO EAT YOUR COOKING SO MUCH...
IS THAT SUPPOSED TO BE HIGH-CLASS TASTE?
IF YOU CONSIDER THE LIQUOR HE BRINGS WITH HIM AND HIS LIKES AND DISLIKES WITH REGARD TO FOOD, YES.
NOT TO MENTION THE GIFTS HE BRINGS.
IT'S ALL PROOF THAT HE EATS NOTHING THAT ISN'T WELL MADE.

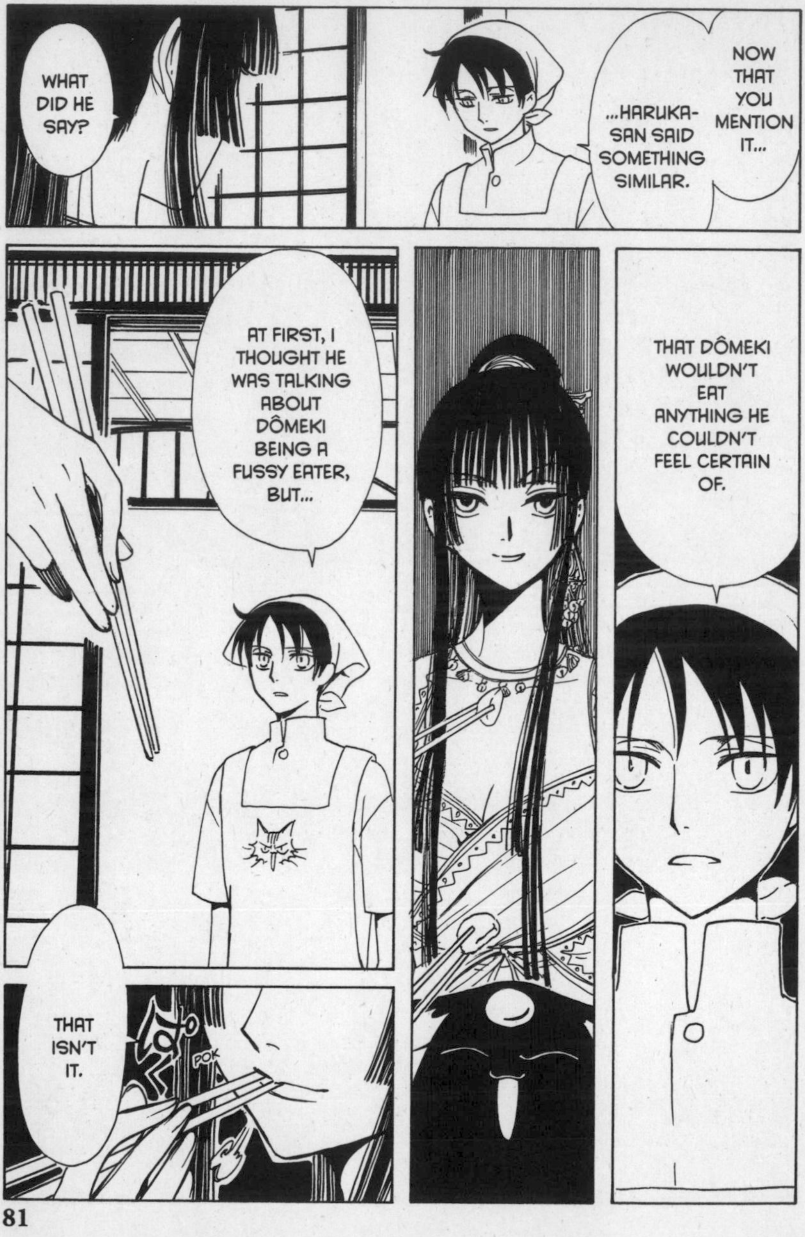
NOW THAT YOU MENTION IT...
...HARUKA-SAN SAID SOMETHING SIMILAR.
WHAT DID HE SAY?
THAT DÔMEKI WOULDN'T EAT ANYTHING HE COULDN'T FEEL CERTAIN OF.
AT FIRST, I THOUGHT HE WAS TALKING ABOUT DÔMEKI BEING A FUSSY EATER, BUT...
THAT ISN'T IT.
POK

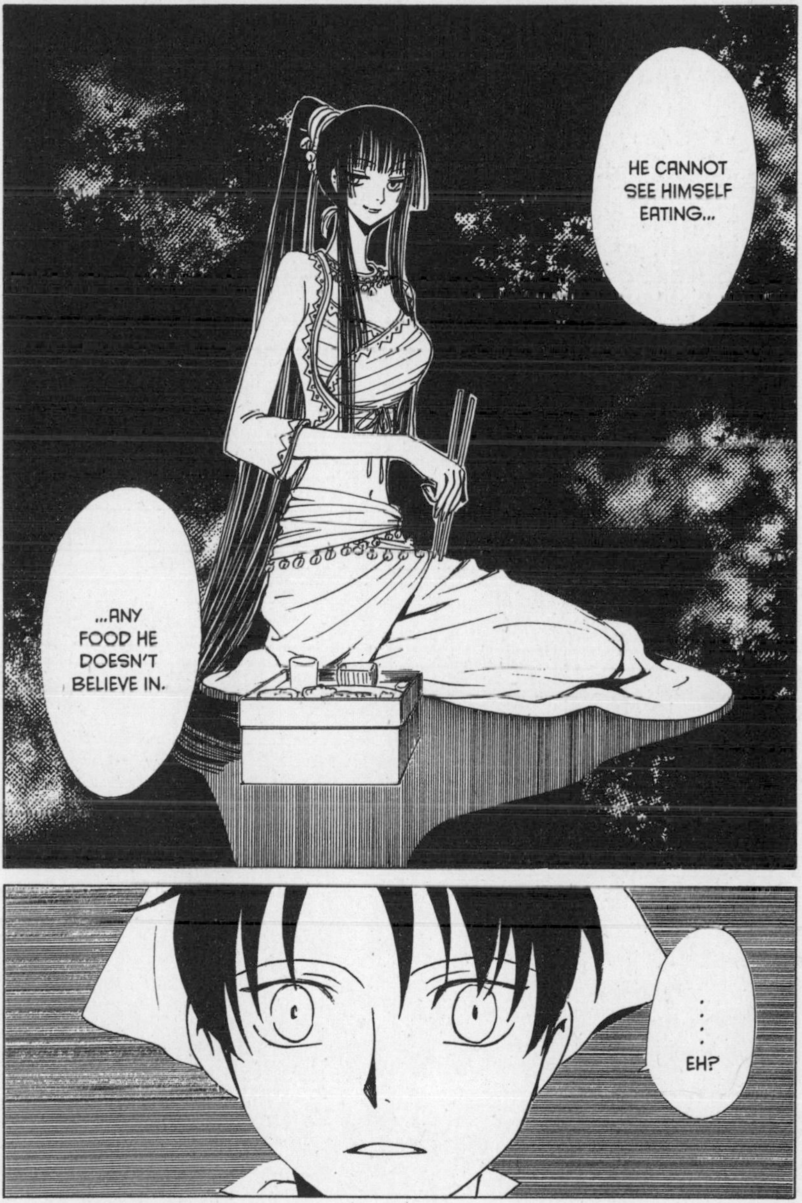
HE CANNOT SEE HIMSELF EATING...
...ANY FOOD HE DOESN'T BELIEVE IN.
.... EH?

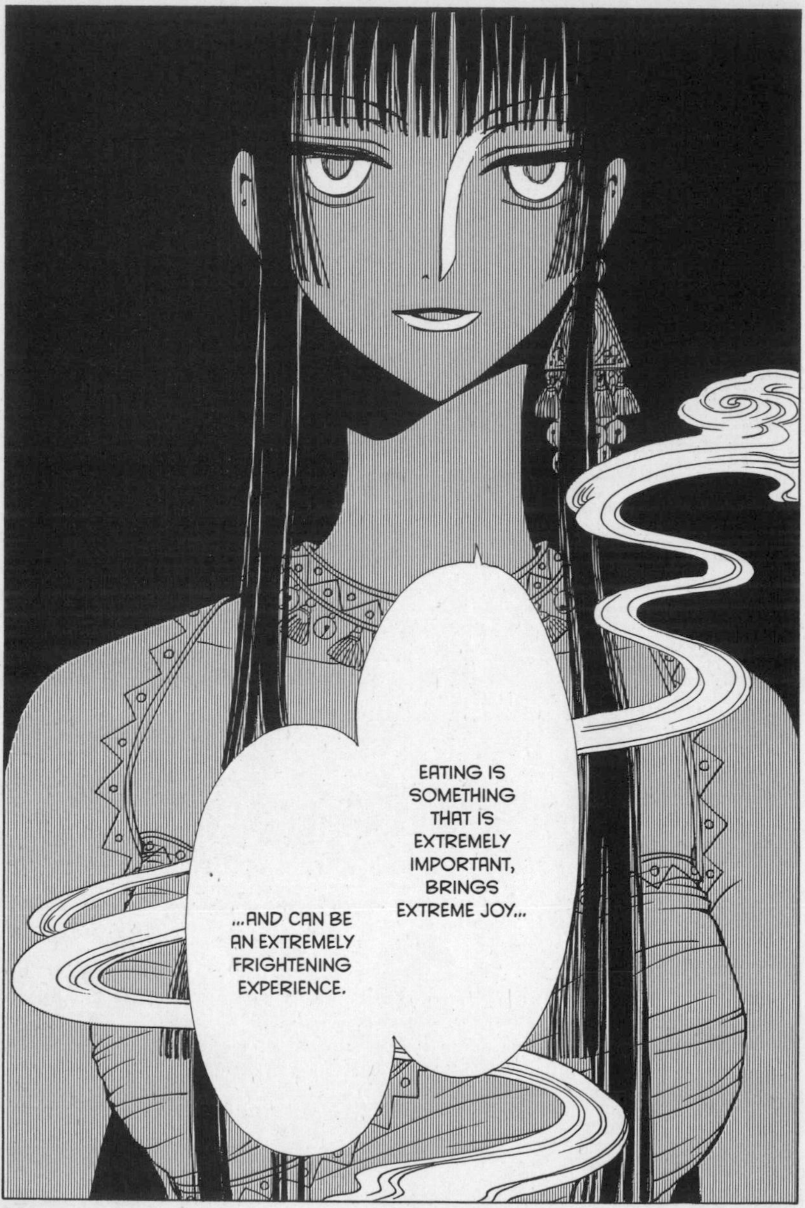
EATING IS SOMETHING THAT IS EXTREMELY IMPORTANT, BRINGS EXTREME JOY...
...AND CAN BE AN EXTREMELY FRIGHTENING EXPERIENCE.

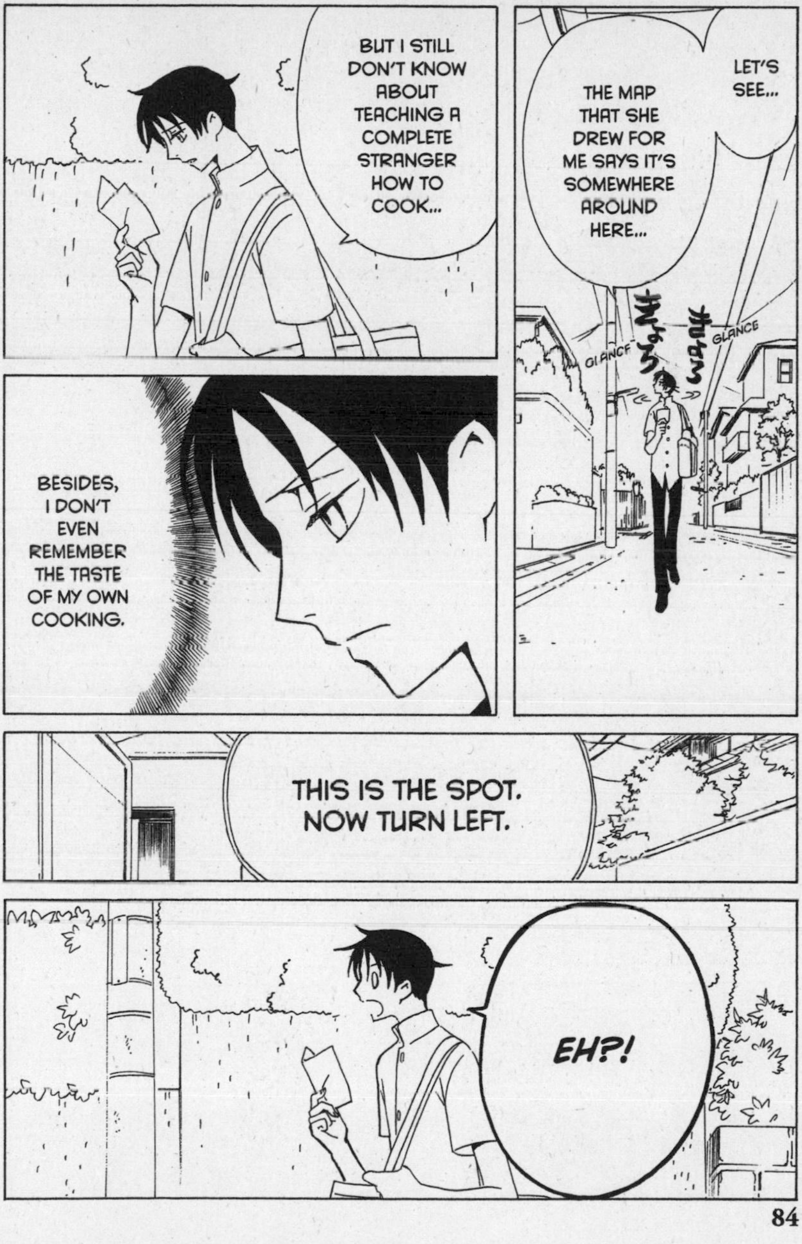
LET'S SEE...
THE MAP THAT SHE DREW FOR ME SAYS IT'S SOMEWHERE AROUND HERE...
GLANCE
GLANCE
BUT I STILL DON'T KNOW ABOUT TEACHING A COMPLETE STRANGER HOW TO COOK...
BESIDES, I DON'T EVEN REMEMBER THE TASTE OF MY OWN COOKING.
THIS IS THE SPOT. NOW TURN LEFT.
EH?!

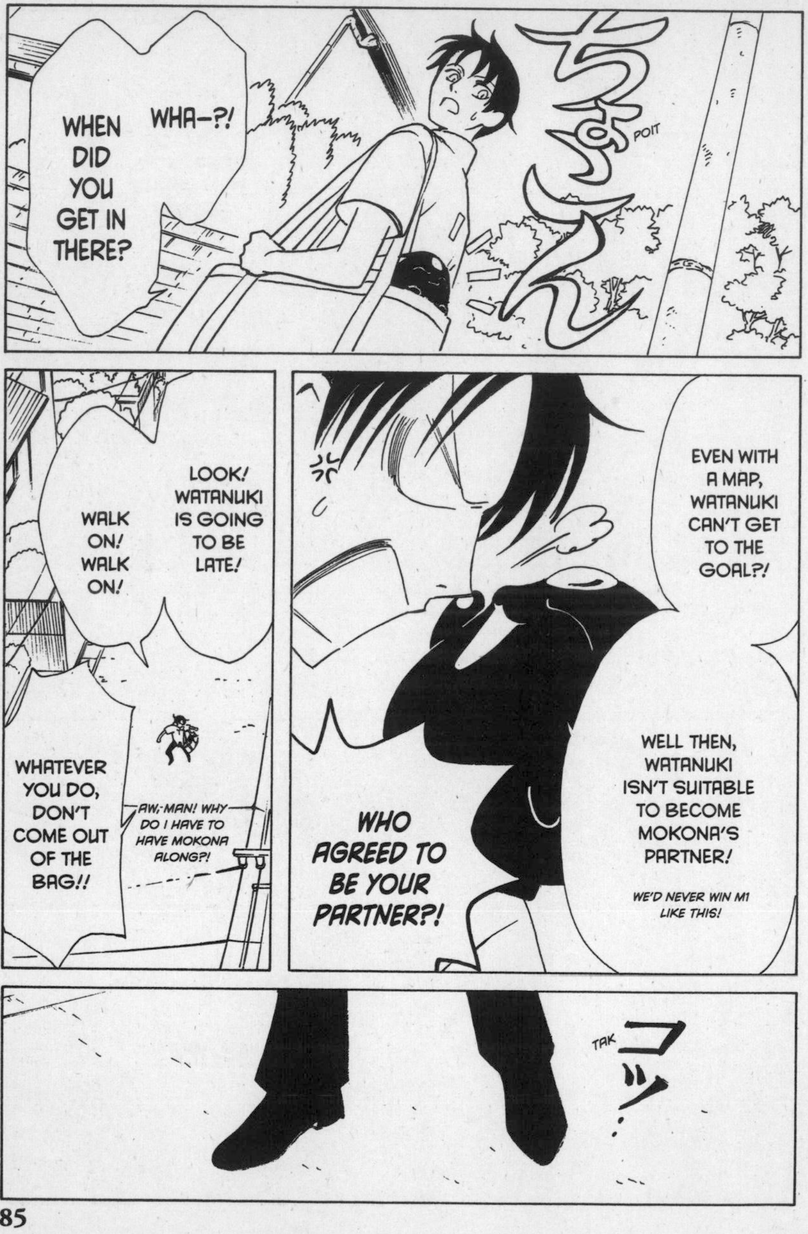
POIT
WHA-?!
WHEN DID YOU GET IN THERE?
EVEN WITH A MAP, WATANUKI CAN'T GET TO THE GOAL?!
WELL THEN, WATANUKI ISN'T SUITABLE TO BECOME MOKONA'S PARTNER!
WE'D NEVER WIN M1 LIKE THIS!
WHO AGREED TO BE YOUR PARTNER?!
LOOK! WATANUKI IS GOING TO BE LATE!
WALK ON! WALK ON!
AW, MAN! WHY DO I HAVE TO HAVE MOKONA ALONG?!
WHATEVER YOU DO, DON'T COME OUT OF THE BAG!!
TAK

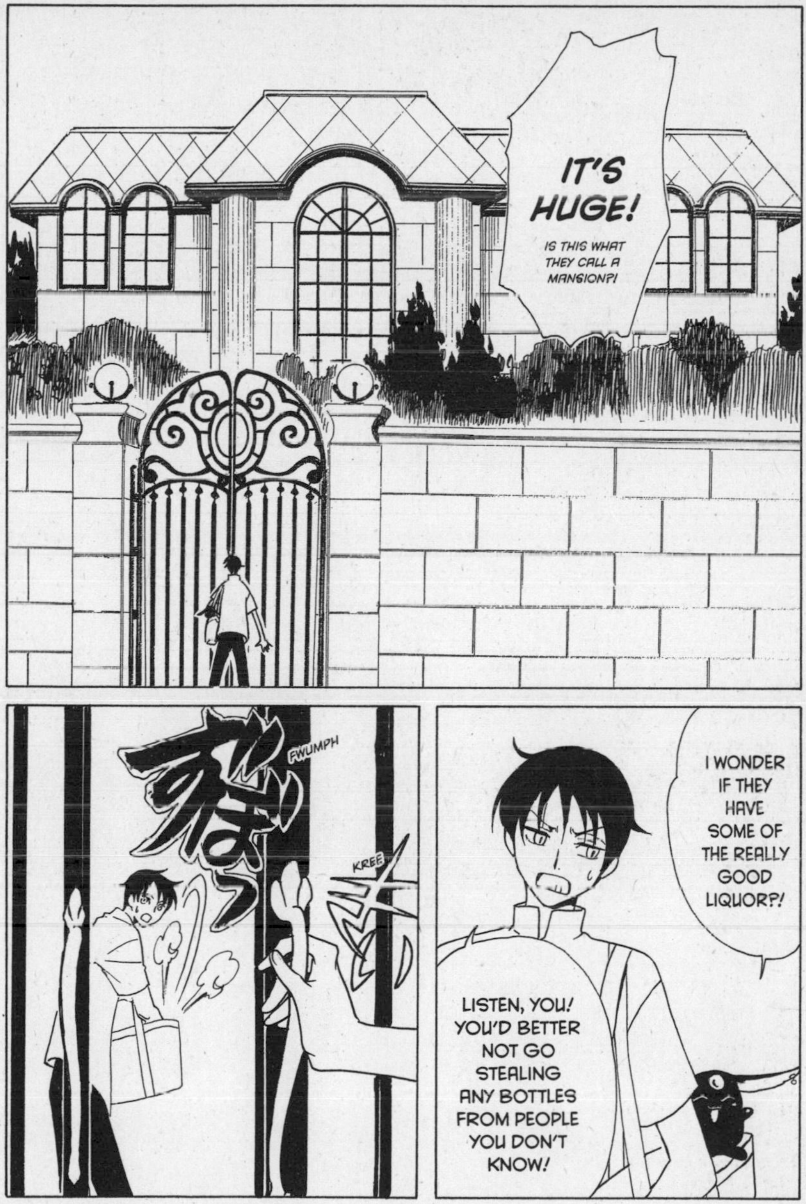
IT'S HUGE!
IS THIS WHAT THEY CALL A MANSION?!
I WONDER IF THEY HAVE SOME OF THE REALLY GOOD LIQUOR?!
LISTEN, YOU! YOU'D BETTER NOT GO STEALING ANY BOTTLES FROM PEOPLE YOU DON'T KNOW!
FWUMPH
KREE

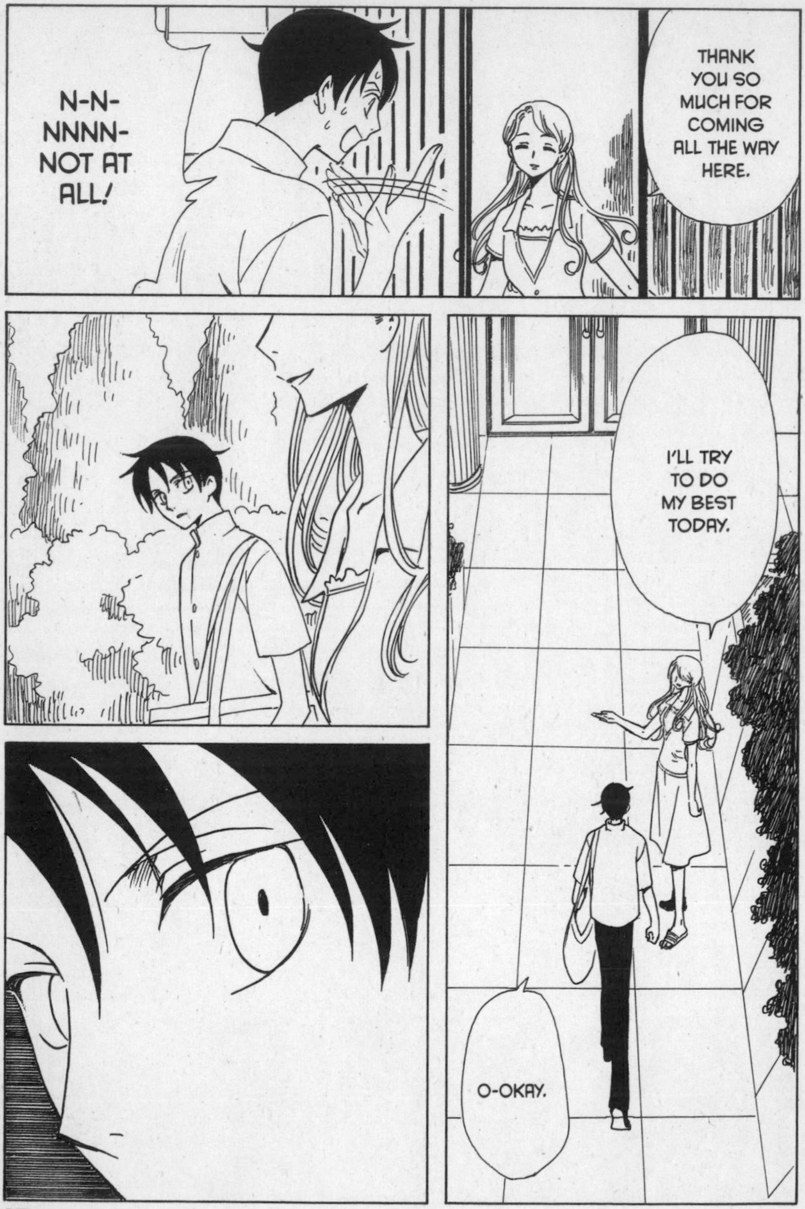
THANK YOU SO MUCH FOR COMING ALL THE WAY HERE.
N-N-NNNN-NOT AT ALL!
I'LL TRY TO DO MY BEST TODAY.
O-OKAY.

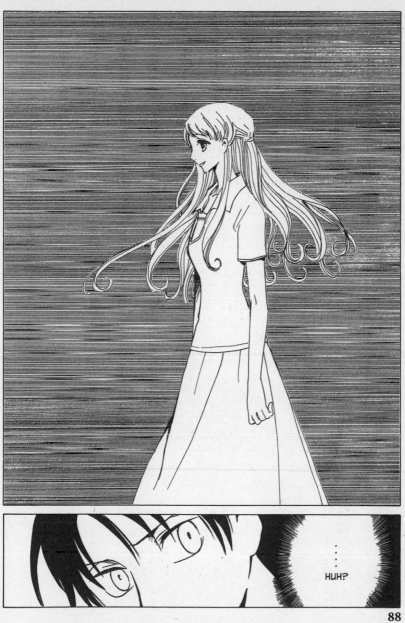

HUH?

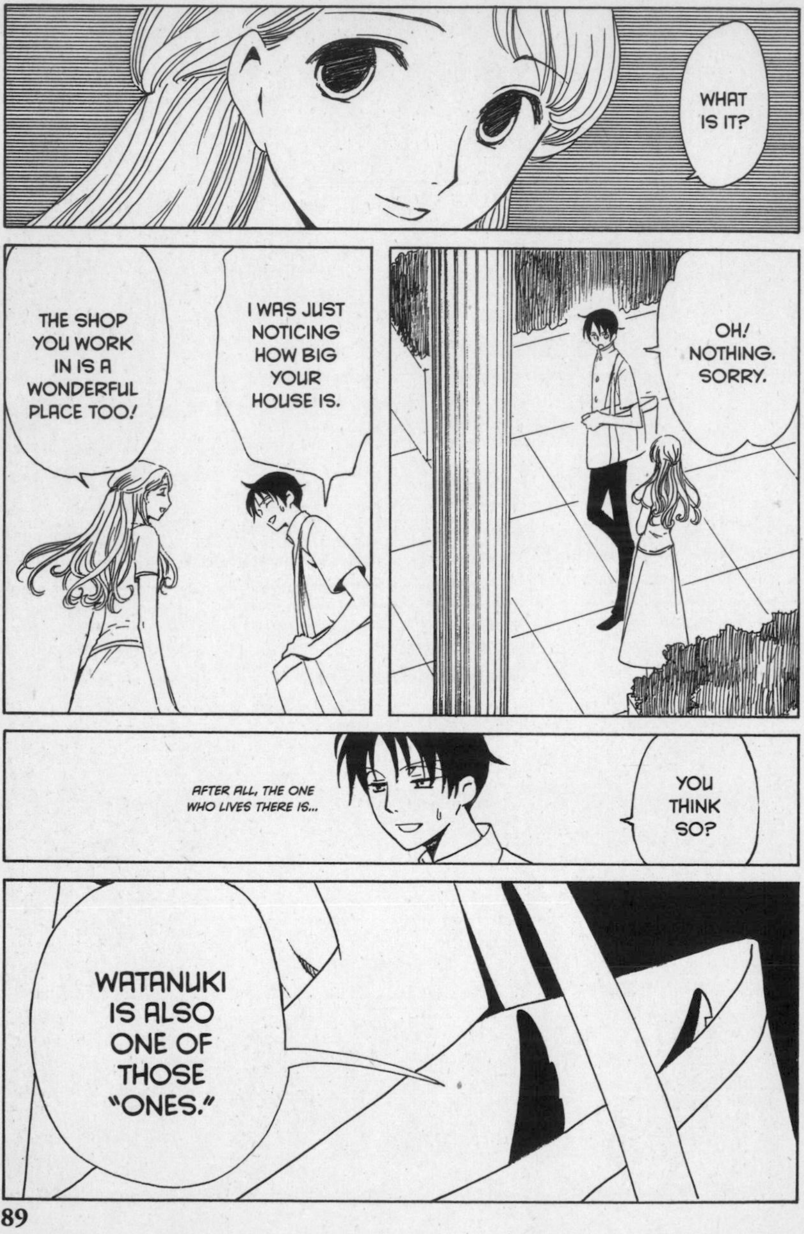
WHAT IS IT?
OH! NOTHING. SORRY.
I WAS JUST NOTICING HOW BIG YOUR HOUSE IS.
THE SHOP YOU WORK IN IS A WONDERFUL PLACE TOO!
YOU THINK SO?
AFTER ALL, THE ONE WHO LIVES THERE IS...
WATANUKI IS ALSO ONE OF THOSE "ONES."

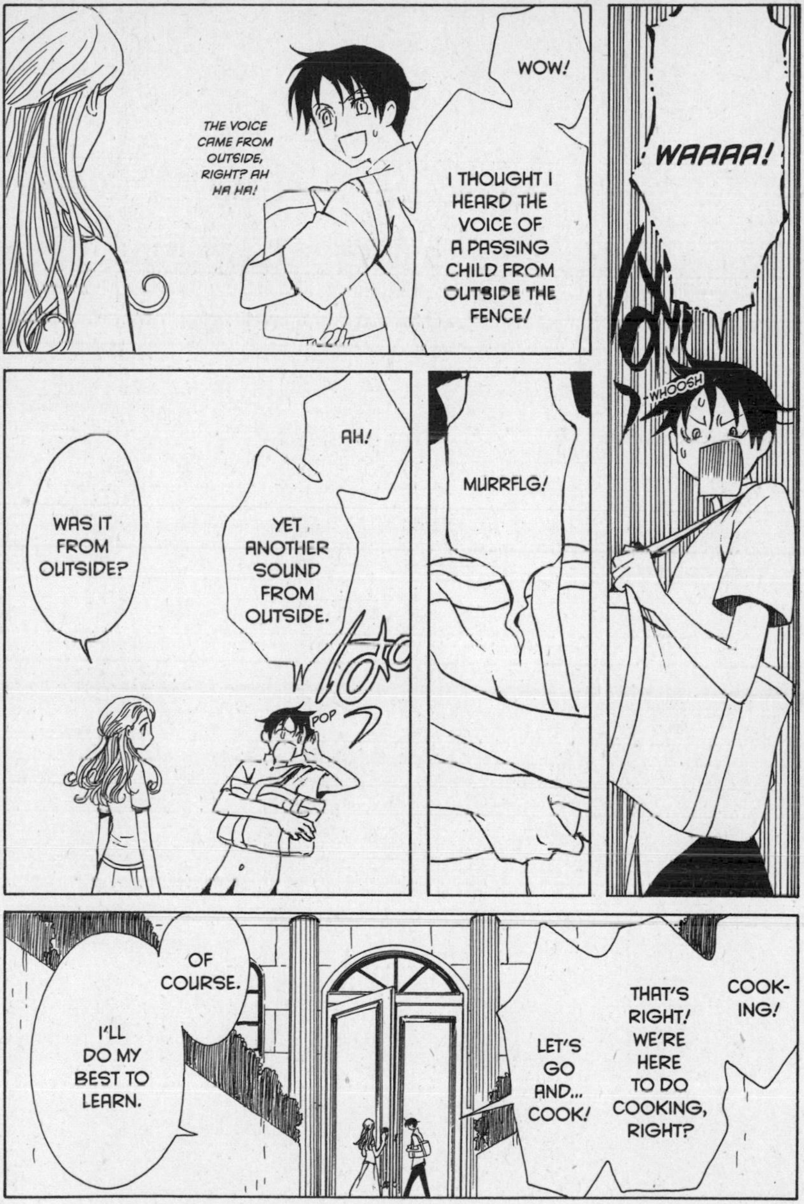
WAAAA!
WHOOSH
WOW!
I THOUGHT I HEARD THE VOICE OF A PASSING CHILD FROM OUTSIDE THE FENCE!
THE VOICE CAME FROM OUTSIDE, RIGHT? AH HA HA!
MURRFLG!
AH!
YET ANOTHER SOUND FROM OUTSIDE.
POP
WAS IT FROM OUTSIDE?
COOK-ING!
THAT'S RIGHT! WE'RE HERE TO DO COOKING, RIGHT?
LET'S GO AND... COOK!
OF COURSE.
I'LL DO MY BEST TO LEARN.

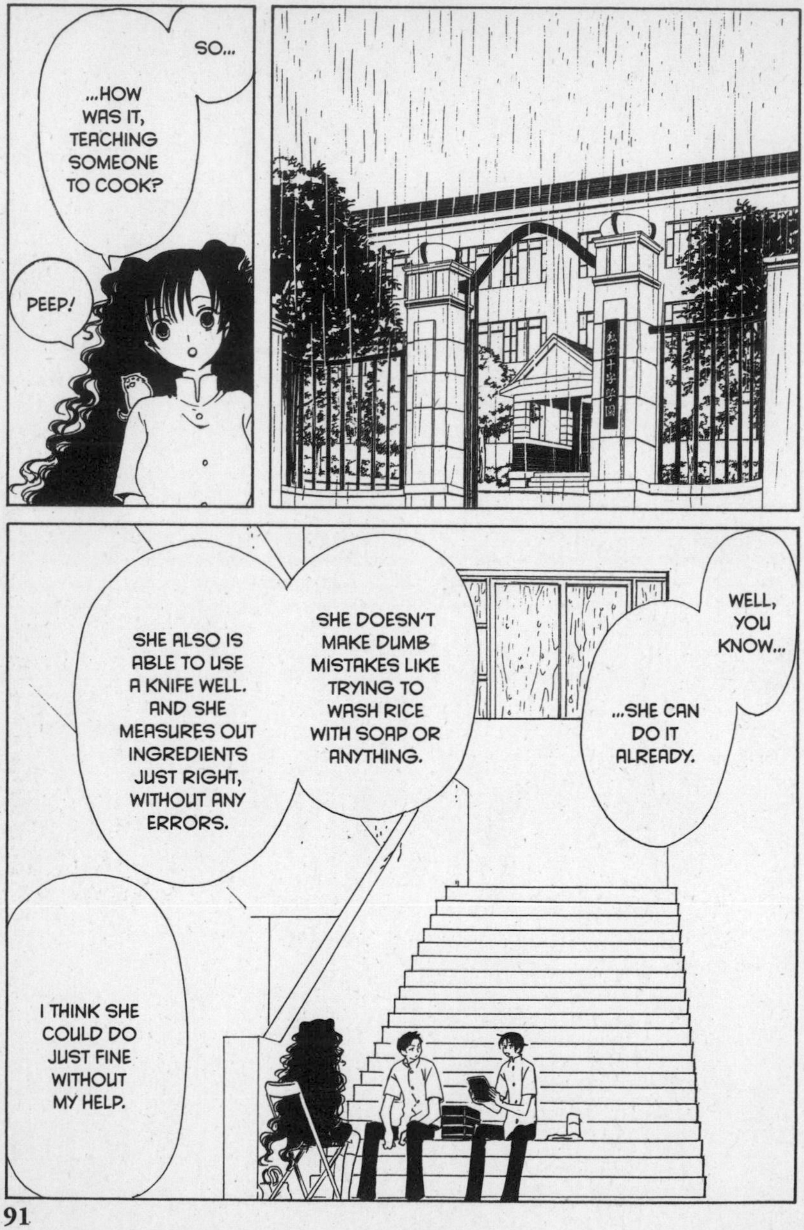
SO...
...HOW WAS IT, TEACHING SOMEONE TO COOK?
PEEP!
WELL, YOU KNOW...
...SHE CAN DO IT ALREADY.
SHE DOESN'T MAKE DUMB MISTAKES LIKE TRYING TO WASH RICE WITH SOAP OR ANYTHING.
SHE ALSO IS ABLE TO USE A KNIFE WELL. AND SHE MEASURES OUT INGREDIENTS JUST RIGHT, WITHOUT ANY ERRORS.
I THINK SHE COULD DO JUST FINE WITHOUT MY HELP.

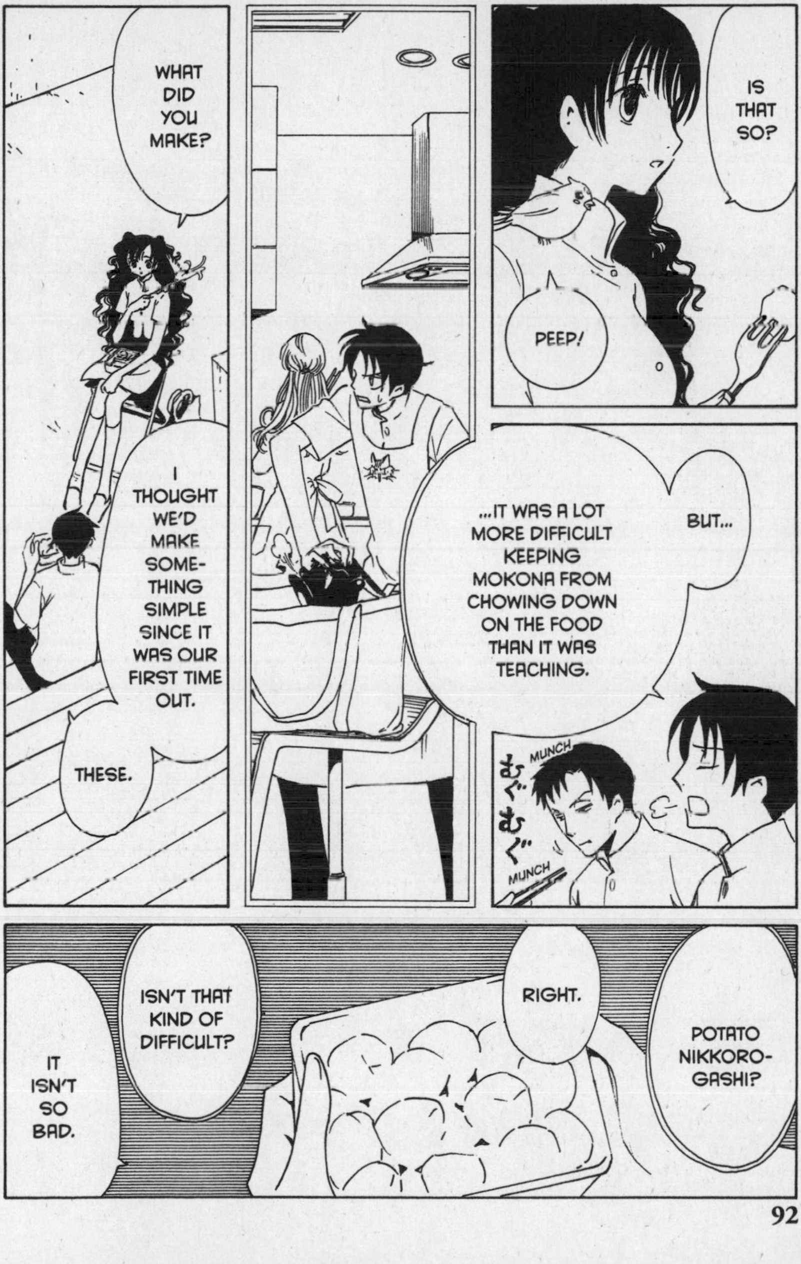
IS THAT SO?
PEEP!
BUT...
...IT WAS A LOT MORE DIFFICULT KEEPING MOKONA FROM CHOWING DOWN ON THE FOOD THAN IT WAS TEACHING.
MUNCH
むぐむぐ
MUNCH
WHAT DID YOU MAKE?
I THOUGHT WE'D MAKE SOME-THING SIMPLE SINCE IT WAS OUR FIRST TIME OUT.
THESE.
POTATO NIKKORO-GASHI?
RIGHT.
ISN'T THAT KIND OF DIFFICULT?
IT ISN'T SO BAD.

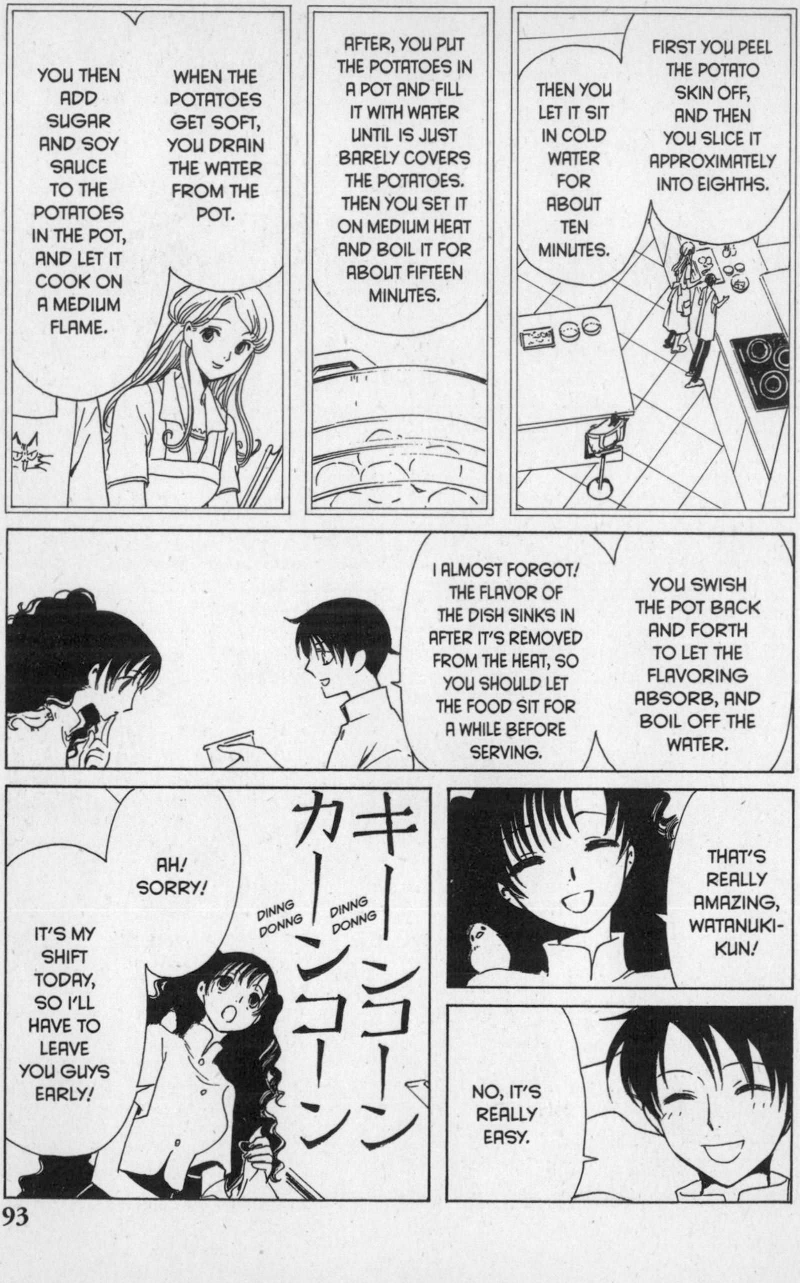
FIRST YOU PEEL THE POTATO SKIN OFF, AND THEN YOU SLICE IT APPROXIMATELY INTO EIGHTHS.
THEN YOU LET IT SIT IN COLD WATER FOR ABOUT TEN MINUTES.
AFTER, YOU PUT THE POTATOES IN A POT AND FILL IT WITH WATER UNTIL IS JUST BARELY COVERS THE POTATOES. THEN YOU SET IT ON MEDIUM HEAT AND BOIL IT FOR ABOUT FIFTEEN MINUTES.
WHEN THE POTATOES GET SOFT, YOU DRAIN THE WATER FROM THE POT.
YOU THEN ADD SUGAR AND SOY SAUCE TO THE POTATOES IN THE POT, AND LET IT COOK ON A MEDIUM FLAME.
YOU SWISH THE POT BACK AND FORTH TO LET THE FLAVORING ABSORB, AND BOIL OFF THE WATER.
I ALMOST FORGOT! THE FLAVOR OF THE DISH SINKS IN AFTER IT'S REMOVED FROM THE HEAT, SO YOU SHOULD LET THE FOOD SIT FOR A WHILE BEFORE SERVING.
THAT'S REALLY AMAZING, WATANUKI-KUN!
NO, IT'S REALLY EASY.
キーンコーン
カーンコーン
DINNG DONNG
DINNG DONNG
AH! SORRY!
IT'S MY SHIFT TODAY, SO I'LL HAVE TO LEAVE YOU GUYS EARLY!

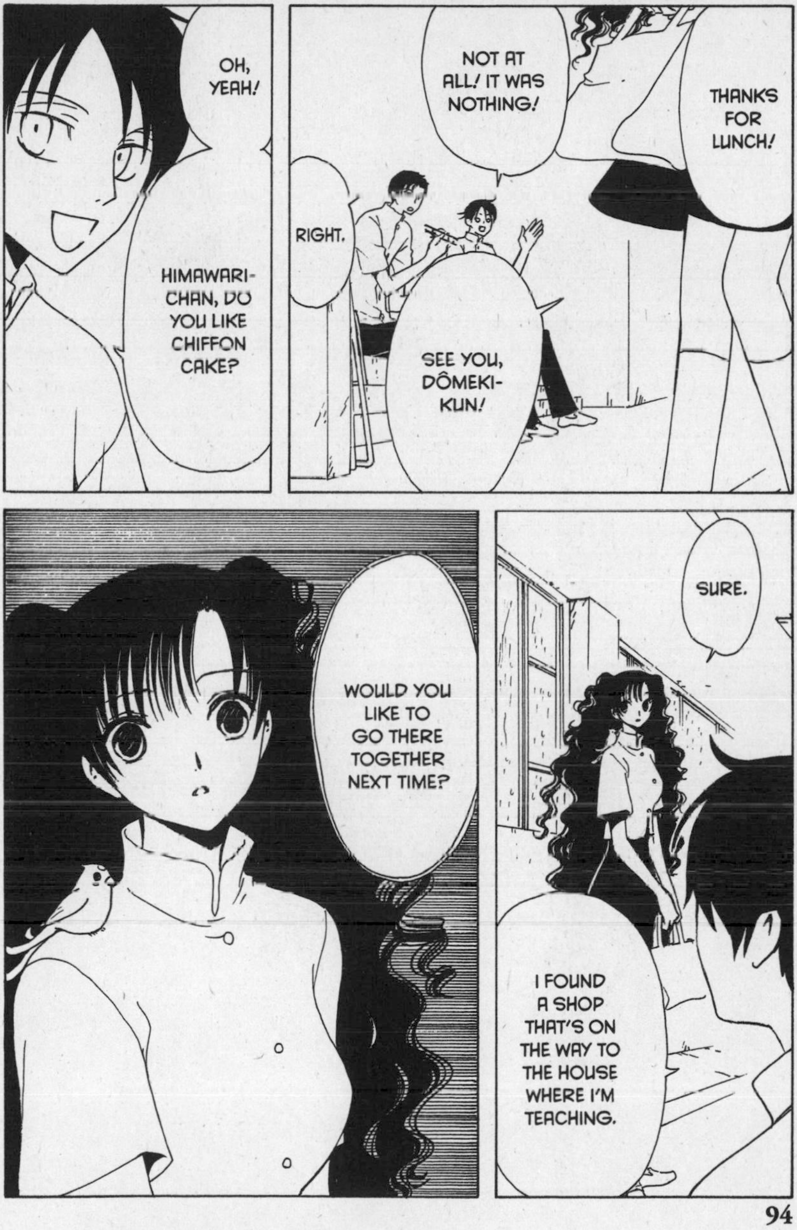
THANKS FOR LUNCH!
NOT AT ALL! IT WAS NOTHING!
SEE YOU, DÔMEKI-KUN!
RIGHT.
OH, YEAH!
HIMAWARI-CHAN, DO YOU LIKE CHIFFON CAKE?
SURE.
I FOUND A SHOP THAT'S ON THE WAY TO THE HOUSE WHERE I'M TEACHING.
WOULD YOU LIKE TO GO THERE TOGETHER NEXT TIME?

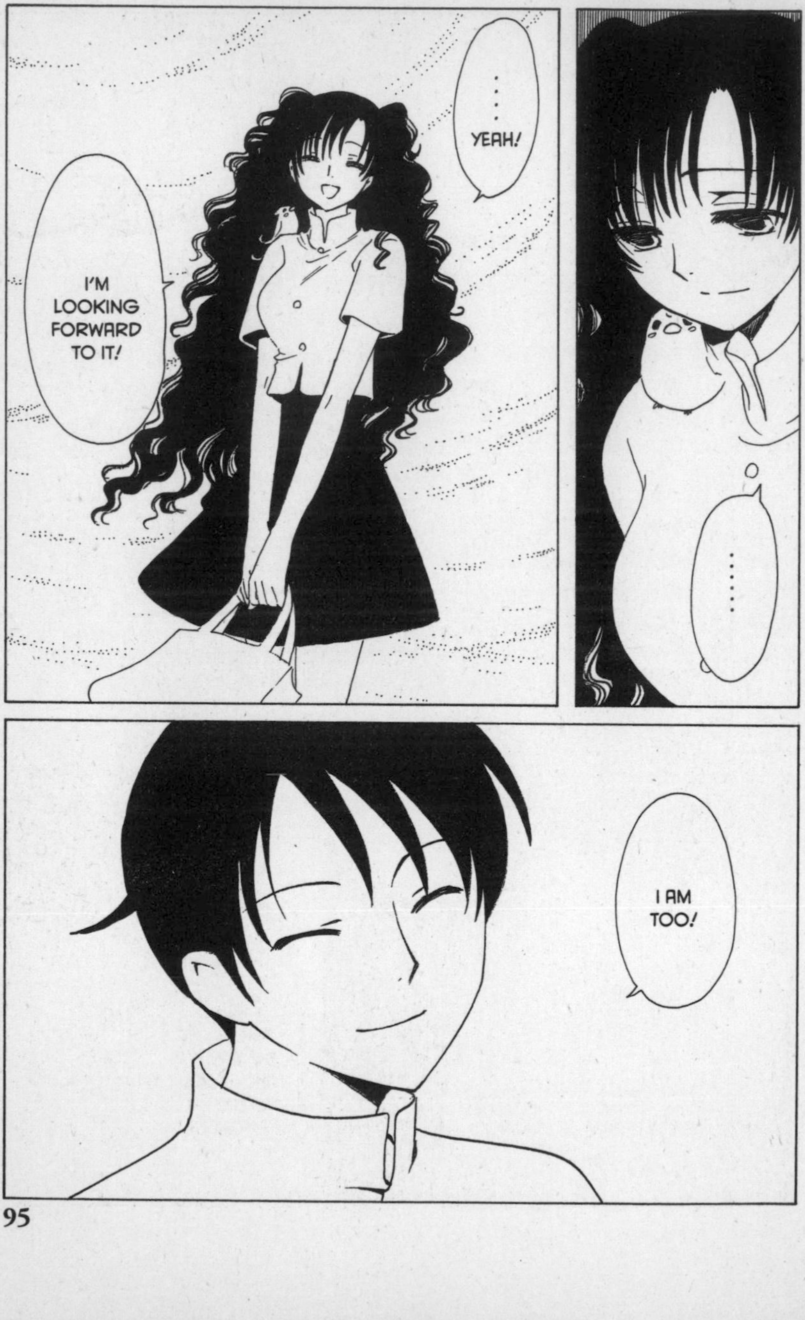
......
....YEAH!
I'M LOOKING FORWARD TO IT!
I AM TOO!

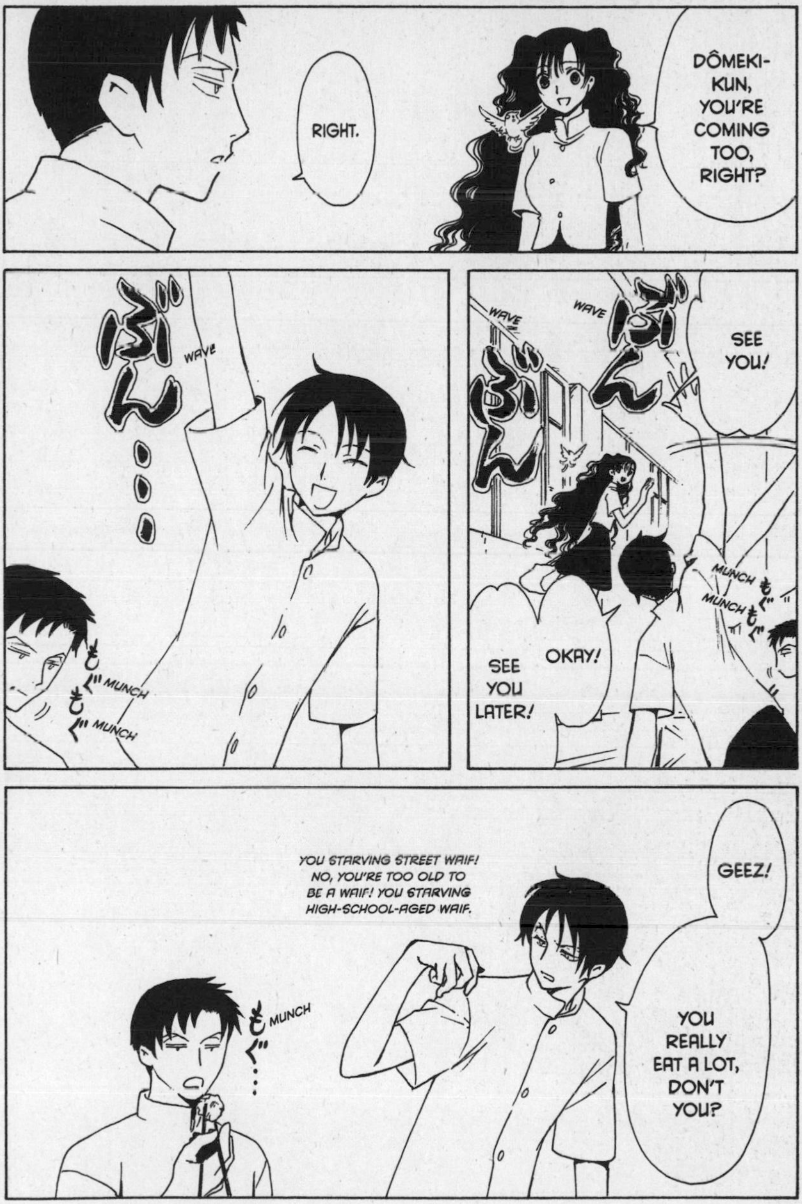
DÔMEKI-KUN, YOU'RE COMING TOO, RIGHT?
RIGHT.
WAVE
WAVE
ぶん
ぶん
SEE YOU!
MUNCH もぐ
MUNCH もぐ
OKAY!
SEE YOU LATER!
ぶん...
WAVE
もぐ MUNCH
もぐ MUNCH
GEEZ!
YOU REALLY EAT A LOT, DON'T YOU?
YOU STARVING STREET WAIF! NO, YOU'RE TOO OLD TO BE A WAIF! YOU STARVING HIGH-SCHOOL-AGED WAIF.
もぐ... MUNCH

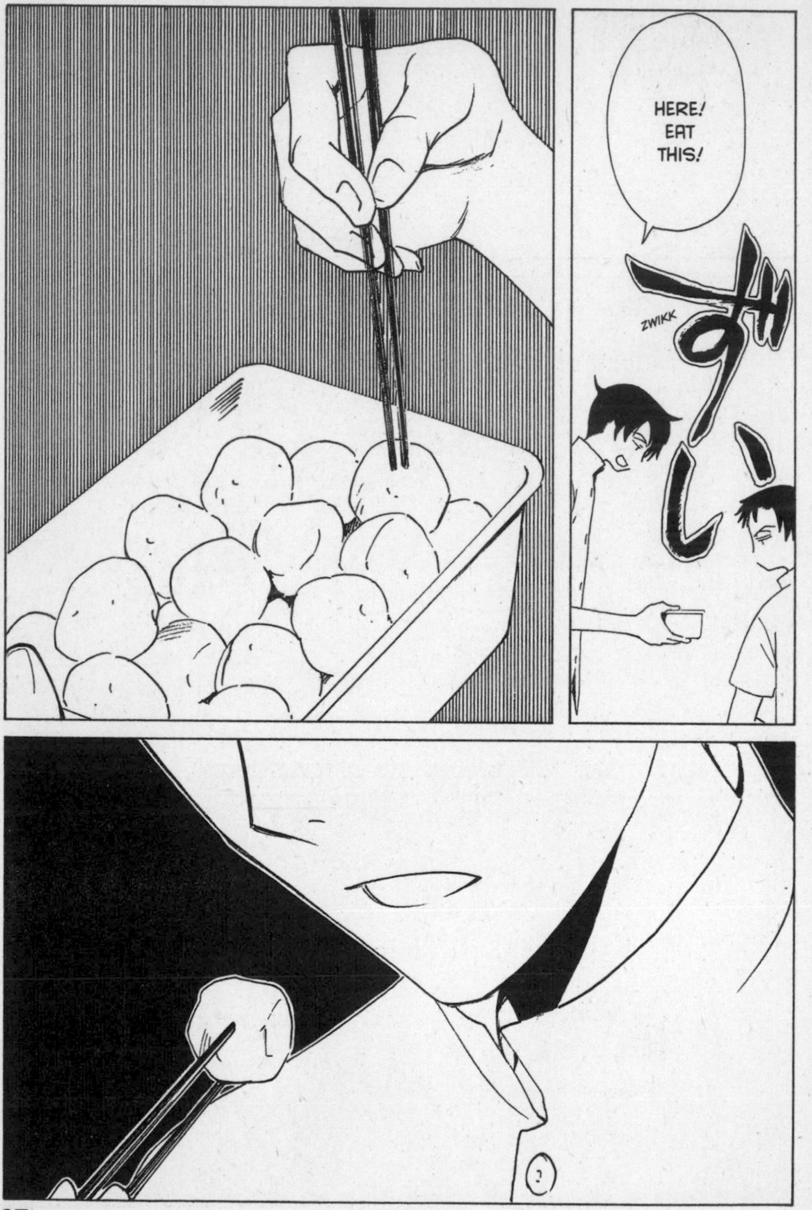
HERE! EAT THIS!
ZWIKK
ずい

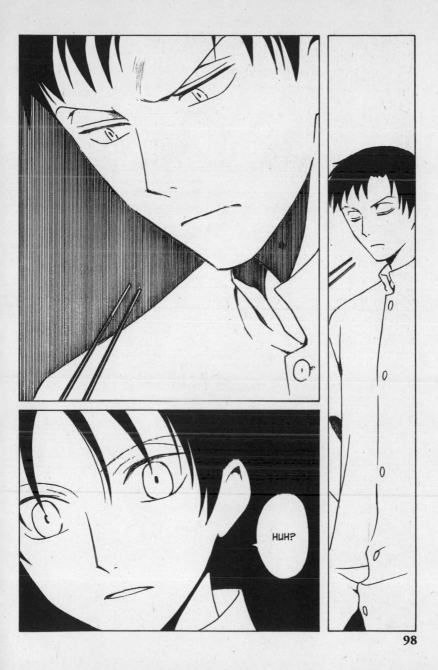

HUH?

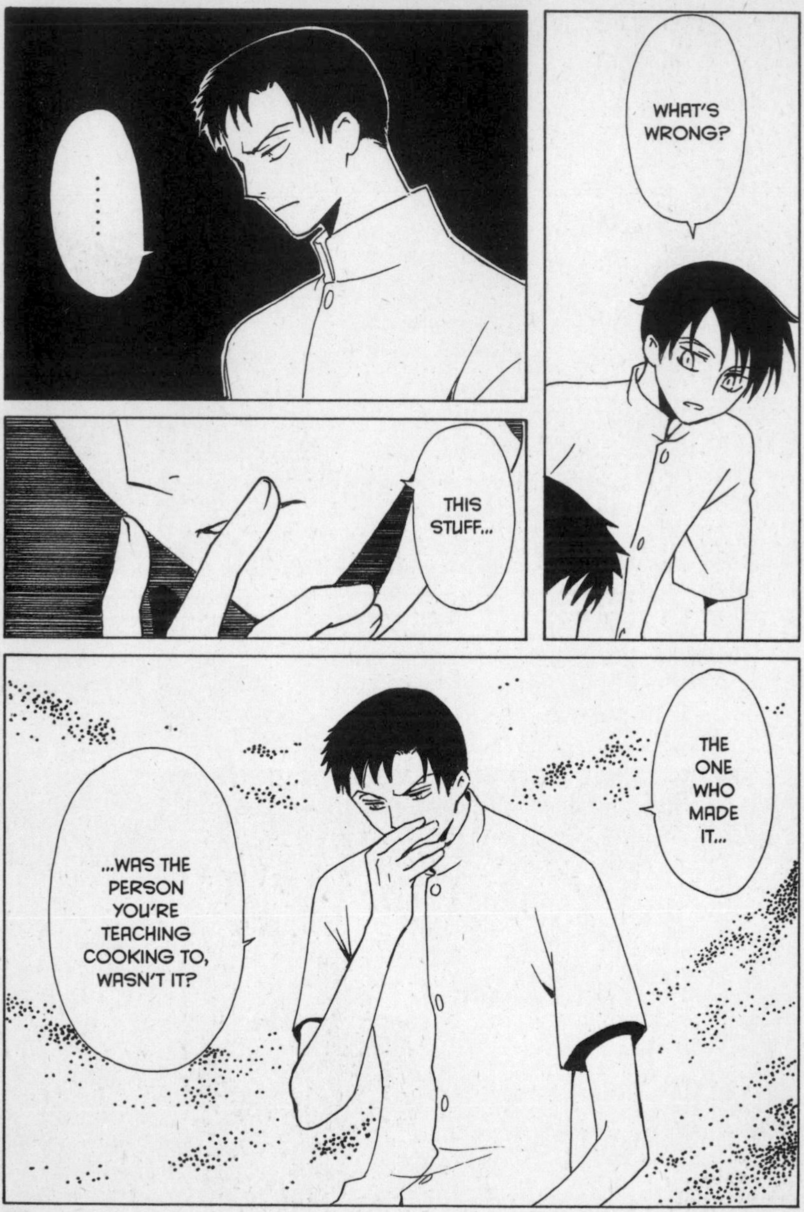
WHAT'S WRONG?
......
THIS STUFF...
THE ONE WHO MADE IT...
...WAS THE PERSON YOU'RE TEACHING COOKING TO, WASN'T IT?

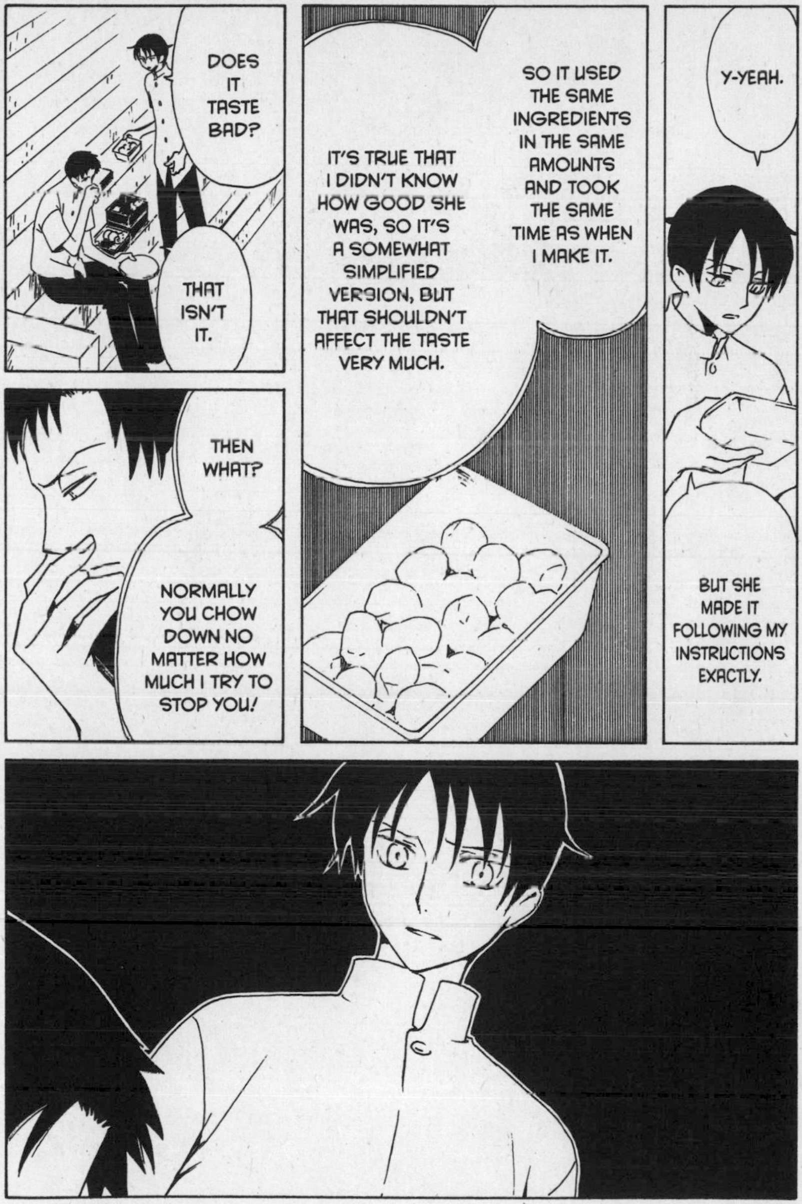
Y-YEAH.
BUT SHE MADE IT FOLLOWING MY INSTRUCTIONS EXACTLY.
SO IT USED THE SAME INGREDIENTS IN THE SAME AMOUNTS AND TOOK THE SAME TIME AS WHEN I MAKE IT.
IT'S TRUE THAT I DIDN'T KNOW HOW GOOD SHE WAS, SO IT'S A SOMEWHAT SIMPLIFIED VERSION, BUT THAT SHOULDN'T AFFECT THE TASTE VERY MUCH.
DOES IT TASTE BAD?
THAT ISN'T IT.
THEN WHAT?
NORMALLY YOU CHOW DOWN NO MATTER HOW MUCH I TRY TO STOP YOU!

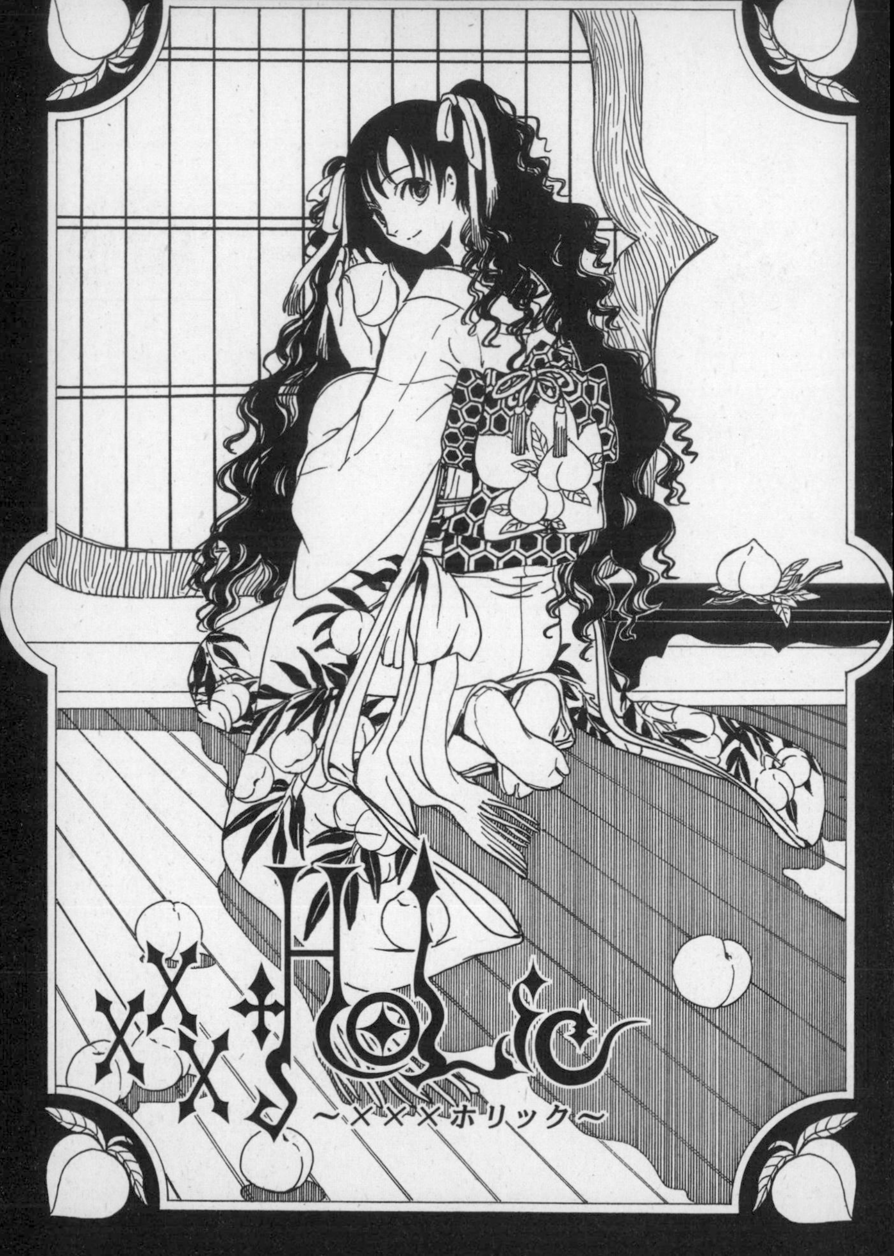
xxxHOLiC
〜××××ホリック〜

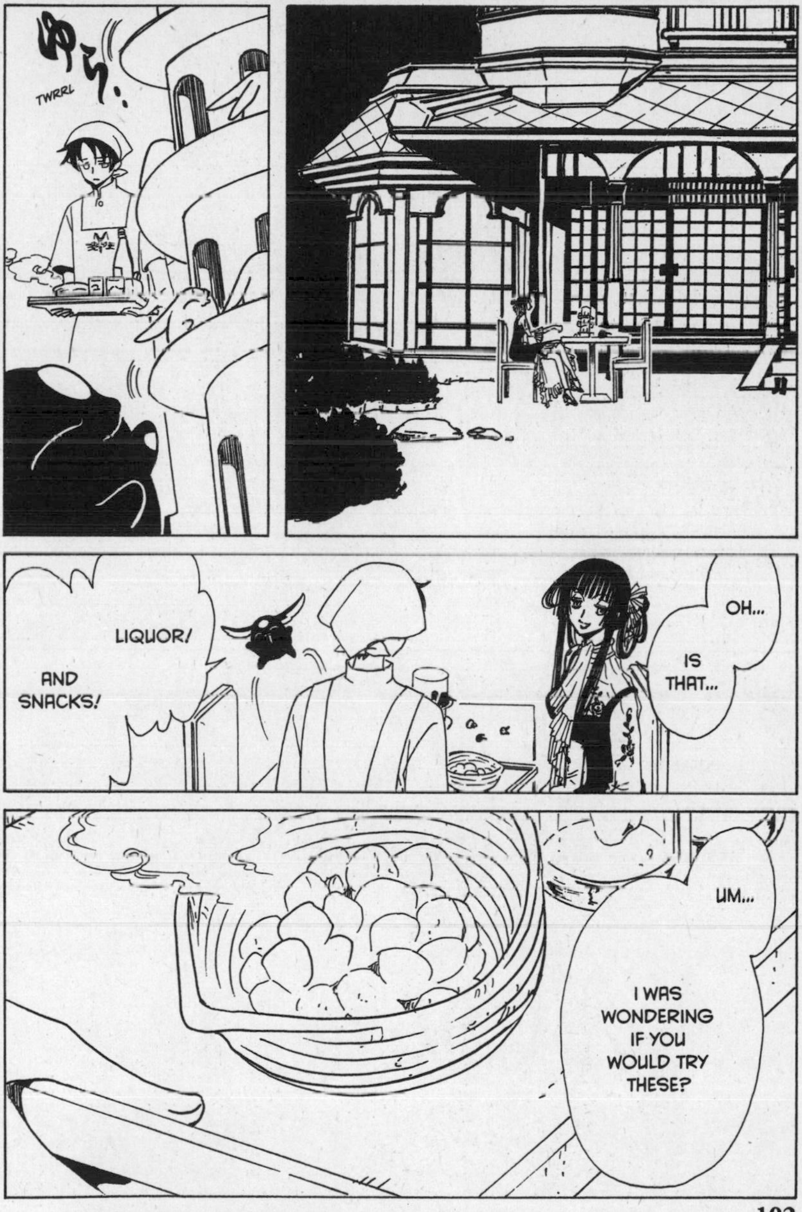
ゆら…
TWRRL
OH...
IS THAT...
LIQUOR!
AND SNACKS!
UM...
I WAS WONDERING IF YOU WOULD TRY THESE?

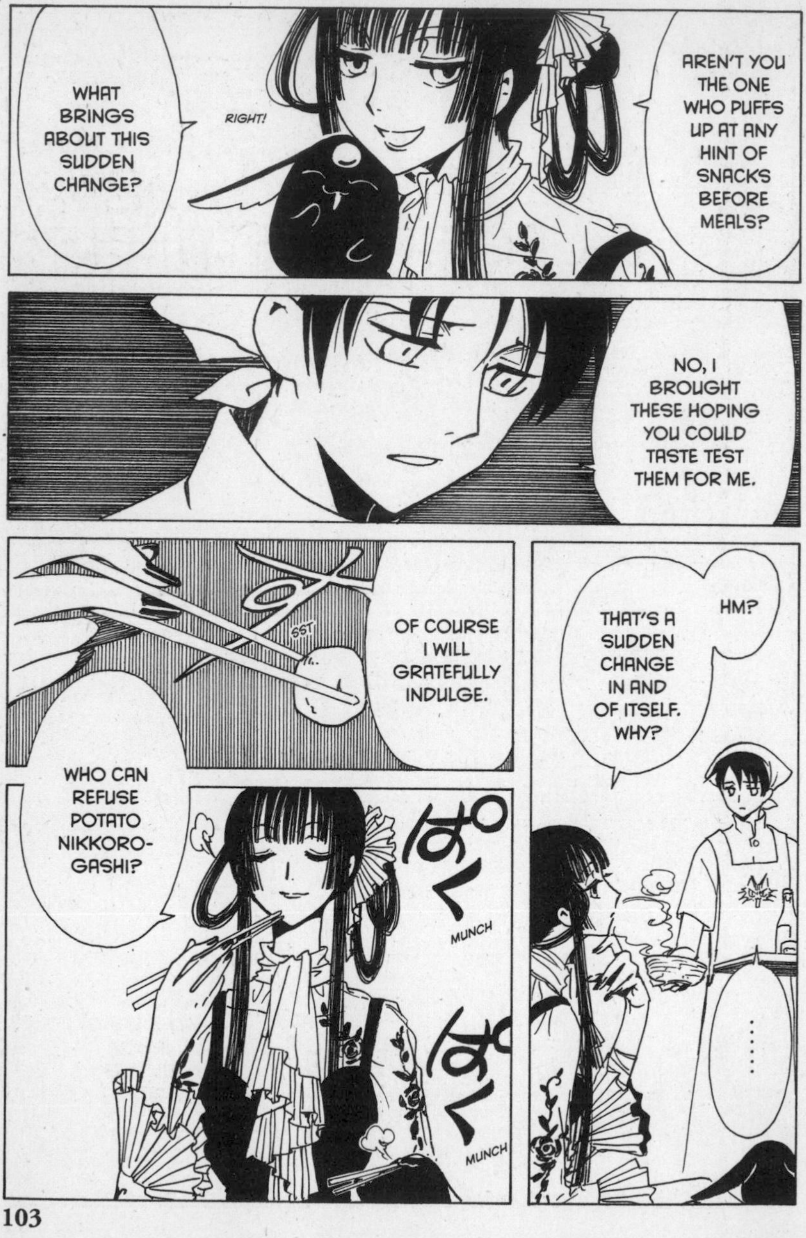
AREN'T YOU THE ONE WHO PUFFS UP AT ANY HINT OF SNACKS BEFORE MEALS?
RIGHT!
WHAT BRINGS ABOUT THIS SUDDEN CHANGE?
NO, I BROUGHT THESE HOPING YOU COULD TASTE TEST THEM FOR ME.
HM?
THAT'S A SUDDEN CHANGE IN AND OF ITSELF. WHY?
......
SST
OF COURSE I WILL GRATEFULLY INDULGE.
WHO CAN REFUSE POTATO NIKKORO-GASHI?
ぱく
MUNCH
ぱく
MUNCH

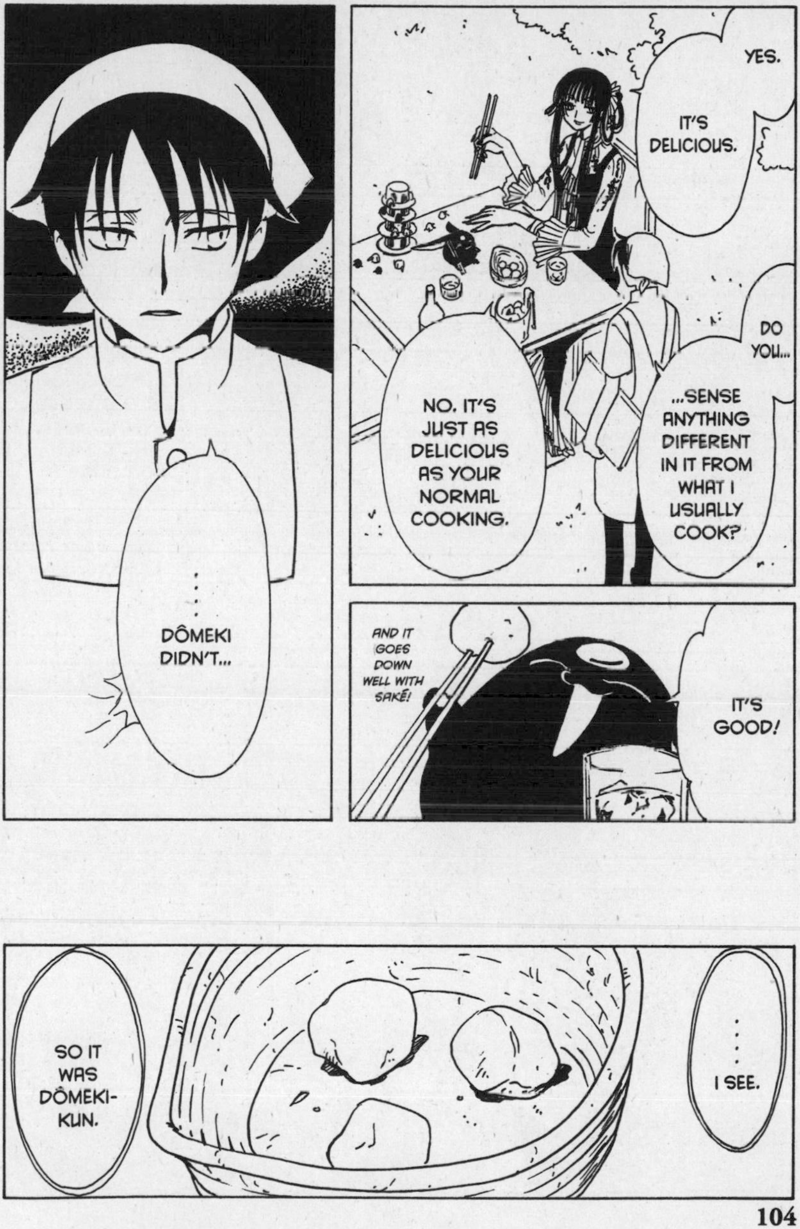
YES.
IT'S DELICIOUS.
DO YOU...
...SENSE ANYTHING DIFFERENT IN IT FROM WHAT I USUALLY COOK?
NO. IT'S JUST AS DELICIOUS AS YOUR NORMAL COOKING.
IT'S GOOD!
AND IT GOES DOWN WELL WITH SAKÉ!
.....
DÔMEKI DIDN'T...
.....
I SEE.
SO IT WAS DÔMEKI-KUN.

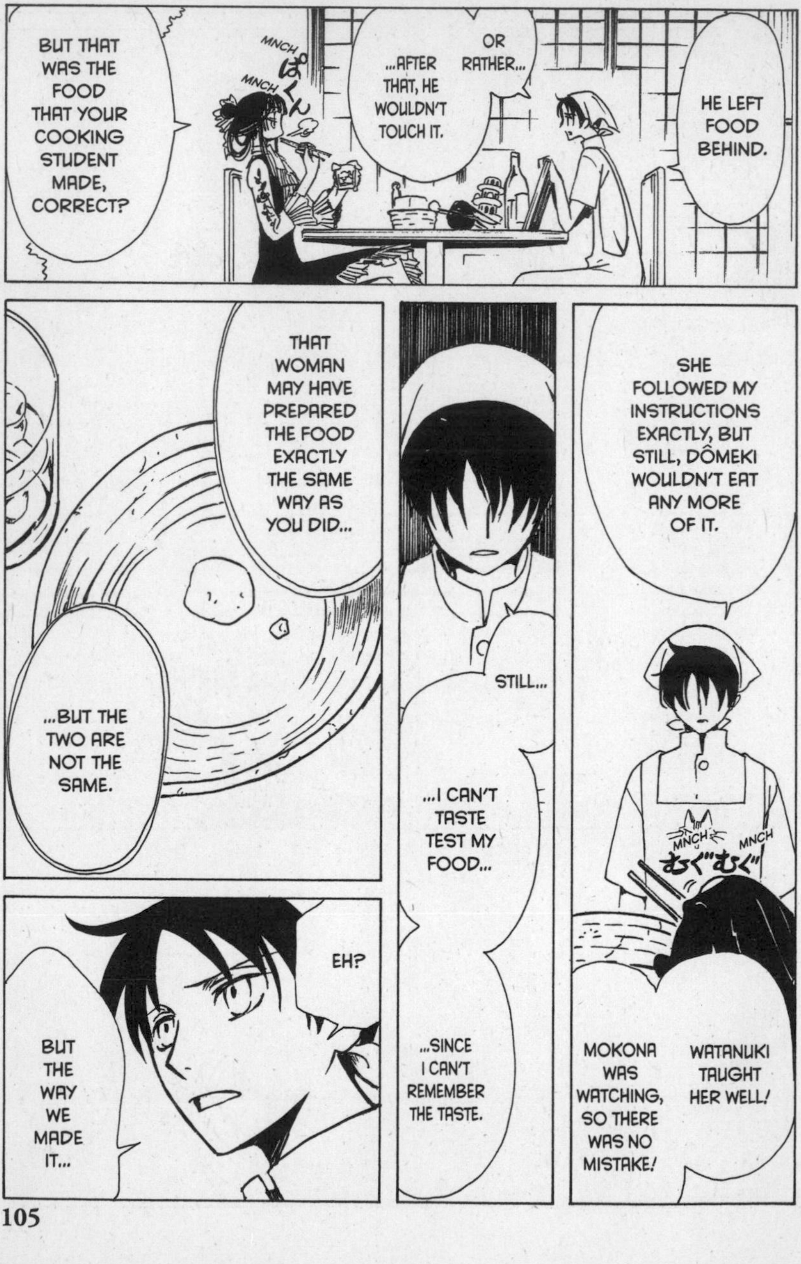
HE LEFT FOOD BEHIND.
OR RATHER...
...AFTER THAT, HE WOULDN'T TOUCH IT.
MNCH ぱくん MNCH
BUT THAT WAS THE FOOD THAT YOUR COOKING STUDENT MADE, CORRECT?
SHE FOLLOWED MY INSTRUCTIONS EXACTLY, BUT STILL, DÔMEKI WOULDN'T EAT ANY MORE OF IT.
MNCH むぐむぐ MNCH
WATANUKI TAUGHT HER WELL!
MOKONA WAS WATCHING, SO THERE WAS NO MISTAKE!
STILL...
...I CAN'T TASTE TEST MY FOOD...
...SINCE I CAN'T REMEMBER THE TASTE.
THAT WOMAN MAY HAVE PREPARED THE FOOD EXACTLY THE SAME WAY AS YOU DID...
...BUT THE TWO ARE NOT THE SAME.
EH?
BUT THE WAY WE MADE IT...

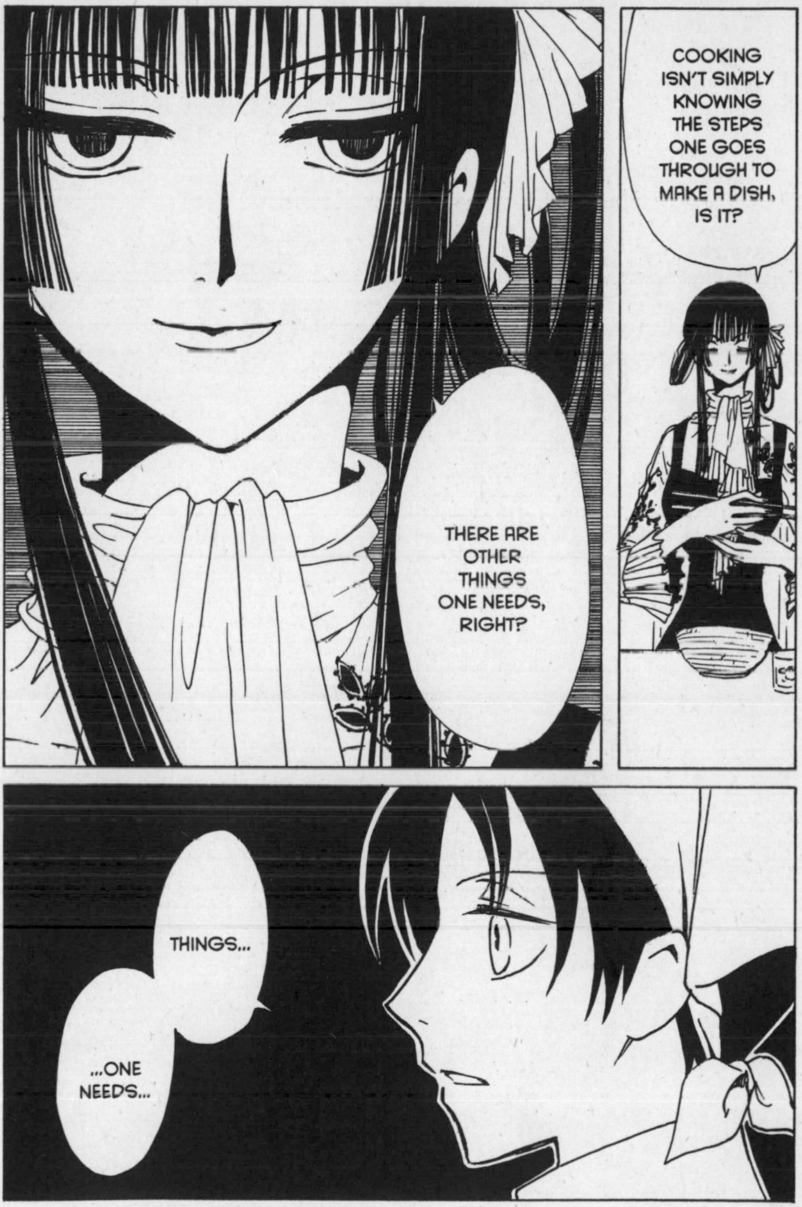
COOKING ISN'T SIMPLY KNOWING THE STEPS ONE GOES THROUGH TO MAKE A DISH, IS IT?
THERE ARE OTHER THINGS ONE NEEDS, RIGHT?
THINGS...
...ONE NEEDS...

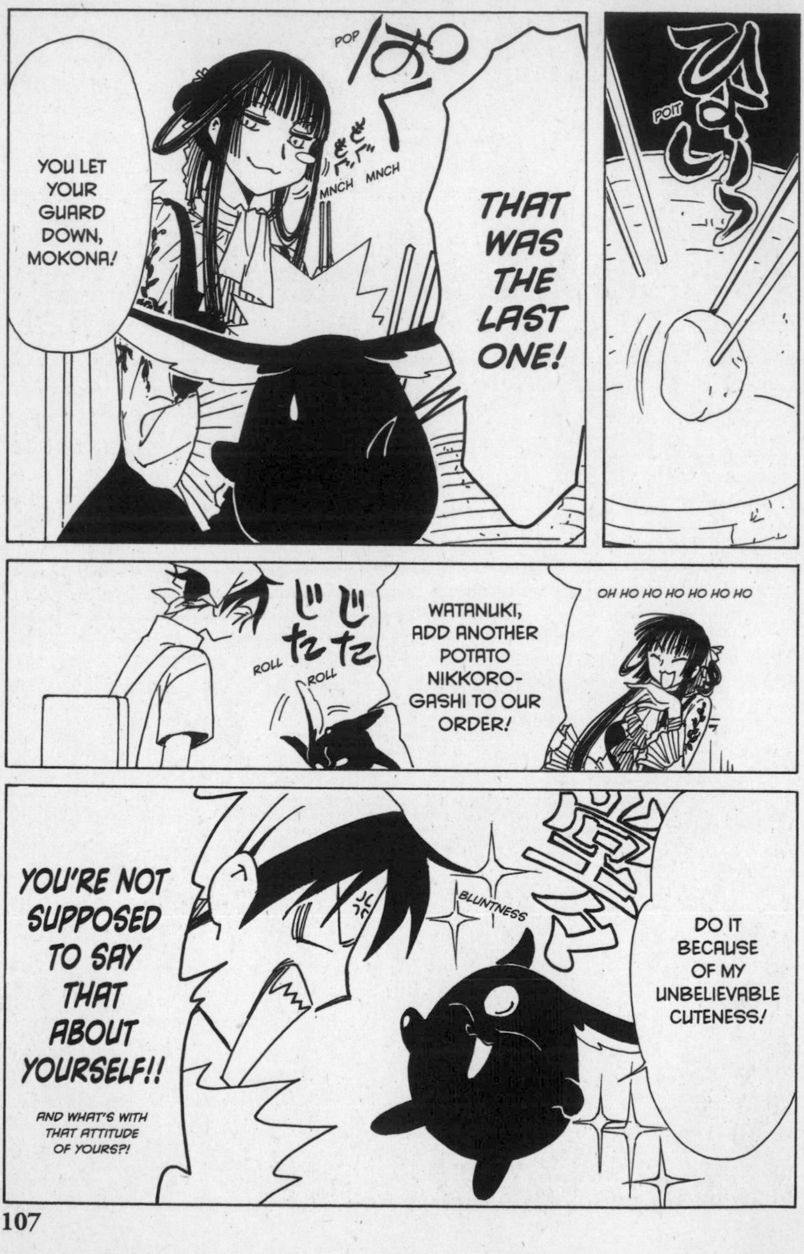
POIT
THAT WAS THE LAST ONE!
POP
MNCH MNCH
YOU LET YOUR GUARD DOWN, MOKONA!
OH HO HO HO HO HO HO
WATANUKI, ADD ANOTHER POTATO NIKKORO-GASHI TO OUR ORDER!
じたじた
ROLL ROLL
DO IT BECAUSE OF MY UNBELIEVABLE CUTENESS!
BLUNTNESS
YOU'RE NOT SUPPOSED TO SAY THAT ABOUT YOURSELF!!
AND WHAT'S WITH THAT ATTITUDE OF YOURS?!

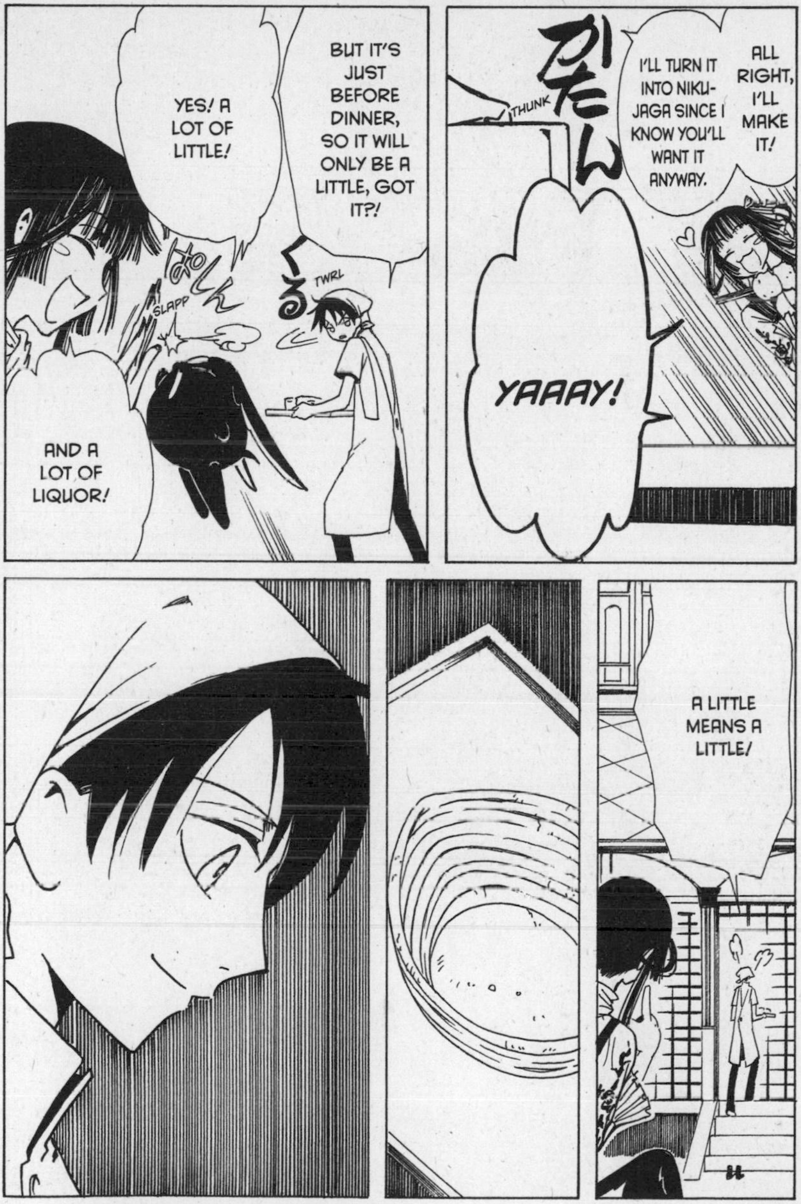
ALL RIGHT, I'LL MAKE IT!
I'LL TURN IT INTO NIKU-JAGA SINCE I KNOW YOU'LL WANT IT ANYWAY.
THUNK
YAAAY!
BUT IT'S JUST BEFORE DINNER, SO IT WILL ONLY BE A LITTLE, GOT IT?!
TWRL
YES! A LOT OF LITTLE!
SLAPP
AND A LOT OF LIQUOR!
A LITTLE MEANS A LITTLE!

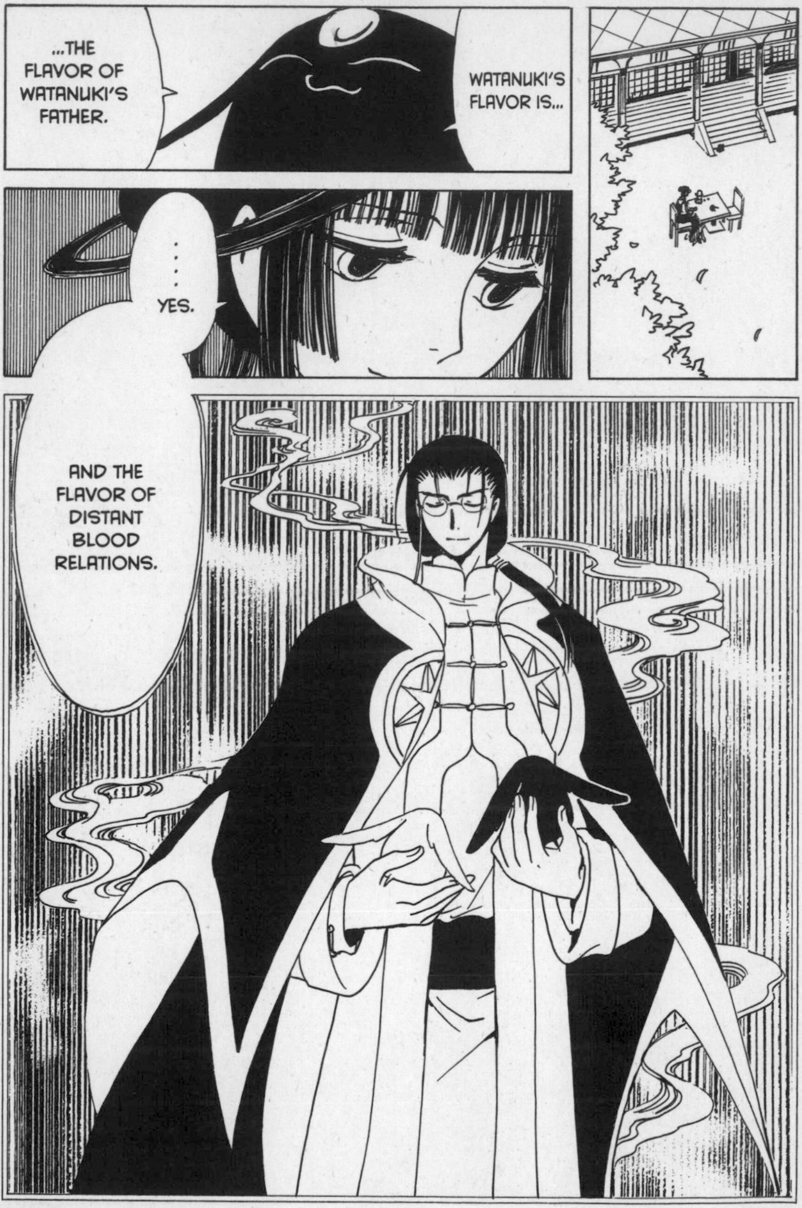
WATANUKI'S FLAVOR IS...
...THE FLAVOR OF WATANUKI'S FATHER.
...... YES.
AND THE FLAVOR OF DISTANT BLOOD RELATIONS.

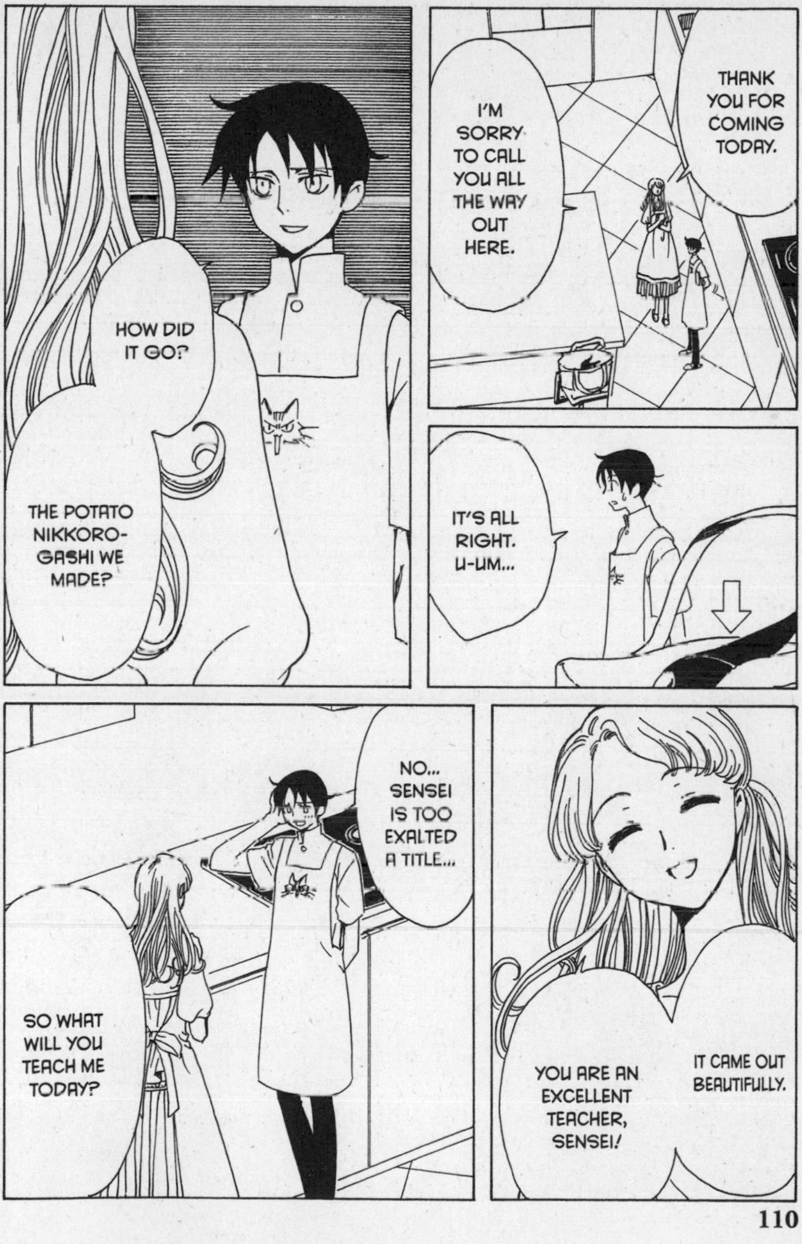
THANK YOU FOR COMING TODAY.
I'M SORRY TO CALL YOU ALL THE WAY OUT HERE.
IT'S ALL RIGHT. U-UM...
HOW DID IT GO?
THE POTATO NIKKOROGASHI WE MADE?
IT CAME OUT BEAUTIFULLY.
YOU ARE AN EXCELLENT TEACHER, SENSEI!
NO... SENSEI IS TOO EXALTED A TITLE...
SO WHAT WILL YOU TEACH ME TODAY?

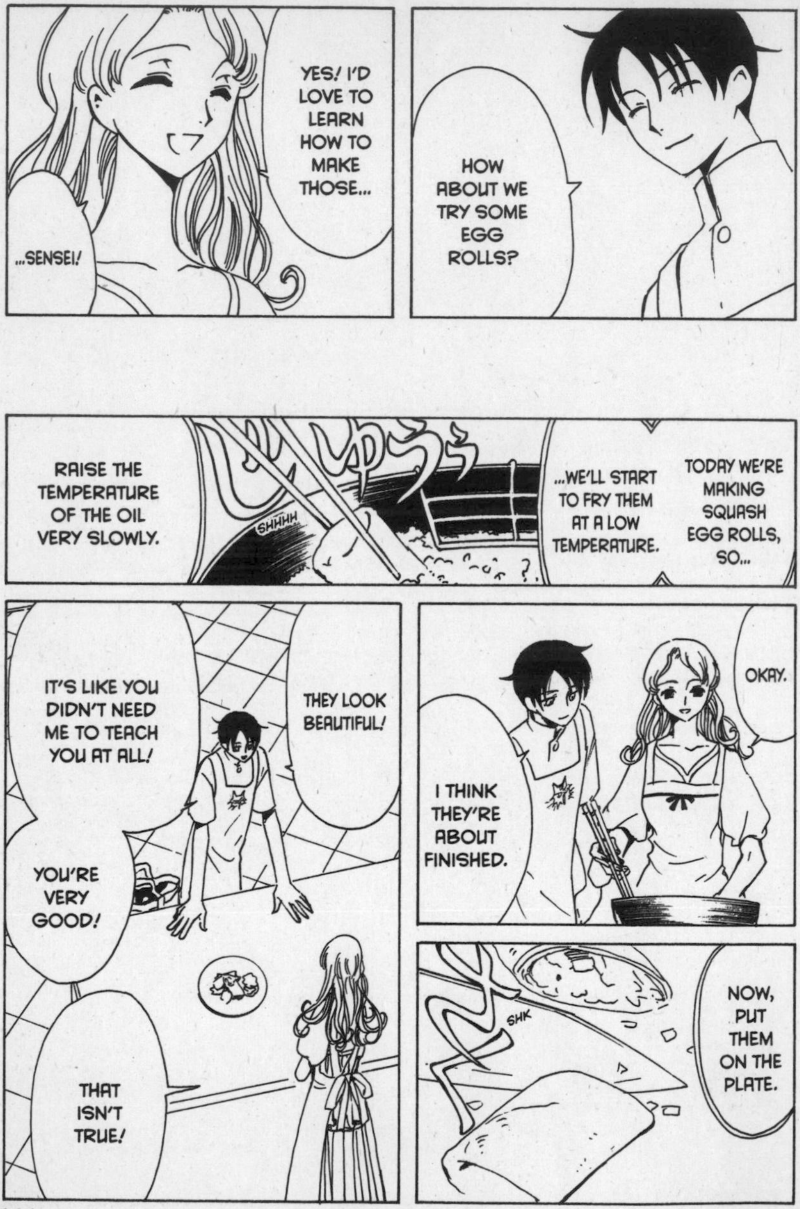
HOW ABOUT WE TRY SOME EGG ROLLS?
YES! I'D LOVE TO LEARN HOW TO MAKE THOSE...
...SENSEI!
TODAY WE'RE MAKING SQUASH EGG ROLLS, SO...
...WE'LL START TO FRY THEM AT A LOW TEMPERATURE.
SHHHH
RAISE THE TEMPERATURE OF THE OIL VERY SLOWLY.
OKAY.
I THINK THEY'RE ABOUT FINISHED.
NOW, PUT THEM ON THE PLATE.
SHK
THEY LOOK BEAUTIFUL!
IT'S LIKE YOU DIDN'T NEED ME TO TEACH YOU AT ALL!
YOU'RE VERY GOOD!
THAT ISN'T TRUE!

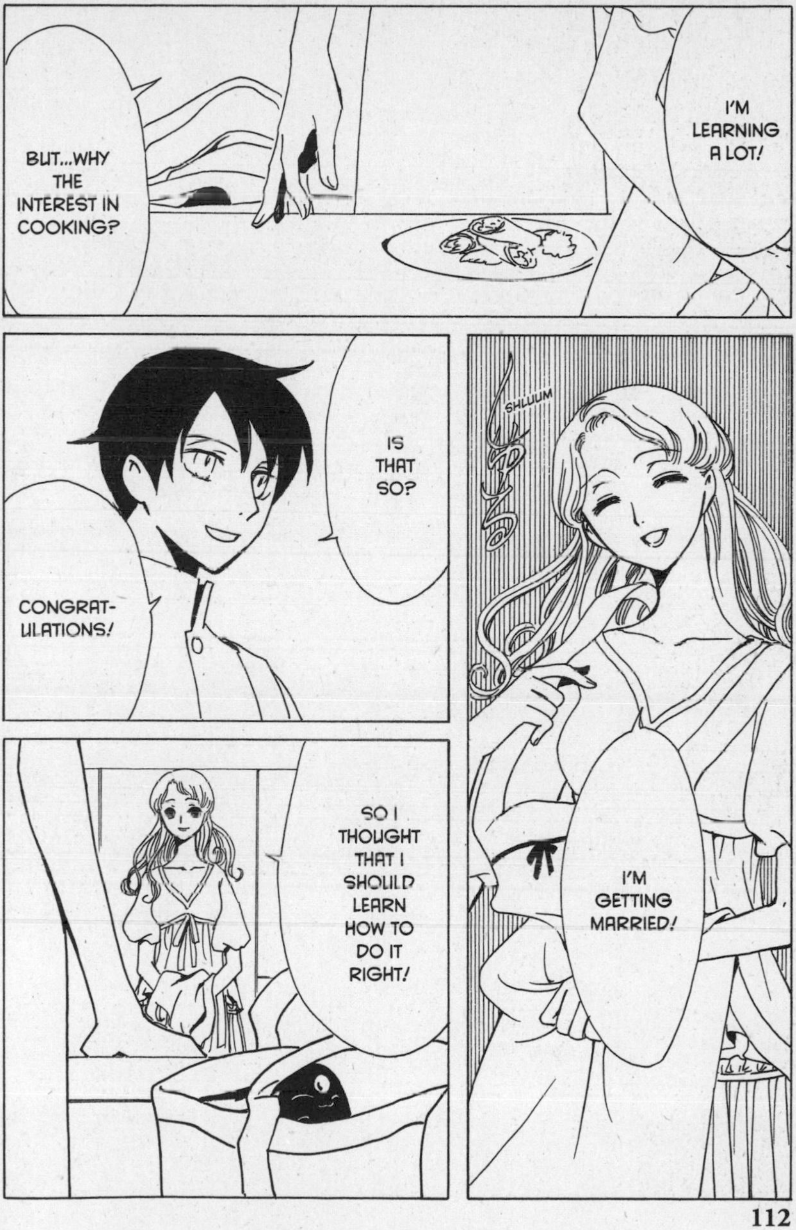
I'M LEARNING A LOT!
BUT...WHY THE INTEREST IN COOKING?
SHLUUM
I'M GETTING MARRIED!
IS THAT SO?
CONGRAT-ULATIONS!
SO I THOUGHT THAT I SHOULD LEARN HOW TO DO IT RIGHT!

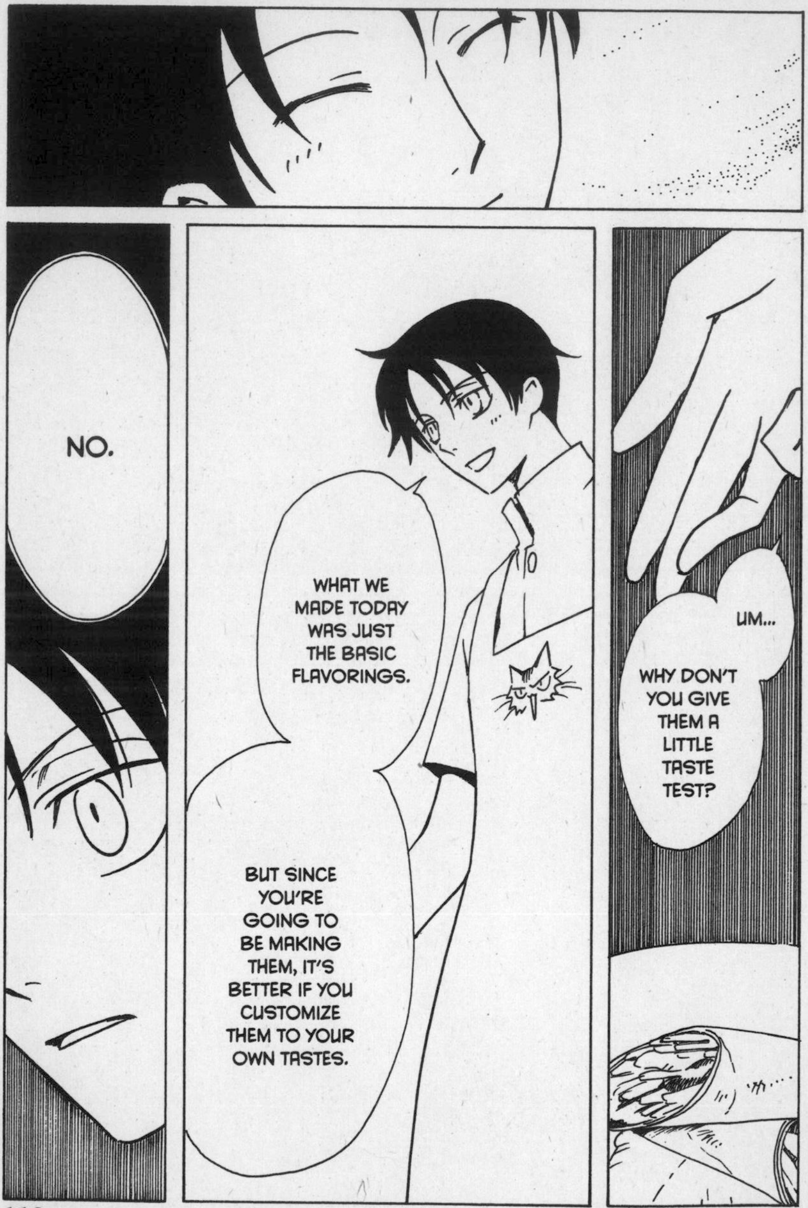
UM...
WHY DON'T YOU GIVE THEM A LITTLE TASTE TEST?
WHAT WE MADE TODAY WAS JUST THE BASIC FLAVORINGS.
BUT SINCE YOU'RE GOING TO BE MAKING THEM, IT'S BETTER IF YOU CUSTOMIZE THEM TO YOUR OWN TASTES.
NO.

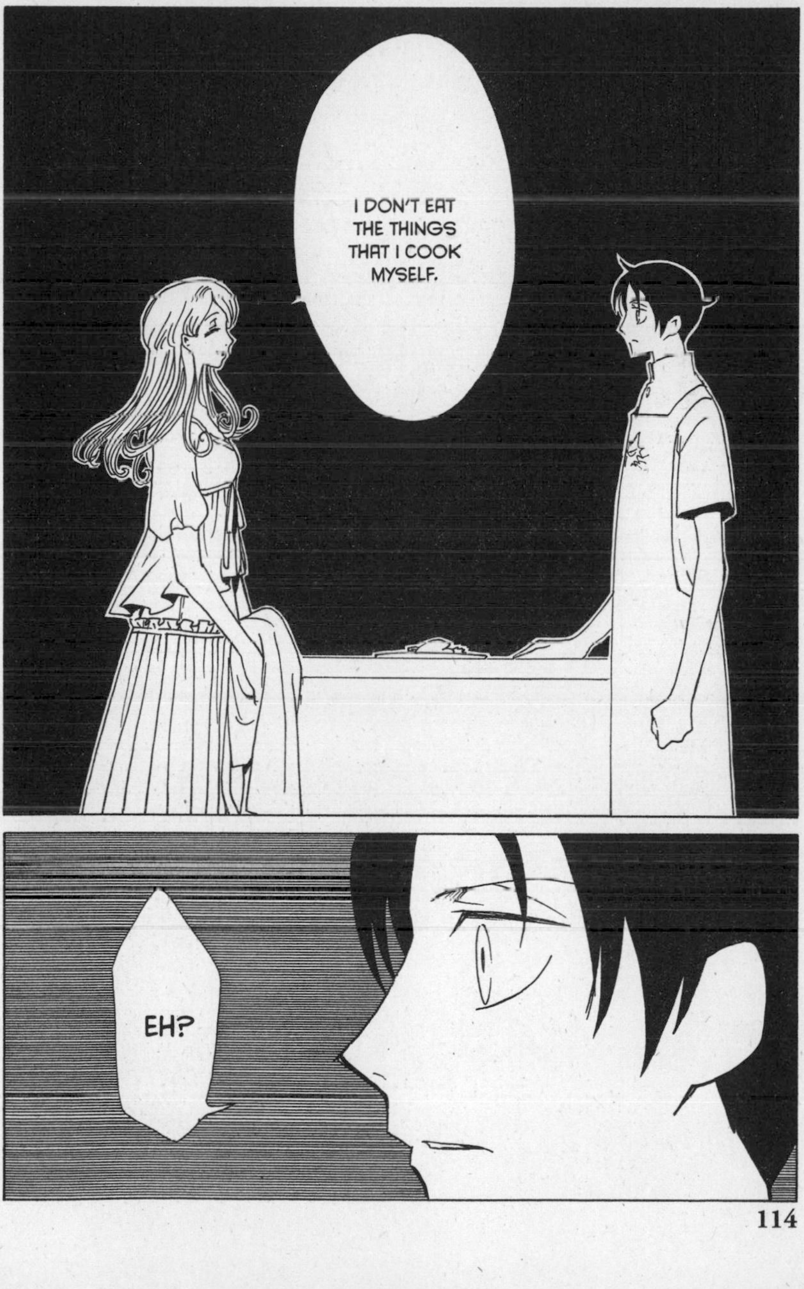

I DON'T EAT THE THINGS THAT I COOK MYSELF.
EH?

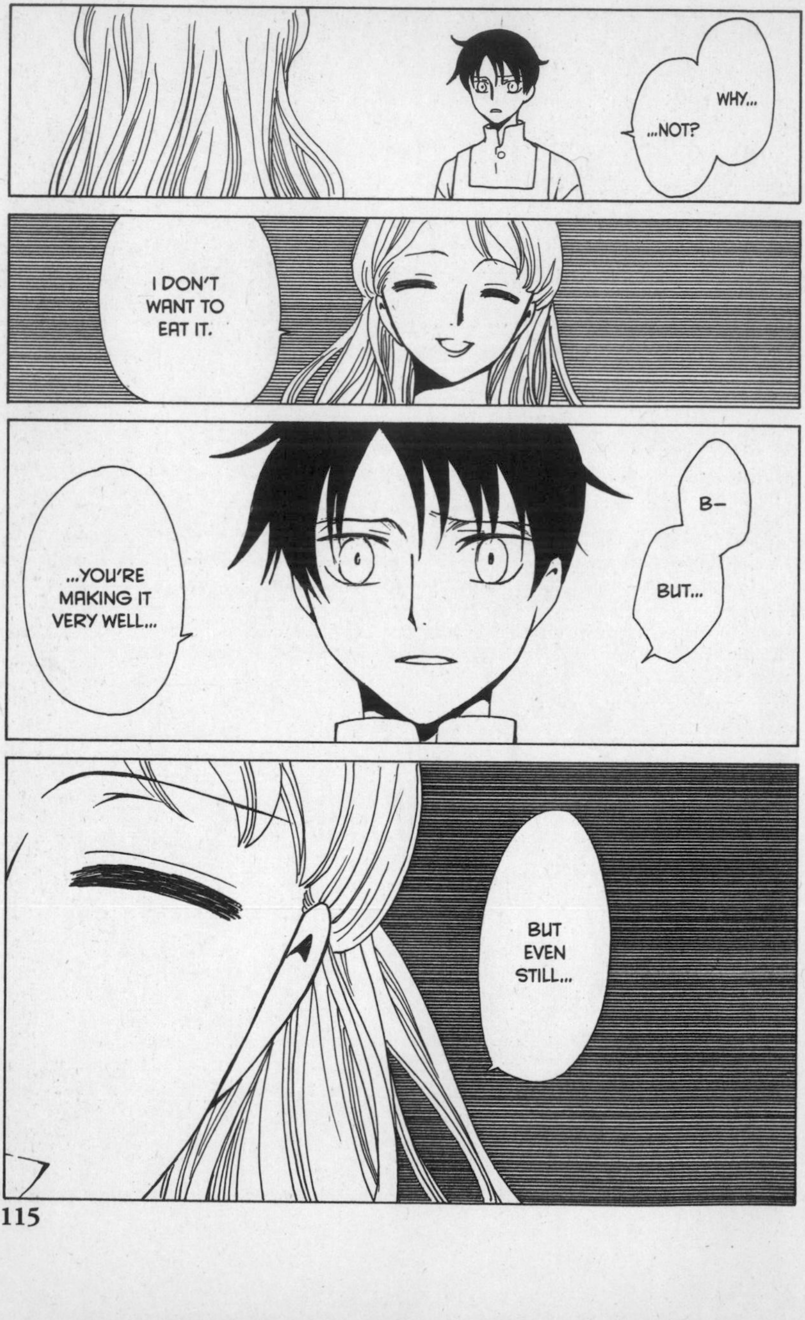
WHY... ...NOT?
I DON'T WANT TO EAT IT.
B— BUT...
...YOU'RE MAKING IT VERY WELL...
BUT EVEN STILL...

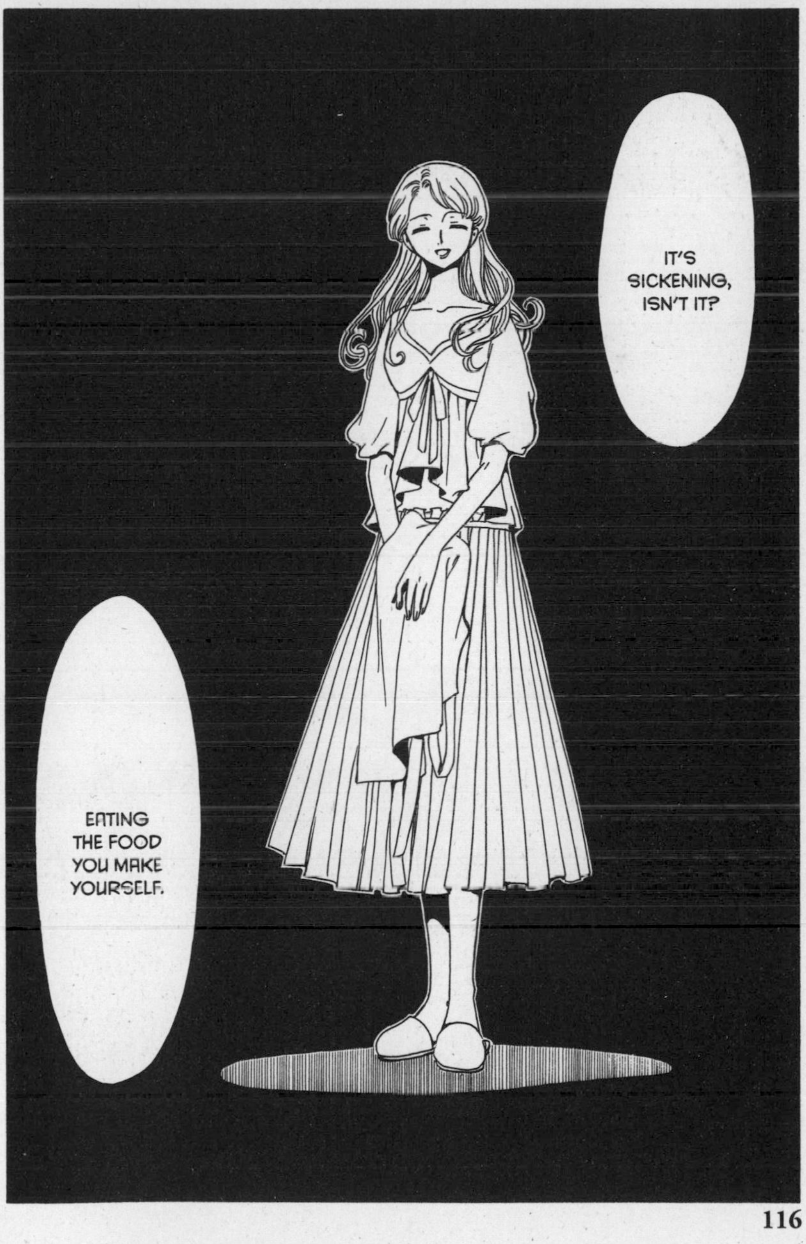
IT'S SICKENING, ISN'T IT?
EATING THE FOOD YOU MAKE YOURSELF.

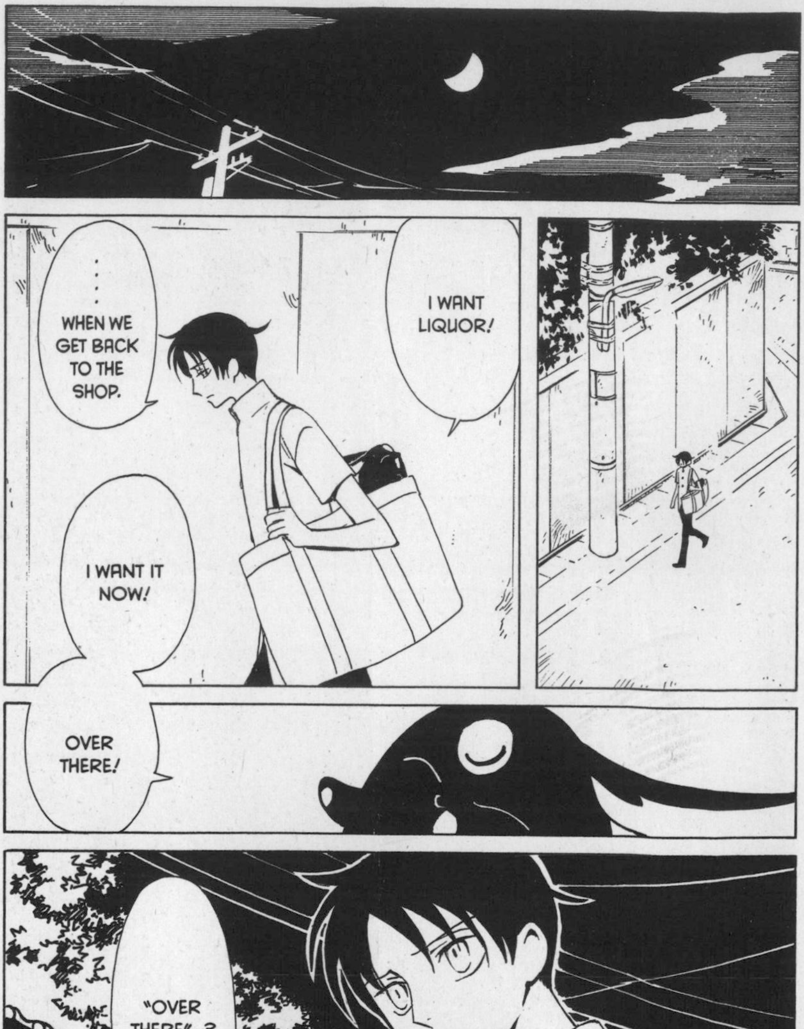
I WANT LIQUOR!
... WHEN WE GET BACK TO THE SHOP.
I WANT IT NOW!
OVER THERE!
"OVER THERE"...?

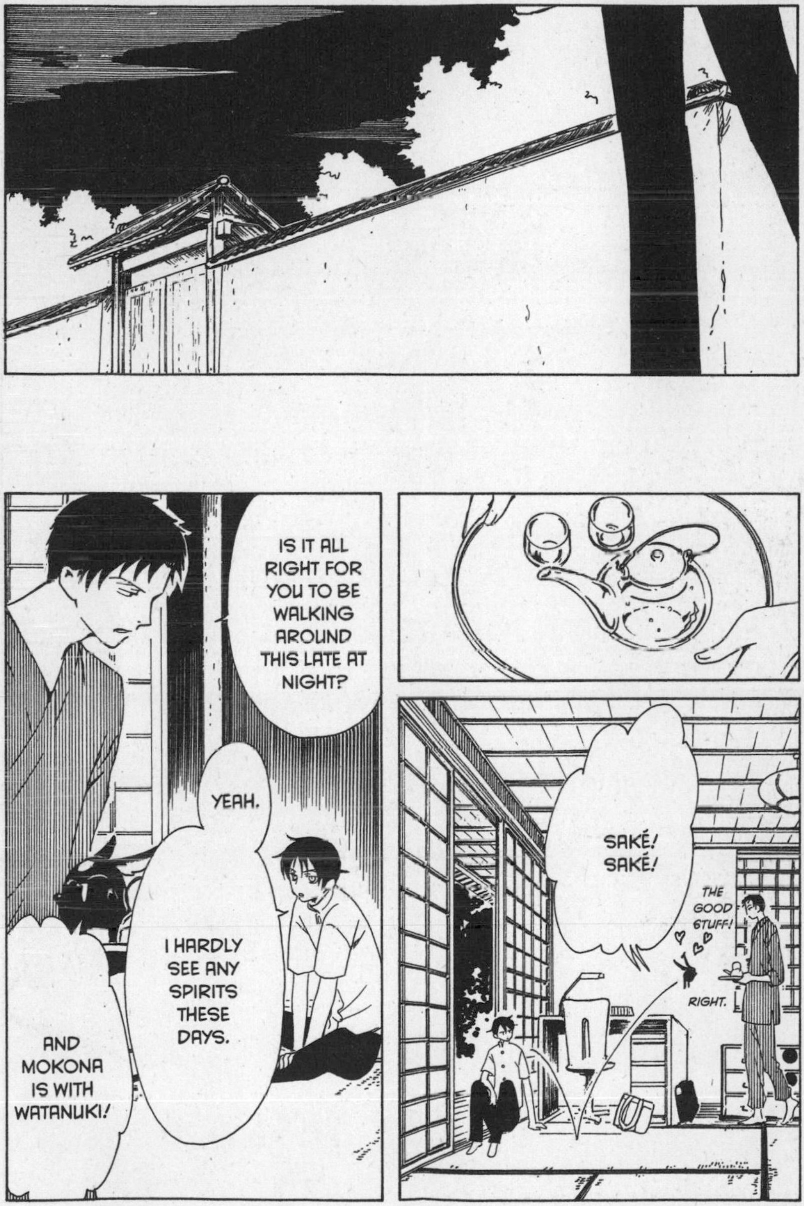
SAKÉ! SAKÉ!
THE GOOD STUFF!
RIGHT.
IS IT ALL RIGHT FOR YOU TO BE WALKING AROUND THIS LATE AT NIGHT?
YEAH.
I HARDLY SEE ANY SPIRITS THESE DAYS.
AND MOKONA IS WITH WATANUKI!

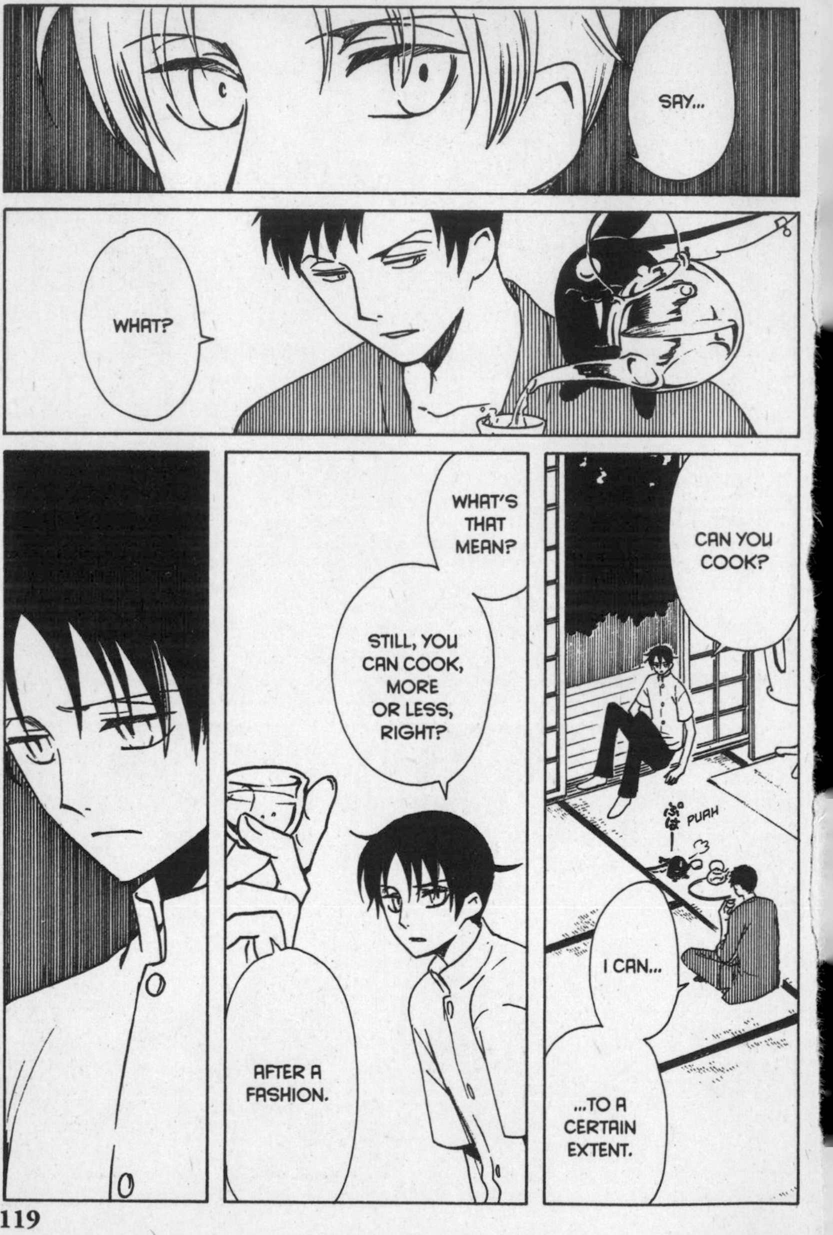
SAY...
WHAT?
CAN YOU COOK?
ぷはー
PUAH
I CAN...
...TO A CERTAIN EXTENT.
WHAT'S THAT MEAN?
STILL, YOU CAN COOK, MORE OR LESS, RIGHT?
AFTER A FASHION.

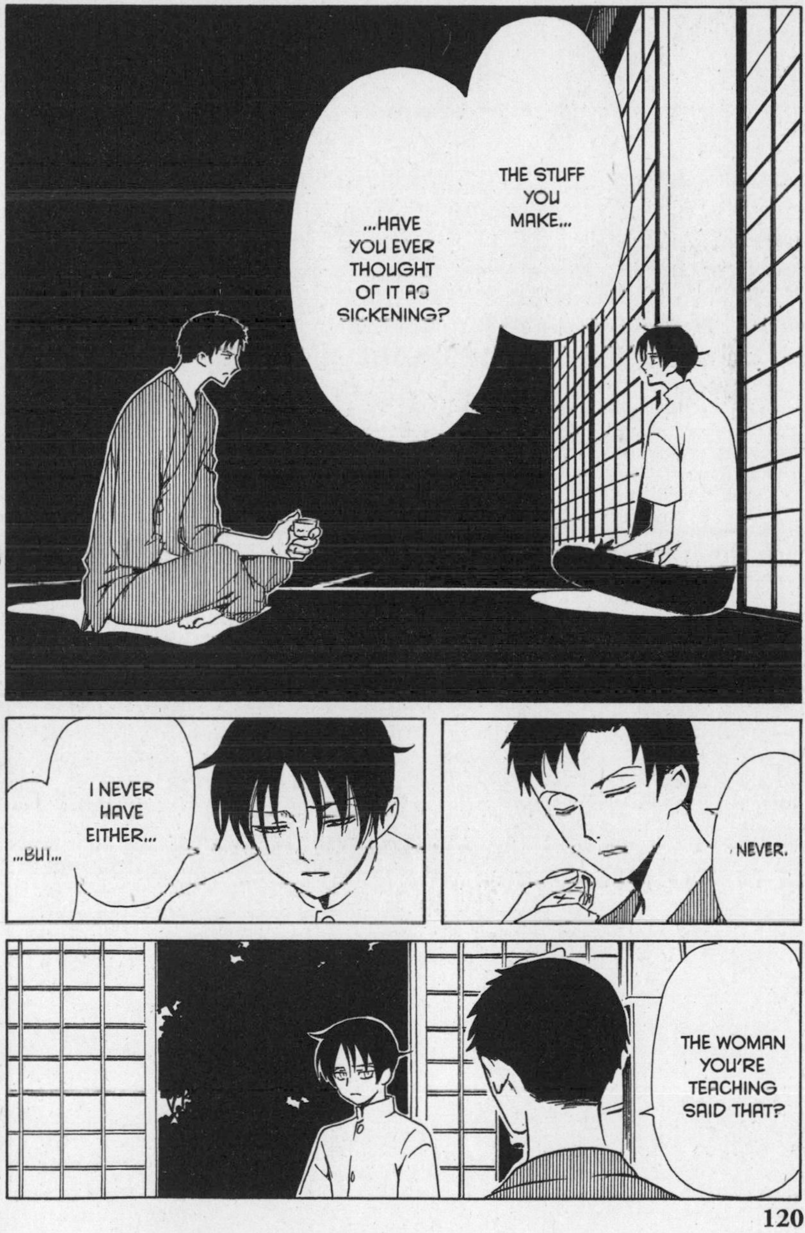
THE STUFF YOU MAKE...
...HAVE YOU EVER THOUGHT OF IT AS SICKENING?
NEVER.
I NEVER HAVE EITHER...
...BUT...
THE WOMAN YOU'RE TEACHING SAID THAT?

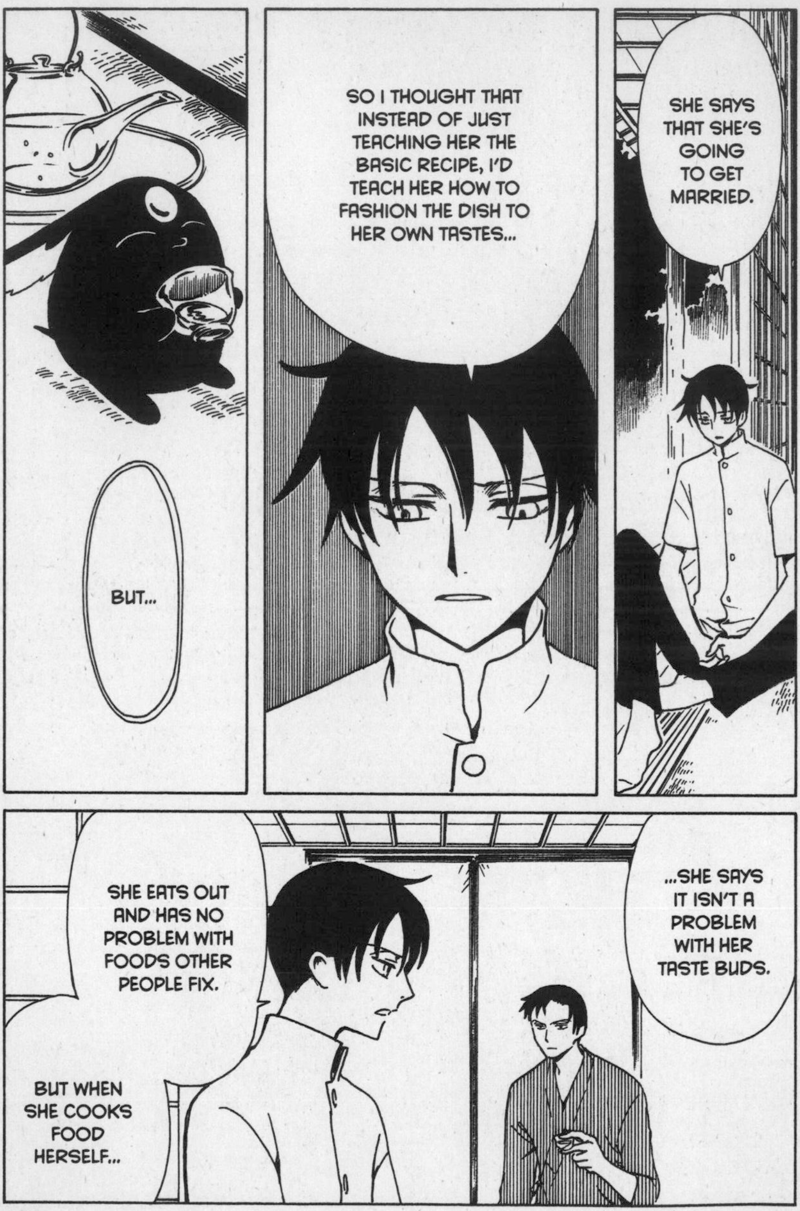
SHE SAYS THAT SHE'S GOING TO GET MARRIED.
SO I THOUGHT THAT INSTEAD OF JUST TEACHING HER THE BASIC RECIPE, I'D TEACH HER HOW TO FASHION THE DISH TO HER OWN TASTES...
BUT...
...SHE SAYS IT ISN'T A PROBLEM WITH HER TASTE BUDS.
SHE EATS OUT AND HAS NO PROBLEM WITH FOODS OTHER PEOPLE FIX.
BUT WHEN SHE COOKS FOOD HERSELF...

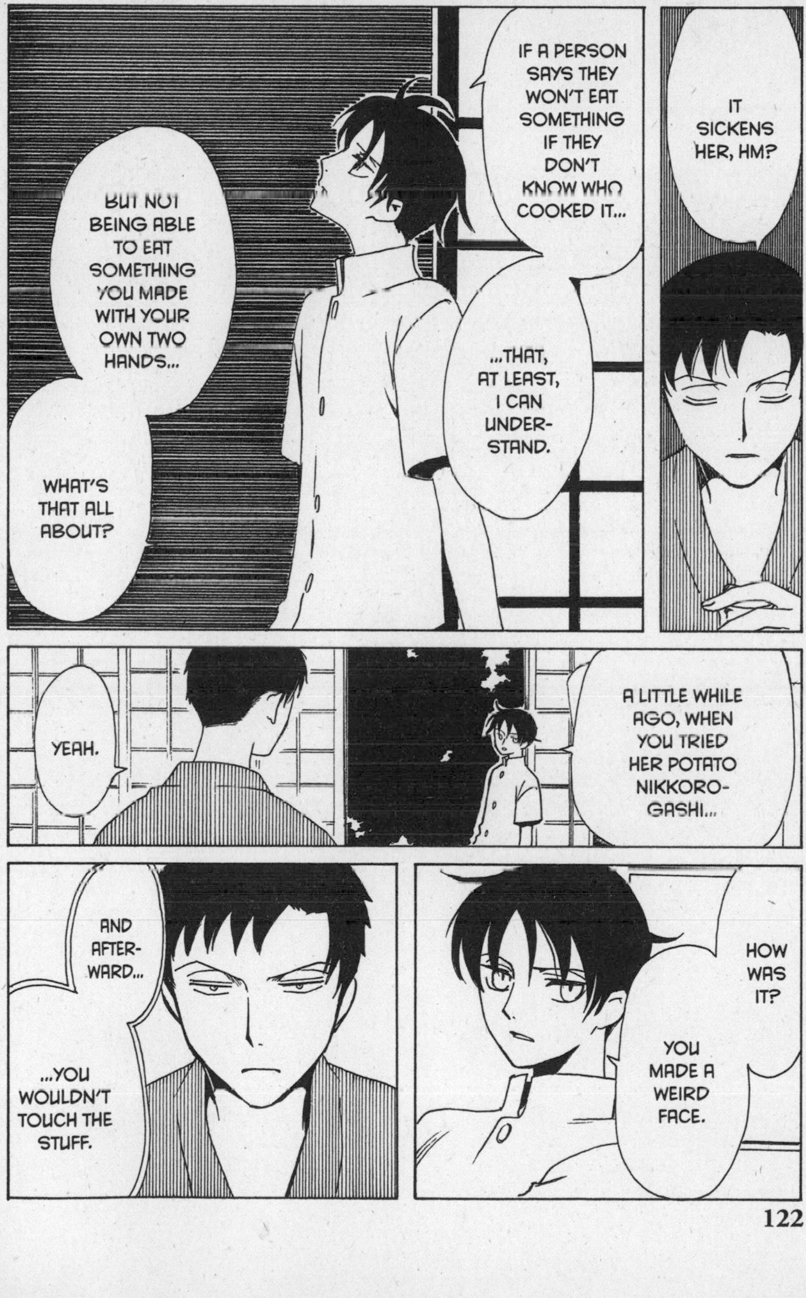
IT SICKENS HER, HM?
IF A PERSON SAYS THEY WON'T EAT SOMETHING IF THEY DON'T KNOW WHO COOKED IT...
...THAT, AT LEAST, I CAN UNDER-STAND.
BUT NOT BEING ABLE TO EAT SOMETHING YOU MADE WITH YOUR OWN TWO HANDS...
WHAT'S THAT ALL ABOUT?
A LITTLE WHILE AGO, WHEN YOU TRIED HER POTATO NIKKORO-GASHI...
YEAH.
HOW WAS IT?
YOU MADE A WEIRD FACE.
AND AFTER-WARD...
...YOU WOULDN'T TOUCH THE STUFF.

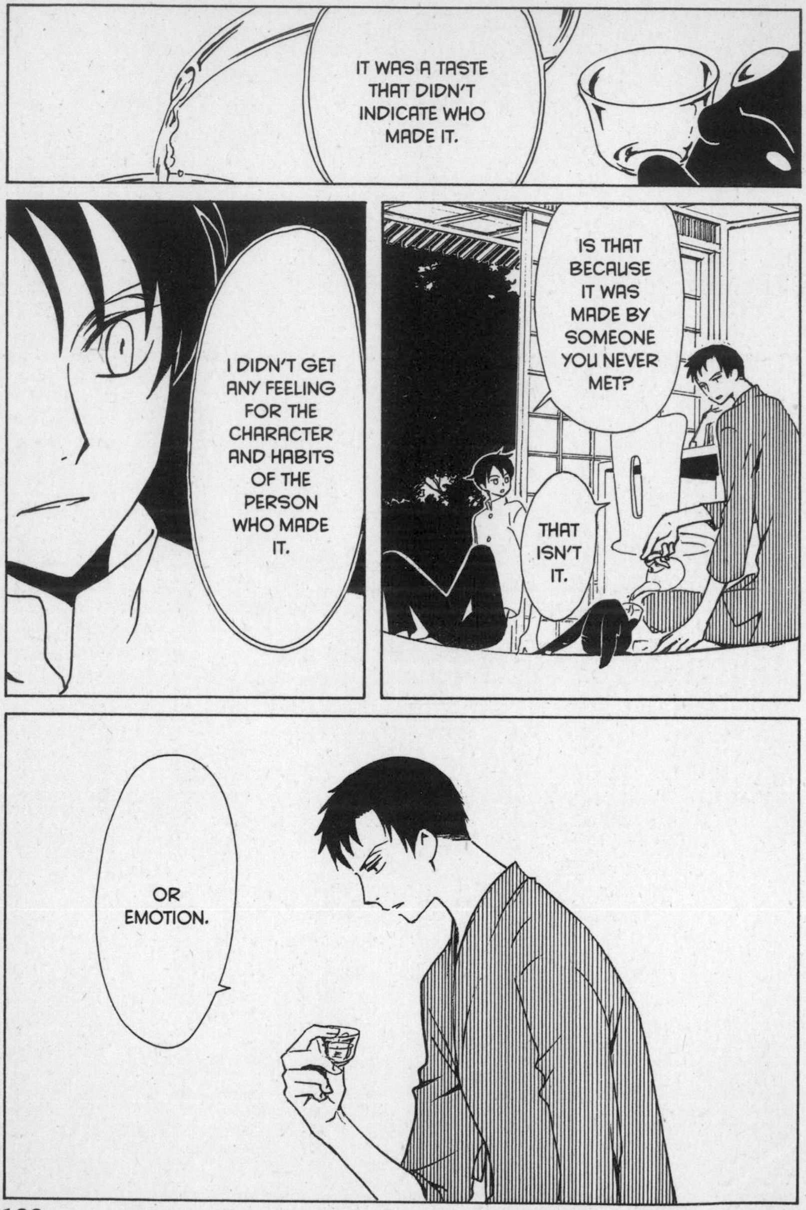
IT WAS A TASTE THAT DIDN'T INDICATE WHO MADE IT.
IS THAT BECAUSE IT WAS MADE BY SOMEONE YOU NEVER MET?
THAT ISN'T IT.
I DIDN'T GET ANY FEELING FOR THE CHARACTER AND HABITS OF THE PERSON WHO MADE IT.
OR EMOTION.

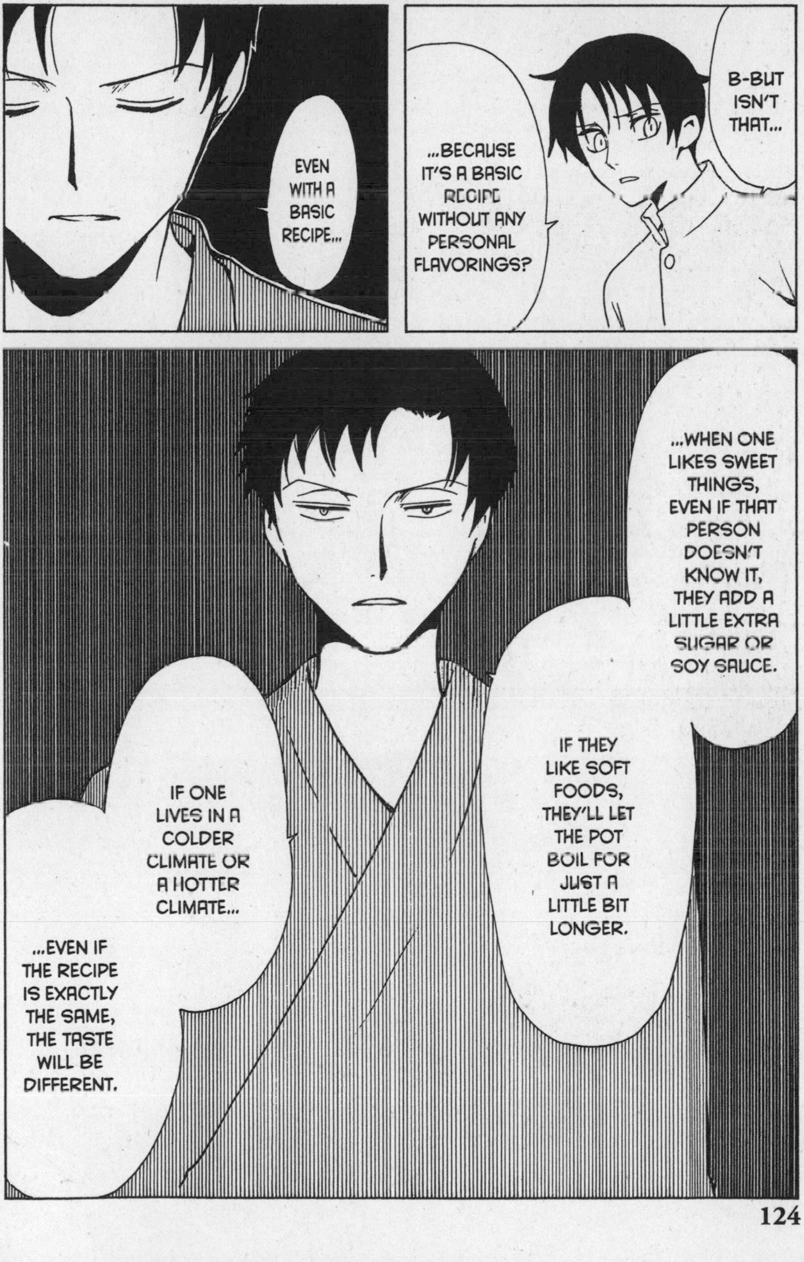
B-BUT ISN'T THAT...
...BECAUSE IT'S A BASIC RECIPE WITHOUT ANY PERSONAL FLAVORINGS?
EVEN WITH A BASIC RECIPE...
...WHEN ONE LIKES SWEET THINGS, EVEN IF THAT PERSON DOESN'T KNOW IT, THEY ADD A LITTLE EXTRA SUGAR OR SOY SAUCE.
IF THEY LIKE SOFT FOODS, THEY'LL LET THE POT BOIL FOR JUST A LITTLE BIT LONGER.
IF ONE LIVES IN A COLDER CLIMATE OR A HOTTER CLIMATE...
...EVEN IF THE RECIPE IS EXACTLY THE SAME, THE TASTE WILL BE DIFFERENT.

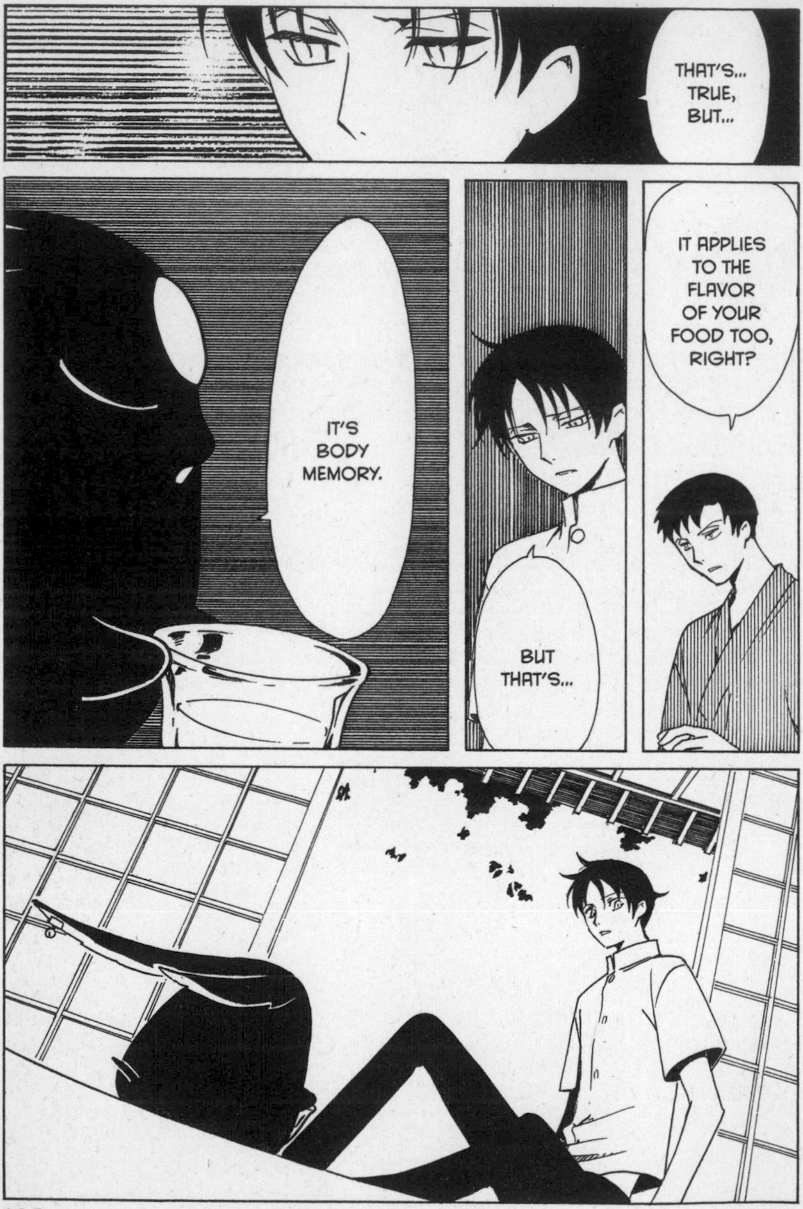
THAT'S... TRUE, BUT...
IT APPLIES TO THE FLAVOR OF YOUR FOOD TOO, RIGHT?
BUT THAT'S...
IT'S BODY MEMORY.

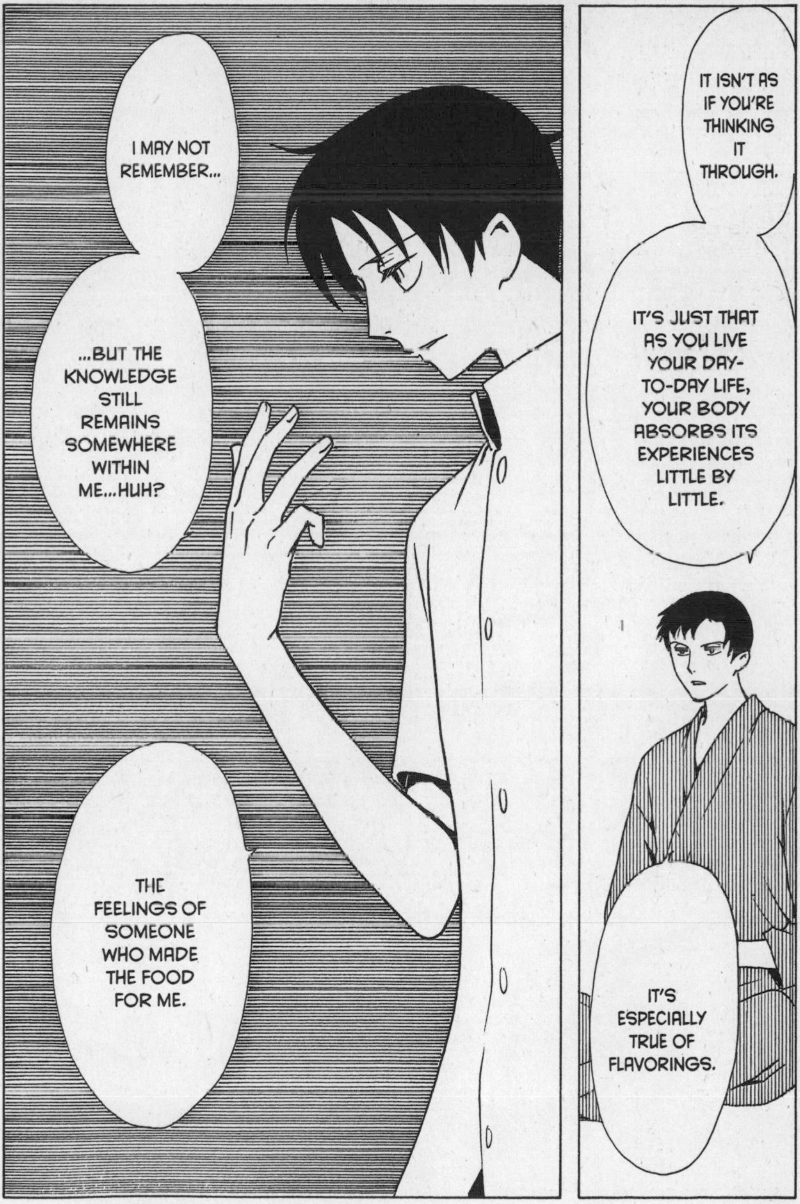
IT ISN'T AS IF YOU'RE THINKING IT THROUGH.
IT'S JUST THAT AS YOU LIVE YOUR DAY-TO-DAY LIFE, YOUR BODY ABSORBS ITS EXPERIENCES LITTLE BY LITTLE.
IT'S ESPECIALLY TRUE OF FLAVORINGS.
I MAY NOT REMEMBER...
...BUT THE KNOWLEDGE STILL REMAINS SOMEWHERE WITHIN ME...HUH?
THE FEELINGS OF SOMEONE WHO MADE THE FOOD FOR ME.

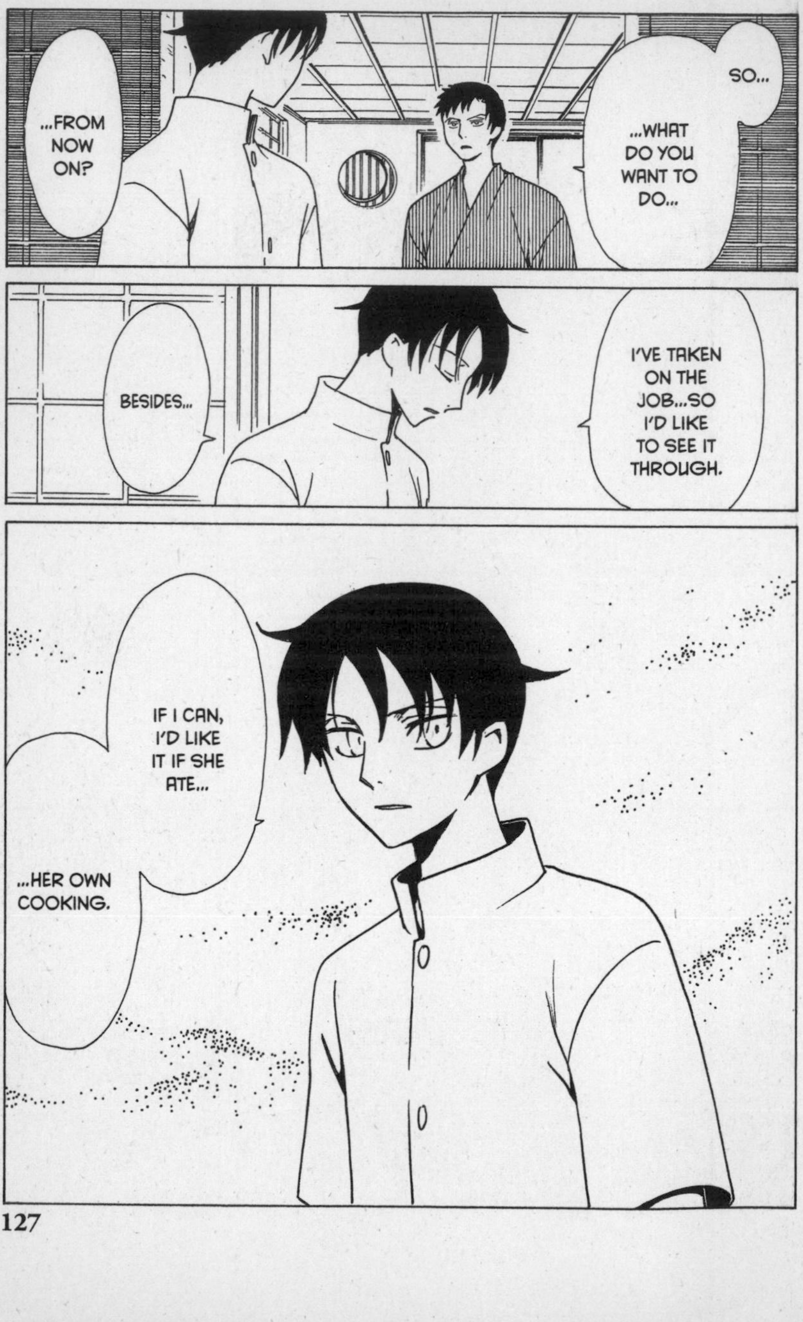
SO... ...WHAT DO YOU WANT TO DO...
...FROM NOW ON?
I'VE TAKEN ON THE JOB...SO I'D LIKE TO SEE IT THROUGH.
BESIDES...
IF I CAN, I'D LIKE IT IF SHE ATE... ...HER OWN COOKING.

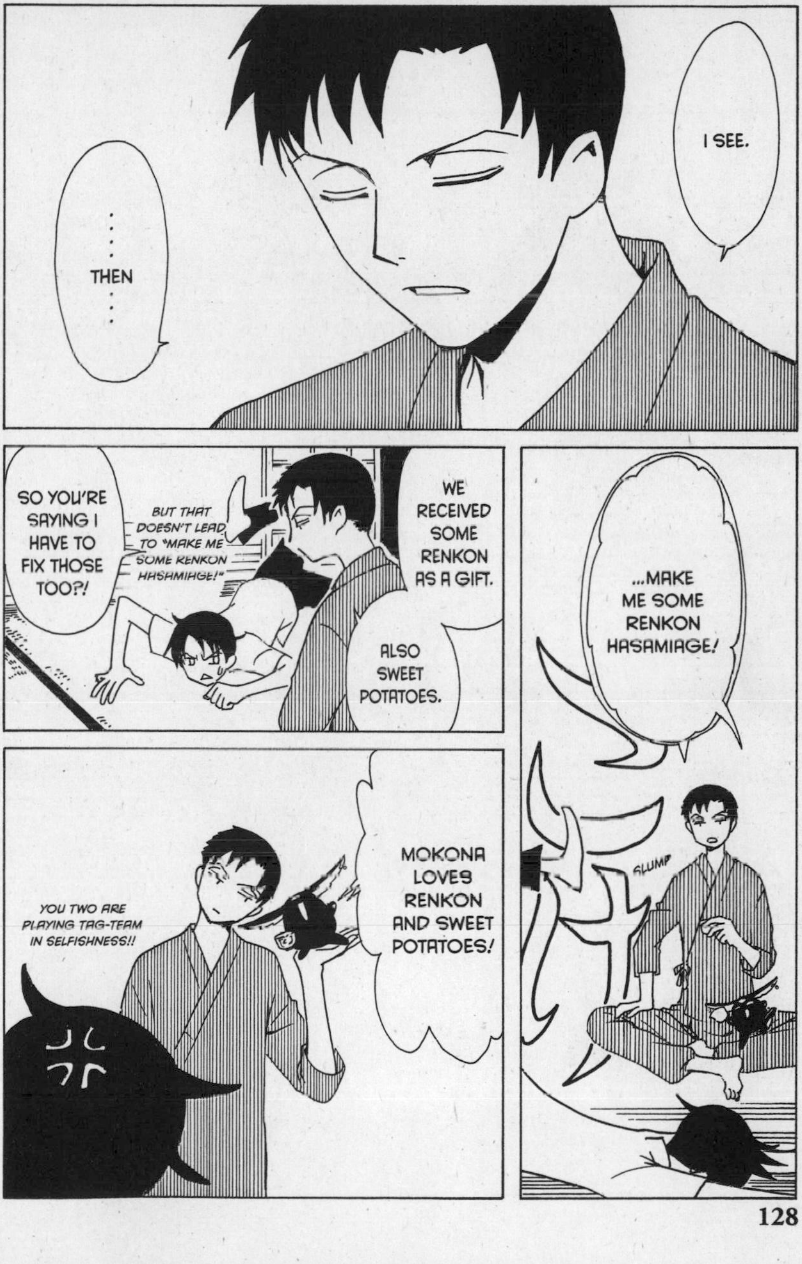
I SEE.
...... THEN ......
...MAKE ME SOME RENKON HASAMIAGE!
SLUMP
WE RECEIVED SOME RENKON AS A GIFT.
ALSO SWEET POTATOES.
BUT THAT DOESN'T LEAD TO "MAKE ME SOME RENKON HASAMIAGE!"
SO YOU'RE SAYING I HAVE TO FIX THOSE TOO?!
MOKONA LOVES RENKON AND SWEET POTATOES!
YOU TWO ARE PLAYING TAG-TEAM IN SELFISHNESS!!

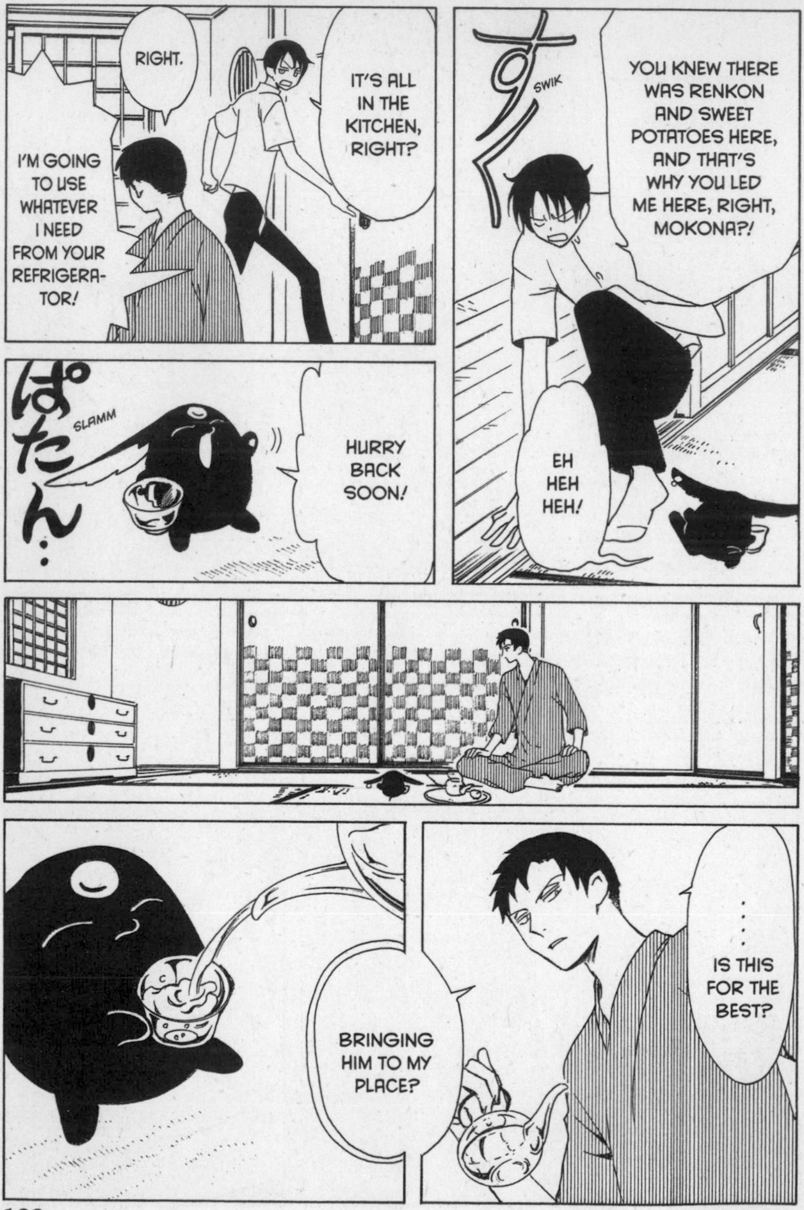
すく
SWIK
YOU KNEW THERE WAS RENKON AND SWEET POTATOES HERE, AND THAT'S WHY YOU LED ME HERE, RIGHT, MOKONA?!
EH HEH HEH!
IT'S ALL IN THE KITCHEN, RIGHT?
RIGHT.
I'M GOING TO USE WHATEVER I NEED FROM YOUR REFRIGERA-TOR!
HURRY BACK SOON!
ぱたん…
SLAMM
...
IS THIS FOR THE BEST?
BRINGING HIM TO MY PLACE?

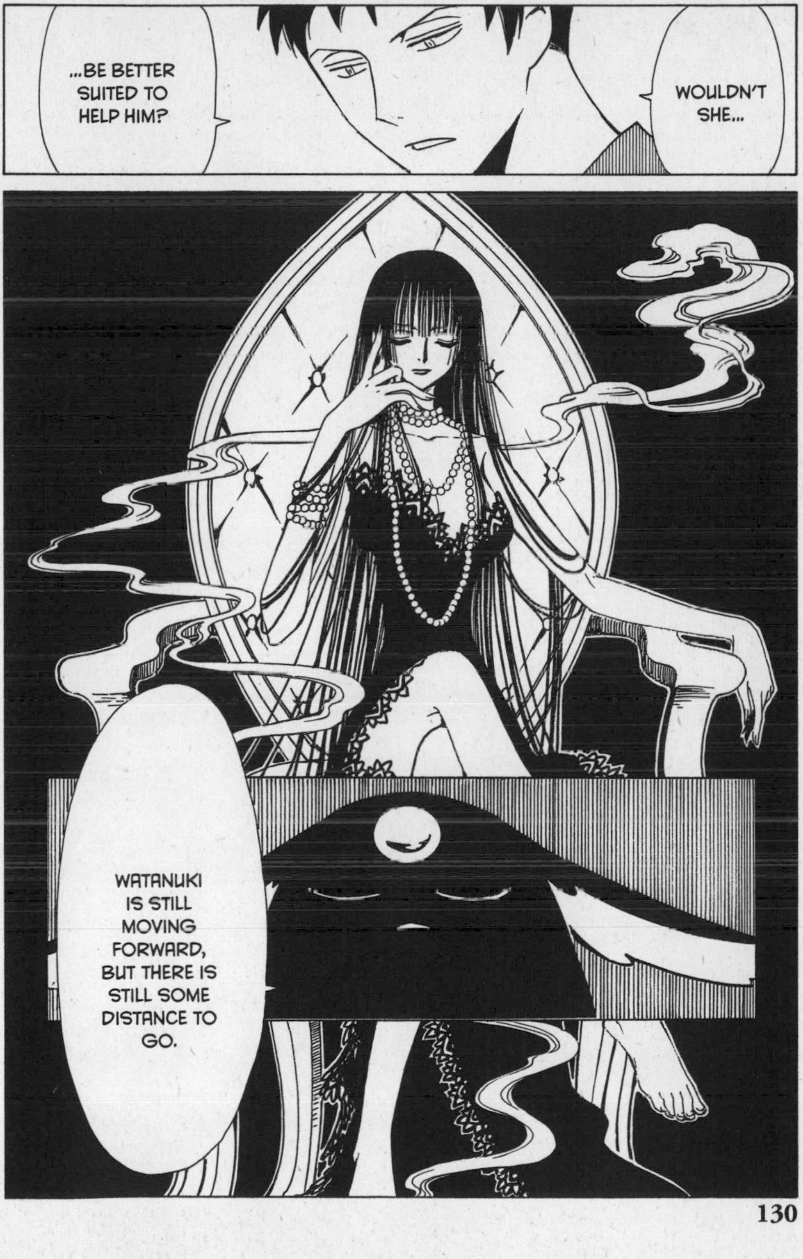
WOULDN'T SHE...
...BE BETTER SUITED TO HELP HIM?
WATANUKI IS STILL MOVING FORWARD, BUT THERE IS STILL SOME DISTANCE TO GO.

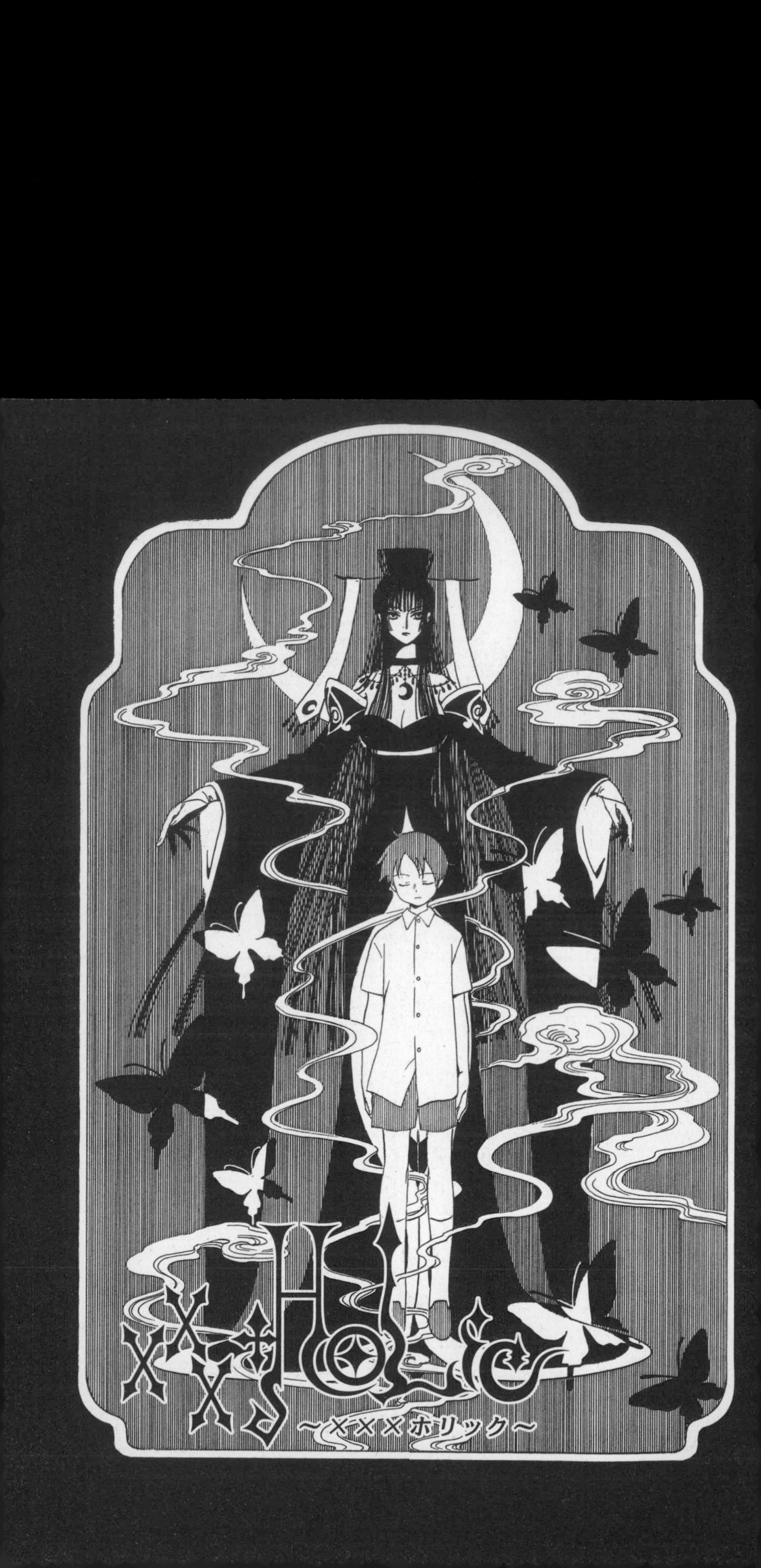
xxxHOLiC
〜×××ホリック〜

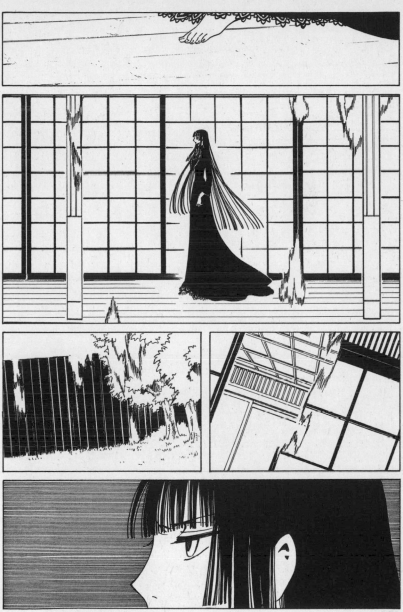

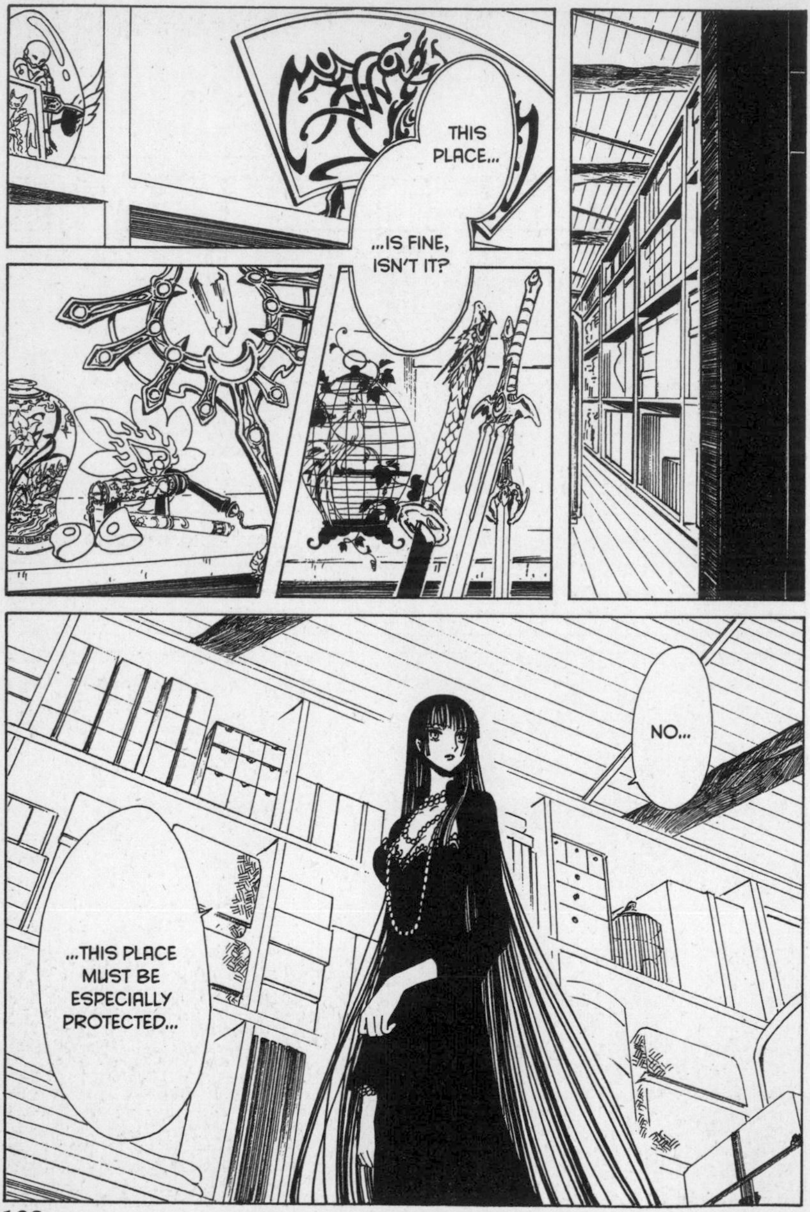
THIS PLACE...
...IS FINE, ISN'T IT?
NO...
...THIS PLACE MUST BE ESPECIALLY PROTECTED...

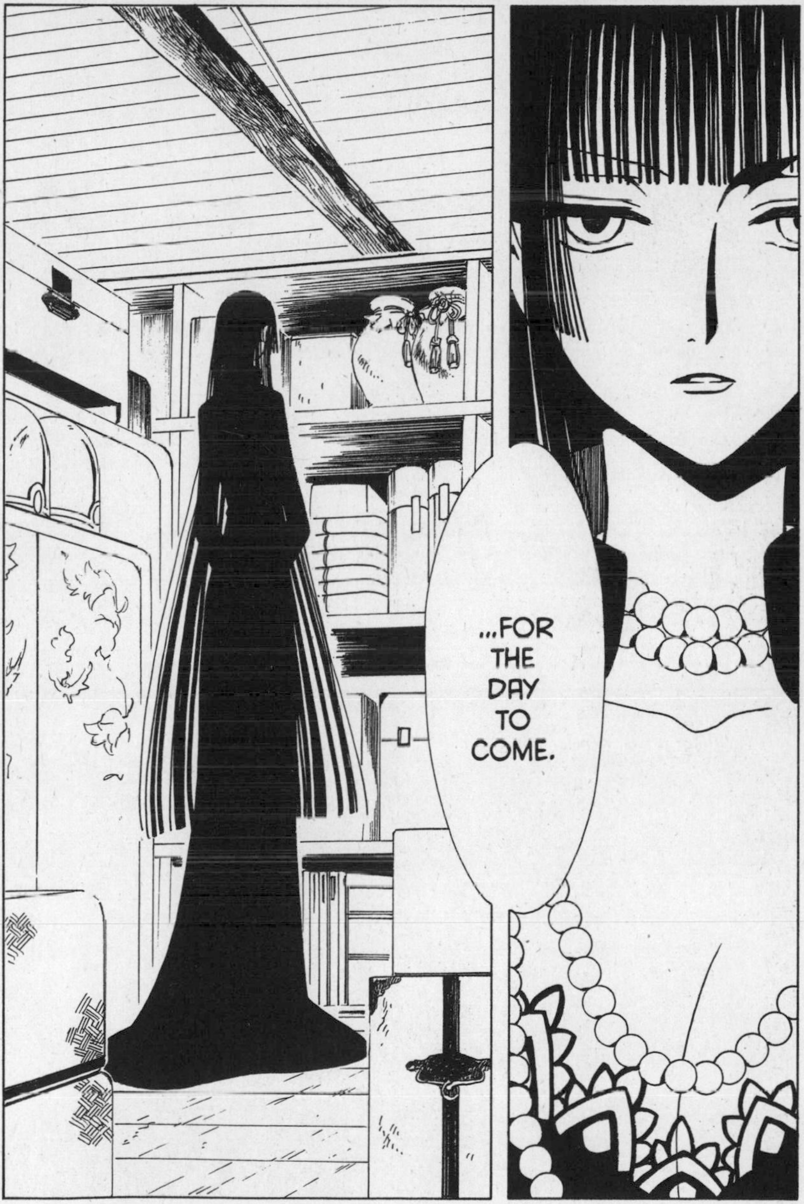
...FOR THE DAY TO COME.

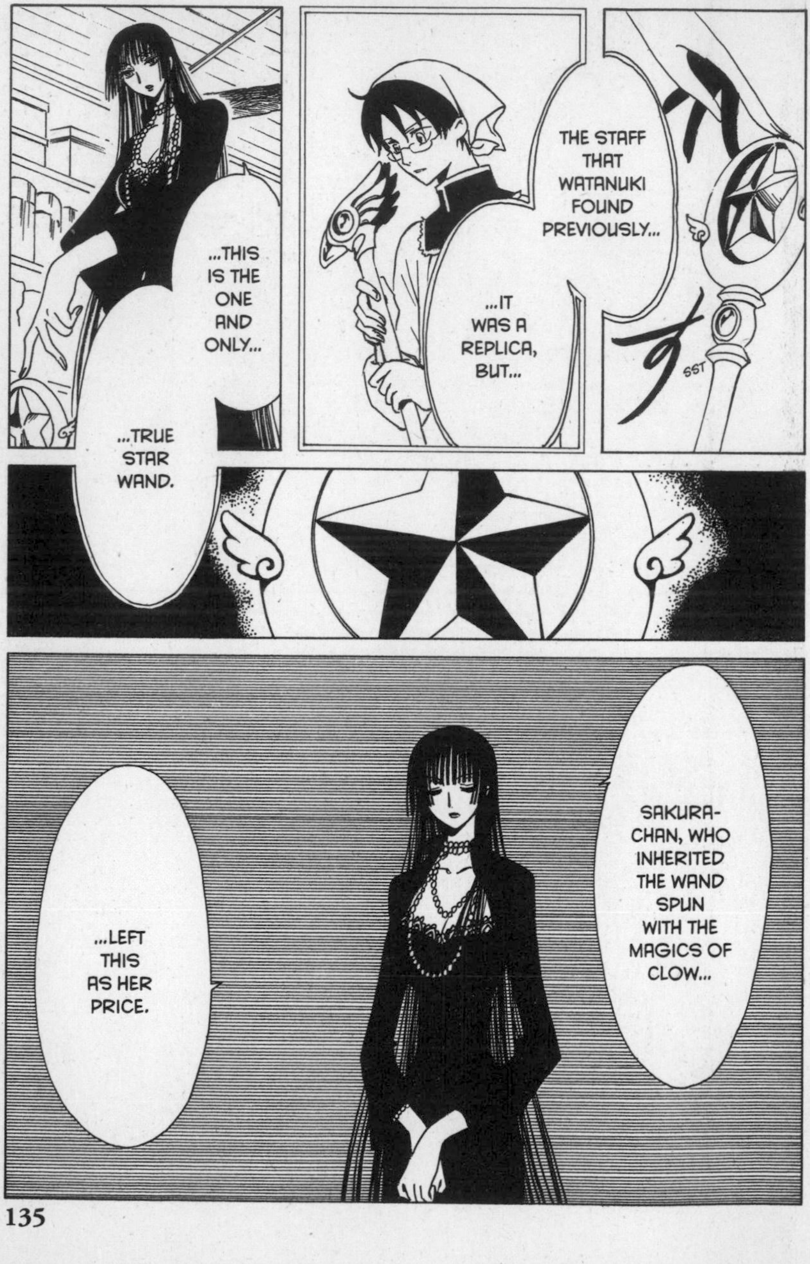
SST
THE STAFF THAT WATANUKI FOUND PREVIOUSLY...
...IT WAS A REPLICA, BUT...
...THIS IS THE ONE AND ONLY...
...TRUE STAR WAND.
SAKURA-CHAN, WHO INHERITED THE WAND SPUN WITH THE MAGICS OF CLOW...
...LEFT THIS AS HER PRICE.

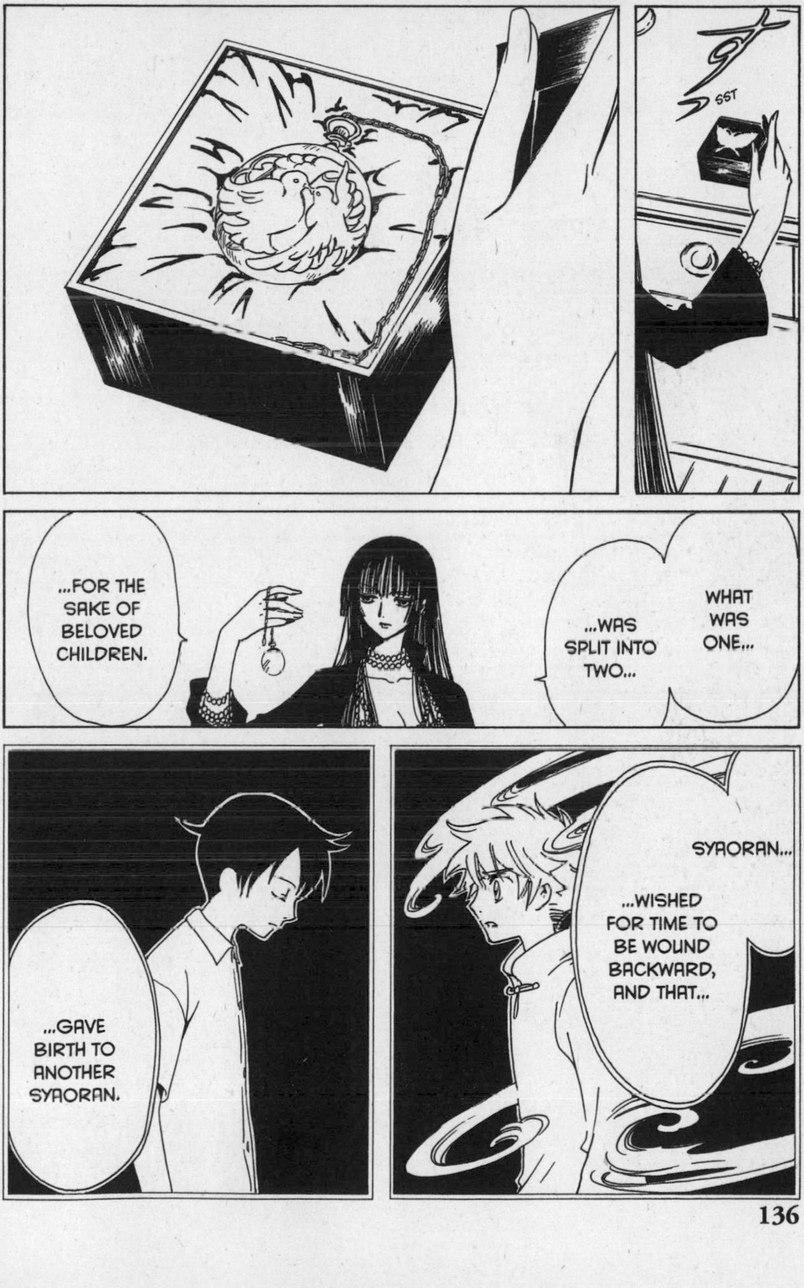
SST
WHAT WAS ONE...
...WAS SPLIT INTO TWO...
...FOR THE SAKE OF BELOVED CHILDREN.
SYAORAN...
...WISHED FOR TIME TO BE WOUND BACKWARD, AND THAT...
...GAVE BIRTH TO ANOTHER SYAORAN.

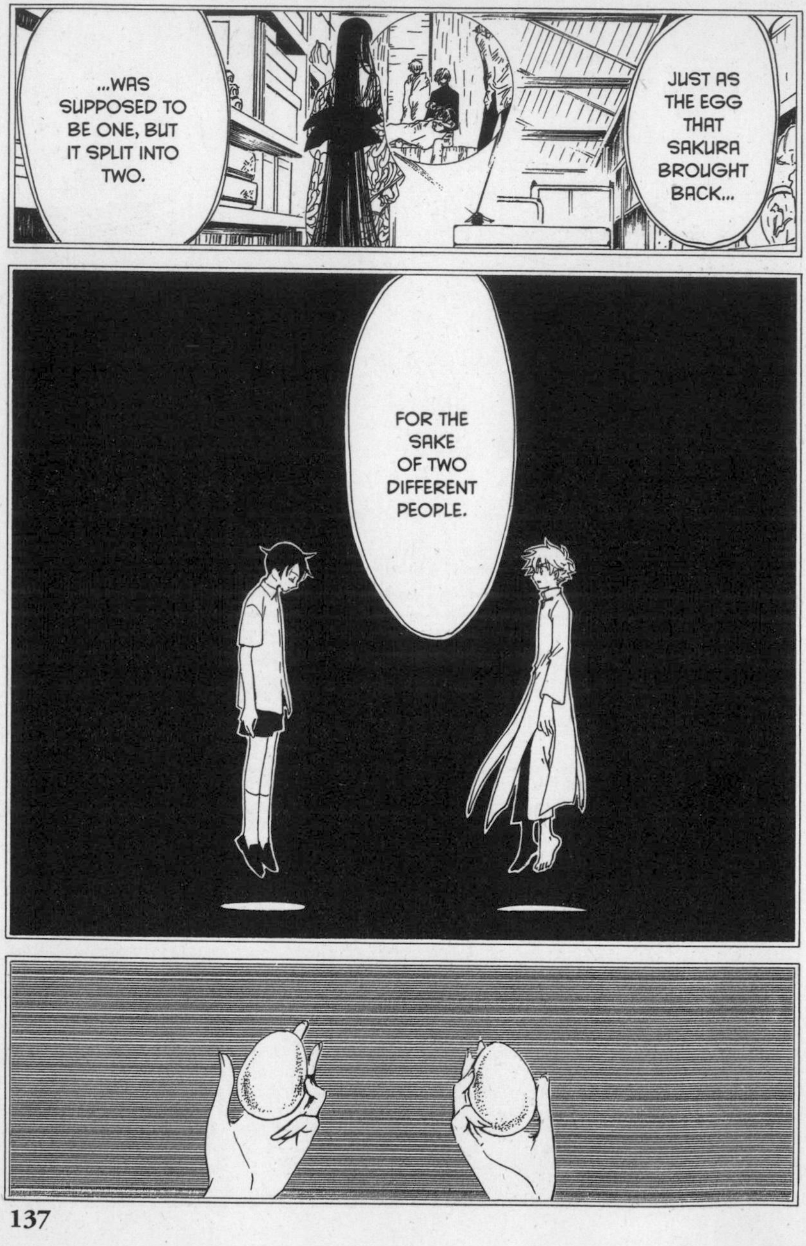
JUST AS THE EGG THAT SAKURA BROUGHT BACK...
...WAS SUPPOSED TO BE ONE, BUT IT SPLIT INTO TWO.
FOR THE SAKE OF TWO DIFFERENT PEOPLE.

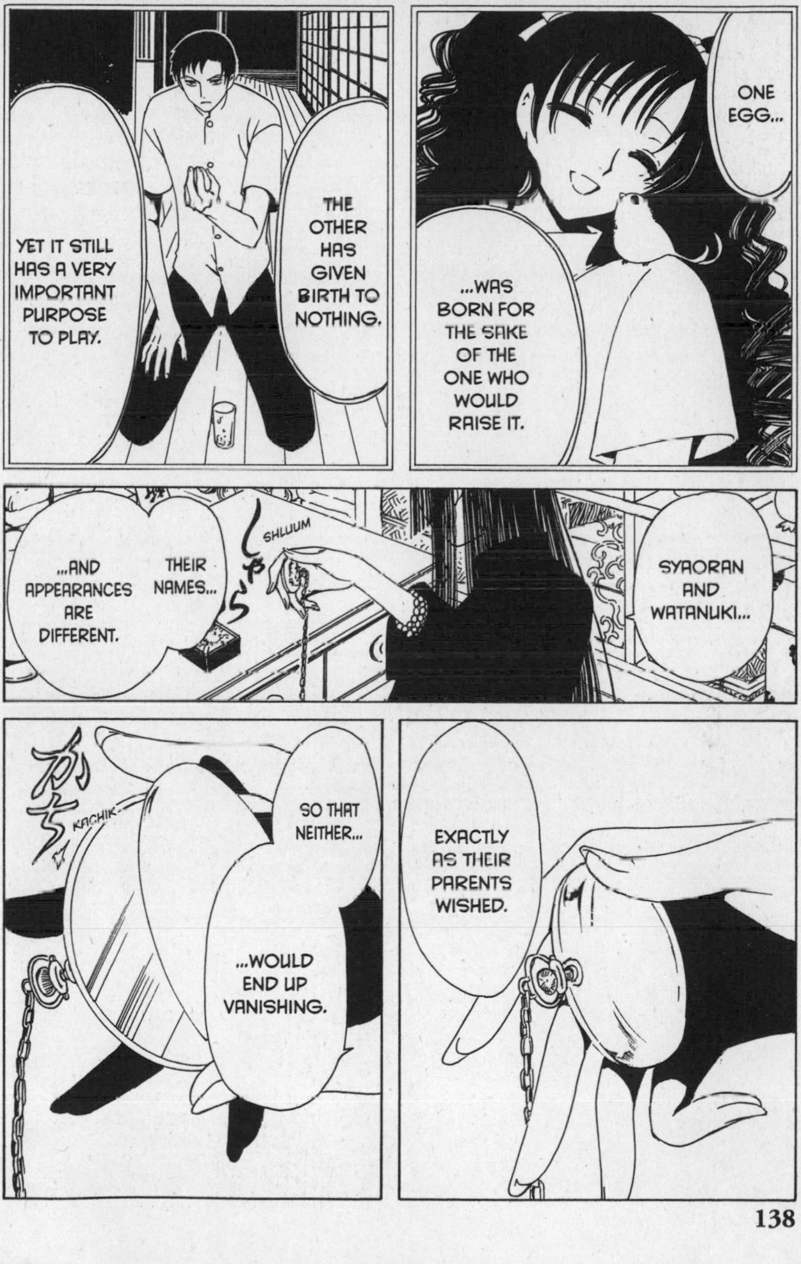
ONE EGG...
...WAS BORN FOR THE SAKE OF THE ONE WHO WOULD RAISE IT.
THE OTHER HAS GIVEN BIRTH TO NOTHING.
YET IT STILL HAS A VERY IMPORTANT PURPOSE TO PLAY.
SYAORAN AND WATANUKI...
SHLUUM
THEIR NAMES...
...AND APPEARANCES ARE DIFFERENT.
EXACTLY AS THEIR PARENTS WISHED.
SO THAT NEITHER...
KACHIK
...WOULD END UP VANISHING.

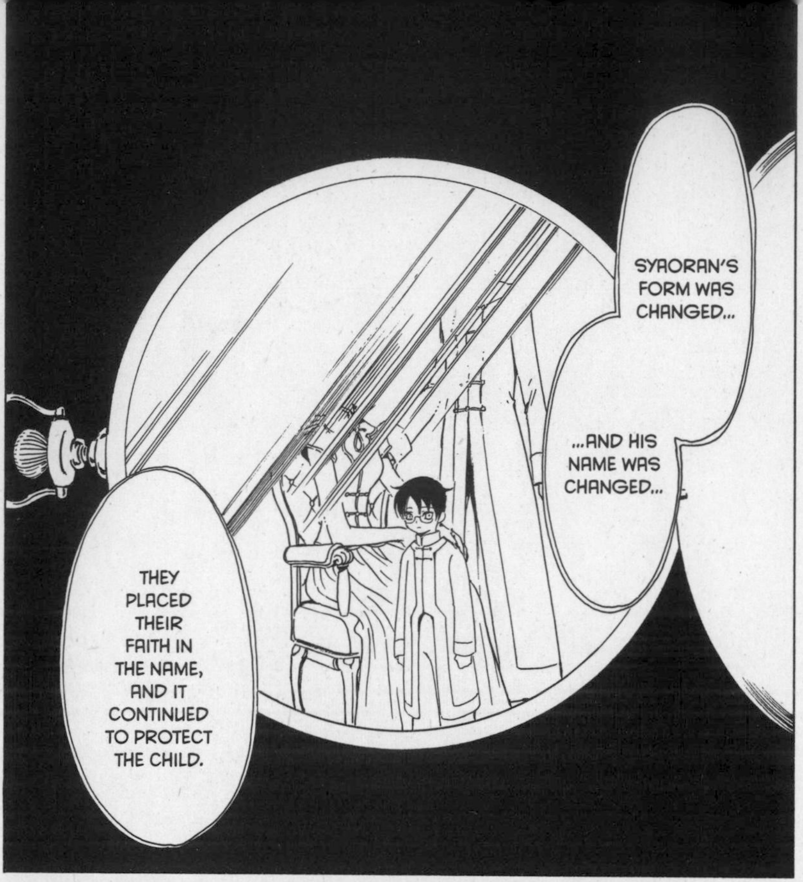
SYAORAN'S FORM WAS CHANGED...
...AND HIS NAME WAS CHANGED...
THEY PLACED THEIR FAITH IN THE NAME, AND IT CONTINUED TO PROTECT THE CHILD.

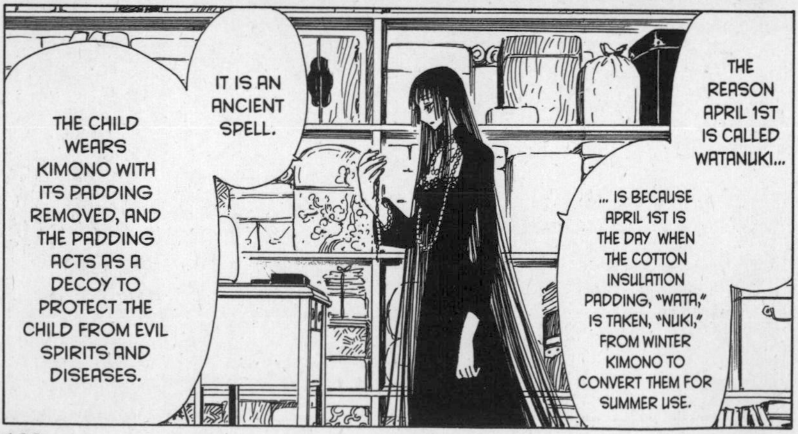
THE REASON APRIL 1ST IS CALLED WATANUKI...
... IS BECAUSE APRIL 1ST IS THE DAY WHEN THE COTTON INSULATION PADDING, "WATA," IS TAKEN, "NUKI," FROM WINTER KIMONO TO CONVERT THEM FOR SUMMER USE.
IT IS AN ANCIENT SPELL.
THE CHILD WEARS KIMONO WITH ITS PADDING REMOVED, AND THE PADDING ACTS AS A DECOY TO PROTECT THE CHILD FROM EVIL SPIRITS AND DISEASES.

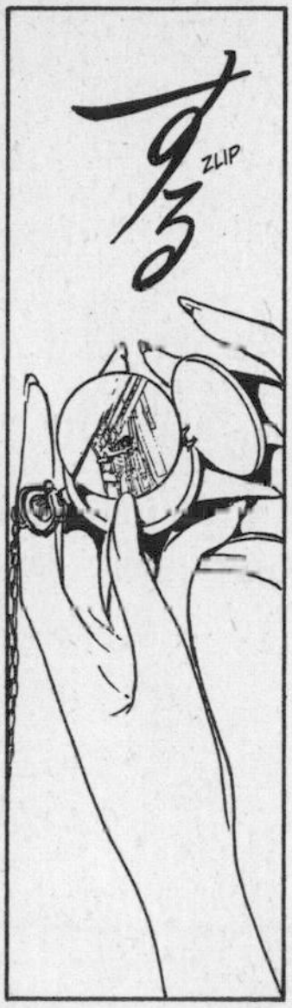
する
ZLIP

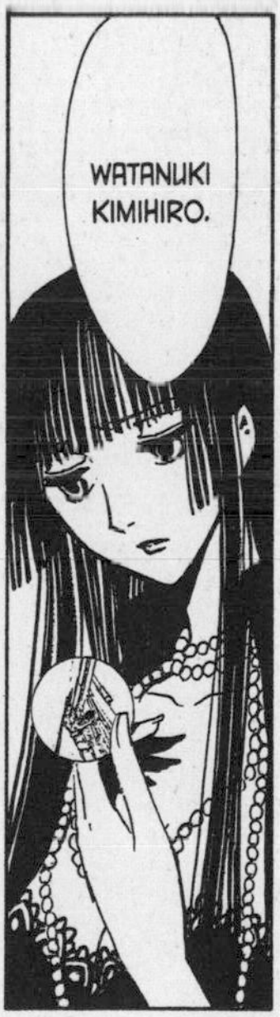
WATANUKI KIMIHIRO.

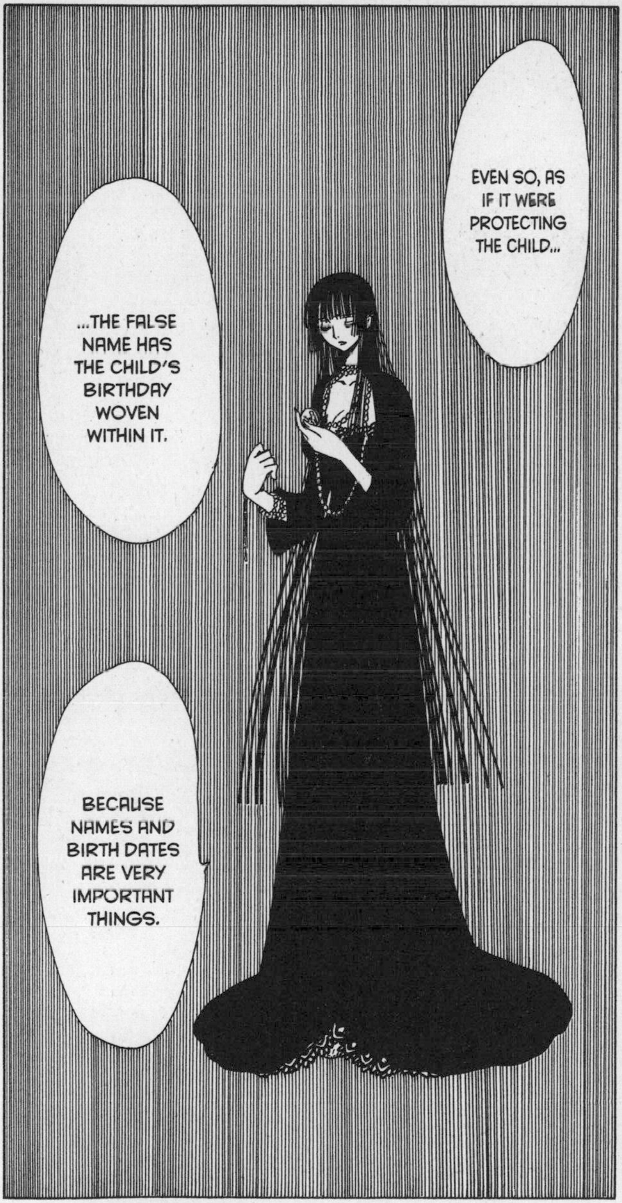
EVEN SO, AS IF IT WERE PROTECTING THE CHILD...
...THE FALSE NAME HAS THE CHILD'S BIRTHDAY WOVEN WITHIN IT.
BECAUSE NAMES AND BIRTH DATES ARE VERY IMPORTANT THINGS.

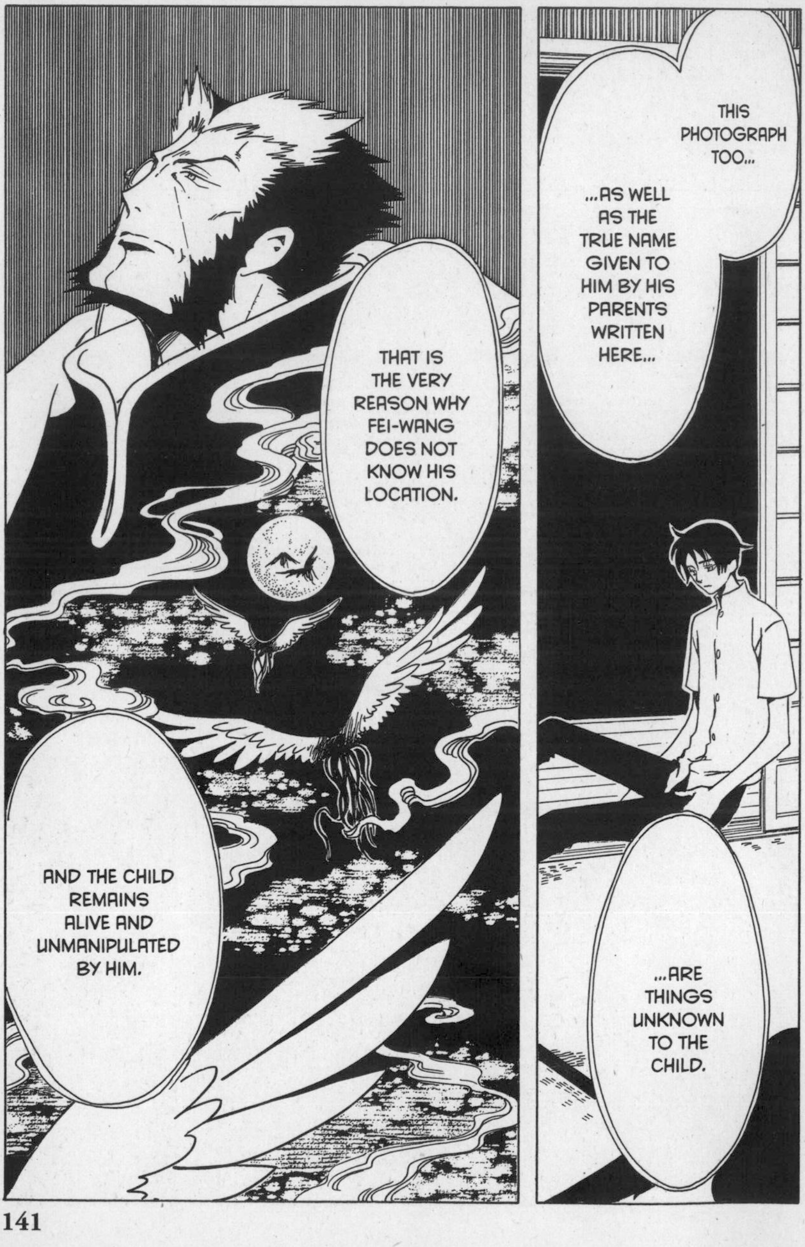
THIS PHOTOGRAPH TOO...
...AS WELL AS THE TRUE NAME GIVEN TO HIM BY HIS PARENTS WRITTEN HERE...
...ARE THINGS UNKNOWN TO THE CHILD.
THAT IS THE VERY REASON WHY FEI-WANG DOES NOT KNOW HIS LOCATION.
AND THE CHILD REMAINS ALIVE AND UNMANIPULATED BY HIM.

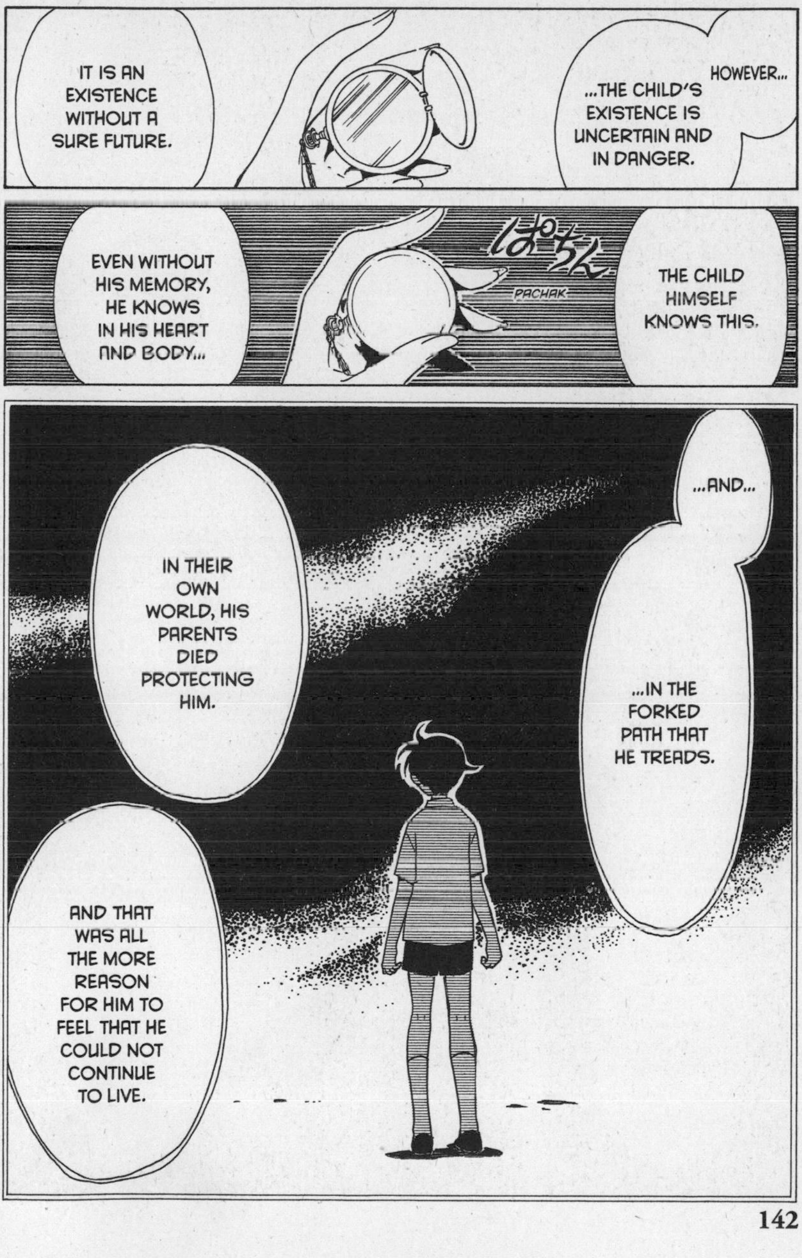
HOWEVER...
...THE CHILD'S EXISTENCE IS UNCERTAIN AND IN DANGER.
IT IS AN EXISTENCE WITHOUT A SURE FUTURE.
THE CHILD HIMSELF KNOWS THIS.
ぱちん
PACHAK
EVEN WITHOUT HIS MEMORY, HE KNOWS IN HIS HEART AND BODY...
...AND...
...IN THE FORKED PATH THAT HE TREADS.
IN THEIR OWN WORLD, HIS PARENTS DIED PROTECTING HIM.
AND THAT WAS ALL THE MORE REASON FOR HIM TO FEEL THAT HE COULD NOT CONTINUE TO LIVE.

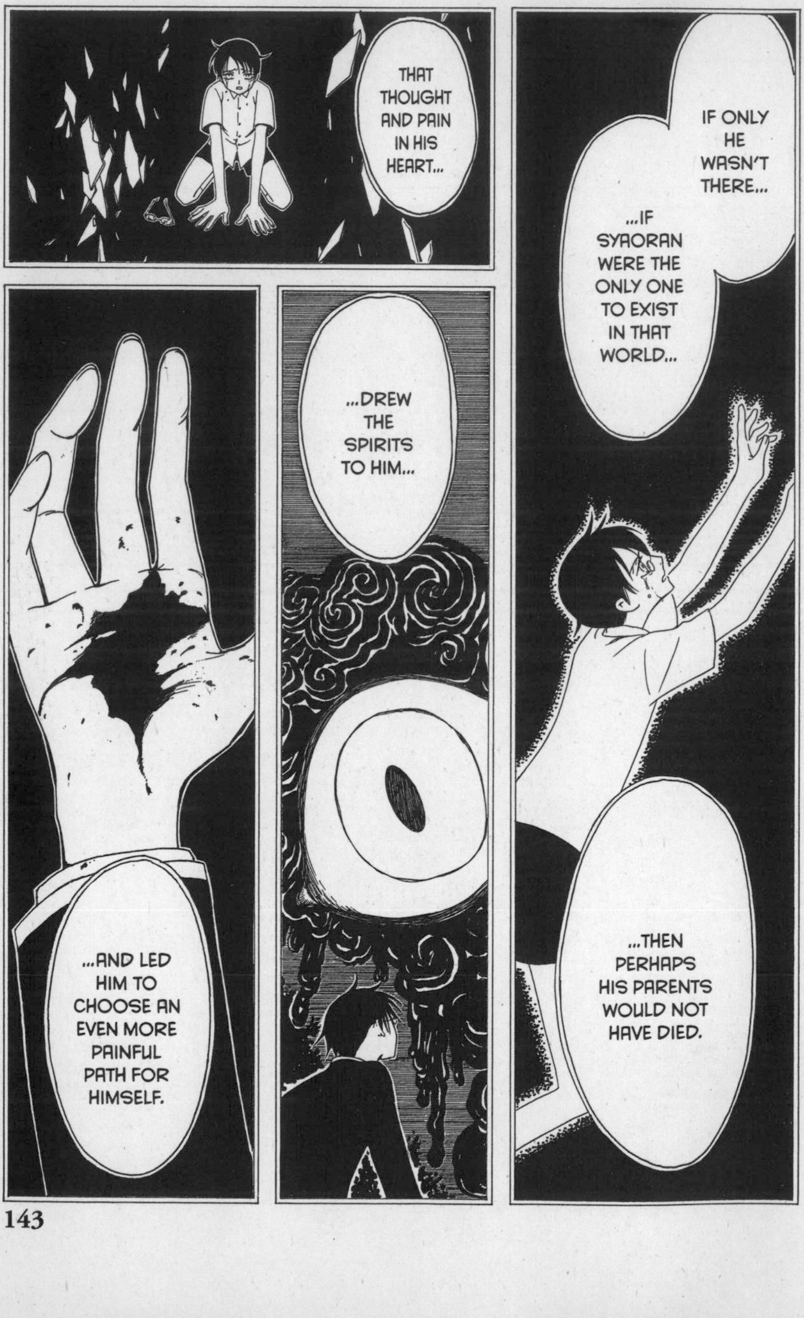
IF ONLY HE WASN'T THERE...
...IF SYAORAN WERE THE ONLY ONE TO EXIST IN THAT WORLD...
...THEN PERHAPS HIS PARENTS WOULD NOT HAVE DIED.
THAT THOUGHT AND PAIN IN HIS HEART...
...DREW THE SPIRITS TO HIM...
...AND LED HIM TO CHOOSE AN EVEN MORE PAINFUL PATH FOR HIMSELF.

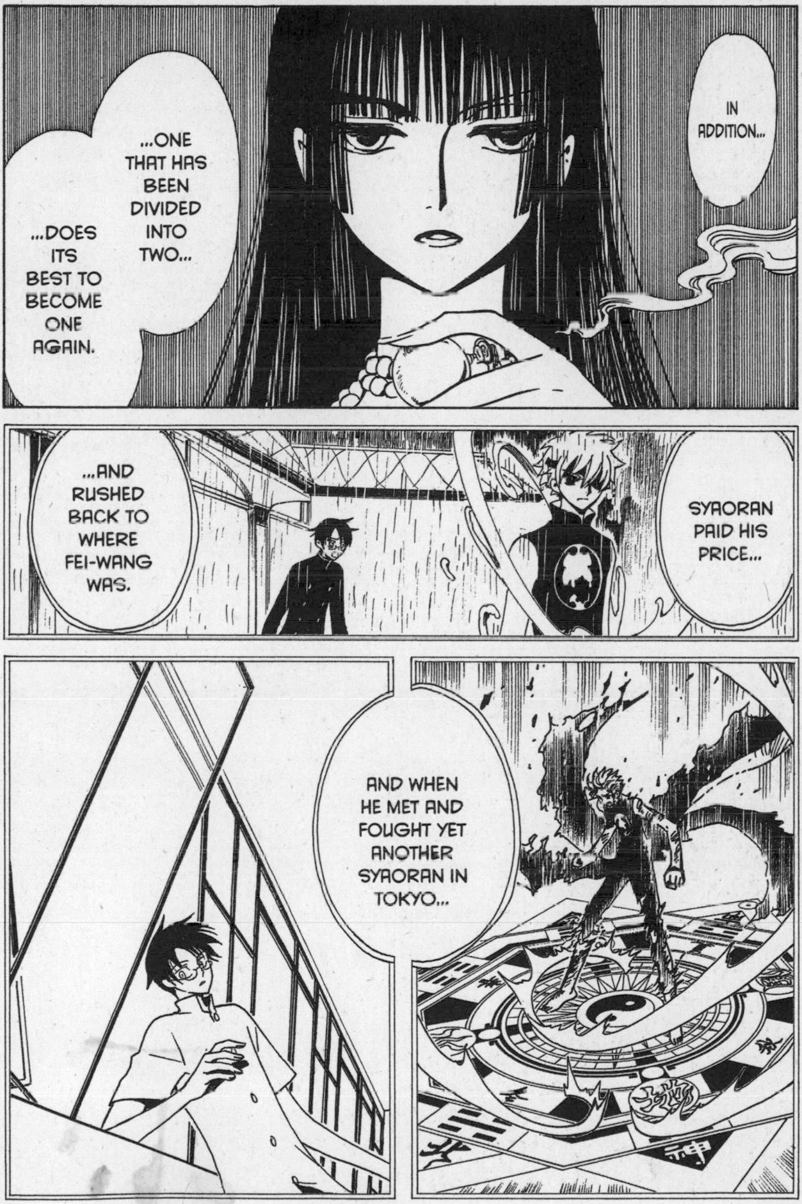
IN ADDITION...
...ONE THAT HAS BEEN DIVIDED INTO TWO...
...DOES ITS BEST TO BECOME ONE AGAIN.
SYAORAN PAID HIS PRICE...
...AND RUSHED BACK TO WHERE FEI-WANG WAS.
AND WHEN HE MET AND FOUGHT YET ANOTHER SYAORAN IN TOKYO...

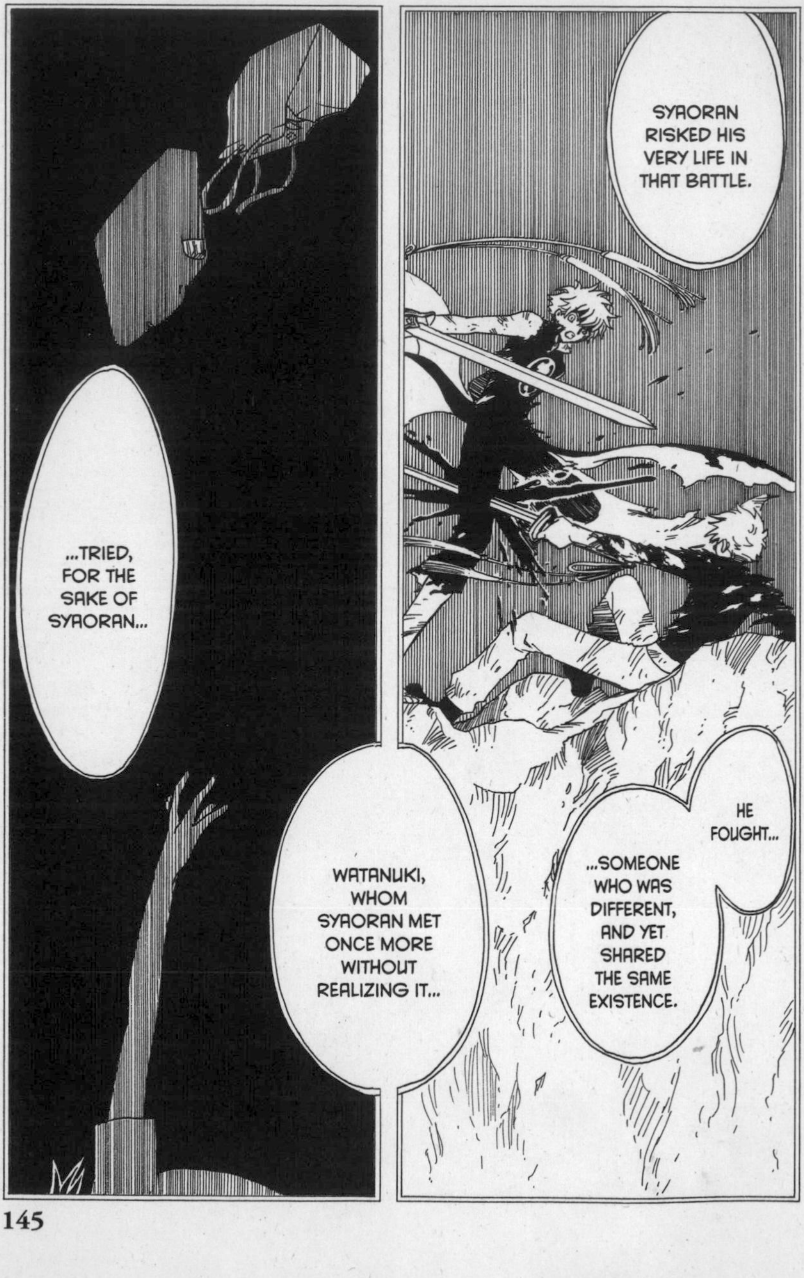
SYAORAN RISKED HIS VERY LIFE IN THAT BATTLE.
HE FOUGHT...
...SOMEONE WHO WAS DIFFERENT, AND YET SHARED THE SAME EXISTENCE.
WATANUKI, WHOM SYAORAN MET ONCE MORE WITHOUT REALIZING IT...
...TRIED, FOR THE SAKE OF SYAORAN...

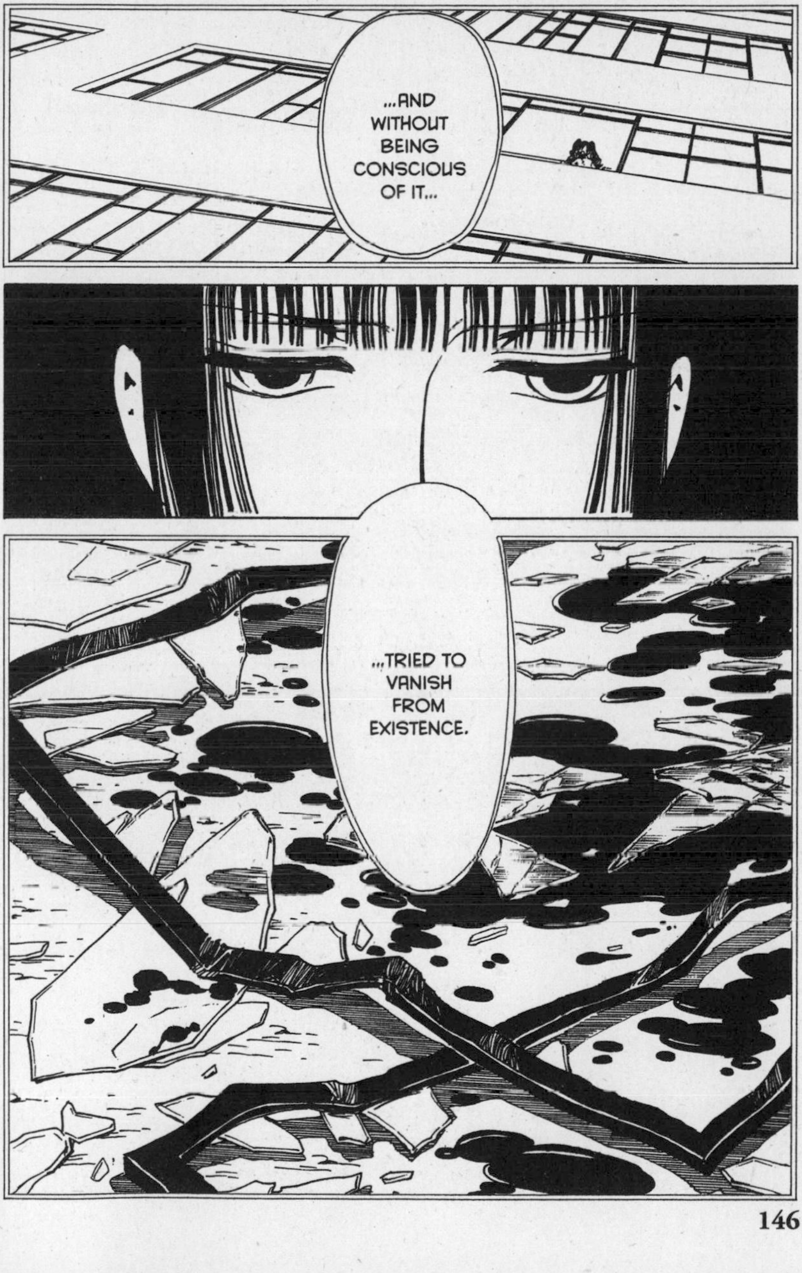
...AND WITHOUT BEING CONSCIOUS OF IT...
...TRIED TO VANISH FROM EXISTENCE.

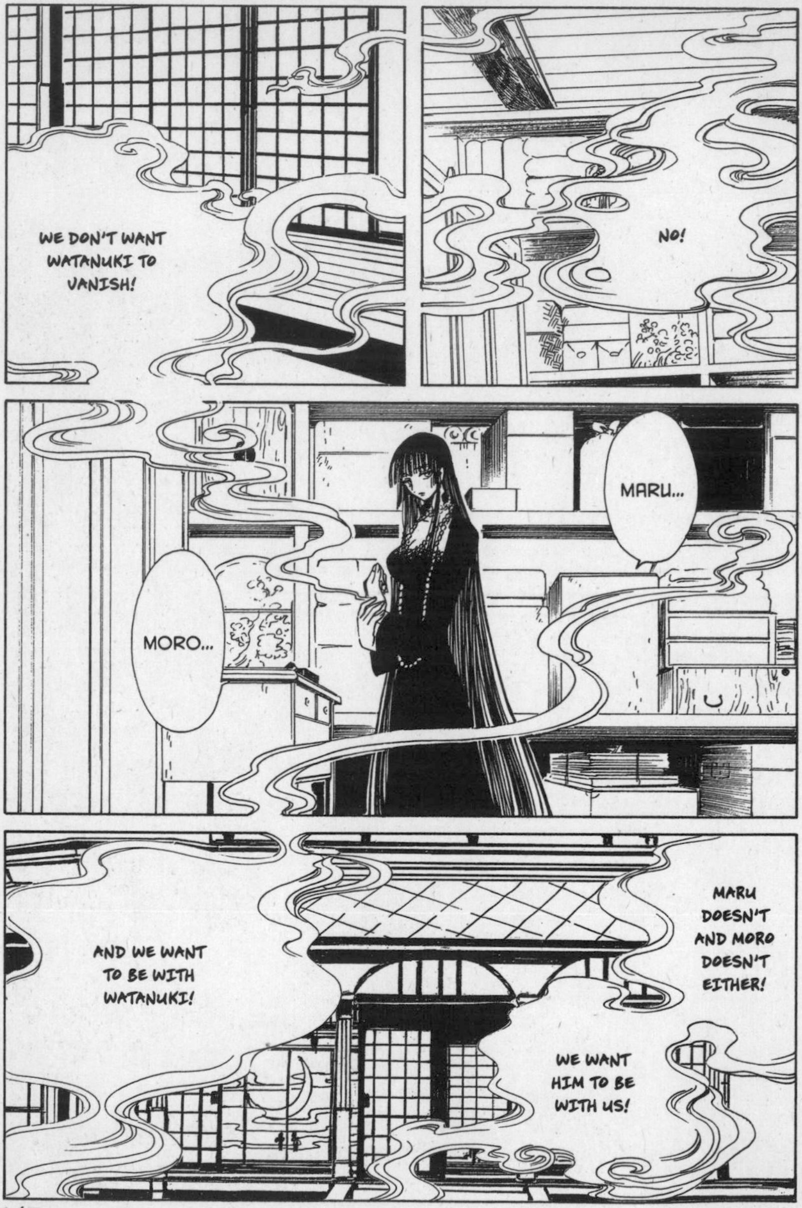
NO!
WE DON'T WANT WATANUKI TO VANISH!
MARU...
MORO...
MARU DOESN'T AND MORO DOESN'T EITHER!
WE WANT HIM TO BE WITH US!
AND WE WANT TO BE WITH WATANUKI!

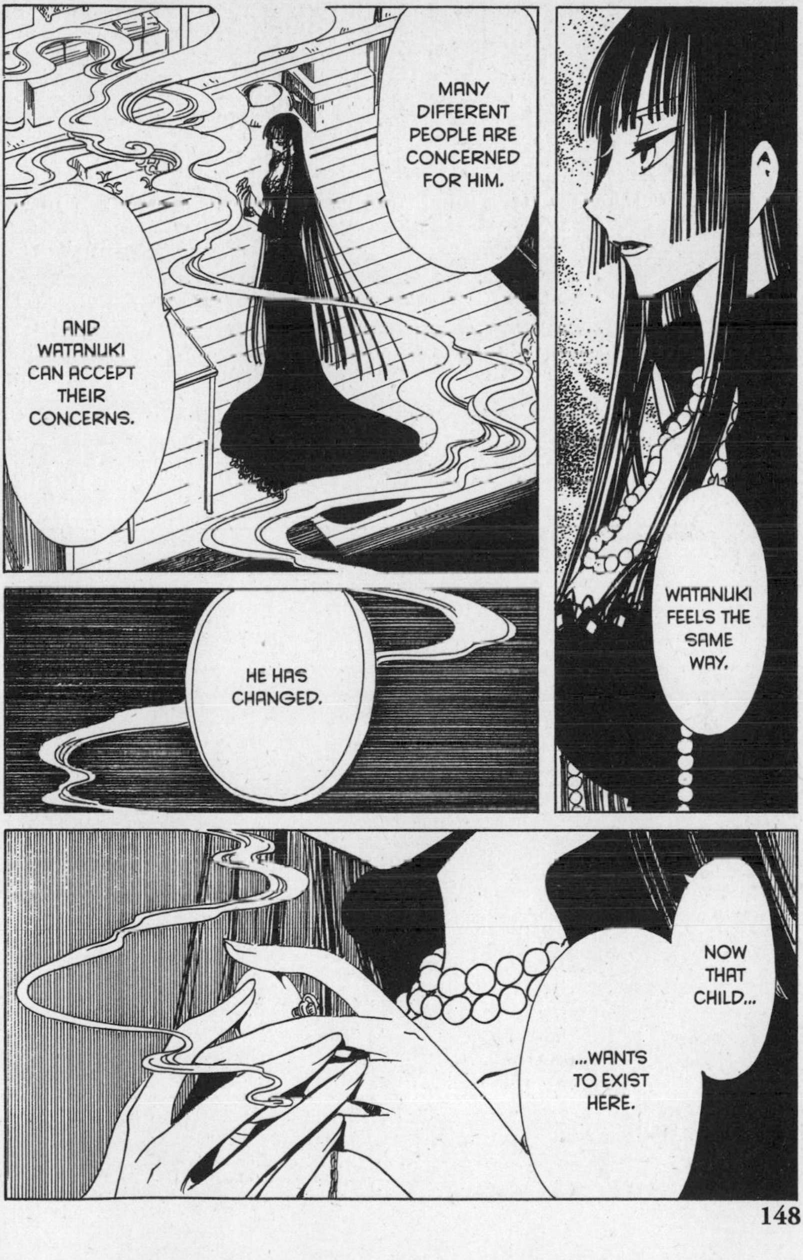
WATANUKI FEELS THE SAME WAY.
MANY DIFFERENT PEOPLE ARE CONCERNED FOR HIM.
AND WATANUKI CAN ACCEPT THEIR CONCERNS.
HE HAS CHANGED.
NOW THAT CHILD...
...WANTS TO EXIST HERE.

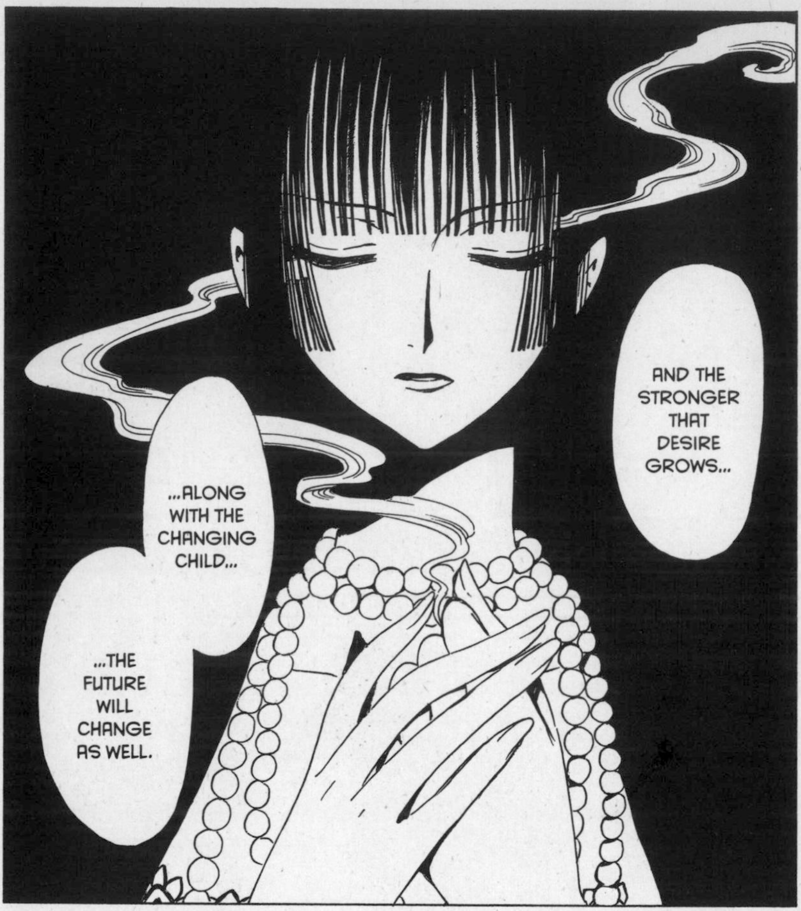
AND THE STRONGER THAT DESIRE GROWS...
...ALONG WITH THE CHANGING CHILD...
...THE FUTURE WILL CHANGE AS WELL.

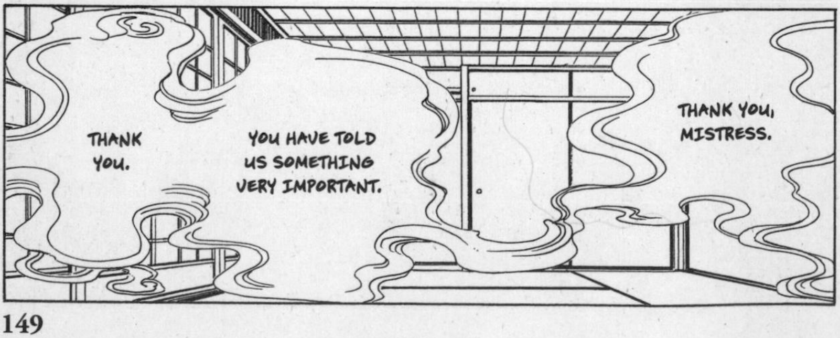
THANK YOU, MISTRESS.
YOU HAVE TOLD US SOMETHING VERY IMPORTANT.
THANK YOU.

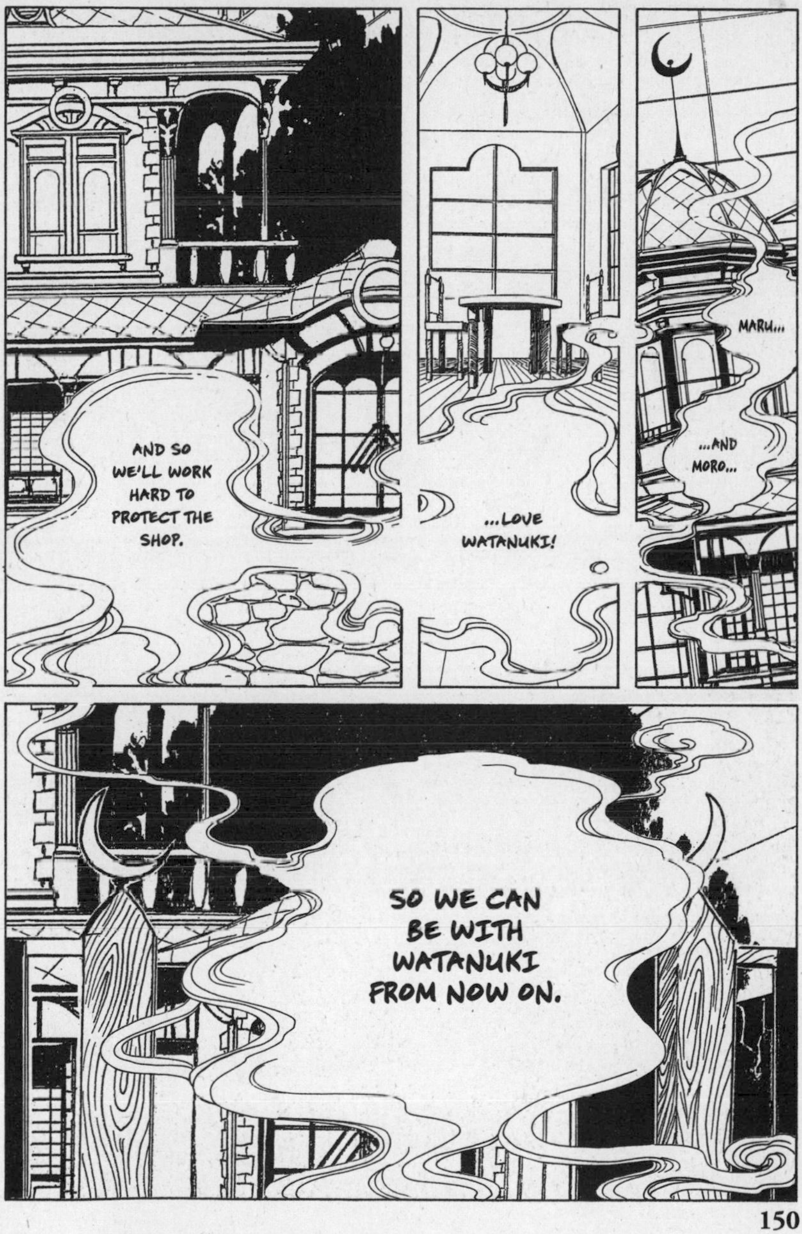
MARU...
...AND MORO...
...LOVE WATANUKI!
AND SO WE'LL WORK HARD TO PROTECT THE SHOP.
SO WE CAN BE WITH WATANUKI FROM NOW ON.

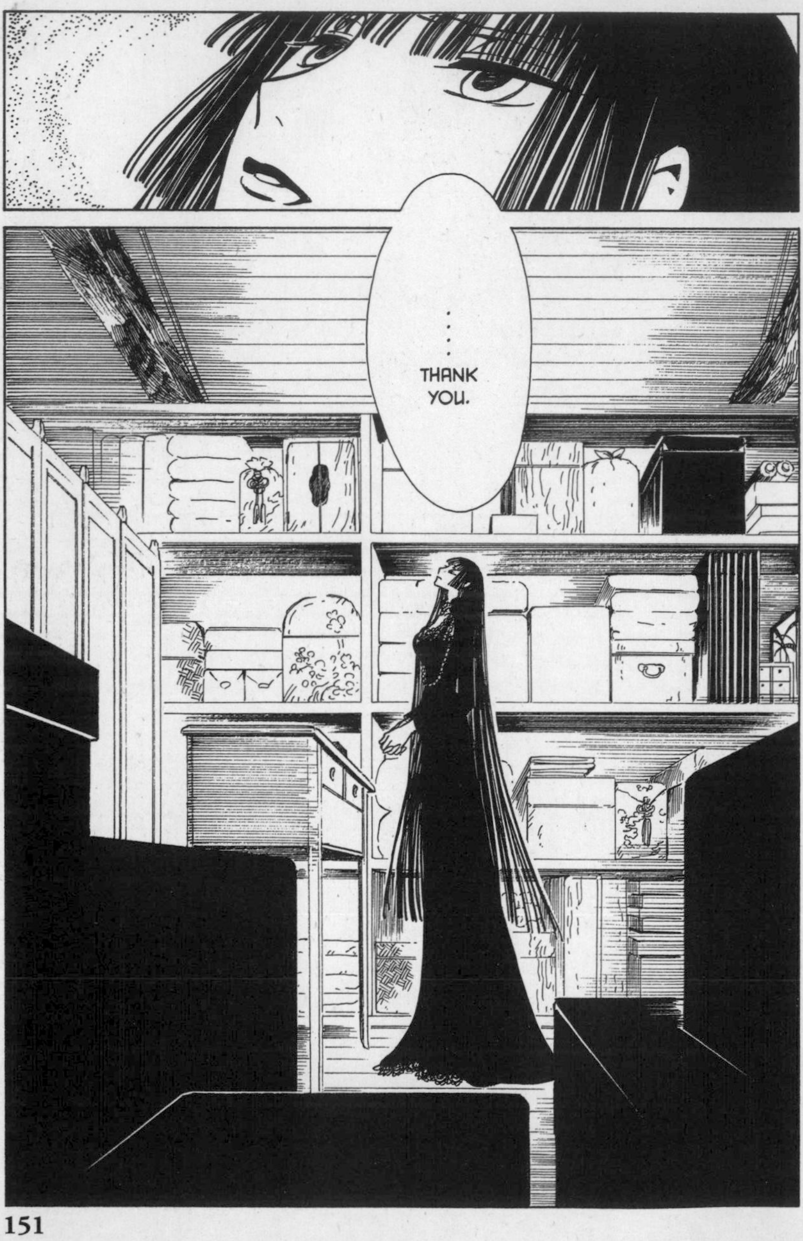
. . . .
THANK YOU.

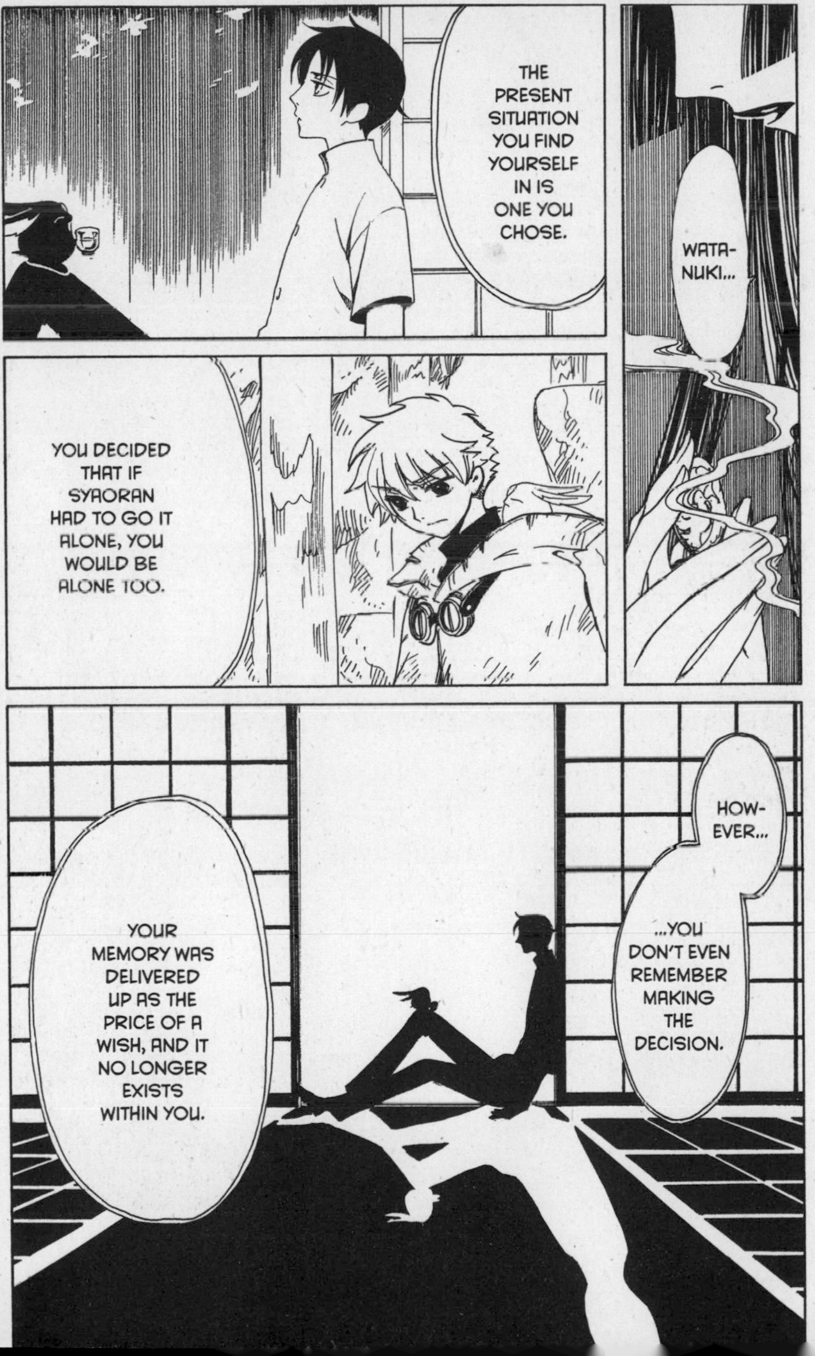
WATA-NUKI...
THE PRESENT SITUATION YOU FIND YOURSELF IN IS ONE YOU CHOSE.
YOU DECIDED THAT IF SYAORAN HAD TO GO IT ALONE, YOU WOULD BE ALONE TOO.
HOW-EVER...
...YOU DON'T EVEN REMEMBER MAKING THE DECISION.
YOUR MEMORY WAS DELIVERED UP AS THE PRICE OF A WISH, AND IT NO LONGER EXISTS WITHIN YOU.

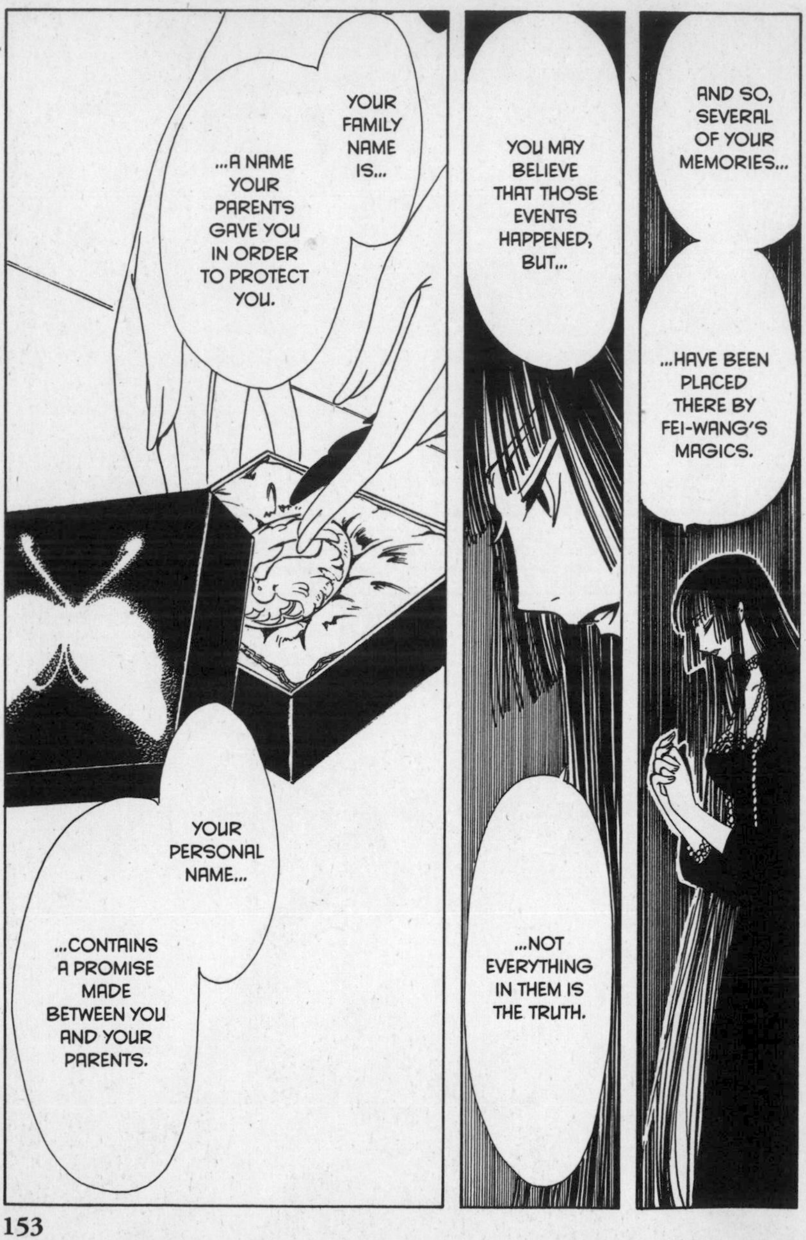
AND SO, SEVERAL OF YOUR MEMORIES...
...HAVE BEEN PLACED THERE BY FEI-WANG'S MAGICS.
YOU MAY BELIEVE THAT THOSE EVENTS HAPPENED, BUT...
...NOT EVERYTHING IN THEM IS THE TRUTH.
YOUR FAMILY NAME IS...
...A NAME YOUR PARENTS GAVE YOU IN ORDER TO PROTECT YOU.
YOUR PERSONAL NAME...
...CONTAINS A PROMISE MADE BETWEEN YOU AND YOUR PARENTS.

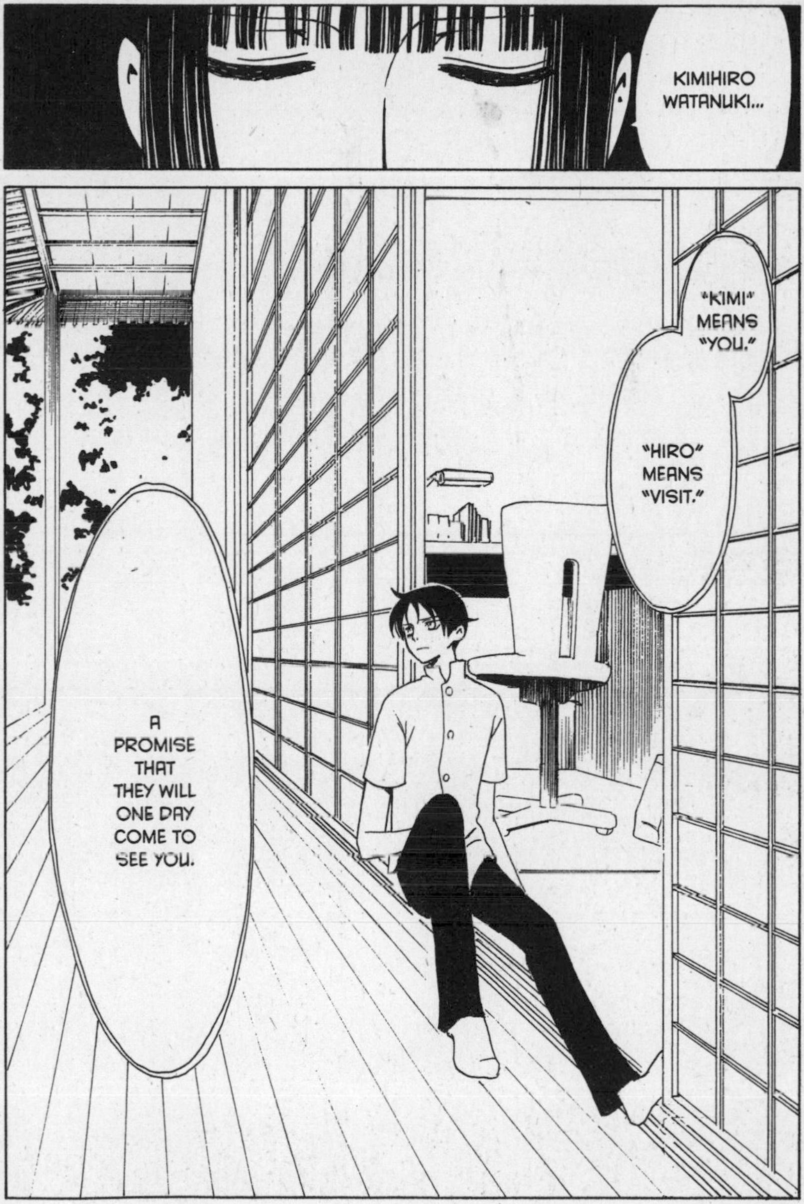
KIMIHIRO WATANUKI...
"KIMI" MEANS "YOU."
"HIRO" MEANS "VISIT."
A PROMISE THAT THEY WILL ONE DAY COME TO SEE YOU.

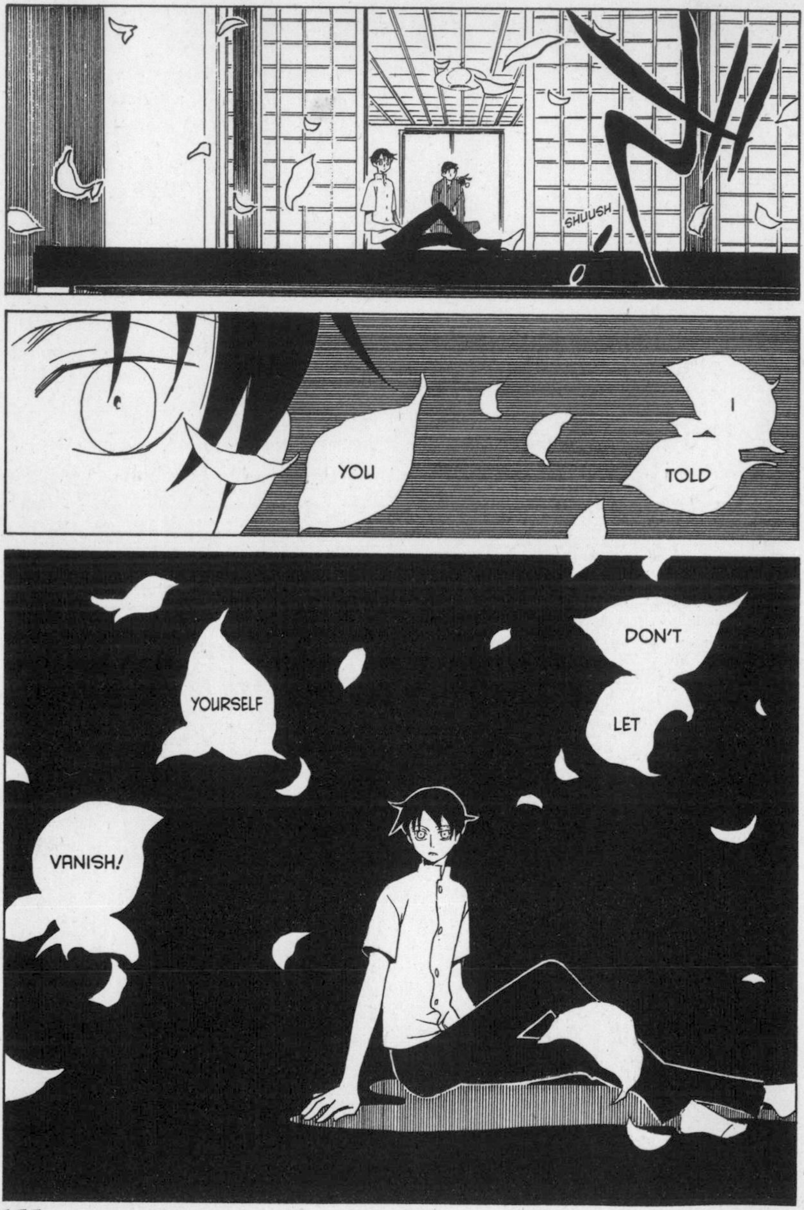
SHUUSH
I
TOLD
YOU
DON'T
LET
YOURSELF
VANISH!

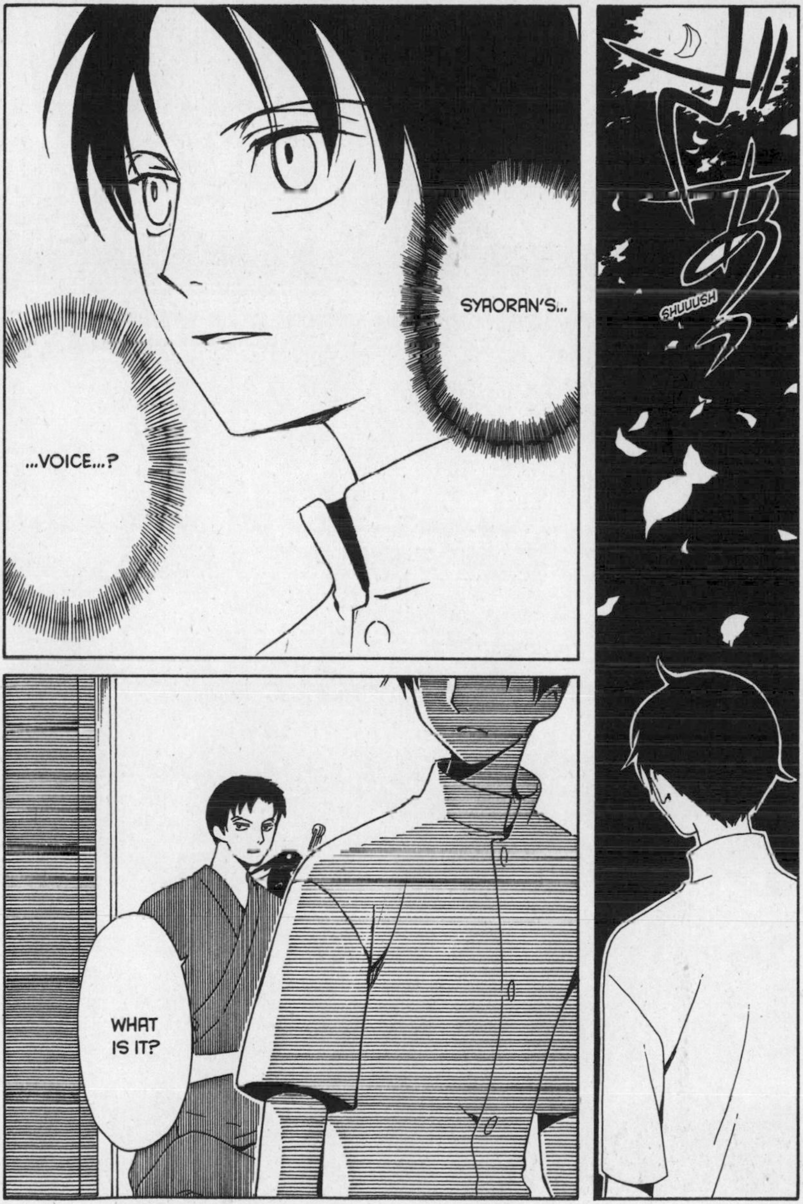
SHUUUSH
SYAORAN'S...
...VOICE...?
WHAT IS IT?

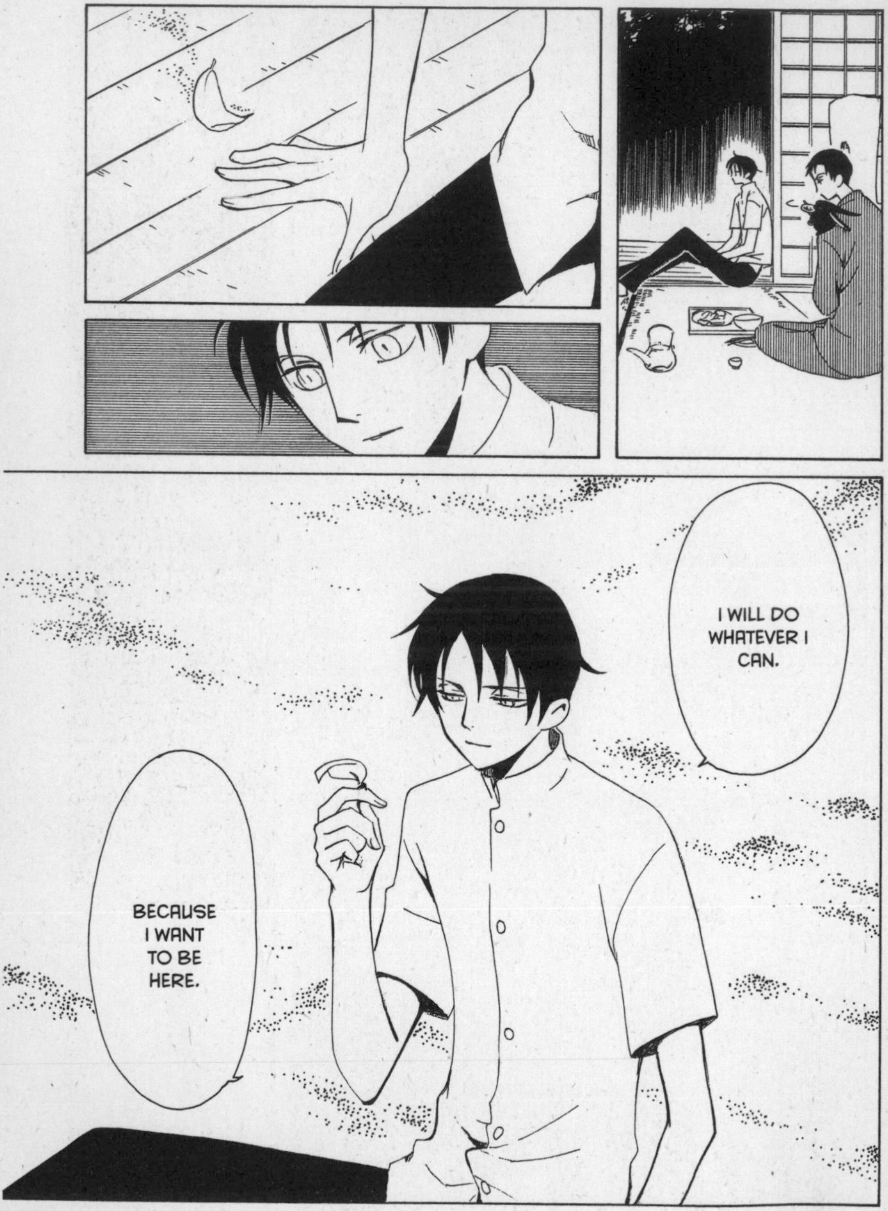
I WILL DO WHATEVER I CAN.
BECAUSE I WANT TO BE HERE.

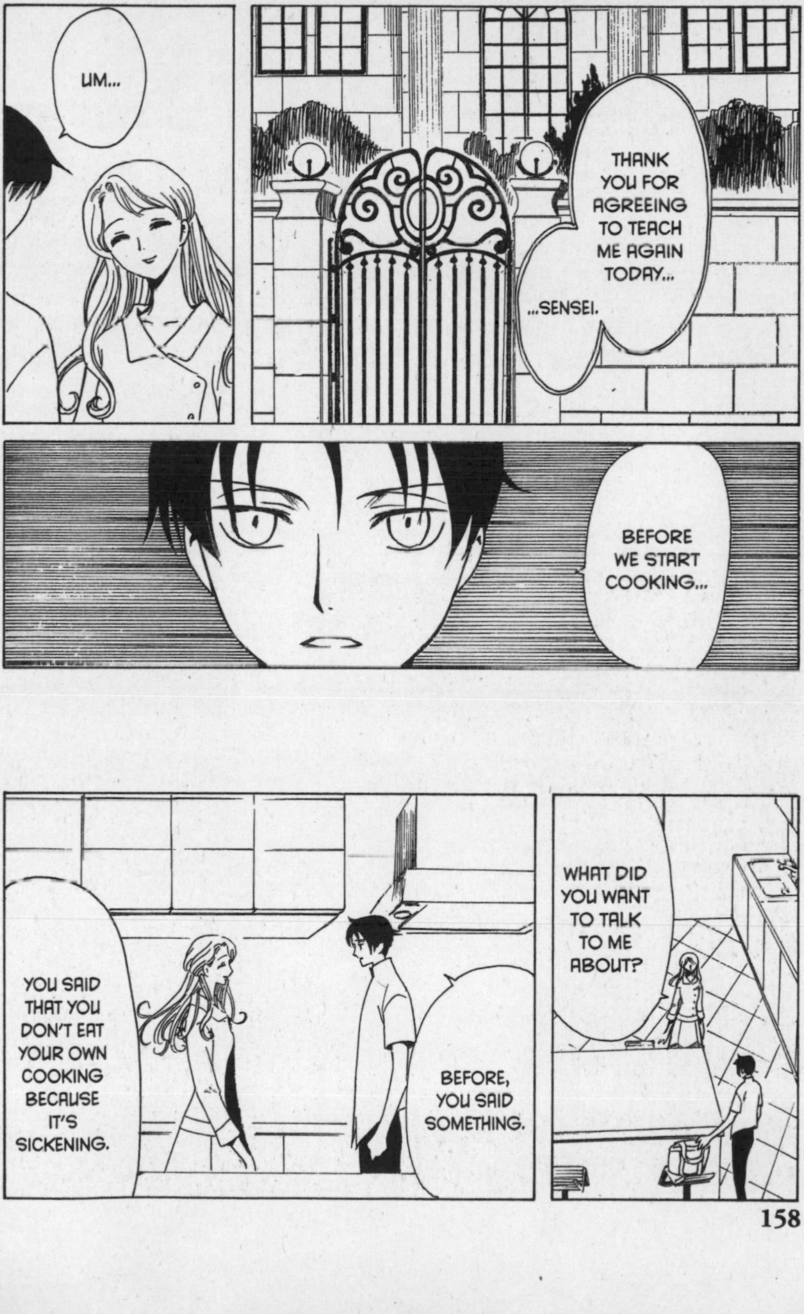
THANK YOU FOR AGREEING TO TEACH ME AGAIN TODAY...
...SENSEI.
UM...
BEFORE WE START COOKING...
WHAT DID YOU WANT TO TALK TO ME ABOUT?
BEFORE, YOU SAID SOMETHING.
YOU SAID THAT YOU DON'T EAT YOUR OWN COOKING BECAUSE IT'S SICKENING.

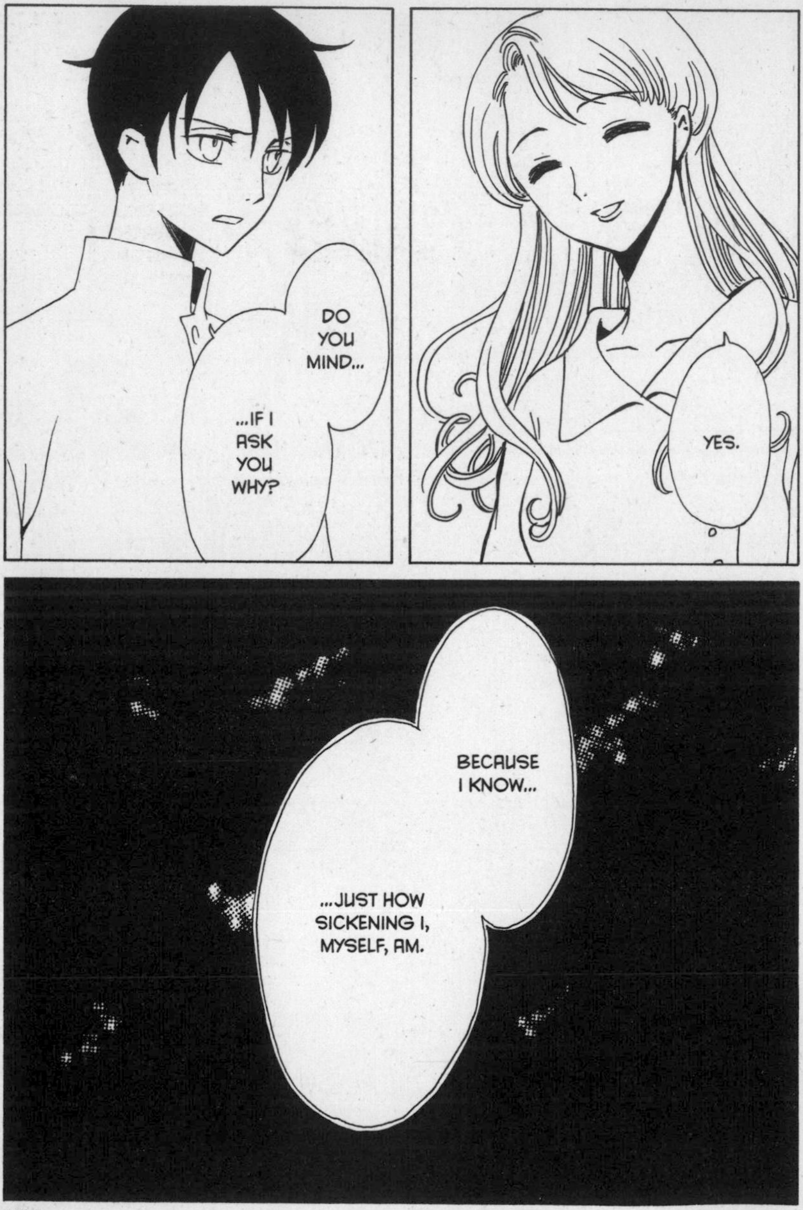
YES.
DO YOU MIND...
...IF I ASK YOU WHY?
BECAUSE I KNOW...
...JUST HOW SICKENING I, MYSELF, AM.

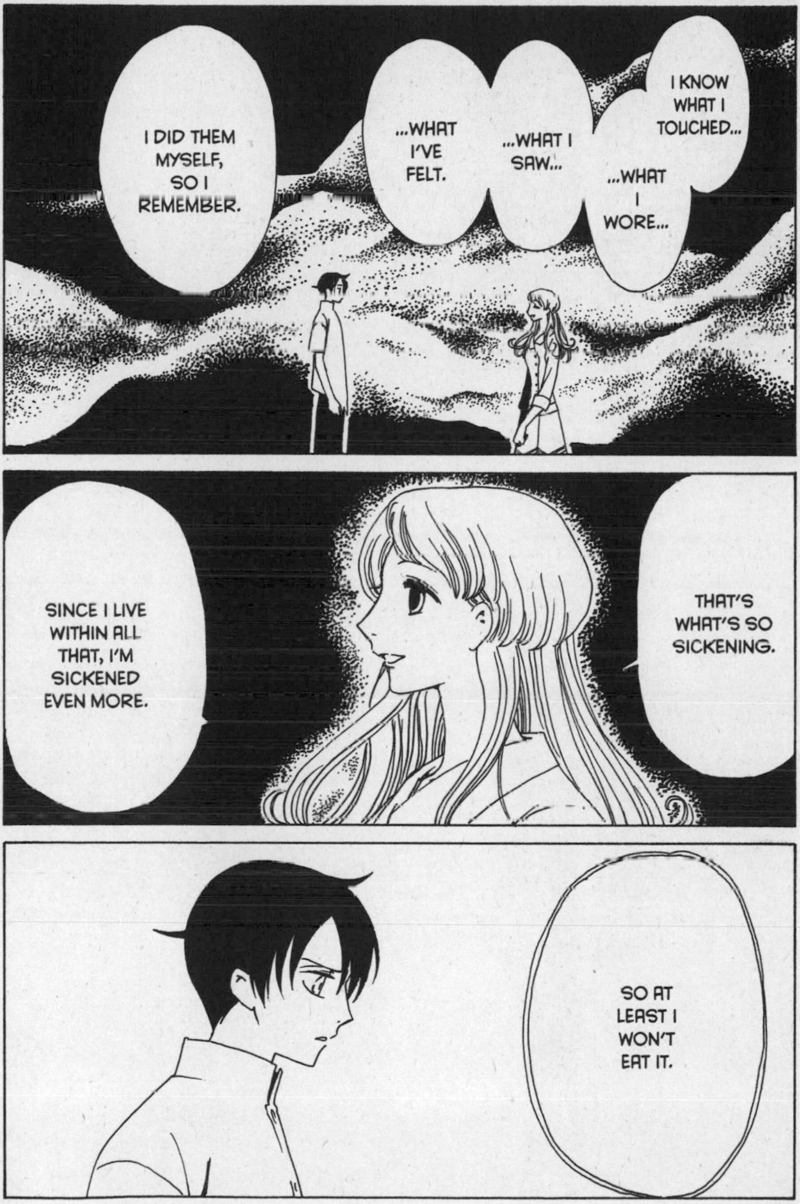
I KNOW WHAT I TOUCHED...
...WHAT I WORE...
...WHAT I SAW...
...WHAT I'VE FELT.
I DID THEM MYSELF, SO I REMEMBER.
THAT'S WHAT'S SO SICKENING.
SINCE I LIVE WITHIN ALL THAT, I'M SICKENED EVEN MORE.
SO AT LEAST I WON'T EAT IT.

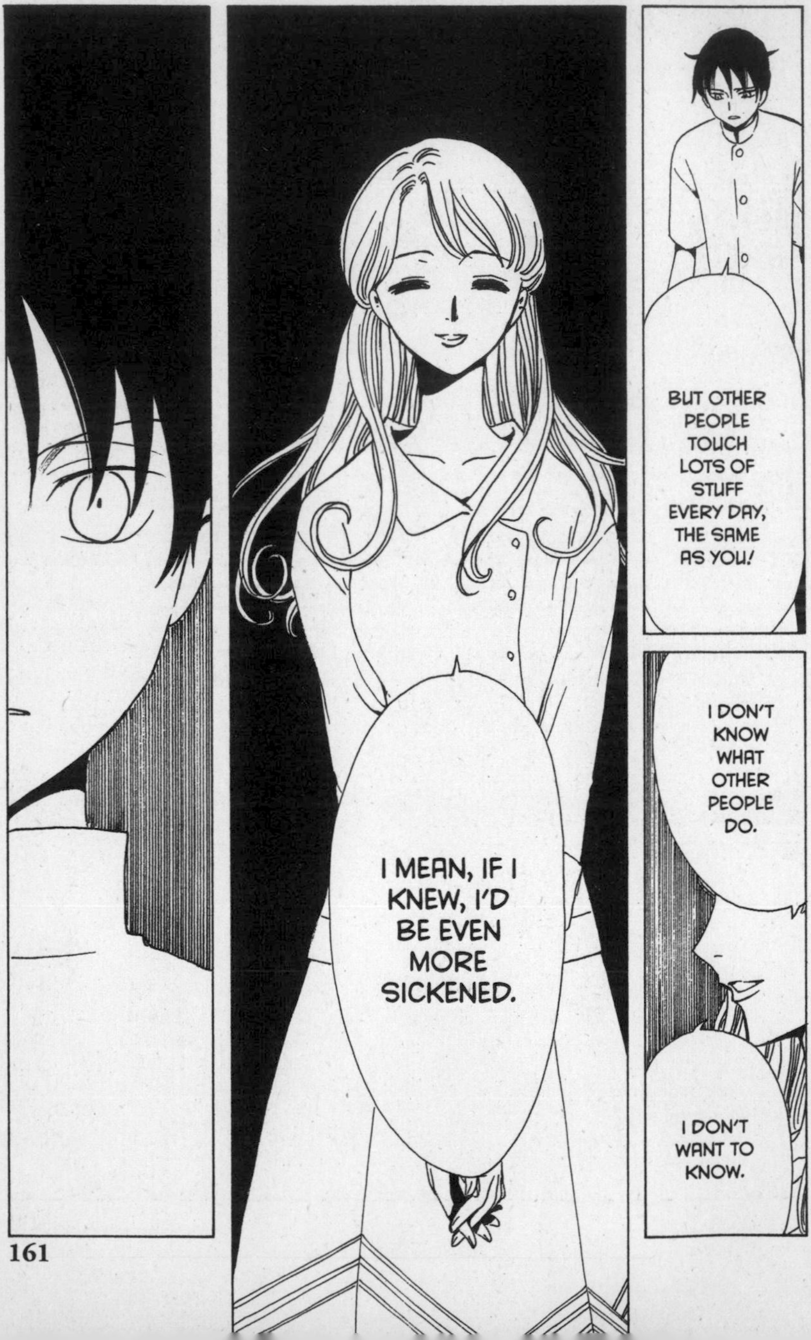
BUT OTHER PEOPLE TOUCH LOTS OF STUFF EVERY DAY, THE SAME AS YOU!
I DON'T KNOW WHAT OTHER PEOPLE DO.
I DON'T WANT TO KNOW.
I MEAN, IF I KNEW, I'D BE EVEN MORE SICKENED.

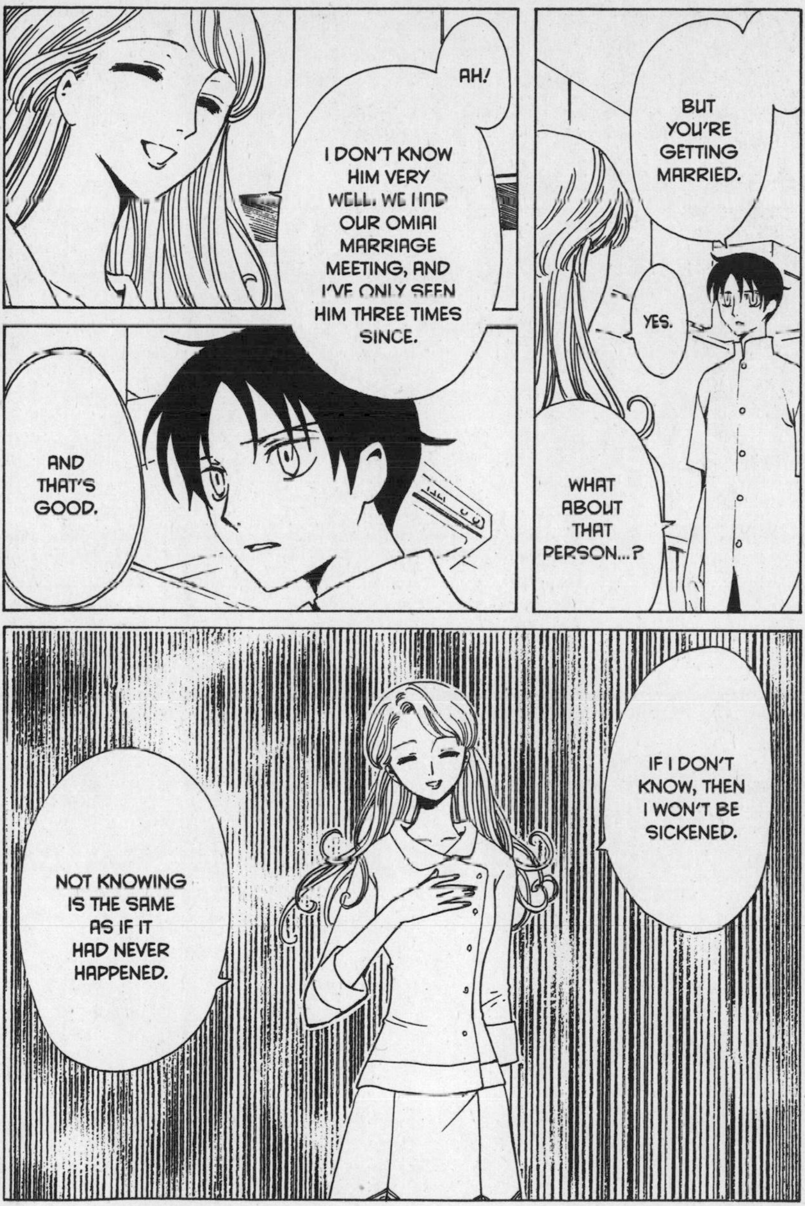
BUT YOU'RE GETTING MARRIED.
YES.
WHAT ABOUT THAT PERSON...?
AH!
I DON'T KNOW HIM VERY WELL. WE HAD OUR OMIAI MARRIAGE MEETING, AND I'VE ONLY SEEN HIM THREE TIMES SINCE.
AND THAT'S GOOD.
IF I DON'T KNOW, THEN I WON'T BE SICKENED.
NOT KNOWING IS THE SAME AS IF IT HAD NEVER HAPPENED.

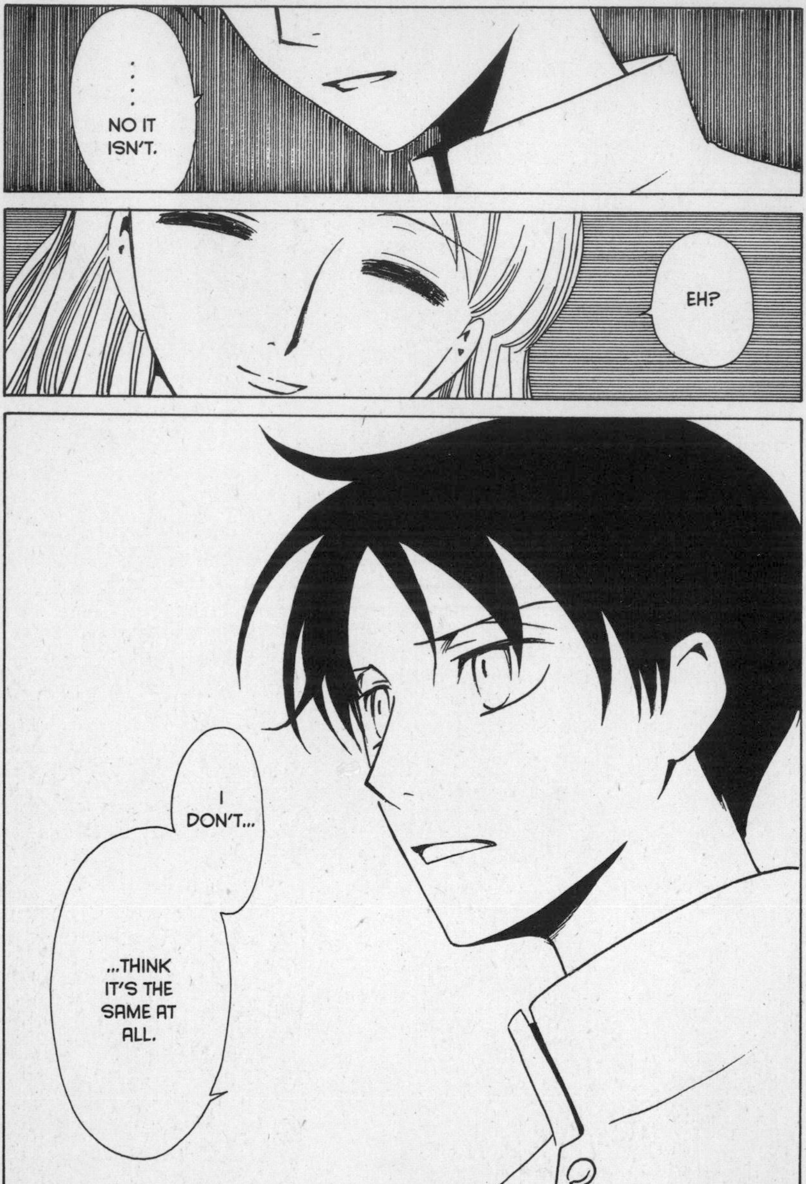

. . . . NO IT ISN'T.
EH?
I DON'T...
...THINK IT'S THE SAME AT ALL.

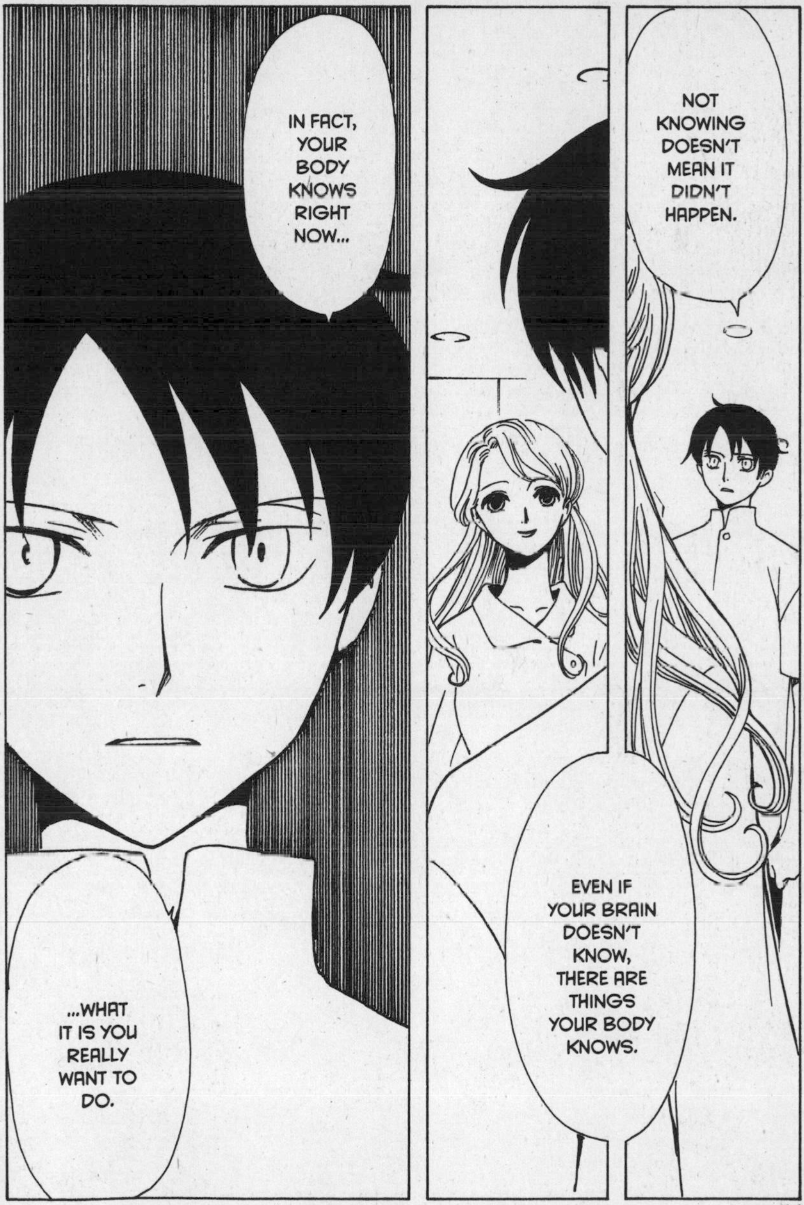
NOT KNOWING DOESN'T MEAN IT DIDN'T HAPPEN.
EVEN IF YOUR BRAIN DOESN'T KNOW, THERE ARE THINGS YOUR BODY KNOWS.
IN FACT, YOUR BODY KNOWS RIGHT NOW...
...WHAT IT IS YOU REALLY WANT TO DO.

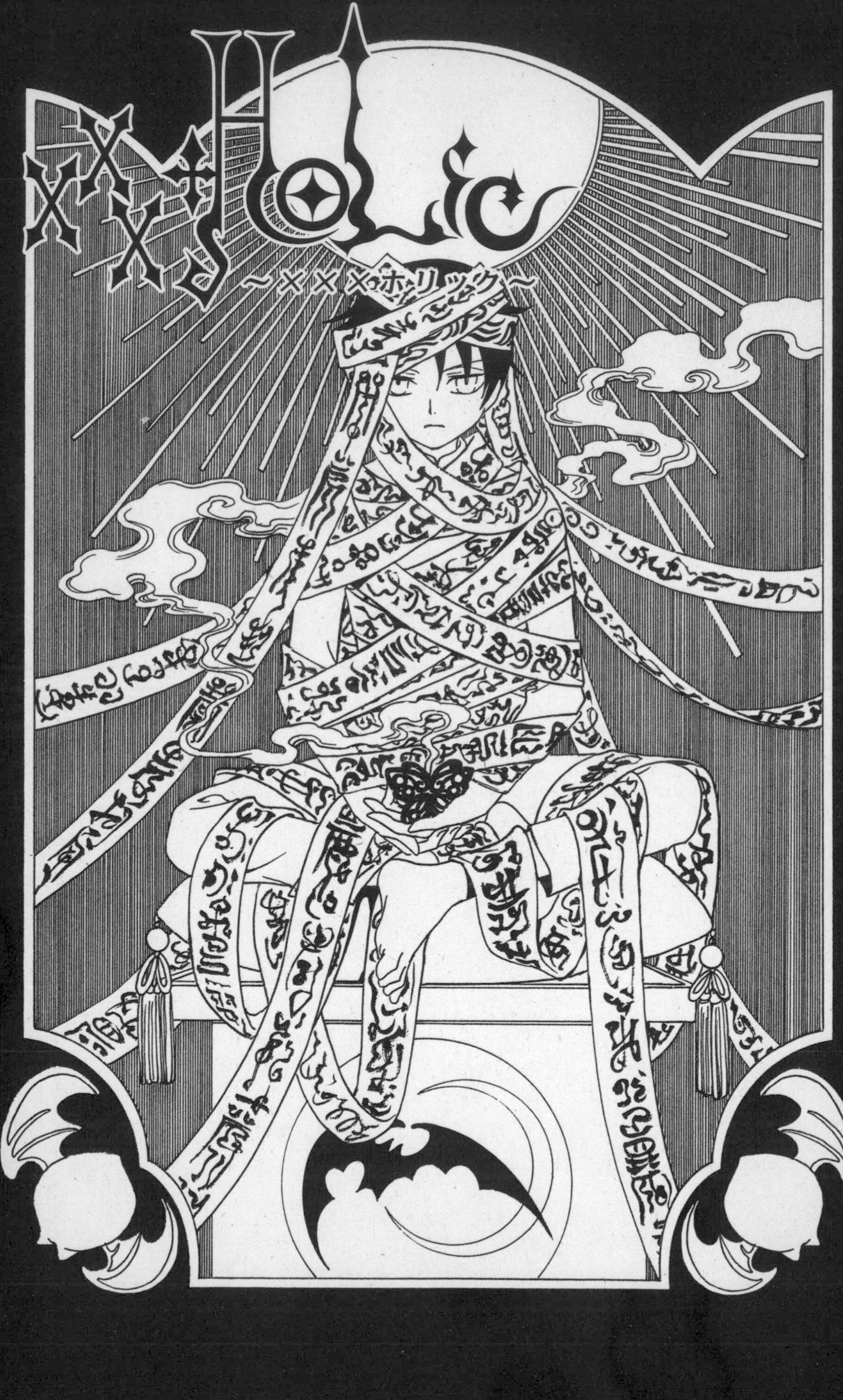
xxxHOLiC
〜×××ホリック〜

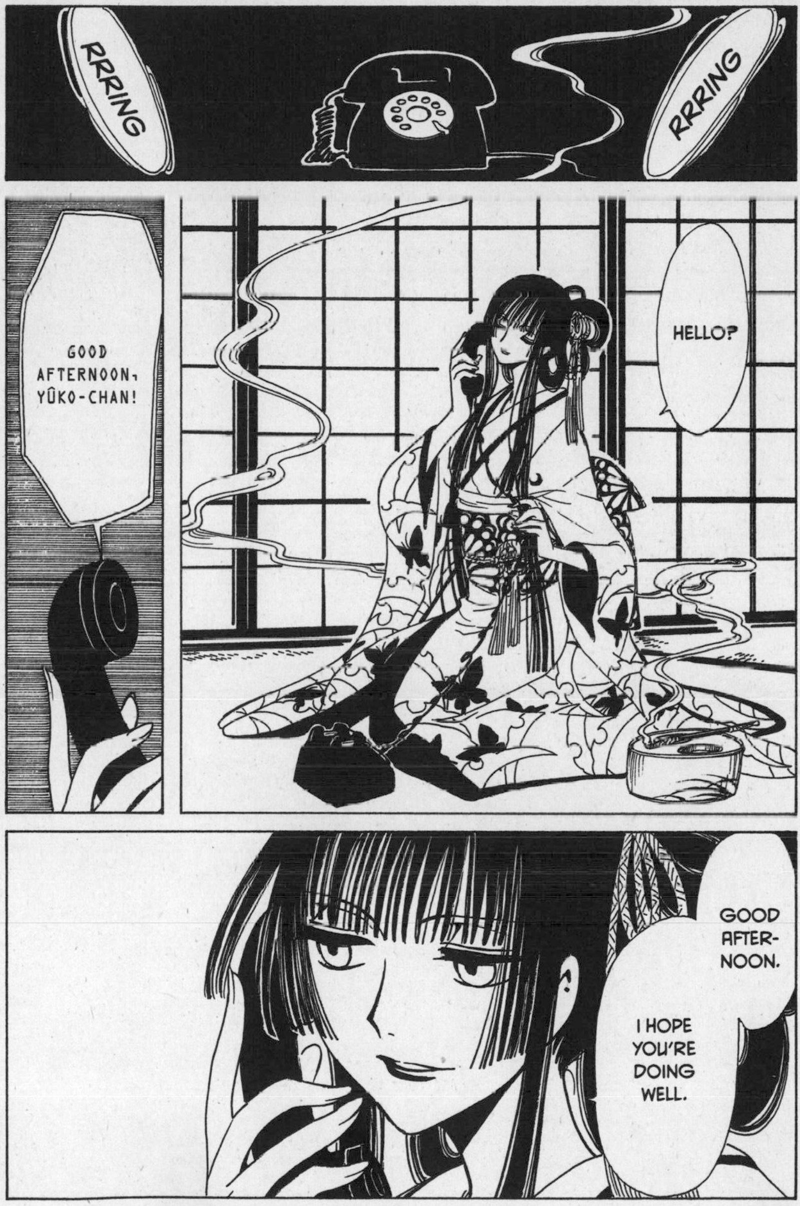
RRRING
RRRING
HELLO?
GOOD AFTERNOON, YÛKO-CHAN!
GOOD AFTER-NOON.
I HOPE YOU'RE DOING WELL.

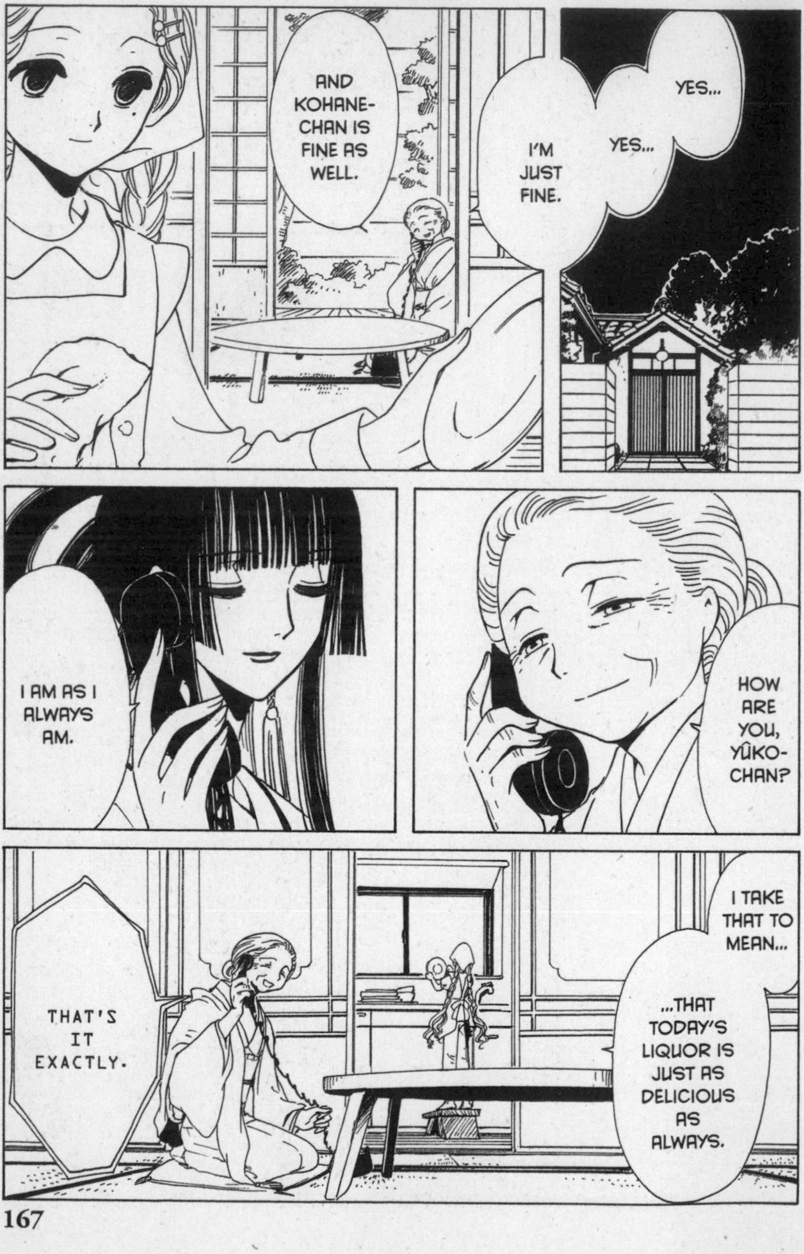
YES...
YES...
I'M JUST FINE.
AND KOHANE-CHAN IS FINE AS WELL.
HOW ARE YOU, YÛKO-CHAN?
I AM AS I ALWAYS AM.
I TAKE THAT TO MEAN...
...THAT TODAY'S LIQUOR IS JUST AS DELICIOUS AS ALWAYS.
THAT'S IT EXACTLY.

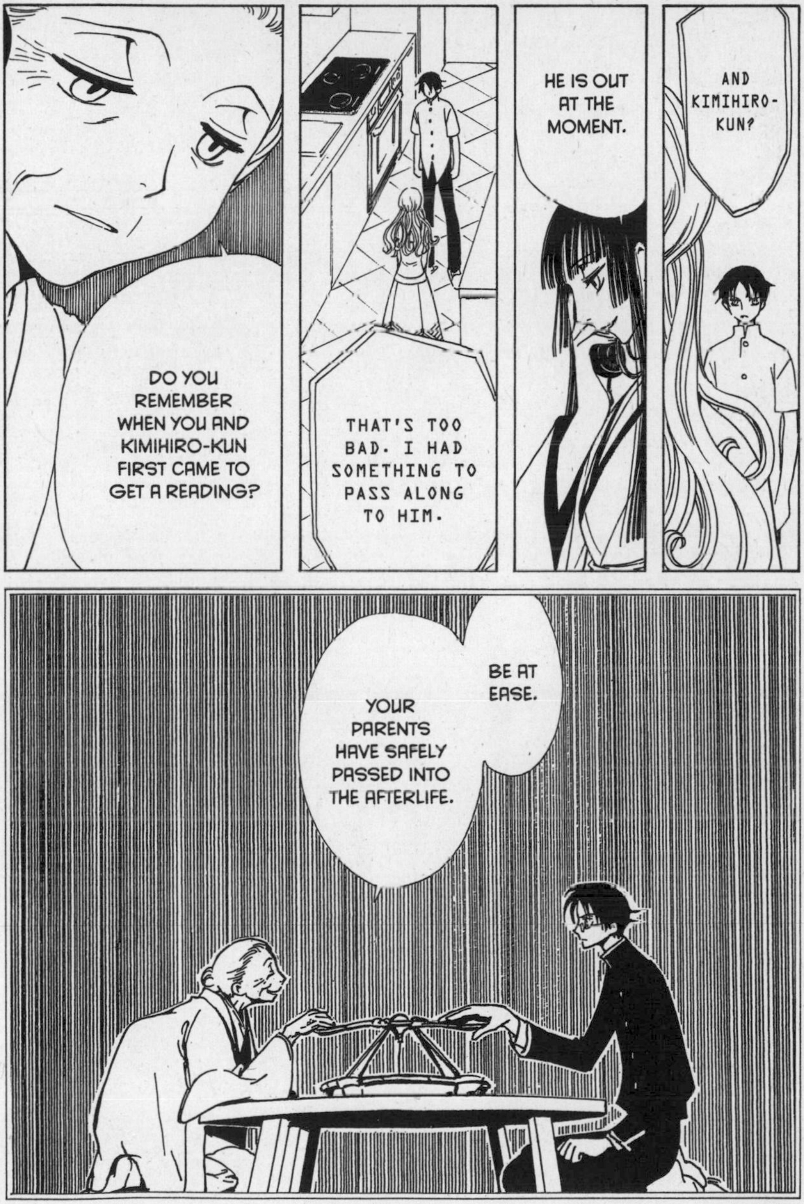
AND KIMIHIRO-KUN?
HE IS OUT AT THE MOMENT.
THAT'S TOO BAD. I HAD SOMETHING TO PASS ALONG TO HIM.
DO YOU REMEMBER WHEN YOU AND KIMIHIRO-KUN FIRST CAME TO GET A READING?
BE AT EASE.
YOUR PARENTS HAVE SAFELY PASSED INTO THE AFTERLIFE.

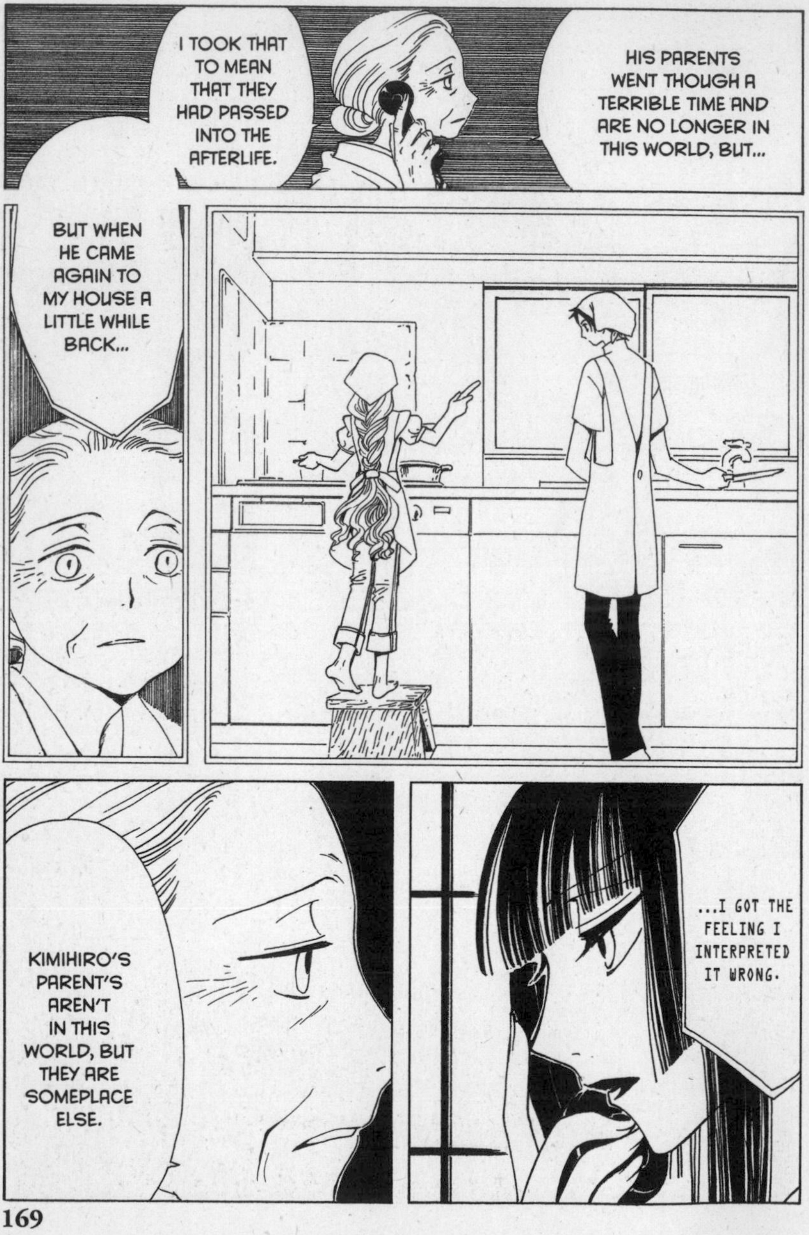
HIS PARENTS WENT THOUGH A TERRIBLE TIME AND ARE NO LONGER IN THIS WORLD, BUT...
I TOOK THAT TO MEAN THAT THEY HAD PASSED INTO THE AFTERLIFE.
BUT WHEN HE CAME AGAIN TO MY HOUSE A LITTLE WHILE BACK...
...I GOT THE FEELING I INTERPRETED IT WRONG.
KIMIHIRO'S PARENT'S AREN'T IN THIS WORLD, BUT THEY ARE SOMEPLACE ELSE.

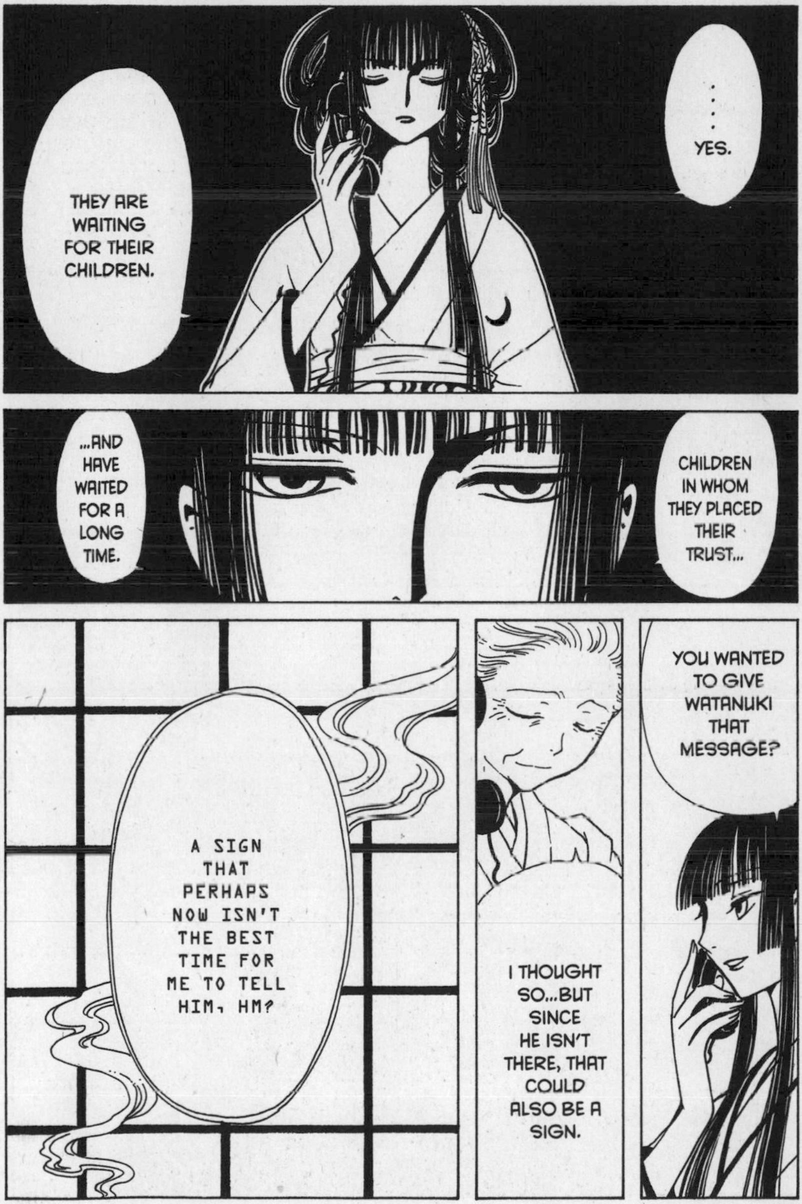
....YES.
THEY ARE WAITING FOR THEIR CHILDREN.
CHILDREN IN WHOM THEY PLACED THEIR TRUST...
...AND HAVE WAITED FOR A LONG TIME.
YOU WANTED TO GIVE WATANUKI THAT MESSAGE?
I THOUGHT SO...BUT SINCE HE ISN'T THERE, THAT COULD ALSO BE A SIGN.
A SIGN THAT PERHAPS NOW ISN'T THE BEST TIME FOR ME TO TELL HIM, HM?

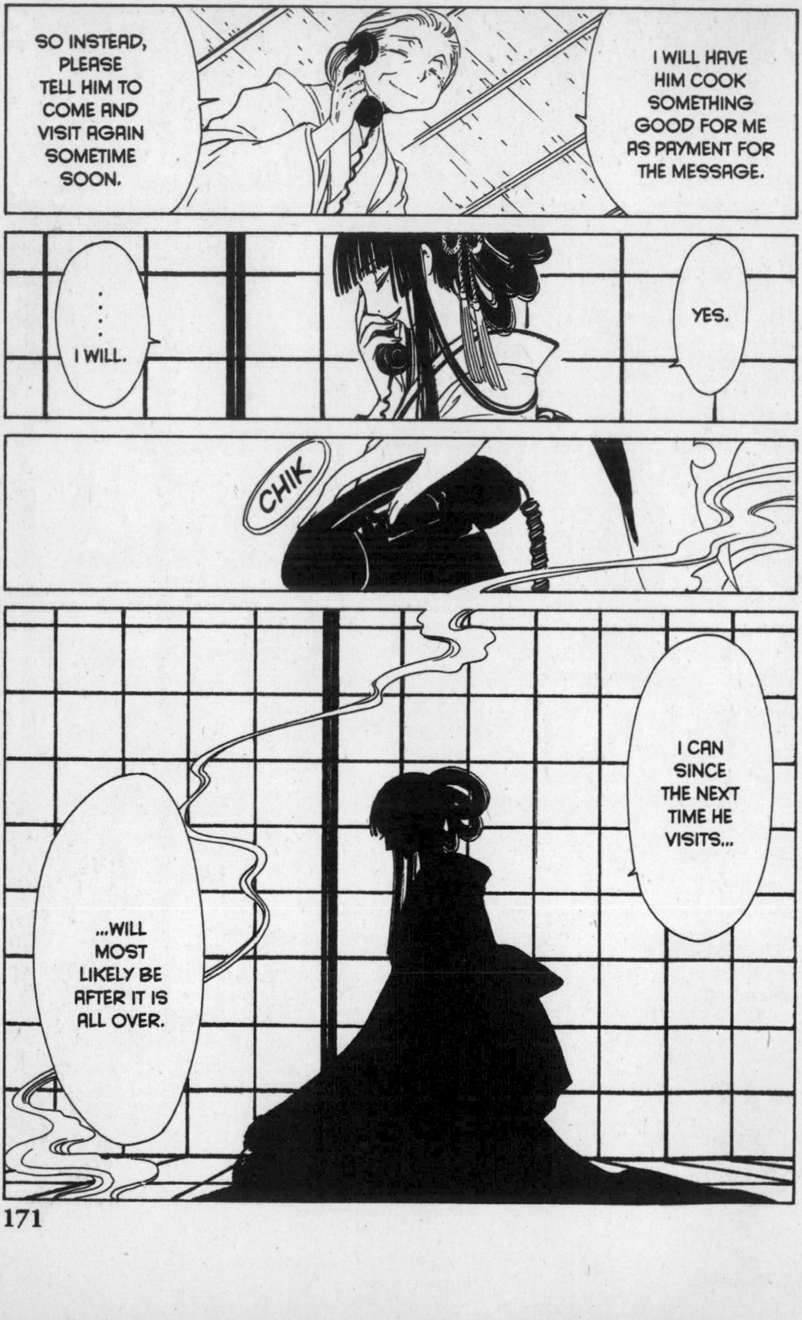
I WILL HAVE HIM COOK SOMETHING GOOD FOR ME AS PAYMENT FOR THE MESSAGE.
SO INSTEAD, PLEASE TELL HIM TO COME AND VISIT AGAIN SOMETIME SOON.
YES.
. . . . I WILL.
CHIK
I CAN SINCE THE NEXT TIME HE VISITS...
...WILL MOST LIKELY BE AFTER IT IS ALL OVER.

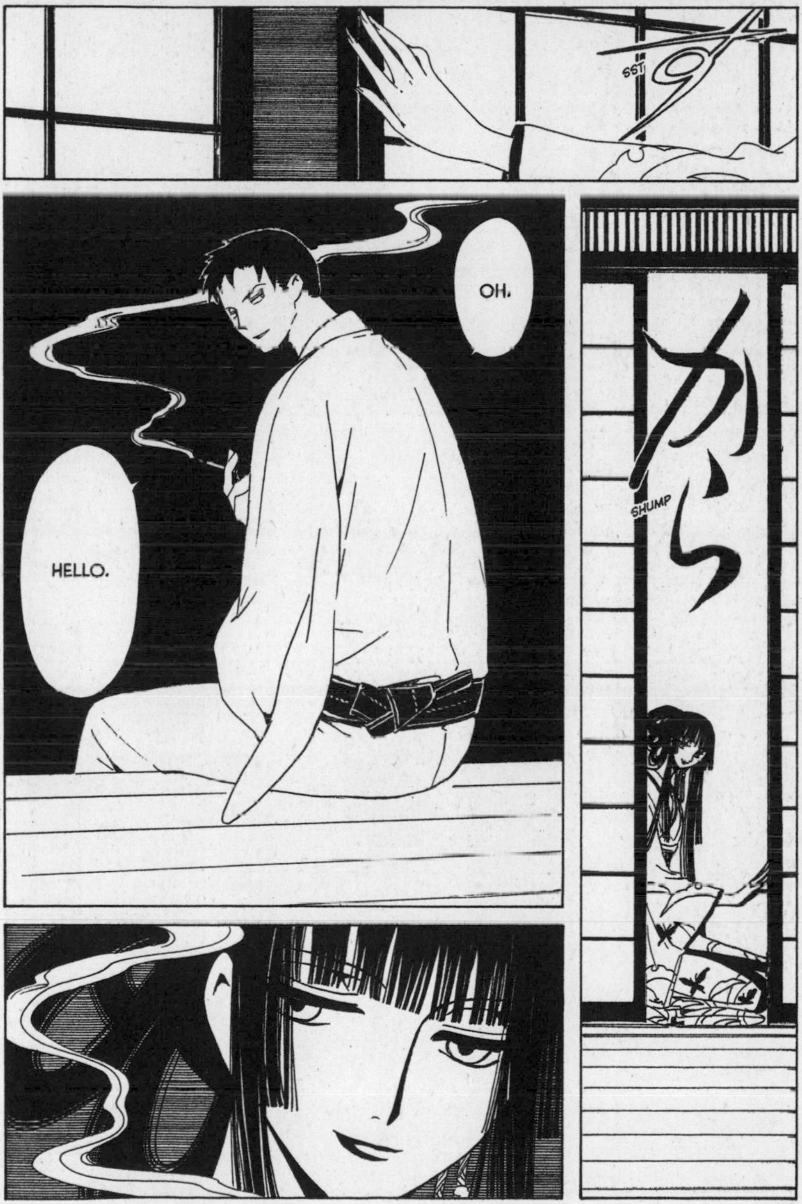
SST
から
SHUMP
OH.
HELLO.

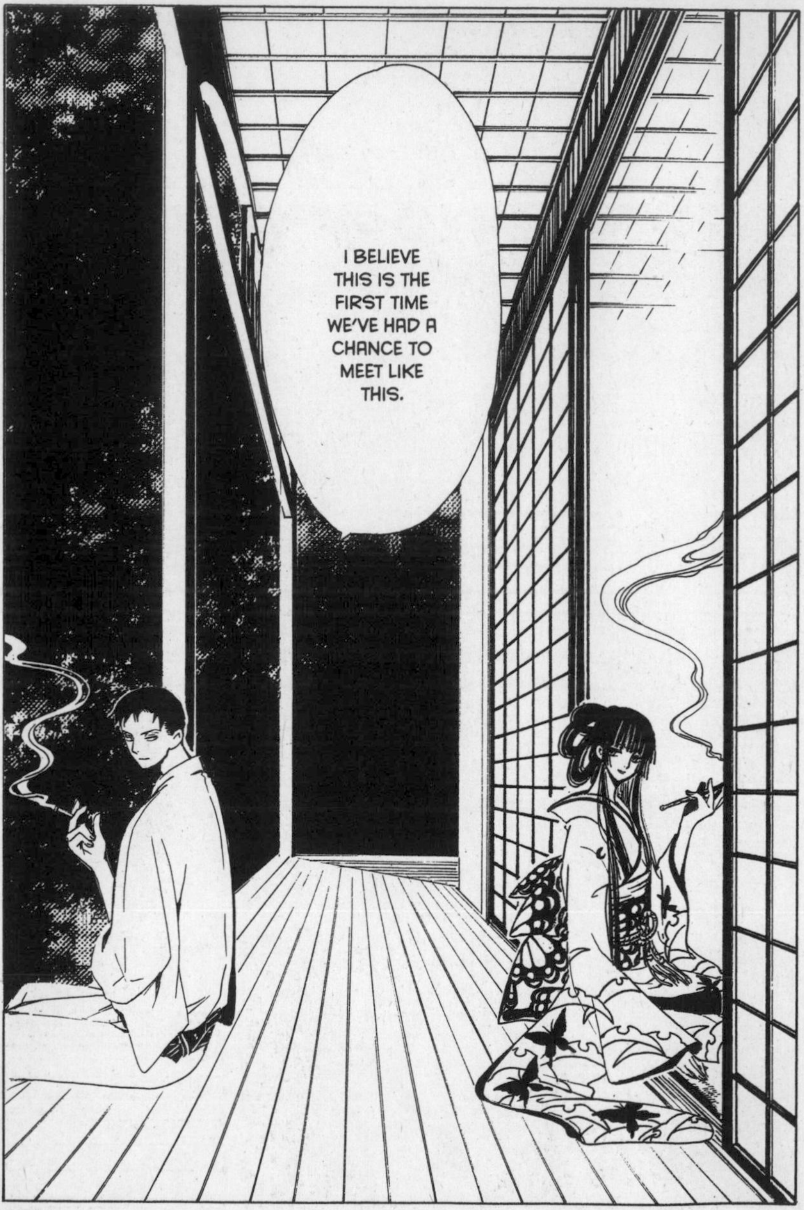
I BELIEVE THIS IS THE FIRST TIME WE'VE HAD A CHANCE TO MEET LIKE THIS.

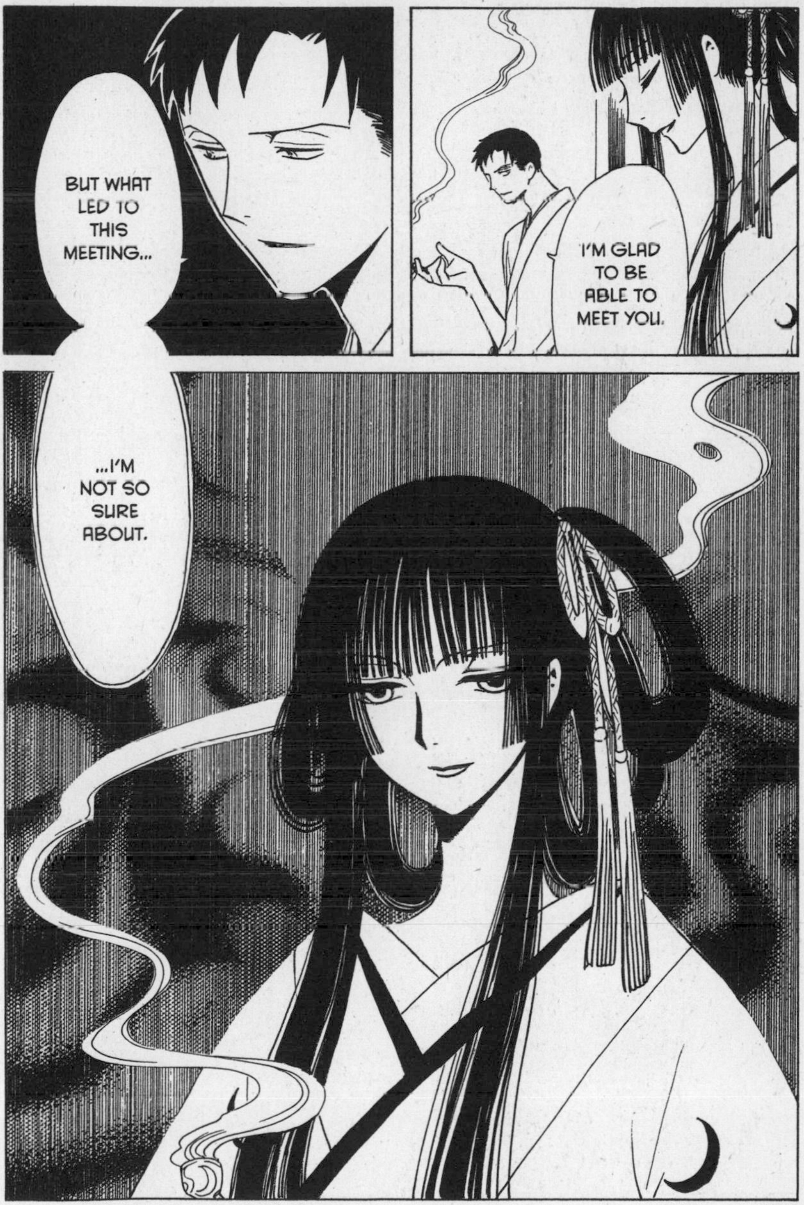
I'M GLAD TO BE ABLE TO MEET YOU.
BUT WHAT LED TO THIS MEETING...
...I'M NOT SO SURE ABOUT.

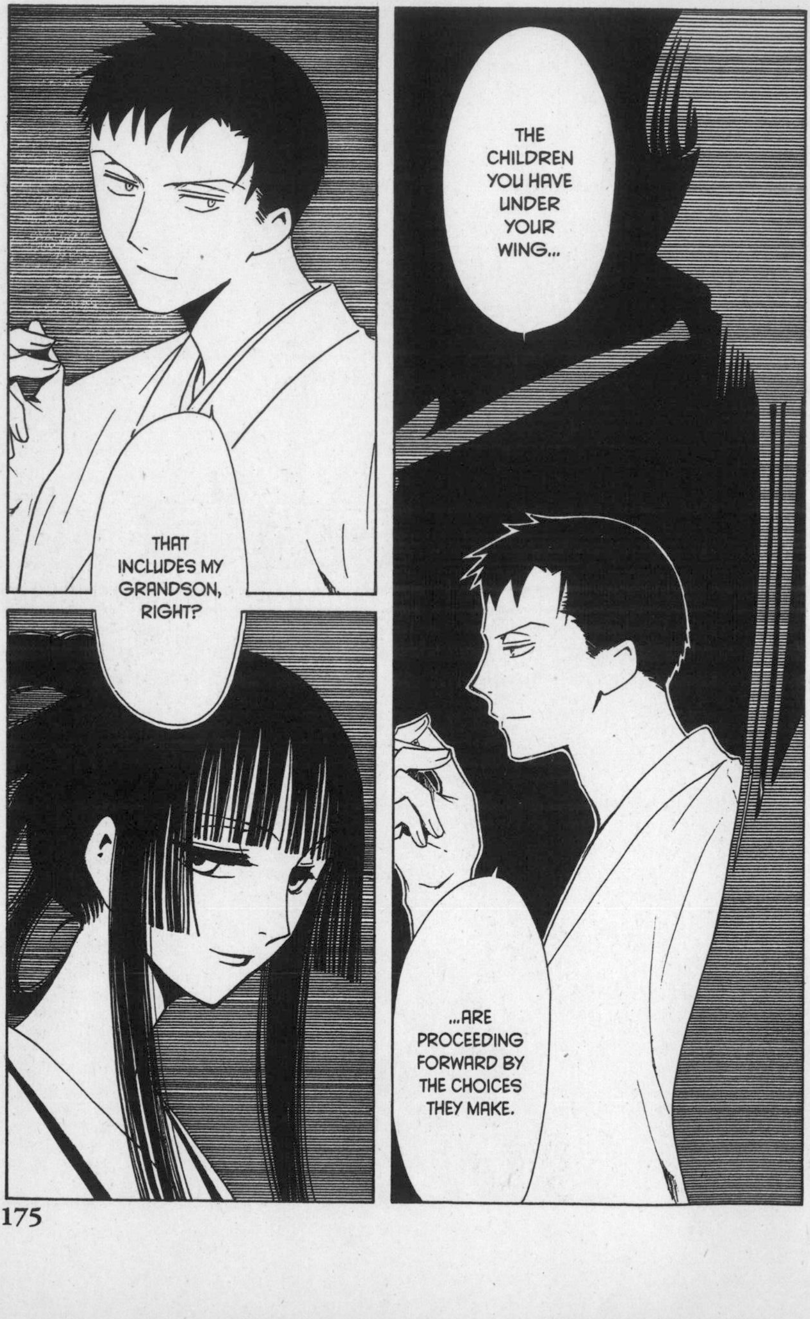
THE CHILDREN YOU HAVE UNDER YOUR WING...
...ARE PROCEEDING FORWARD BY THE CHOICES THEY MAKE.
THAT INCLUDES MY GRANDSON, RIGHT?

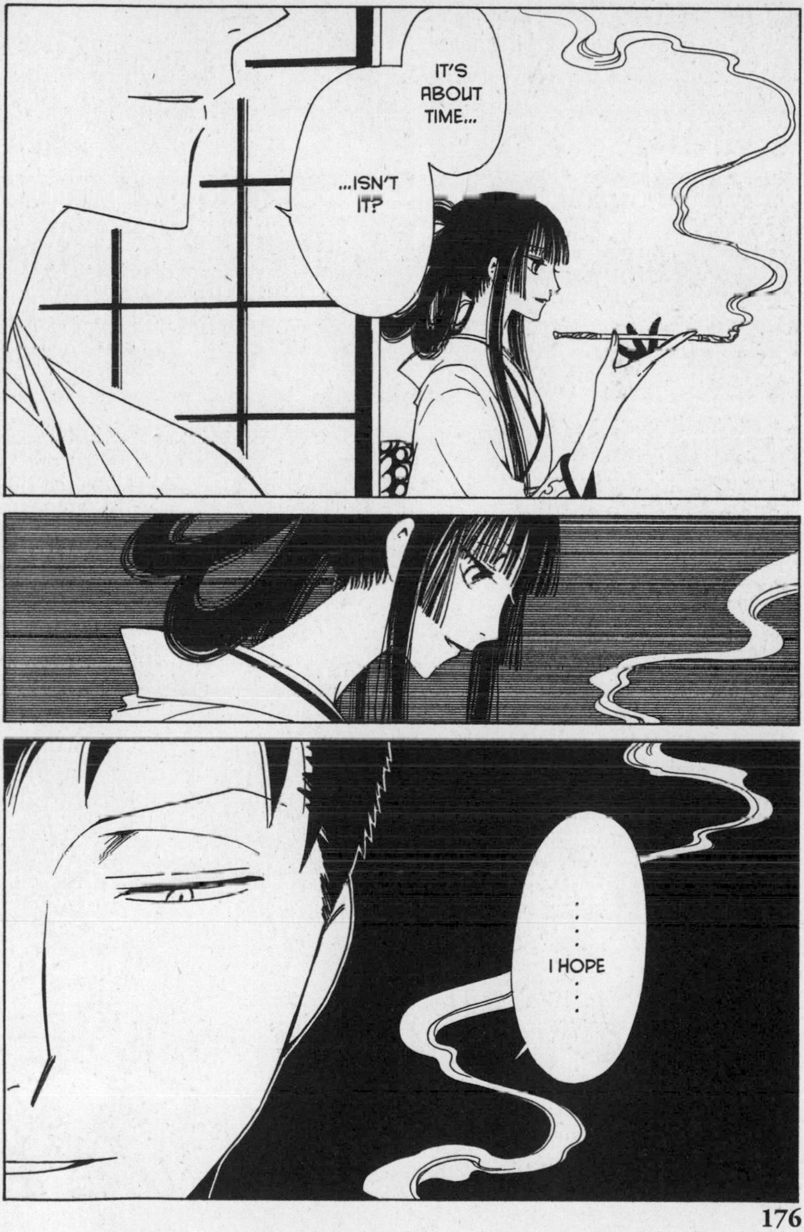
IT'S ABOUT TIME...
...ISN'T IT?
......I HOPE......

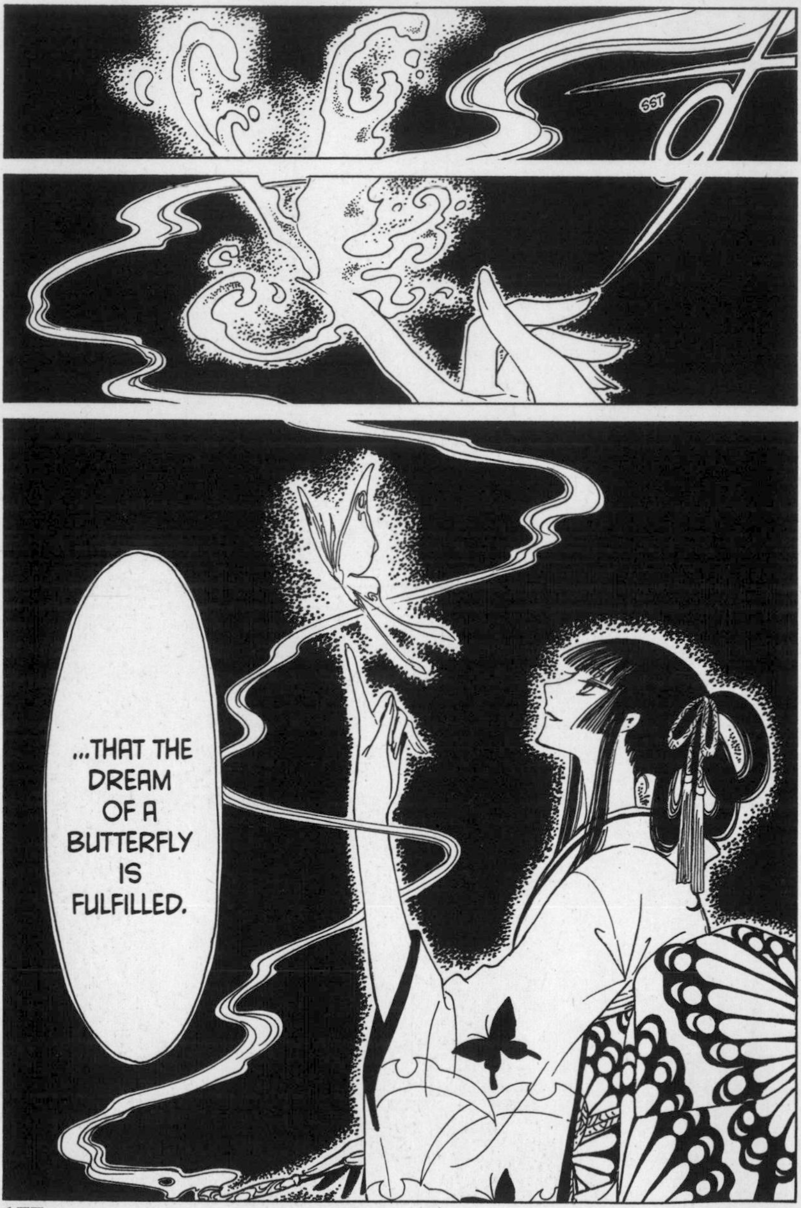
SST
...THAT THE DREAM OF A BUTTERFLY IS FULFILLED.

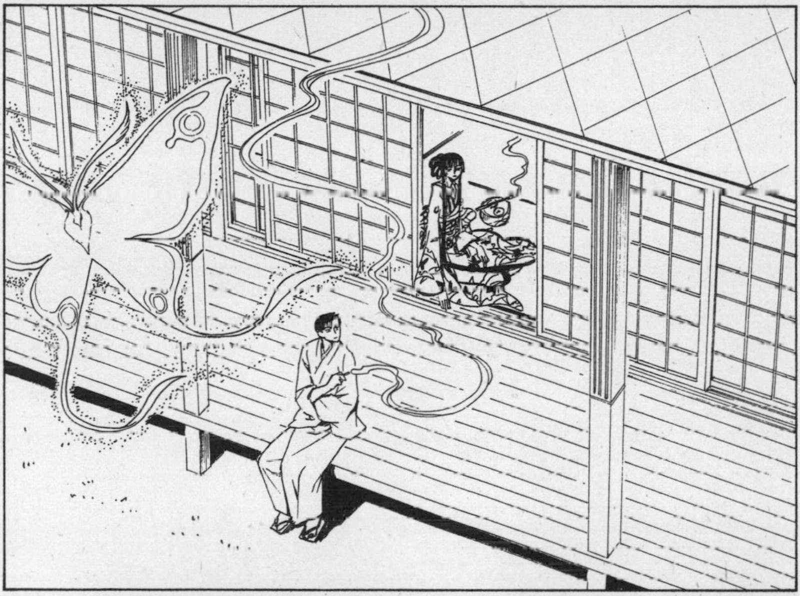
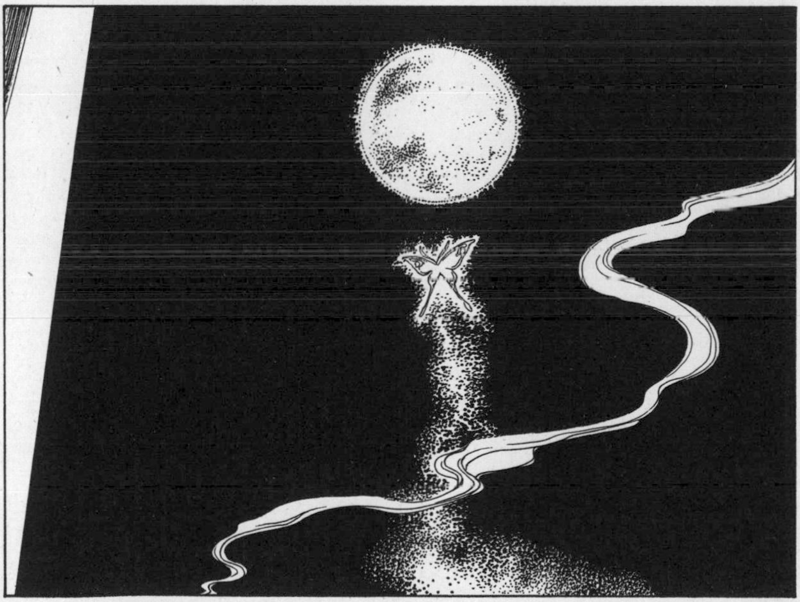

❧ Continued ❧

in *xxxHOLiC,* volume 15

About the Creators

CLAMP is a group of four women who have become the most popular manga artists in America— Nanase Ohkawa, Mokona, Satsuki Igarashi, and Tsubaki Nekoi. They started out as *doujinshi* (fan comics) creators, but their skill and craft brought them to the attention of publishers very quickly. Their first work from a major publisher was *RG Veda*, but their first mass success was with *Magic Knight Rayearth*. From there, they went on to write many series, including Cardcaptor Sakura and Chobits, two of the most popular manga in the United States. Like many Japanese manga artists, they prefer to avoid the spotlight, and little is known about them personally.

CLAMP is currently publishing three series in Japan: Tsubasa and xxxHOLiC with Kodansha, and Kobato with Kadokawa.

Translation Notes

Japanese is a tricky language for most Westerners, and translation is often more art than science. For your edification and reading pleasure, here are notes on some of the places where we could have gone in a different direction or where a Japanese cultural reference is used.

Page 5, Spinach and Meatballs *Fukume-ni*

Fukume-ni is the Japanese word for mixed simmering. The veggies and meatballs are placed in a simmering soup, and the taste of the soup is infused through the ingredients. After one removes it from the heat and allows the dish to cool, then the dish may be reheated just prior to serving to set the flavor.

Page 6, *Sembei*

Sembei is a rice-based snack that is baked or fried to a very crisp texture. They come in flavors from sweet to spicy, and are a standard snack to place on the table when company comes to visit. If one is not careful, the crunch of *sembei* can be very loud.

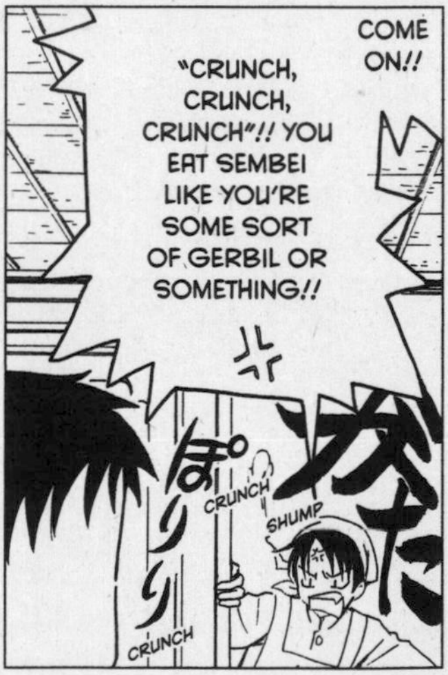
COME ON!!
"CRUNCH, CRUNCH, CRUNCH"!! YOU EAT SEMBEI LIKE YOU'RE SOME SORT OF GERBIL OR SOMETHING!!
SHUMP
CRUNCH
CRUNCH

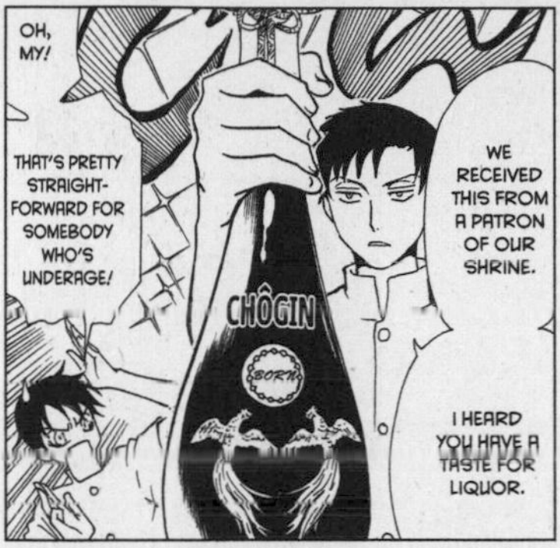
WE RECEIVED THIS FROM A PATRON OF OUR SHRINE.
I HEARD YOU HAVE A TASTE FOR LIQUOR.
OH, MY!
THAT'S PRETTY STRAIGHT-FORWARD FOR SOMEBODY WHO'S UNDERAGE!
CHÔGIN
BORN

Page 15, Born Chôgin

The Born Brewery (using the *bon kanji*, which means "purity," but makes use of an official spelling of "Born") is located in Sabe-shi city of Fukui Prefecture. It makes a very rare saké, Chôgin, that has a very high reputation. Chôgin is given to the Japanese Imperial family for its own use.

Page 36, Awamori

Awamori is a liquor that is similar to *shôchû* saké, but made differently. Both are made from rice, but while *shôchû* (what we normally think of as saké) is brewed, Awamori is distilled. It reportedly originated in Thailand, but it is now considered an Okinawan liquor.

Page 64, Angry Guy (*Tsukkomi*)

As described in the notes of previous volumes, a *manzai* comedy act is made up of the angry guy (*tsukkomi*) and the dumb guy (*boké*). As the angry guy, Watanuki is constantly snapping at Dômeki.

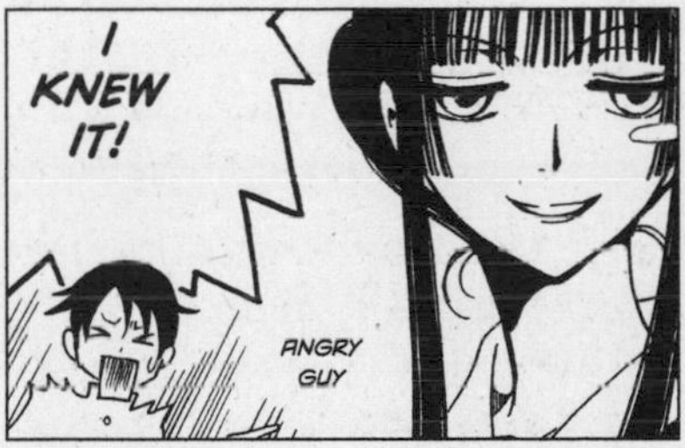
I KNEW IT!
ANGRY GUY

Page 74, Four-Level Bento Box

Bento boxes come in all sizes from kids' lunch boxes to stackable party trays for huge parties and gatherings. The four-level bento box is usually a set of four lacquered boxes around nine inches square that are stacked together, each upper box forming the lid for the box beneath. These boxes can carry a surprisingly large amount of food.

Page 79, *Rakugo*

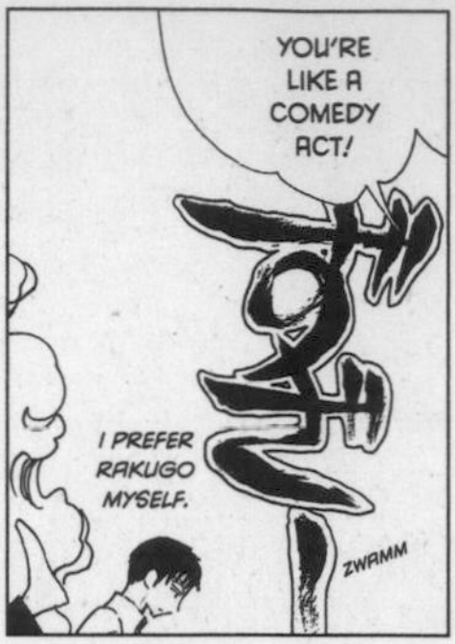

YOU'RE LIKE A COMEDY ACT!
I PREFER RAKUGO MYSELF.
ZWAMM

Rakugo is a traditional Japanese one-man comedy performance. A kimono-clad man (women *rakugo* performers are not unknown, but they are uncommon) sits on a *zabuton* cushion onstage and tells amusing stories. The stories tend to be longer and more subdued than the frenetic *manzai* acts or Western stand-up comedy.

Page 80, *Manzai*, M1

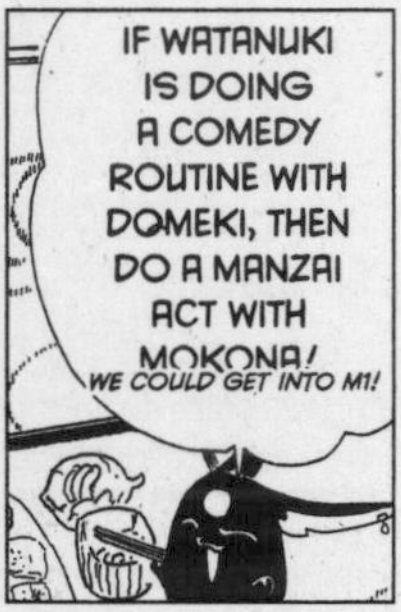

IF WATANUKI IS DOING A COMEDY ROUTINE WITH DOMEKI, THEN DO A MANZAI ACT WITH MOKONA!
WE COULD GET INTO M1!

As stated above, *manzai* is a two-man comedy performance. This is one of the most popular Japanese stand-up comedy combinations, and successful *manzai* acts have gone on to extremely successful television and movie careers. One of the ways for a *manzai* act to break out is through the annual M1 competition (a riff on F1 car racing, but the *F* for "formula" is replaced by the *M* for "*manzai*"). New and established two-man combinations compete to be awarded the prize for best *manzai* act of the year.

Page 91, Washing Rice with Soap

Before being put into the pot to cook, rice should be rinsed in a particular way. However, the act of rinsing the rice uses the same word (*arau*) as is used for washing such things as dishes, clothing, hands, etc. When told to wash the rice, people who have no experience with cooking have a tendency to break out the dish soap and give the rice a thorough scrubbing. This is considered a classic mistake and one way to judge the lack of experience of a cook.

Page 91, How to Use a Knife

The Japanese kitchen knife, the *hôchô*, is a very sharp cutting instrument, and even experienced amateur chefs can cut their fingers while doing the thin slicing that Japanese cooking requires. The way one holds one's fingers while slicing is a sure indicator of the experience of the cook.

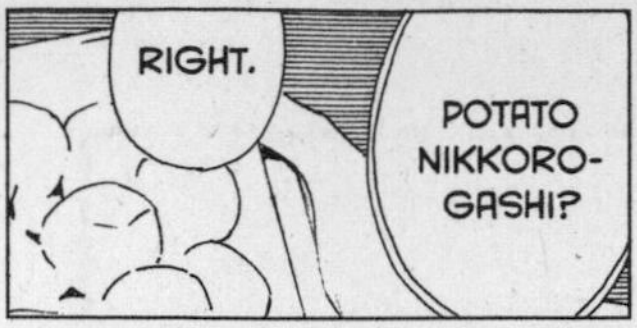
RIGHT.
POTATO NIKKORO-GASHI?

Page 92, Potato *Nikkoro-gashi*

Nikkoro-gashi is a dish in which potatoes (in this case, taro) are boiled and then simmered in a mixture of flavorings, including sugar and soy sauce.

Page 108, *Niku-jaga*

A stew made with meat (*niku*) and potatoes (*jagaimo*) seems more like a Western dish than a typical Japanese traditional meal. But *nikujaga* is one of those meals that nearly every Japanese person has grown up with. Like miso soup, the average Japanese person considers the best-tasting *nikujaga* to be the one Mom always used to make.

Page 128, *Renkon Hasamiage*

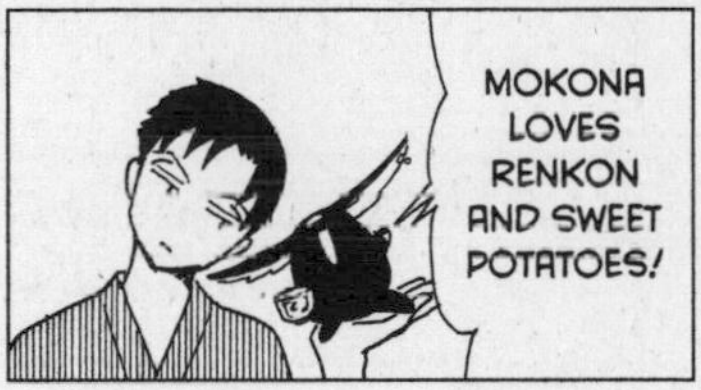
MOKONA LOVES RENKON AND SWEET POTATOES!

Renkon is a tuber that has a stiff, crunchy texture. *Hasamiage* means "sandwiched and fried." One takes two slices of *renkon* and places between them meats, cheeses, veggies, mushrooms, or other ingredients, and fries the sandwich in a light batter. The crunchy texture of the *renkon* goes well with the chewy, rich interior.

Page 162, *Omiai* Marriage Meeting

Although love marriages are becoming more and more popular, arranged marriages (*omiai*) are still a large part of Japanese culture. The two prospective marriage candidates meet each other, usually surrounded by family and go-betweens, and have a short conversation regarding such topics as school/work history and hobbies. After the first meeting, they are expected to accept or refuse the offer of marriage. Either candidate has the ability to refuse. There may be more than one meeting, but the more meetings there are, the harder it is to refuse because of the large number of people involved and the raised expectations. Arranged marriages are considered "safer"—less prone to divorce—than love marriages since both families are invested in making sure the marriage works.

TOMARE!

[STOP!]

You're goir...

Manga is a completely
different type of reading

To sta...

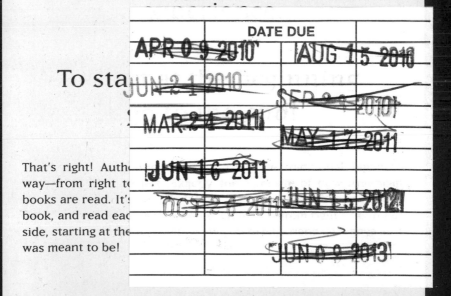

DATE DUE		
APR 0 9 2010		AUG 1 5 2010
JUN 2 1 2010		
		SEP 2 2010
MAR 2 4 2011		
		MAY 1 7 2011
JUN 1 6 2011		
OCT 2 6 2011		JUN 1 5 2012
		JUN 0 9 2013

That's right! Auth...
way—from right t...
books are read. It'...
book, and read eac...
side, starting at the...
was meant to be!